STANDING ON
THE SHOULDERS OF GIANTS

To Christopher,

Best Wishes,

F Rafters

Frank Rafters

Grosvenor House
Publishing Limited

This book is published by
Grosvenor House Publishing Ltd
28-30 High Street, Guildford, Surrey, GU1 3EL.
www.grosvenorhousepublishing.co.uk

A CIP record for this book
is available from the British Library

ISBN 978-1-78148-645-0

To my family and friends – Without you,
I would not be who I am today.

Contents

Acknowledgements

My thanks to Josh Gaffney, "The Glasgow Herald", "The Evening Times", "The Scotsman", "www.thecelticwiki.com", "www.londonhearts.com", "The Story Of The Celtic (W. Maley)", "The Celtic Story (J.E. Handley)", "Celtic 1888–1995 – The Official Illustrated History (G. McColl)" and, last but not least, "The Scottish Football Museum" at Hampden Park.

"The Celtic Effect"

"If I have seen further, it is by standing on the shoulders of giants." – Sir Isaac Newton

"Celtic."

There are few individual words in the sporting world which mean so much to so many, and there are perhaps even less which continue to spawn countless others to be written about them throughout the generations. Without **"Celtic"**, then it is almost certain that I would have written none of the following one hundred and sixty-eight thousand words. Without **"Celtic"**, the very fabrics of not only Glasgow but Scotland, Europe and even the world as a whole would not be quite as they are today. Yes, the differences without **"Celtic"** would be most pronounced in Glasgow, particularly in the East End of the city, but nonetheless, the point stands. Without Celtic Football Club, our world would not be the same.

Now, that may sound like a rather grand and extravagant statement to make, but I stand by it resolutely. To consider **"Celtic"** to be the name of **"just another Football Club"** would be an incidence not only of underestimation of the highest order, but also of a general lack of knowledge. Presumably, the vast majority of you reading this will be Celtic supporters, and therefore you are likely to agree with the above sentiments more than someone who has no affiliation with the Club. Regardless, whether you haven't missed a Celtic game in decades or whether you've never seen a football match in your life, I hope that by the time you finish reading this book, you will be able to understand this strong belief, which is held by thousands, if not millions, of people across the globe.

Presently, many of you will establish that I possess an interest in science. After all, the name of this book is derived from a famous quote of Sir Isaac Newton (previously mentioned), the man who famously discovered gravity, amongst many other wonderful things. Much later, as you read the final pages of this piece, I shall discuss my decision to give the book its particular title. However, for now, I shall simply highlight the fact that I have always held an interest in physics and science as a whole.

Please, relax. In a couple of paragraphs time my focus will be firmly on football, but indulge me for a moment. Now, we all know that life can be chaotic. Whether you're running late for work, trying to get the kids ready for another day at school or frantically searching for your season ticket when the new campaign's kick-off is only hours away, we've all felt frazzled at times.

During my school life and a relatively short time at university, one particular matter which caught my attention above most others was **"Chaos Theory"**. Essentially, this states that even minute changes within a given situation, whether it happens to be an experiment in a laboratory or an incident in your day to day life, can lead to massively different outcomes. Such events have been widely popularised in all forms of media in the modern day, with this being more commonly referred to as **"The Butterfly Effect."** In fact, novels such as **"Harry Potter"** and television series like **"Doctor Who"** have based entire storylines around this.

Anyway, the idea for this stems from an example whereby a butterfly flaps its wings, causing the air around it to move just a little bit in doing so. On its own, such a movement is seen by the vast majority as negligible, but in reality every little motion or change in our lives can, and often do, make a difference. For example, when a defender receives the ball whilst he is under pressure from an opponent, he can often simply clear the ball into touch, handing possession back to the other team, or try to pass to a teammate. Now, as it is impossible to predict the future, the defender cannot foresee which scenario will follow his choice – he can only use his best judgement to do what he thinks is correct. However, his decision, or any of the countless others involved in any football match, could ultimately determine the eventual result of the game. After all, attempting to pass the ball out from the back could backfire and lead to the concession of a goal, or equally well, it could have quite the opposite effect – and therefore we have chaos.

Of course, nobody can fully embrace the idea of **"The Butterfly Effect"** and base their lives around it – otherwise they would most likely lose their minds. I am merely trying to highlight the fact that, without the presence of a particular person, group or action, regardless of whoever or whatever they may be, the world we live in, which is innately chaotic, could be a very different place.

Returning to the topic of this book (I assure you that is the physics lesson done), I ask you to consider it for a moment – a world without Celtic.

From the earliest days of the Football Club, the much needed funds raised by Brother Walfrid, John Glass and several other important figures would not have been provided to various charities without the presence of Celtic. With this in mind, it is almost certain that some of the people they did assist would have perished without them. Had this been the case, family trees would read differently and in all likelihood some of the people in Glasgow today would never have been born. In all seriousness, I know it may sound like a somewhat pedantic point, but I believe it to be a critically important one. I feel James E. Handley, the author of **"The Celtic Story"** (published several decades ago now), summed it up perfectly when he began his book with the following line: **"The Celtic Football and Athletic Club had its origin in the cause of charity."**

Without Celtic, the poor children's dinner tables of the East End of Glasgow would never have been able to help as many people as they eventually did. For example, in the Club's first year in existence, it donated a little over four hundred and twenty pounds to charitable causes, the equivalent of almost fifty thousand pounds in today's money. Now, extrapolate that figure over the long history of the Football Club and you will likely conclude that Celtic's influence, on charity alone for the moment, has played an integral part in many people's lives.

Without Celtic, it is likely that, whilst some of the men now regarded as sporting icons may have gone on to become involved with football in some manner, there is no way they could have all achieved the levels of success they did at Celtic Park. Equally, some of those who wore the Hoops may never have become professional footballers if Celtic had not been there to give them the opportunity. After all, without Celtic, nobody can know for certain whether the names of Jock Stein and many others would have become famous and lived on, long beyond the men themselves.

Without Celtic, a factory, industrial unit or supermarket may now occupy the sacred ground we regard as **"Paradise"** – if it hadn't simply been left to rot over the years like many other large pieces of ground in the inner city of course – a dreadful thought yes, but a valid one nonetheless.

Without Celtic, throughout the course of one hundred and twenty-five years, countless individuals would have supported other football teams, and many would have developed no interest in the game at all. An infinite number of cherished memories would not exist, and endless friendships and romances would never have taken root and prospered. People would never have met, and therefore the world would be a different place.

Without Celtic, the game of football in Scotland would likely never have reached its pinnacle, with a home-grown side being crowned the Champions of Europe.

And, without Celtic, my life would not be the same – I am certain of that. Equally, I don't think it would be an unreasonable presumption on my part that neither would many of your lives.

It was Celtic's first manager, Willie Maley (a man whom, unsurprisingly, I haven't taken too long to mention) who said:

"The Club has been my life, and I feel without it, my existence would be empty indeed."

And now, even in the modern era, that point will still resonate with thousands upon thousands of people, and undoubtedly it shall continue to do so long into the future. From a personal point of view, it speaks to me with a stark clarity. I am all too aware of the fact that Celtic Football Club has always been there for me, throughout the highs and lows of my life, like a much loved relative, with the potential to bring unbridled joy but also occasional bouts of frustration and even, at times, despair.

For the record, as of this book's publication towards the end of 2013, I am only twenty-three years of age. I have been a season ticket holder at Celtic Park for almost a decade, and even from my earliest days on this Earth, Celtic have been a notable presence in my life. Born and bred in the west of Scotland, I have witnessed the great and the good that associations with the Football Club can bring to my life, as well as the uglier side of things too.

I have met countless fantastic people in my time as a Celtic supporter, both those who only entered my life for a brief moment, perhaps amongst a chaotic goal celebration, and those who have gone on to become firm, much loved friends of mine. Equally, I have had sectarian slurs directed towards me from others because I happen to support a particular football team, and therefore I am perceived to come from a particular background. I have also learned the many unwritten rules of life in and around Glasgow. In my early years, these tended to involve things such as being told to cover up my Celtic shirt by my parents if I was going to be out and about, whilst in more recent times, I have become aware that certain places and particular pubs are simply considered to be **"no-go areas"**.

Away from football for a moment, whilst I cannot say that my life so far has been perfect, I feel I must acknowledge the fact that, on the whole, I have many reasons to feel tremendously lucky. I am blessed with a family whom I love fiercely, and several good friends whom I have known for many years. I have never gone hungry, and there has always been a roof over my head, thanks largely to hard work of my parents, whom I cannot thank enough for what they have done for me.

However, as tends to be the case for many people, there have been times in my life when I have felt far from lucky. My own personal battles with depression and anxiety have taken me to places which I hope and pray I shall never return to. At points, in times gone by, I have been truly miserable – I am not concerned about highlighting that. However, I was fortunate enough to have wonderful support around me which enabled me to recover and, more recently, to overcome the challenges posed when writing this book also.

I have seen beloved relatives die and new family members born. I have watched my father overcome cancer, and, as I have alluded to, I have faced my own personal battles. I have experienced immense highs and sickening lows, but such is life. If there were no bad times for any of us, we would likely take the good times for granted. And yet, all of these experiences have shaped me into the man I am at this point in my life and, critically, Celtic Football Club has always played its own role too.

Regardless of whether times were tough or not, the thought of the next match, potential signings, different tactics, exciting youth players, and the memories of victories long gone by have always been there to take my mind off things. To support Celtic is to have an escape, and to be part of a larger family. Yes, there are disagreements from time to time within the family but, fundamentally, the family unit holds firm. Whenever one of us is faced with adversity, the rest will rally to protect and support them, whether it is our manager or an impoverished child in a distant land.

And so, returning to my initial point, through this book, I intend to examine not only the history of Celtic, but how its presence has affected individuals, ranging from legendary players to average supporters, as well as collective groups. You will read not only of the giants of our Club's past, but of the people who stand on their shoulders in the present day. My hope is that as you travel through these pages, you may all learn something, not only about Celtic Football Club, but perhaps about life as well.

Whilst the air displaced by the flap of a butterfly's wings may not make much of a difference on the grand scheme of things, I wholeheartedly believe that the existence of a living, breathing entity such as Celtic Football Club has, and continues to have, a tremendous impact on the lives of so, so many people. This belief, ladies and gentlemen, is what I consider to be **"The Celtic Effect".**

"My First Steps"

Sunday, April 20th 1997
Celtic 3, Aberdeen 0
(Cadete 24, 63, Donnelly 51)

Perhaps the match detailed above isn't a game that many people will remember. In fact, I would go so far to say that relatively few folk will have any significant recollection of it, despite over forty-seven thousand packing themselves inside an ever-changing Celtic Park to see it at the time. After all, it was then, and remains to this day, a virtually meaningless affair, at least on the surface. Rangers had all but officially sealed their ninth league title in a row only days earlier, equalling Celtic's long cherished record from the 1960's and 1970's, and whilst the mood may have been defiant at Parkhead, it was far from jubilant. Celtic had not won the Championship since 1988, and every solitary one of the Club's supporters was all too aware that the Bhoys only had one more chance to stop their rivals. Equalling Celtic's record was one thing, but the prospect of it being bettered by the Ibrox side was unthinkable, and yet, for a while, it was a terrifying possibility.

However, ignoring the previously mentioned apathy regarding the match against Aberdeen, I can say with certainty that the twentieth of April 1997 is a date that I shall never forget. There is, of course, a very good reason for that, as on that day, this six year old was lucky enough to have his first taste of the place we call **"Paradise"**. I sat with my dad in the South Stand, where he had his seat for some sixteen years prior to my first visit, and where he continues sit, week in, week out, to this very day.

I remember being overawed by the whole experience; the people, the noise, the sights, the sounds, the smells – everything – and that was before the game had even started. As I stood there prior to kick-off, I can still recall gazing up at the relatively newly constructed North Stand and being truly staggered by its size and colouring. For the record, whilst I was a child I automatically loved anything green and white or anything with the word **"Celtic"** emblazoned upon it, so to find myself staring at what seemed to be an utterly enormous green stand with six giant white letters spelling out my favourite word was like a vision of heaven for me. Little did I know then that less than ten years later, I would become a season ticket holder and sit within ten rows of the top of the upper tier at every home game.

Anyway, returning to 1997, whilst many people may not have been too excited that day, I was, as I'm sure you can imagine, absolutely ecstatic. The prospect of seeing the team I already adored so much in person was truly mind-blowing. As the sides emerged from the tunnel, I stood on the seat next to my father, holding onto his arm to balance myself, all to catch my first glimpse of the famous Glasgow Celtic, as they strolled out into the spring sunshine before me.

Looking back on it, one of my most enduring impressions of that day was that everything seemed larger then than it does now. At the age of twenty-three, I now stand somewhere around the six feet and three inches mark in terms of height, but then I was, of course, much smaller. The partially completed stadium seemed vast, and yet the atmosphere somehow felt intimate, and oddly, it still feels similar today.

Focusing on the match itself, my memories of the first goal are as follows – Tosh McKinlay played a long ball forwards through the air towards Jorge Cadete, who proceeded to sprint after it, with his hair bouncing behind him in a sight not dissimilar to the modern day Georgios Samaras. Anyway, as he chased down the ball before him, I remember everyone around me leaping to their feet in anticipation, staring towards the far end of the ground where the action was unfolding. Whilst this occurred, time seemed to slow down, and I found myself straining my neck in all directions in search of a gap large enough to see through the crowd of bodies in front of me. Eventually, as if by some incidence of destiny or fate, a small opening appeared just in time for me to watch the Portuguese striker run on to the pass and coolly chip the ball over the oncoming Aberdeen goalkeeper Derek Stillie.

To this day, I can still close my eyes and see the aftermath, as my dad picked me up and hugged me, amidst what I recall as one of the craziest goal celebrations I have ever been a part of. In reality, it was a good, but otherwise 'normal' goal, and did not spark anything like the scenes I have witnessed against sides such as AC Milan, Manchester United, Porto and, of course, Rangers. However, to a small Bhoy, it seemed as if the place had just erupted. Only moments later, for the first time, I was treated to a live rendition of one of my favourite songs:

"There's only one Jorge Cadete,
He puts the ball in the netty,
He's Portuguese, and he scores with ease,
Walking in a Cadete wonderland."

In all honesty, it was simply magnificent. As the match continued, Simon Donnelly made it two-nil to Celtic, before Jorge Cadete scored once again midway through the second half to put the icing on the cake for the victorious Hoops. As I walked out of Celtic Park for the first time, I felt certain that I would return – I was hooked. In truth, I have loved Celtic for as long as I can remember, but I believe (from personal experience at least) that the first time you see them live is something truly special, regardless of what age you happen to be when you have the pleasure of doing so.

In truth, when I shut my eyes and remember that day in 1997, there is a little part of me that wants to well up with a tear or two, and I'm not entirely sure as to why. Perhaps the raw emotion involved has stuck with me, or perhaps it is simply because the entire experience retains a special place as one of my happiest memories. To wander up Kerrydale Street and watch Celtic play was a tremendous privilege – and it still is. If I am ever blessed with the opportunity to repeat this feat not only with my father beside me, but with a child (or children) of my own in tow then I will, for those few moments, hold a place as one of the happiest people on the face of the Earth, because it will mean more to me than I can express with mere words. People with no love of football or Celtic Football Club may, understandably, find this idea somewhat difficult to grasp. However, I have no doubts that the vast majority of you reading this will know exactly what I mean.

Anyway, from that day onwards, I have always held a particular liking for matches against Aberdeen. I suppose the sight of the two side's kits takes me back on every occasion upon which I see the two teams face each other, although I must confess that the feeling isn't quite so nice whenever they beat us.

In hindsight, I imagined I bored both my mum and my late gran to tears by talking endlessly about my first steps at Paradise in the days following my trip to Parkhead. Hell, it's more than fifteen years later as I write this, and yet here I am, still talking about it, albeit with a slightly larger vocabulary and an audience who haven't heard this story before.

However, one thing I had always regretted was the fact I did not have a copy of the programme from my first game. I imagine my dad bought me one, but either it got thrown away over the years or simply lost to the family's 'land that time forgot' – the loft. Regardless, a few months after I started the **"Maley's Bhoys"** website I put a request out on Twitter to see if, by any chance, someone still had that programme. Amazingly, it didn't take long before one kind hearted soul contacted me and posted it through from his personal collection, entirely free of charge. Rest assured, I treasure that programme to this day, and will continue to do so as long as I live, having read it from cover to cover on several occasions.

As I have said, most supporters won't remember that day in 1997, and in the vast majority of history books it will be classed as nothing more than an average game. However, it will remain forever sacred to me, for it was a day when I had the privilege of combining two of my favourite things in life, watching the world renowned Celtic play, and spending a bit of quality time with the greatest fans on Earth.

"What A Side That Would Have Been"

Eleven years ago, in 2002, the members of the Celtic support were given the opportunity to vote not only for their greatest Celtic team, but for their greatest player (Jimmy Johnstone), greatest foreign player (Henrik Larsson), and greatest Club captain (Billy McNeill) respectively. By this reckoning, the greatest ever Celtic side was as follows: Ronnie Simpson, Danny McGrain, Billy McNeill, Tommy Gemmell, Bobby Murdoch, Paul McStay, Bertie Auld, Jimmy Johnstone, Henrik Larsson, Kenny Dalglish and Bobby Lennox.

Immediately, several thoughts will undoubtedly stir in many of your minds. Some of you will remember great goals, mesmerising pieces of skill and men who utterly adored all things Celtic; others will ponder the selections, perhaps feeling that an unnamed player would have been more worthy of a place than one of the individuals listed above; whilst others will simply think, **"what a side that would have been"** – and they would be right to do so.

However, whilst all of these thoughts and more stirred in my head as I considered the possibility of writing this book, three words stood out in my mind – **"The Lisbon Lions"**. This is not because I am about to tell you that the greatest eleven should have been made up entirely by the men who took to the field in Lisbon that day, although they were very possibly the greatest eleven to have ever played at the same time. No, my thoughts of the Lisbon Lions were somewhat broader than that, as I immediately realised that there was not a single member of the greatest Celtic team listed above who was a member of any side prior to that of the Lisbon Lions. This meant that over half of the Football Club's history, and therefore hundreds of the players to have pulled on a Celtic jersey during that time were wholly unrepresented.

Now, there are, of course, several contributory factors to this, with perhaps the most notable being found in the sands of time. As the years and decades pass, fewer and fewer of the supporters of old, who had the pleasure of enjoying some of the incredible footballing talent of their times, live to tell their fantastic tales. This loss, combined with the significant lack of recording technology until fairly recently, has allowed some of the true greats to slip through the proverbial net. This is not to say they are forgotten, as the names of men like Willie Maley continue to be sung at Celtic Park to this day, but because only a small number of us (if any in some cases) have any direct experience of watching them.

However, it did prompt me to consider a simple, yet intriguing question. Ignoring the men mentioned above, and only focusing on the players who plied their trade prior to the era of the Lisbon Lions, who would have made the greatest Celtic team of that time? And so, with this in mind, I set myself a cut-off point in the form of the year of 1960, and decided that all of those who would feature in my greatest eleven could only have stayed with the Club until that point and no later, before the Lions truly began to take shape.

Therefore, ladies and gentlemen, allow me to present my take on the greatest Celtic team ever (1888–1960).

"Our Bright And Shining Star"

"A young lad named John Thomson,
From the west of Fife he came,
To play for Glasgow Celtic,
And to build himself a name."

"On the fifth day of September,
'gainst the Rangers club he played,
From defeat he saved the Celtic,
Ah but what a price he paid."

"The ball rolled out from centre,
Young John ran out and dived,
The ball rolled by; young John lay still,
For his club this hero died."

John Thomson was born on the twenty-eighth of January 1909, in the small town of Kirkcaldy, Fife. The son of John and Jean, he attended Denend Primary School and Auchterderran High School, and would go on to become a legendary figure in the world of Scottish Football, although no one knew that at the time he grasped his first trophy. Auchterderran High School won the Lochgelly Times Cup with John between the posts as a young teenager, and even at this stage, his talent was clear to see, with one teacher, Mr Lawton, describing him as **"a born goalkeeper".**

He spent his early life, from the age of only fourteen years old, working in his local coal pit – Bowhill Colliery near Cardendan – alongside his father. John spent much of this time coupling and uncoupling carts several hundred feet below ground level, assisting the transit of coal around the mine to operate as smoothly as possible in the process. Of course, John was not alone in this regard, as so many other young men of the time who lived in the area found similar employment. Away from the mine though, John continued with his favourite pastime, playing for junior sides Bowhill Rovers in 1924 and mid-1925, and latterly, Wellesley Juniors between mid-1925 and 1927.

Nowadays, with young goalkeepers such as David De Gea being transferred for tens of millions of pounds, it may surprise you to hear that one of, if not the, greatest goalkeeper to ever pull on a Celtic strip was purchased for the mammoth figure of just ten pounds sterling.

Having heard the talk of a great young goalkeeper playing with a junior side in Fife, Willie Maley dispatched his chief scout at the time, Steve Callaghan, to watch a tie in which Wellesley went up against Denbeath Star in October 1926. Remarkably, Mr Callaghan's initial instructions were to watch Denbeath's goalkeeper and report back on his performance. However, it is clear that John must have impressed Mr Callaghan, as Celtic quickly altered their transfer target and pounced to sign the then seventeen year old boy, before any other professional side could take an interest or make him a counter offer.

In February 1927, after an unimpressive performance from then first choice goalkeeper Peter Shevlin against Brechin City, Willie Maley made one his famously radical changes to his team selection for the Celts' next match, by handing the eighteen year old John Thomson his Celtic debut. Clearly, it was a wise decision, as Celtic won by two goals to one at Dens Park, in front of a little under twenty thousand spectators.

Only forty minutes into his senior Celtic career, John conceded his first goal, but there was no shame in this. Dundee were a good side at the time, and newspaper reports from the time described the goal as **"having an element of luck in it, as the ball struck the bar before passing into the net."** By this reckoning, there was likely little that John could have done to prevent the goal. However, he kept the ball out of his net for the remainder of the match, and helped the Celts to an important victory.

Interestingly, whilst John Thomson attempted to prevent the ball from going in at one end, his teammate Alec Thomson, who had signed from Wellesley Juniors (just like John, but five years previous), was trying to put the ball in the back of the net at the other, and he was successful in this regard, scoring the equaliser, before Jimmy McGrory scored the winning goal.

By the time John kept his first senior clean sheet, he had played six matches with the Hoops, conceding eleven goals, before a goalless draw against Aberdeen at Celtic Park put an end to that run. This is not to say that John was playing badly – far from it, in fact. Newspaper correspondents speak of him **"saving in clever fashion"** and, when speaking of certain goals he conceded, claim **"Thomson was powerless to save."** However, he was not incapable of making an error, for even during the aforementioned goalless draw, John dropped the ball when stopping a shot, and it was only thanks to his defenders quick thinking that the threat to his goal was nullified. With time though, John would gain experience, and such errors would become an increasingly rare sight.

Over the remainder of the 1926–27 season, John made what is now colloquially known as the **"number one jersey"** his own, by playing in every single match throughout the campaign. He suffered his first defeat as a Celtic player at the hands of Cowdenbeath, who were then a mid-table side. This was the first time the Hoops had lost in Thomson's eight matches as goalkeeper. Comparing this with the latter stewardship of Peter Shevlin, when Celtic lost three times in nine outings, Maley would have noted the difference in the team's fortunes, although it would be unfair of me to pin the blame for those defeats solely on Shevlin, as the Hoops' defence was not exactly watertight in those days.

This would become clear when Celtic travelled to Tynecastle at the end of March, where they lost by three goals to nil. Had it not been for Thomson, as well as a missed penalty which was blazed over high over his crossbar, Celtic could have been on the receiving end of a rather hefty defeat. In the following weeks, another loss against Falkirk and a three-all draw with Dundee United meant that Celtic had conceded eleven goals in their last four games, as the Scottish Cup Final grew closer by the day. Their opponents at Hampden were to be second tier East Fife, and whilst Celtic were, unsurprisingly, heavy favourites, their defensive record of late would have undoubtedly concerned a few of their supporters.

Thankfully, their fears were to remain unrealised, as Thomson and Celtic defeated East Fife by three goals to one in the end, in front of approximately eighty thousand fans. However, Celtic were given a fright by the Second Division side, who took the lead only seven minutes into the match. A minute later though, Celtic were somewhat fortunate as a shot from winger Patrick Connolly struck an East Fife man and bounced past their helpless goalkeeper into the net to level the scores.

It is often said that mental toughness matters a great deal with regards to sporting success, and whilst this may not always be the case, it certainly seems to have been a factor in the Scottish Cup Final of 1927. East Fife, the massive underdogs, had scored early. By all accounts, it was a dream start for them. However, the elation of an early goal (and all of the hard work they put in to achieve it) was lost after only a moment or two, through nothing other than bad luck. Whilst many great teams throughout history could have recovered from this unlucky turn of events, East Fife, who were caught in the heat of the moment, became rattled, and never truly recovered, despite it still being early in the tie, as the following newspaper report from the time explains:

"Misfortune, however, befell East Fife the next minute with Robertson, their right back, inadvertently turning a shot from Connolly, the Celtic outside-right, past his own goalkeeper. This mistake was not only disastrous in its immediate consequences, but practically disintegrated the East Fife team, who abandoned their own style of play and sought vainly to rival the artistry of opponents superior to them in experience and skill."

Despite the generally one-sided nature of the play from that point onwards, East Fife continued to mount counter attacks on a few occasions, forcing Thomson into action, as he **"saved brilliantly"** when called upon. The following passage, taken from the same article in **"The Glasgow Herald"** as the previous quote, alludes not only to the physical performance of Thomson, but also to his remarkable mental toughness. At the age of only eighteen, and only months after emerging from the junior game, he found himself in the biggest match in the whole of Scottish Football. Not only that, but he had conceded to a lower league side after less than ten minutes. Many would have crumbled in John's position, knowing that the hopes and dreams of thousands rested upon their shoulders, but he took it in his stride, and allowed it only to motivate him to improve and show the world just how good he could be.

"East Fife's virtues were their energy and indomitable spirit, which enabled them to turn the run of play for a brief period, during which they harassed the Celtic backs and succeeded twice through Weir and Wood in seriously testing the Celtic goalkeeper, a youth recently recruited from the junior ranks and whose display in this nerve-testing event proved him a custodian of distinction."

In the following season, 1927–28, John went on to establish himself as the best goalkeeper in Scotland in the minds of many football fans. As the season progressed, newspaper plaudits such as this, written after Celtic had won three-nil away at Raith Rovers after a nervy start to the game, began to become increasingly common reading: **"The Rovers were the more aggressive side in the first half, and only good goalkeeping [from Thomson] prevented them from taking the lead in the early stages."**

In the autumn of 1927, John was selected as the goalkeeper for a combined Glasgow team which would travel to Sheffield for the traditional match between the best players plying their trade in the two cities, held annually. Initially, John was only set to be joined by one teammate for this match, Adam McLean, but Francis Doyle would soon accompany the two Celts when the revised line-up was released closer to match day.

For those of you who may not know, Adam McLean was a Celtic great often forgotten by some of the support. In fact, McLean could well have featured in this imaginary side of mine. An incredibly talented winger, with feet which could mesmerise defenders from the first minute of a match to the last, McLean was regularly the supplier of crosses for the Club's all time leading goalscorer, Jimmy McGrory. McLean spent eleven years of his life with Celtic, before leaving for Sunderland, after scoring one hundred and thirty-eight times in four hundred and eight appearances – certainly a not bad ratio for a winger!

As for Francis Doyle, he was, well, somewhat less memorable. He spent the majority of his time playing with the reserves during his relatively short spell at the Club. In truth, it was difficult for him to break into the first team, when wingers of the standard of Gallacher and McLean were his rivals for places in the first team. In saying that, he did play twenty-one times in all, scoring three goals, which is something most of us will never achieve, and is therefore rather admirable.

Moving on to the match in Sheffield, Glasgow had not lost the annual fixture since 1914. However, in the driving autumnal rain of the Steel City, a stagnant looking Glasgow side would succumb to a determined home team playing to their strengths. The match ended four-one in favour of the hosts, and despite the scoreline (it was the first time Sheffield had put four goals past their rivals since 1896), Thomson was largely praised by the media both north and south of the border as having had **"a cool, confident game."**

In one newspapers' description of the first Sheffield goal, we have the opportunity to attain a rare glimpse of Thomson's fearless goalkeeping style; a fearlessness which would, one day, tragically, conspire with fate to cost him his young life.

"The first came after thirty seven minutes play, when Tunstall lunged the ball forwards, and into the goal area. Trotter dashed forward and, with great daring, Thomson ran out to thwart him. However, the goalkeeper came a cropper for his pains, and the forward drove the ball home – a good goal. Thomson was slightly hurt."

Another continued, **"Thomson in the Glasgow goal reminded one of the old Wednesday favourite, Davison, by his nimbleness and pluck."**

Having returned to Scotland, Thomson featured again as Celtic annihilated Third Lanark by seven goals to nil in the semi-finals of the Glasgow Cup. The Hoops would soon meet rivals Rangers in the final, who defeated Clyde by the same scoreline at Ibrox Park.

And so, the sides ran out in front of approximately eighty-four thousand people at Hampden Park, on the eighth of October 1927. In the first half, Celtic would rely heavily on Thomson as Rangers pushed strongly for the opening goal. One sports column reported: **"...but for the superlative goalkeeping of Thomson, Rangers powerful and accurate shooting must have had reward."**

Celtic then scored twice, somewhat against the run of play, through Jimmy McGrory and Patrick Connolly. The report continues: **"Rangers restarted strongly, but were again baffled and discouraged by the very fine goalkeeping of Thomson."**

Despite the fact the Ibrox side eventually managed to pull one goal back, the final whistle soon signalled that it was Celtic's day, as they won the Glasgow Cup for the fifteenth time.

"The personality of the match was undoubtedly Thomson, the Celtic goalkeeper, whose judgement, ability, and agility can scarcely be over praised."

Over the coming years, the plaudits would fly in for Celtic's young goalkeeper, whose hands would come to be described by the immortal Jimmy McGrory as **"artist's hands"**. Celtic conceded sixteen less goals in the league campaign of 1927–28 than that of the previous year, as Thomson made numerous vital saves which kept their season alive. This included heaps of praise for John's performance against Queen's Park in the Glasgow Cup Final of 1928. Celtic won two-nil, but reports from the time tell us that, without Thomson, it would have been simply impossible for Celtic to have triumphed.

"It was a game in which all the honours lay with the losers. It is scarcely too much to say that Celtic were never so thoroughly outplayed by opponents as they were in the first half. The play of the Amateurs' half-backs and forwards in that period was beyond all criticism in clever ball control, shooting, and general all round excellence, and only phenomenal goalkeeping by the youthful Celtic custodian, Thomson, denied Queen's Park a lead...the final will be recalled primarily as a goalkeeper's triumph."

Early in 1930, John would suffer his first serious injury as a professional goalkeeper, breaking his jaw and a few ribs, as well as damaging his collarbone and losing a couple of teeth, during a loss against Airdrieonians. He did this whilst making one his characteristic diving saves, where he would throw himself at the feet of an opposing player. Sadly, this would not be the last time John would suffer a serious injury playing the game he adored, for the Club he loved. A newspaper report described the incident as follows:

"Airdrieonians beat Celtic by two goals to one in a very ordinary game at Parkhead yesterday. Play never at any time reached a high level, but perhaps this can be attributed to the unfortunate accident which befell John Thomson, the Celtic goalkeeper, seven minutes after the start. The goalkeeper was assisted from the field after being injured in a collision with the Airdrie outside-right, and it was afterwards learned that a jawbone had been fractured. The Celtic team had to be rearranged, and Hughes was brought back to partner Barrie (the former Queen's Park player), while McGonagle went in goal. The deputy goalkeeper gave a good display, and was congratulated by Paterson, the Airdrie keeper, as the teams retired at the interval."

Only a couple of months later, John returned to the Celtic squad as the Hoops defeated St Johnstone by six goals to two at Celtic Park. During his absence, back up goalkeeper John Kelly made eight of the ten appearances he would eventually make as a Celtic player and, to his credit, he kept a clean sheet on five of those eight outings. However, in only his second match of that eight game run, Celtic disappointingly crashed out of the Scottish Cup to St Mirren by virtue of a three-one home defeat. Whilst he was not the only one who had to shoulder some degree of blame for the defeat, the differences between himself and Celtic's regular keeper were clear to see: **"...when he was beaten it was apparent that he lacked the agility and anticipation which can only be acquired from experience."**

In saying that, Kelly was generally reliable and calm, for he was a competent enough goalkeeper, and somewhat unfortunate to find a truly special individual in the form of Thomson keeping him out of the senior side. He left for Carlisle United at the end of the season in search of more regular senior appearances, after he came to the realisation that John would likely be Celtic's main goalkeeper for many years to come.

Returning to the match against St Johnstone, Jimmy McGrory was also returning from injury, and thus the Celtic supporters were in a buoyant mood that day, as the goals flew in and two of their heroes re-established themselves in the Celtic line-up after notable absences. One newspaper report read: **"Both received a great welcome, which was renewed at intervals when each demonstrated his complete recovery by masterly play."**

On the eighteenth of May 1930, John Thomson made his international debut against France, and kept a clean sheet, as Scotland won by two goals to nil. John played his part, as one article written regarding the match describes: **"At the other end it was Thomson's turn to distinguish himself when, from a free kick near the corner flag, a Frenchman banged the ball in from only eight yards. Thomson, however, leaped high up to punch the ball out with both hands."**

John would go on to make three more appearances for his country, against each of the home nations, keeping two more clean sheets, against Ireland and, famously, against England, as goals from George Stevenson and Jimmy McGrory propelled Scotland to a two-nil win, and a share of the British Home Championship title. Regarding that legendary victory over the English opposition, one newspaper columnist wrote: **"Over the whole game Thomson, the goal-keeper, had an easy time of it so well was he covered by his colleagues. On the occasions when he was called into action, however, he cleared in a style which justified the selectors' confidence in him."**

Interestingly, **"The Glasgow Herald"** goes on not only to list the teams, but the respective height and weight of each player also. In modern times, we have Fraser Forster in goal at Celtic Park, who is not only the tallest goalkeeper, but the tallest player to have played for the Football Club, standing at an impressive six feet and seven inches in height. In 2012–13, Forster was also the tallest goalkeeper to feature in the UEFA Champions League that season. His sterling performances, particularly against Barcelona, earned him the nickname of **"La Gran Muralla"** in the Catalan newspapers, a phrase meaning **"The Great Wall"** – I have no doubts that John Thomson would have admired the acquisition of such an accolade in a great footballing city like Barcelona.

Nowadays, with the benefit of hindsight, it is often intriguing to consider how the game of football has changed. One notable difference is that, generally, footballers (especially defenders and goalkeepers) have become taller. Of course, whilst the average height of human beings on Earth has increased, it has not risen as dramatically as the average height of many professional footballers. In the modern era, there are certainly coaches who believe that bigger players are better players when it comes to the issues of protecting one's goalmouth. However, had John Thomson played in the Champions League in the aforementioned season of 2012–13, he would have been the smallest of all of the goalkeepers by some distance, standing at only five feet and eight inches tall, almost a foot short of Fraser Forster. Statistics such as these highlight that the game of football is continuously changing and adapting, developing by the day, and this is no bad thing – it is like a dynamic organism – no two seasons are the same, and nor should they be.

Returning to the tale of John Thomson, at the end of 1930–31, which would be his last full season, John helped Celtic to win their second major trophy of his time at the Club, as the Celts defeated Motherwell by four goals to two in the replay which followed the Scottish Cup Final of 1931. Despite his handling error allowing Motherwell to equalise midway through the first half, Thomson had a relatively good game, throwing himself across his goalmouth and courageously diving at the feet of his opponents in order to defend the lead Celtic would go on to build. It is perhaps a fitting tribute that eighty years later, in 2011, Celtic would repeat the feat against the Steelmen, albeit by a different scoreline.

Interestingly, had Celtic lost to Motherwell in 1931, then the Club, incredibly, would have found itself in breach of contract – or so the popular joke of the time went, as it is described here in one Glaswegian newspaper.

"Mr Tom White, who accepted the Cup on behalf of Celtic, humorously explained that it was necessary for Celtic to have the Cup, since it was part of a contract into which they had entered. Their American tour had been arranged on the assumption that they would take either the Cup or the League flag across the Atlantic with them. They had, therefore, made sure of the first thing down for decision."

At the start of the 1931–32 campaign, there was only one thing on the minds of those at Celtic Football Club. Rivals Rangers had now won the past five league Championships, and were aiming to make this a record equalling 'six in a row' (remember Celtic had previously become the first and only Club to achieve this feat, at that point in time, between 1904–05 and 1909–10). As between seventy-five and eighty thousand supporters travelled to Ibrox on the fifth of September 1931 for the first Glasgow derby of the new season, many predicted it would be a match to remember, and they were right – but tragically, not for any enjoyable reason. As the following quotes highlight, the match itself turned out to be a fairly haphazard affair in the first half, with the importance of the game being personified by the anxious style of football on display.

"Nervousness was obvious in every movement. Free kicks were numerous, and the number of throw-ins in the early stages was phenomenal. The teams were as boxers trying to "size up" each other, and then when they tried to land blows they struck air."

"And so the game went on for half an hour in wild bursts with science thrown to the winds. Yet the crowd with their partisanship to buoy them up seemed to be enjoying themselves; they howled loudly enough anyway."

"Some idea of the drabness of the play may be gathered from the fact that the first decent shot to trouble either of the goalkeepers came after thirty-five minutes play..."

Early in the second half of the game, with the tight match still goalless, a ball played through the Celtic defence was chased down by Rangers striker Sam English. However, English was not the only player determined to make the ball his own, as the Celtic goalkeeper Thomson rushed forward in an attempt to quell the threat to his goalmouth. John then made the last of his famous saves at the feet of an opponent, stopping Rangers from taking the lead, but paying the ultimate sacrifice in the process.

As both players stretched for the ball, John's head collided with English's knee, dealing a fatal blow to the young goalkeeper. This was, of course, a horrific accident. In a sense it was football at its purest; a striker chasing down a pass as an athletic goalkeeper hurled himself at the ball, as the crowd drew breath with excitement and anticipation. However, it was also luck at its most terrible.

One Glaswegian newspaper reported the incident as follows: **"Shortly after the interval, the Rangers centre-forward, English, worked past the Celtic backs, and in a desperate and daring effort to save his goal from imminent downfall, John Thomson, the brilliant young Celtic goalkeeper, threw himself at the forward's feet as the latter delivered his shot, and received the impact of the kick as both players fell to the ground."**

There was nothing either player, nor any of medical staff present, could do. Once the collision had occurred, John Thomson was left with a fractured skull and a ruptured artery. His colleagues and friends in the Celtic team found him unconscious with blood escaping from his head wound. He was stretchered from the field with some of the crowd unaware of the fact such a serious injury had just occurred before their very eyes.

Another newspaper journalist wrote: **"The ball curled past the far post, but Thomson lay limp, while English, who had also fallen, rose and bent over him. Trainers immediately rushed onto the field, followed by doctors and the managers of both teams."**

"Behind the goals were massed the followers of Rangers, and a section of these commenced to cheer. Meiklejohn [the famous Rangers captain, David Meiklejohn] left the group round the stricken player, and, with arms outstretched, made a mute appeal. It was effective, and amid tense silence, Thomson was carried off the pitch on a stretcher."

However, as John left a football pitch for the last time, it is said that **"a single piercing scream"** emanating from a woman in the main stand broke the awkward silence that had descended soon after the collision. Tragically, this was not the scream of a random woman as she saw the severity of Thomson's injuries, but that of John's fiancée, Margaret Findlay, whom he was set to marry later that year.

John was swiftly taken to the Victoria Infirmary in Glasgow's Southside where, despite the valiant efforts of surgeons there to lessen the pressure being imposed upon the brain by severe swelling, he died at around twenty-five minutes past nine in the evening. Upon the reception of his injury, word was quickly sent from Glasgow to Cardendan for John's parents. They arrived at his bedside only moments before John passed away. The match itself finished goalless, with John Thomson's final clean sheet remaining intact – and, in time, Rangers would fail to equal Celtic's run of six consecutive titles, as Motherwell won the League Championship for the one and only time in their history.

"I took a trip to Parkhead,
To the dear old Paradise,
And as the players came out,
Sure the tears fell from my eyes."

"For a famous face was missing,
From the Green and White Brigade,
And they told me Johnny Thomson,
His last game he had played."

And so Celtic Football Club, Scotland, and the game of football as a whole had lost one of the most promising goalkeepers they had ever seen. When he died, twenty-two year old John Thomson had already played over two hundred times for Celtic, picking up two Scottish Cup winners medals along the way, having also featured four times for his country, keeping three clean sheets. More importantly though, a young woman had lost her fiancé, two parents had lost their child, siblings had lost their brother, others had lost their friend, and thousands had lost their idol.

Reflecting on the tragedy, one journalist wrote of his personal memories of the incident:

"Perched away up on the roof of the grandstand, away from the immediate touch of the crowd and it's enthusiasms, pressmen are apt to become cold and cynical, they get a bird's eye view and see many petty actions that escape the eyes of the crowd – and the referee."

"Yet the news that John Thomson had received a depressed fracture of the skull caused sadness; the end of a great, if somewhat short, career had come, and Thomson had always played the game the way it should be played – keenly and cleanly."

It is believed that somewhere between thirty and forty thousand people attended John's funeral in Fife. Not only did special trains have to be scheduled to meet demand, but it is reported that many people who could not afford the railway fares felt it necessary to walk the whole way (some fifty-five miles) from Glasgow to Cardendan just to be there. As Thomson's coffin was carried through the village streets by his teammates, people stood not only on the pavements, but also on walls and rooftops to pay their final respects.

One week on from the match at Ibrox, Celtic took to the field for the first time hence to face Queen's Park at Celtic Park. Prior to the beginning of sporting proceedings, everybody in attendance, players and spectators alike, took a few moments to remember their fallen goalkeeper, as the following exert from **"The Glasgow Herald"** describes:

"Impressive tribute was paid to John Thomson at Celtic Park on Saturday. The flags were at half-mast, and all round the ground there was a subdued air. Celtic came out first filing slowly from the pavilion, followed by Queen's Park, the 22 players forming an unbroken line as they walked to the field and took up their positions. All wore black armlets."

"The crowd did not know how to welcome the players – there was a moment's hesitation, and then a half-hearted cheer rippled round the field. Players and spectators stood while a lament, the Last Post, and "Lead, Kindly Light" were played. There was silence for a moment, then a cheer for the teams and another for Falconer as he ran towards the west goal. Then play began."

A few weeks later, as the Scottish Football Association held its first meeting since the accident, all of the members conveyed their sympathies officially, as can be found in the minutes of the meeting at Hampden Park. They said:

"61. Sympathy. Desired to record the loss which the game sustained by the tragic death of John Thomson (Celtic F.C.) on the 5th September, 1931, following an accidental injury sustained by him at Ibrox Park, Glasgow, on that day, and to extend the deep sympathy of this Association to the parents of John Thomson, and to the Celtic and Rangers Clubs."

Perhaps the best way to honour the memory and legacy of John Thomson is through the words of those close to him and to the world of Scottish Football:

"He was the best keeper I had ever seen." – Desmond White, future Celtic chairman

"Graceful, athletic, very brave and courageous." – Robert McElroy, Historian

"A great player who came to the game as a boy and left it still a boy; he had no predecessor, no successor, he was unique." – John Arlott, Journalist

"Among the galaxy of talented goalkeepers whom Celtic have had, the late lamented Thomson was the greatest...A most likable lad, modest and unassuming, he was popular wherever he went... Never was there a keeper who caught and held the fastest shots with such grace and ease...Among the great Celts who have passed over, he has an honoured place." – Willie Maley, Celtic Manager

However, this was not the end of the John Thomson story, for in 2008, he was posthumously inducted into the Scottish Football Hall of Fame. He is still remembered to this day by the Celtic support, and the people of Cardendan, with football tournaments, charity walks, and even a play at the King's Theatre in Glasgow taking place in his honour.

Finally, let us also remember the other man tragically involved in this accident, a figure whom the incident seemingly had a tremendous impact on. Sam English, a striker originally from Aghadowey across the Irish Sea, was forced to leave Scotland not long after the death of John, as football crowds around the country regularly subjected him to abuse which was entirely unfounded. After a spell with Liverpool, English retired, telling a friend that since the death of Thomson, he had experienced **"seven years of joyless sport"**. Sam died in April 1967, still haunted by the events of that day at Ibrox Park.

"Farewell my darling Johnny,
Prince of players we must part,
No more we'll stand and cheer you,
On the slopes of Celtic Park."

"Now the fans they all are silent,
As they travel near and far,
No more they'll cheer John Thomson,
Our bright and shining star."

"So come all you Glasgow Celtic,
Stand up and play the game,
For between your posts, there stands a ghost,
Johnny Thomson is his name."

"We Have No Intention of Stopping"

The stretch of Glasgow's Gallowgate outside the famous Barrowland Ballroom has always been one of my favourite places in the city. Yes, there are nicer areas and yes, there are most certainly more affluent areas, but nonetheless I've always enjoyed my time there, regardless of whether it consisted of a few pints in one of the local bars, or a stroll around the Barras Market at the weekend, picking up everything from dodgy DVD's to some fantastic doughnuts. However, I suppose the main reason for my liking of the area is a simple case of identity.

Anyone who has ever lived in Greater Glasgow will know that there are certain areas which are far friendlier to Celtic supporters than others, as a lack of wealth often combined with blatant socio-religious stigma forced many of the communities which possessed a natural affinity towards Celtic Football Club into the same areas or towns as each other in decades long gone by – many of which remain green and white strongholds to this day. The belief that there is strength in numbers has been held by many downtrodden people across the world throughout the sands of time, as such groups naturally polarise towards each other when they perceive a threat to themselves and/or their families.

The area of the Gallowgate which I alluded to earlier is one of the most visible strongholds to a passer-by, with Irish tricolours fluttering above bars and shops often painted with the colours of Celtic Football Club and many of which have names referencing the Club or a moment in its history – **"Hoops Bar"**, **"Tim Land"** etc. However, earlier this summer I was not destined for either of the two aforementioned examples but for **"Bar 67"**, aptly named after the year of Celtic's greatest triumph.

Inside, I was set to meet two gentlemen who travelled to Lithuania in early October 2002 to see Celtic finish off their hosts F.K. Suduva before progressing to the second round of the UEFA Cup competition. Having spoken to one of the two men, Frank Mullen, on the phone and arranged the meeting, I had been told to simply ask for him at the bar when I arrived. And so, as I entered the pub on a Thursday afternoon, I was not overly surprised to find that it was rather quiet. Perhaps that sounds somewhat obvious, but as someone who had only ever been in **"Bar 67"** in the hours before big matches at Celtic Park previously, it allowed me a new view of the premises. For example, whilst I'd seen the large mural painting of several Celtic greats (many of which are featured in this book) on prior visits, I'd never really had the time to truly appreciate it. Likewise, the array of old programmes, photographs and scarves covering not only the other walls but also the ceiling took my interest. Anyway, as I stood there at the bar waiting to be served, a man in a suit jacket and tie finished his phone call in the corner and quickly introduced himself as Frank, or **"Wee Franny"** as he is more commonly known.

Having sat down at a table in the corner of the bar, we were soon joined by Franny's pal (and one of his many travelling companions over the years), Hughie Connolly, who set a large bag down on the table beside him. Previously, Franny had said that he believed Hughie still had his ticket from that night in Lithuania and, having opened his bag and pulled out a folder which was literally bursting full of old programmes and tickets enclosed in plastic pockets, Hughie produced it in utterly pristine condition, alongside programmes, tickets and newspapers from every European match Celtic played that season. As he did so, I couldn't help but notice an original programme from the European Cup Final in 1967 flick by – something I had never seen previously in the flesh, but was privileged enough to that day.

Before proceeding any further, I should highlight that these two gentlemen were unique characters, and I'm sure neither of them would dispute the fact that once they start talking about Celtic Football Club and trips of old, they could talk for Scotland. Of course, as a young man, I found this all to be tremendously interesting, but after extensive tangents and stories of days gone by, one of us, whether it was myself, Franny or Hughie would be forced to say **"Anyway, back to Suduva!"** If we had not, then we would have likely still been sitting there discussing Celtic upon closing time at the pub – I kid you not.

Franny and Hughie first travelled to an away European game in 1966, as Celtic narrowly lost to Liverpool in the semi-finals of the European Cup Winners' Cup at Anfield, and even now, almost fifty years on, the late away goal which was disallowed that would have set up a European Final with Borussia Dortmund at Hampden still grates with the two men (I expect I may feel somewhat similar about Seville in my later life, but that's another story entirely). Anyway, ever since then, they have travelled across the length and breadth of Europe, taking in not only the **"popular destinations"** but also many of the others, some of which lay behind the **"Iron Curtain"**. In truth, an author could likely write a book on these two men and their experiences alone.

Returning to 2002, both men had travelled to Switzerland where they had seen Celtic crash out of the UEFA Champions League on away goals after a disappointing three-all aggregate draw with F.C. Basel. Unfazed by this, only hours after Celtic had drawn F.K. Suduva; Franny received a phone call from a friend chartering a plane to Lithuania, a country with a far bigger interest in basketball than any other sport, asking if he would be able to fill a batch of seats for him. Despite the fact the plane was set to fly from Gatwick International Airport, a little under thirty miles south of Central London, Franny had no problems with regards to filling the spaces with regular European travellers from both Scotland and Ireland – in fact, he eventually asked for extra places to accommodate demand, as the deal on offer (excluding return travel to Gatwick) came in at half of what was being charged for the official away trip. Having gathered in the money, Franny chuckled slightly as he recalled walking down the Gallowgate with all of the cash inside a carrier bag, within which he estimated there would have been several thousand pounds in total.

And so, as supporters from both Scotland and Ireland headed for Gatwick one day prior to Celtic's tie with F.K. Suduva, they felt safe in the knowledge that their side had all but officially secured their place in the next round thanks to an emphatic first leg victory which saw them run out eight-one winners at Celtic Park (meaning Suduva would need to produce an utterly miraculous, nigh on impossible result such as a seven-nil scoreline to cause an upset). Having travelled down to Gatwick on the train, Franny and the rest of the Scottish party had arrived at the airport in plenty of time, without any incident of note. However, as the deadline for check-in drew closer, a group of Irish supporters, who had initially flown into Luton International Airport, some seventy miles away, were yet to arrive.

Across London, members of the aforementioned Irish group were looking at their watches with increasingly anxious expressions on their faces. They had just discovered that due to an ongoing strike, no trains were running between the two airports, meaning they would need to find an alternative means of traversing the seventy miles or face the prospect of missing their flight – and they would need to be fast. With this in mind, they dashed outside the front of the arrivals hall, with one of them jumping in front of a Black Hackney Cab that was just pulling away from the kerb, placing his hands on the bonnet as he did so. Within seconds, they all struck up a conversation with the initially irate driver, whom they believed to be of Turkish origin. Having explained the seriousness of their situation, they offered the man one hundred pounds if he could get them to Gatwick on time, and he duly accepted.

Now, that may sound as if that was that. However, the more observant among you will have noted that the taxi was pulling away from the kerb when they Irish lads halted its progress, meaning that the driver already had a fare in the back of the vehicle. The individual in question, an English gentleman in a pinstripe suit with a briefcase, was left rather stunned as, only moments later, the driver virtually hauled him out of the cab as his new Hooped passengers leapt in, before returning to the driver's seat and speeding off as if he was destined for Silverstone rather than Gatwick. Incredibly, the group made their check-in deadline with only moments to spare, and the Turkish taxi driver received his large reward for his valiant efforts.

That incident aside, it was a smooth trip to Lithuania for all involved, as the group, including Franny and Hughie, touched down at Vilnius Airport, just outside of Lithuania's capital city.

Having arrived at their hotel and dropped off their bags, Franny and Hughie went out for a meal along with a few others, before retiring to bed.

The next day, the pair awoke and wandered around the city, before spending some time with the larger party at a local bar. Now, some of you may have noticed that whilst the party were staying in Vilnius, the match itself was actually played in Kaunas, Lithuania's second largest city, some sixty miles away. F.K. Suduva actually ply their trade in the town of Marijampolé, a settlement with a population of less than fifty thousand people, but whilst their new stadium (opened in 2008) is occasionally the host of international matches, their old home was not deemed fit for the first round of the UEFA Cup.

For this reason, Celtic's tie against the Lithuanian side was held at the Darius and Girėnas Stadium, the ground named after two pilots, Steponas Darius and Stasys Girėnas, who were killed as they attempted to become the first people to fly directly from New York to Kaunas. The stadium remains the home of F.B.K. Kaunas and with a maximum capacity of a little over eight thousand spectators, it is situated almost exactly one thousand, one hundred miles away from Celtic Park.

Returning to the tale of Franny and Hughie, they still had to make their way from Vilnius to Kaunas, with a few hours left to go before kick-off. Whilst they had initially considered the use of public transport, they instead asked a taxi driver how much it would cost them to be driven there, knowing that many things were fairly cheap in the country (between ten and fifteen pence for a pint of lager, for example) and that it would, potentially, save them a lot of hassle. Incredibly, the answer given to the men was that it would cost them the equivalent of only four or five pounds for a sixty mile journey down the Lithuanian motorway. Of course, they accepted this offer and once they arrived at the stadium, they asked their driver where they could find a bus or a cab for a return journey, and were amazed when he subsequently offered to wait for them for several hours before driving them back personally – all for the relatively measly sum of only another fifteen pounds.

With that organised, the attention of Franny, Hughie and all the rest of the travelling supporters turned to the match itself. According to Hughie, there were a little less than one hundred and twenty Celtic fans in total that made the journey, and, with the greatest respect to the Lithuanian people, whom they described as friendly and jovial, it appears none of the travelling support were particularly impressed with the stadium they visited. **"It was like a public park"**, reflected Franny, **"I'd say it was like a junior ground, but in all honesty I thought it was worse than a junior ground – the playing surface was terrible."**

"Of course, the tie was over and done with at Celtic Park, so when I found there was a bar underneath our little stand with televisions, a fair amount of our supporters simply headed down there to watch the match and have a drink," continued Franny.

By the time the game was over, Franny and Hughie returned to their taxi along with a couple of mates after witnessing Celtic win a fairly drab encounter by two goals to nil. As promised, the driver was still there, and soon they were on the road back to Vilnius. However, sometime into the journey, one of the other men announced that he desperately needed the toilet, and so the taxi slowed to a halt on the hard shoulder of the motorway in order to allow nature to take its course.

The individual in question, who shall remain nameless, had perhaps had one too many drinks by this point, and proceeded to fall into a drainage ditch which he had failed to spot by the roadside. However, this went unnoticed by the others until they returned to their vehicle and realised they were a man short. As they turned around, the whole group (the driver included) saw a set of legs flailing up from the drainage ditch a short distance away. Of course, this incident provided great hilarity for everyone other than the victim himself, but this emotional high would soon take a notable downturn, once the men finally left their driver, having handed him his fee, and headed back to the restaurant which Franny and Hughie had eaten in the night before, simply hoping for a quick meal before bed.

Upon entering the building, the bouncer (yes, the restaurant had a bouncer) seized Franny by the throat, forcing him up against the doorway wall and demanding, via broken English, that he told him about the counterfeit dollars which had appeared in the restaurant last night. As Franny and Hughie had previously explained to me, they always took a mixture of Pounds Sterling, U.S. Dollars and German Deutsche Marks whenever they had travelled to the Eastern Block in the past, rather than using the local currency. With relatively few tourists in town, and none more memorable than the green and white clad Celtic supporters, the restaurant staff clearly presumed it had been the two Glaswegians who had paid them with counterfeit money, although they both strenuously denied this. Eventually, after an exchange of views and, notably, an exchange of cash, Franny was set free and they found somewhere else to eat instead.

However, the Celtic supporters in Vilnius would soon be the subject of more scrutiny, as later, a bar full of supporters would be visited by a group of Lithuanian police who, by all accounts, looked like they would have been right at home in a James Bond movie, with long leather coats, matching gloves, traditional fur hats and shiny black boots which made a distinctive sound as they struck the floor of the bar. In Franny's own words: **"It was a very frightening experience. These guys looked like they had come straight from an old film where they played members of the K.G.B., with the hats and the gloves and everything else. They began to ask about fake money and, because I was one of the guys who hadn't been drinking, I did my best to act as one of the spokesmen for the group. They produced a few notes of varying currencies and then compared them closely with some of those we had on us, and for a time we were all awfully nervous."**

Thankfully, after around half an hour of questioning, the Celtic support were vindicated as no evidence of any wrongdoing (or any counterfeit money for that matter) was ever found, and they were left to enjoy what remained of their trip to the country.

Finally, I suppose I should conclude this chapter with the pair's reflections on Lithuania, a country which regrettably boasts the highest homicide rate in the European Union and also the third highest suicide rate on the face of the Earth. Of course, there are a plethora of reasons for this, and in all honesty, one could probably pen a university dissertation regarding this. However, one thing is clear – poverty plays a role.

Whilst Hughie recalled that Lithuania was not as poor as some of the countries they had visited previously when Europe was truly divided, it was clear that many of the people there were very poor. However, over the last ten years, the gross domestic product of the country has quadrupled, and gradually, this prosperity appears to be seeping down to the average Lithuanian. Whether this ties in with Franny's feeling that the country was **"a bit more westernised than he had expected"** is up for debate, but both men said they would **"have no hesitations about returning to the country."**

"The majority of the people were lovely," reflected Franny, **"stereotypes can say whatever they like about countries like Lithuania, but in my opinion, you can never truly appreciate a place or the people who live there until you have visited it and spoken to them in person. Yes, the country had its problems – but show me a country which does not. I thought things were changing for the better and I hope that continues."**

As for football, the sport remains in the long shadow of basketball in Lithuania, but it appears to be on the right track and perhaps, one day, Celtic shall see F.K. Suduva again. One thing is certain though, Franny and Hughie have lived long and interesting lives following Celtic Football Club, making many friends both foreign and domestic in the process, and I hope they'll continue to follow the team around Scotland and Europe for many years to come – **"we have no intention of stopping,"** the pair told me. They are both incredibly friendly gentlemen, and if you ever happen to meet either of them, be sure to put some time aside and take an opportunity to listen to some fantastic stories.

"Don't Judge A Book By Its Cover"

Flurries of snow in late March – ah, Scotland at its finest.

Unsurprisingly, in the midst of one of the coldest March's on record, the sight of a boiling hot cup of tea was a welcome one, as I sat down for a 'face to face' discussion with a very interesting man. In all likelihood, very few of you will know Kevin, but because of his name alone, most would, correctly, predict that he is a Celtic supporter (admittedly, the fact he is featured in this book probably suggested that in itself, but you know what I mean). However, if I were to use Kevin's full working title instead, which is **"Sergeant McAuley"**, then many of you may have made another prediction.

In truth, by making such a presumption either way, we would have all been somewhat guilty of stereotyping. It's the sort of thing people's mothers tend to say: **"Don't judge a book by its cover"**. And so, in the case of Kevin McAuley, the book you are currently reading and life in general, it's just another situation when mums are proven to be correct. Kevin is an avid Celtic supporter, and a member of the British Armed Forces, and whilst that should not be a contradiction in terms, there will be some who feel it is. They are, of course, entirely entitled to their opinion, but on a personal level I would have to strongly disagree with them.

Born in the late 1970's, Kevin grew up in Motherwell before an eventual move to Hamilton. In respect of this, the first football matches he ever took in were at Fir Park in the early 1980's, as his father's friend was the Head of Security for Motherwell Football Club, and he would often allow them to take any empty seats in the stand on match days free of charge. Kevin's family were all diehard Celtic fans themselves, but decided to **"try him out"** in a local stadium before dragging him all the way into Glasgow on the off chance that he couldn't sit still for ninety minutes to watch a game. On one occasion, Celtic travelled to Fir Park, and, as was so often the case, Kevin's father's friend allowed the pair access to the players' lounge after the match. And so, with his treasured autograph book in hand, Kevin – still a child – began to wander around the visiting team asking for their respective signatures.

Soon, he approached Maurice Johnston, who proceeded to flick through the pages of Kevin's book, laugh, and hand it back to him unsigned before returning to his conversation as if nothing had happened. Naturally, this upset Kevin, but it is probably fair to say that it upset Kevin's father more, who was incensed by the Celtic striker's reaction. As he remonstrated with Johnston, the disagreement led to an argument, which in turn led them to the verge of a physical altercation.

Thankfully though, the peace was quickly restored before things got too out of hand by none other than the Celtic captain, Roy Aitken. Despite his tough characteristics on the field of play, **"The Bear"** showed off his famously nice nature that day, and was incredibly apologetic to both Kevin and his father – so much so that he led the pair over to the table filled with the other Celtic players, and sat them down. As Kevin's autograph book worked its way around the table, more and more signatures were added to it, as, some distance away, the Celtic captain had a quiet word in Maurice Johnston's ear regarding his conduct. Regardless, the main thing Kevin took from that day was not the ignorance of one player, but the kindness and respect shown to him by the Celtic captain, and the group as a whole. **"From then on in I knew I truly was a Celtic supporter,"** said Kevin, **"Obviously, that was the first time I'd seen Celtic, and despite the incident with Johnston, I was hooked. I knew there was something special about them"**.

Not long after that, he saw his **"first proper Celtic game"** (i.e. one away from Fir Park) as Celtic won by five goals to nil at Clydebank in March 1986, thanks to a hat-trick from Brian McClair as well as a goal each from Tommy Burns and Alan McInally. Within a couple of years, Kevin and his late uncle were travelling to matches regularly. Initially he did so with the **"Motherwell Nine-In-A-Row Celtic Supporters Club"** (out of the Railway Tavern, Motherwell), before his move to Hamilton where he travelled in by train for home games and jumped on whichever supporters bus would take him to away games.

Over the years, as with most supporters, he has watched some better Celtic sides than others, but regardless of the results and the performances, Kevin was often there to support his team. When he rejoined the British Army in 2001 (having previously served during the 1990's), he was, of course, unable to attend as many matches, but he still did all he could to keep updated with the team news and results. This determination to remain **"in the loop"** with all things Celtic led to a few incidents of note during his military career, some of which I will describe to you now.

As Celtic progressed through the rounds of the UEFA Cup as 2002 became 2003, Kevin was based in Kuwait, awaiting the increasingly likely order to move over the border into Iraq. As an electrical engineer, he had been sent to the country around the turn of the year in order to become accustomed with how the combination of searing heat and endless drifting sand affected the technology being used by his colleagues. For this reason, as the Hoops ran out against Stuttgart on the twentieth of February, Kevin wasn't expecting to have any opportunity to watch the game. Anyway, on his route back from the mess hall that night, he decided to check the book which logged all the electrical faults in need of repair for the following day, and in doing so, he passed the control room of the American command centre at the base. As he glanced through a large window, he spotted a familiar shirt on one of the countless televisions attached to the opposite wall, which were broadcasting various channels from around the globe.

Now, as the room was the American command centre at the Kuwaiti base, Kevin wasn't allowed to simply wander in and sit down in front of his chosen screen. However, as he was an electrical engineer, he was allowed access to that room if any of the numerous electrical components within required his services. Having relayed his situation to his fellow engineers, suddenly a plethora of things required **"checked"** and **"fixed"** in the command room that night, and Kevin was sent to do the jobs, and do them he did – albeit rather slowly. This allowed him to see a large part of the Hoops' three-one victory – I suppose it makes a change from a pub in Hamilton, eh?

Around a fortnight later, Celtic and Rangers faced each other at Parkhead as the battle for the Scottish Premier League title heated up. Without Henrik Larsson, Celtic weren't as strong as they could be, but they did manage to grind out a one-nil victory nonetheless thanks to a strike from a Welshman, John Hartson, who would go on to write his name into the history books of Celtic Football Club only weeks later. Unable to watch the match live, Kevin had been saving up his allotted minutes of satellite phone usage, and booked himself in for a call to coincide with the end of the game. Upon saying **"Hello"** to his father for the first time in weeks, Kevin's first questions were **"What was the score?"** and **"Who scored?"** – it was only after this that he went on to ask how his son, daughter and the rest of the family were doing, but such was life on the days of the old Glasgow derbies between Celtic and Rangers, regardless of whether you were in Kilmarnock, Kilsyth or Kuwait.

The remainder of spring would be eventful not only for Celtic, who smashed their way past Liverpool at Anfield thanks partly to John Hartson's wonder goal, but also for Kevin. On the same day as the second leg against the Merseyside Club, Kevin crossed the border into Iraq. A little over a month later, he joined several hundred colleagues in the outdoor cookhouse where they were based, and began to stare at the big screen which was set up there intently. Celtic, the team whom he had supported since he was a child, found themselves in the second leg of a UEFA Cup semi-final. All that stood in the Hoops' way were Boavista, and as the game kicked off and wore on, Kevin's emotions began to run higher and higher. Being the only Celtic fan there, he was as much a focus of attention as the match itself for his colleagues, who watched his nervous agony as it inevitably turned into absolute elation. Seconds after Henrik Larsson found the back of the net, the Celtic supporting world was in bedlam, and in the early hours of the morning in the Middle East, it was no different, as Kevin celebrated like he had never celebrated before.

"I was jumping around like a lunatic while everyone else just sat there looking at me! I couldn't have cared less, mind. It was amazing, a European final, I could barely believe it! All of these

folk who supported English teams were left staring at a Scottish team in the UEFA Cup Final. It was magnificent," said Kevin. Continuing on from this, Kevin then described the somewhat nasty events of the week which followed:

"A few days later, a lot of the lads, including me, were struck down with D&V [that's diarrhoea and vomiting to the rest of us], **so we weren't allowed anywhere near the cookhouse. Now, that was a problem for me considering Celtic were set to play Rangers at Ibrox, and the only television screen was in the aforementioned cookhouse. I wasn't allowed anywhere near the big screen, so I ended up having to use a pair of 'bino's'** [binoculars] **to try and see it from our quarantine area. I could hear the commentary easily since the sound was funnelled out of the three sided hangar, but I couldn't see anything. Still, a win was a win. It certainly made me feel a bit better for the first time in days!"**

And so, on the twenty-first of May 2003, as thousands of Celtic fans completed their journeys to Seville, Kevin completed his own trip – his trip home to Scotland, that is. Arriving back in Hamilton, he went home, threw his bags in the house, got changed, and headed to the local pub to meet his mates following a **"Hi mum! Bye mum!"** style conversation. Having gone without a drink for months, he openly admits that the alcohol had more of an effect on him than it usually had and, sober or not, I know he wasn't the only grown man (or woman) who cried at full time that night.

Later that year, as autumn turned to winter, Celtic travelled to Ibrox once more as they looked to reclaim the Scottish Premier League title from their rivals. Due to injuries, Chris Sutton made one of his famous appearances at centre half, and Liam Miller featured in the midfield line. Of course, whilst this wasn't ideal, Rangers clearly did not benefit from **"any unfair competitive advantage"** (yes, I can be a tad sarcastic at times, you'll need to forgive me), as a single goal from John Hartson once again meant the points would return to Parkhead with the visitors.

Now, at this point a few of you are probably thinking, **"Ok, so where was Kevin this time?"** and you'd be right to do so, but I doubt many of you (if any), would have guessed correctly. As the

Glasgow derby kicked off, Kevin was absolutely Baltic, and there's a good reason for that, because he found himself on a yacht in the middle of the Baltic Sea on **"Adventure Training"**.

Prior to leaving the port of Kiel (which is, coincidentally, the host of the biggest annual sailing event in the world, **"Kiel Week"**), Kevin and his colleagues were given a briefing by their civilian instructor for the voyage. During this talk, all of the important pieces of kit on the yacht that they would be sailing on were pointed out to the lads, and Kevin, who was already so concerned about the upcoming Glasgow derby that he had asked if there would be any stopovers along the way to their destination in Denmark, took particular note of the vessel's emergency radio.

As the group set sail onto the Baltic in late October, Kevin watched his mobile phone signal waning before it disappeared entirely when they finally lost sight of land. He knew this would happen, and was therefore unperturbed by it. However, as kick-off approached, Kevin saw his instructor enjoying an **"herbal cigarette"** on the deck of the yacht. Presuming he would be preoccupied for some time, Kevin couldn't help himself, and he began to fiddle about with the emergency radio, hoping that, with his history as an electrical engineer (albeit unfamiliar with the frequency range), he could find some coverage of the match.

As he scanned the airwaves, desperately hoping for a report from Ibrox, a booming voice thundered out from behind him: **"McAuley! What the fuck are you doing touching that emergency radio?!"** cried the instructor. Unsurprisingly, he wasn't too impressed when he discovered Kevin had been using the emergency technology in order to attempt to hear the commentary of a football match, and after giving **"McAuley"** a **"right royal roasting"** in front of his mates, he sent the guilty party outside onto the deck, to steer the yacht for the next stage of the voyage.

"I sat there in a huff," recalled Kevin, **"he'd just ripped right into me in front of the boys so I felt pretty crap. In desperation I pulled my phone out of my pocket to see if there was a signal but there wasn't even a hint of it. I'd virtually given up, until I spotted some land away off to my side some time later. By this stage, the instructor was away up the other end of the yacht enjoying one of**

his "herbal cigarettes" again, and although I knew I was meant to keep a steady heading, I began to wonder..."

"I nudged the boat slightly off course so we could head a bit closer to the land, hoping I could pick up enough of a mobile phone signal for a text to come through. I had the Celtic score updates system set up on my phone at that point, so the Club always messaged me with any goals and the final score. I knew the civvy [again, that's a civilian to you and me] **leading us wouldn't be happy with me if I got caught, but I couldn't help chancing my arm..."**

And so, as the vessel began to creep gradually closer and closer to the land in the distance, Kevin kept one eye on his phone, and another on the instructor whom he'd angered earlier. Eventually, the distinctive buzz of his mobile told him that not only had he got a signal, but he had a text. As he opened it, he saw that Celtic had beaten Rangers at Ibrox, and let out a whoop of delight. This was to be a mistake on Kevin's part, as it drew the attention of his colleagues, and critically, the attention of his instructor.

"We won! One-nil! We won!" Kevin told his mates, before the instructor appeared demanding to know what all the noise was about. A moment later, as he awaited an answer, the instructor exclaimed, **"Wait! Why the hell are we so close to land? McAuley?!"** He paused as he realised what Kevin had done, and to say he was unhappy would have been an understatement.

"He would have made me walk the plank there and then if he could have gotten away with it," said Kevin, **"and he went on to make my life a misery for the rest of the trip, but it was well worth it just to know that the Bhoys back home had went to Ibrox and done the business. Not even a raging instructor with a vendetta could wipe the smile off my face, although having to stay onboard and guard the yacht that night whilst my mates were allowed ashore for a beer almost did."**

In more recent years, Kevin has qualified as a nurse and studied **"Battlefield Advanced Trauma and Life Support"**, whilst working in the Accident and Emergency departments at a few hospitals during his time back on home soil. When I first met him, Kevin was considering his future in the military. However, having now been promoted to Sergeant and selected to study specialist Accident and Emergency training, he has no plans to leave the services at this point in time. Whilst at home, Kevin does all he can to spend time with his teenage son and daughter, however, he reflected that apparently it's **"not cool"** for teenagers to be seen hanging around with their dad nowadays – the wry smile on his face perhaps alluding to some of his escapades in his younger years. Having said all of this though, it doesn't mean that there isn't time for one last story from Kevin's past, as we recall the occasion upon which he visited the Andes Mountains in Peru.

Having already visited what claims to be the **"highest Irish bar in the world"** (**"Paddy Flaherty's"**, which I'm reliably informed sits at ten thousand, seven hundred and thirty-nine feet above sea level in Cusco) whilst on exercise in the country, Kevin found himself with some time off on the day that Manchester United were set to welcome Gordon Strachan's Celtic to Old Trafford for the first time. Obviously, Kevin was willing to go to great lengths to see the match as ever, and began to wander aimlessly around the town of Cusco in search of somewhere to watch it.

Having shown me a picture of the street he eventually found the game on, my suspicions that his story may turn out to be somewhat surreal were confirmed. Many of the structures were pieced together with a mixture of scrap metal and brick. With no windows in sight and no lighting switched on as it was the afternoon in Peru, every building appeared to be nothing other than a darkened doorway from street level.

"I was wandering up and down these streets, looking into all the wee bars, but I couldn't find anywhere with any customers, let alone the match on the television," said Kevin. **"I was roasting, fed up and just about to give up when this local bar owner, who had clearly caught sight of my Celtic top, shouted from the dark opening to one building and motioned to me to come inside. Once my eyes adjusted to the lighting, low and behold, there was this lad, in his Manchester United shirt, with this wee television in the corner. We were the only ones there, and as the game kicked off, we both started drinking shots of this clear local stuff. To be**

honest, I still don't know what it was, but it was lethal. By the end of the game, which we lost three-two, I reckon we were both pretty hammered. The altitude didn't help me!"

And so, presumably, Kevin stumbled back to his station and awoke with a nasty hangover – a hangover similar to those suffered by thousands of Celtic fans on such occasions, regardless of who they are or where they live. To this day, Kevin McAuley remains a passionate Celtic supporter, and, in my mind at least, he is just as welcome at Celtic Park as anyone else. Proverbially speaking, this military and civilian medic **"bleeds green and white"**.

"The Wild Rover"

As I write this, Celtic are fortunate to have a few incredible talents playing at full-back for the Football Club, with an enthusiastic little Honduran (Emilio Izaguirre), a determined young Welshman (Adam Matthews), and an increasingly experienced Swede (Mikael Lustig) regularly flying up and down the wings across Scotland and Europe. In young Joe Chalmers and Darnell Fisher too, we may see other gifted players emerge onto the big stage in the years to come. However, they are far from the first Celts to play in the full-back position and become well loved amongst the Club's supporters. Thankfully, they are also much less controversial figures than one of their earliest predecessors; the man who was the first player to truly become a 'Celtic star', Daniel Doyle.

Dan was born in Paisley on the sixteenth of September 1864, almost a century and a half ago, to parents Allan and Janet. In his younger life, I doubt Dan, nor the majority of other young men growing up in the area, felt that they would be remembered for generations to come. His early footballing career involved spells with Broxburn Shamrock, East Stirlingshire and, eventually, Hibernian of Edinburgh. During his time at Hibs, he played in the first match ever to take place at the newly built Celtic Park, on the eighth of May 1888. This match against Cowlairs was, of course, on the site of the original Celtic Park, a short distance from where the current stadium stands, but nevertheless it is an interesting fact to note. For the record, the tie finished goalless.

From Hibernian, Doyle headed south of the border to the potentially lucrative professional leagues in England, as he joined Newcastle East End (one of the two teams, along with Newcastle West End, that combined to form the Club we know today as Newcastle United) before moving on to Grimsby Town. It was during Dan's time at Grimsby that he was directly involved in a tragic accident, which many believe changed Daniel Doyle forever.

As Grimsby Town took on Staveley on the twelfth of January 1889, Dan collided with a well-known cricketer (a lot of cricketers were involved in the early days of football as people experimented with the new game and as many matches were initially staged on cricket grounds, especially in England where they formed ideal alternatives for Club's unable to construct a purpose built stadium) by the name of William Cropper. As the two men came together as they battled for possession of the ball, Doyle made contact with Cropper's stomach with some force. Within moments, Cropper writhed around on the turf in agony, before being carried off of the field to the dressing rooms whilst he was still in obvious distress. Without any modern day form of medical assistance, the internal injuries (believed to have been a ruptured bowel) which twenty-six year old Cropper received resulted in his death sometime later. He never left the dressing rooms alive, passing away whilst in the arms of Staveley's goalkeeper, his friend and fellow cricketer, George Hay.

The tragic incident was, of course, totally accidental and Dan was cleared of any wrongdoing, but undoubtedly it must have had a tremendous impact on the then twenty-four year old. It has been widely reported since then that, for one reason or another, Cropper did not actually want to play that day, but was persuaded to do so against his wishes, and repeated references to this fact (regardless of their veracity) could not have helped Dan to feel any better about the horrible situation he found himself cruelly entangled in.

Returning to the field of play later that year, as a different person but the same player, Dan Doyle's talents won him a place with Everton Football Club. In the next couple of seasons, he would not only go on to captain the Club, but to help Everton win their first English League Championship in 1891 (the Merseyside club have only repeated this feat on eight occasions since then, and they would not do so again until 1914–15). Only months after this historic triumph, Doyle decided to return to his native Scotland to play for the still recently formed Celtic Football Club. During the off season, Dan had actually agreed three contracts – with Everton, Celtic, and even Bolton Wanderers – although privately, he knew exactly where he would be playing his football at the start of the coming season. I suppose a lot of us would take what was, essentially, triple wages for the course of the summer if we knew we could get away with it! In 1892 though, Everton's financial accounts showed that they recovered a fee of almost seventy pounds from **"Mr Doyle"**, so it appears he was not fully successful in this respect.

Regardless, Dan Doyle officially signed for Celtic Football Club on the tenth of August 1891, and began a stint which would last almost exactly eight years. Whilst his capture was a massive coup for Celtic, it did go to show two important things about Scottish Football at that time, and it also alluded to where its ultimate destiny would lie in the future. In 1891, Scottish Football was, at least officially, a purely amateur affair (i.e. the clubs could not pay players for their services) whilst in England teams had been professional organisations for sometime.

In order to assure Dan Doyle's services, Celtic made use of a tactic employed by several 'amateur' clubs back then, and exploited a loophole by giving Dan a pub in Airdrie which he would own and run. This provided him with a steady stream of income while he played the game he loved. In the coming years, once Scottish Football had finally allowed the introduction of professionalism in 1893, senior figures with connections to several clubs would confirm that this had been a regular practice. However, it is worth highlighting that, as I'm sure many of you will know, there is one club in the professional leagues in Scotland who stood firmly by their beliefs and who remain amateurs to this day – Queen's Park Football Club. In modern times, when some players can be paid hundreds of thousands of pounds every week simply to kick a ball about (albeit with incredible skill), I can't help but wonder whether, at least in certain aspects, Queen's Park didn't have the wrong idea after all.

And so, as the 1891–92 season began, Celtic faced a trip to Tynecastle for their opening match of the campaign. In front of what was described by one newspaper as **"an immense crowd"**, Dan Doyle, the ex-captain of the reigning English Champions, made his Celtic debut. However, by all accounts, Dan, as well as many of his new teammates, had a noticeably poor day as Celtic lost by three goals to one. Dan was reported to have miskicked the ball on several occasions, and almost scored an own goal on another.

Despite this though, Dan Doyle's talents had an almost instantaneous effect on Celtic and their performances. Only a week after his first outing, Celtic faced Rangers for one of the final times at the old Celtic Park and, with **"a good defence in Doyle and Kelly"**, the Celts not only kept a clean sheet, but scored a few goals themselves, as they defeated their opponents by three goals to nil.

Anyway, in his first season with the Club, the man the Celtic support would flock from miles around to see helped his new side lift the Glasgow Cup, the Glasgow Charity Cup and, perhaps most importantly, their first Scottish Cup, in 1892. It took two attempts for Celtic to defeat their opponents Queen's Park, because the 'first final' was declared a friendly match as police and authorities could not deal with the truly vast number of supporters who made their way to Ibrox to watch the game (approximately forty thousand, which was considered an enormous crowd at that time) – Celtic prevailed one-nil regardless.

The events of that day at Ibrox though are of some interest, to my mind at least. In anticipation of a large attendance, Rangers had two new stands specially constructed, and according to one newspaper, the Club felt **"that 36,000 could be accommodated comfortably"**. However, upon further research, I feel that it is safe to say that at least one of two beliefs must have been false, if not both. Either the official attendance was incorrect, which is a distinct possibility, or the Rangers committee was wholly wrong in its estimations.

With this in mind, let me take you back to that day for a moment. Imagine it, the late throngs of a freezing winter in Scotland's largest city. There's still some snow on the ground, and as usual, there's a bitterly cold chill in the air. Celtic defeated Rangers by five goals to three in the semi-final a little over a month earlier, and you've been looking forward to this day for some time now. Kick-off is scheduled for four o'clock, and you've heard there are no less than thirteen special trains which have been laid in order to carry over ten thousand spectators to Ibrox

Park. And so, you make your way to stadium, arriving about two o'clock. Already, the ground is almost at capacity, and you enter to find the Celtic support singing what has since been described as **"stretches of popular airs"**.

An hour later, the pressure at the gates outside becomes so great that one of them bursts open, allowing thousands of spectators to stream in free of charge. As members of the crowd strained for a view of the field, the Celtic team emerge from the main stand to a rapturous reception. The match begins, but due to unavoidable incursions by the crowd onto the field of play, it is agreed the match will be regarded as a friendly. Despite this, you see Celtic win one-nil, and look forward to the second attempt at the final, knowing your team have the measure of their opponents.

When the match was replayed, a superior Celtic side came from a goal down at half time and scored five goals without reply in the second half to win the match and lift the famous old trophy, adding the first to a tally which now stands at an incredible thirty-six Scottish Cup triumphs. Dan Doyle played alongside the likes of Willie Maley and Sandy McMahon (who scored two goals) that day, in front of about twenty thousand people at Ibrox. Whilst several newspapers raved about the forward play of **"the Celtic"**, Dan was praised briefly by **"The Glasgow Herald"**:

"Doyle was also in great form, his kicking and tackling at times being magnificent."

In a sight that would become customary for some years to come, as the victorious Celtic team returned to Celtic Park with a trophy, the locals (some without shoes on their feet) would pour on to the streets to catch sight of their conquering heroes. As the Lisbon Lions would go on to do with the European Cup on a more widely publicised scale, the earliest successes of Celtic sides provided some respite to the impoverished people of the East End. Through their achievements, they brought hope to the lives of many which were all too hopeless in many senses.

Imagine it – Celtic, the Football Club created only years previously for the maintenance of dinner tables and with the aim of battling sickening levels of poverty, in a somewhat divided society, had just won the greatest prize in Scottish Football. People who had nothing, and I truly mean nothing, danced and sang the night away without a care in the world, all for one night, and all because of Celtic. There is something very special about that thought, and it is another reason for us all to be proud of what Celts before us have achieved, even in the distant past beyond any of our lifetimes.

The 1891–92 season would also see Dan Doyle receive his first international cap, as Scotland lost by four goals to one to England at Ibrox in April. The fact Doyle was only selected nine times for Scotland is still much maligned to this day within the Celtic support, who believe that he, like many others, was often overlooked because of who he was and who he played for, rather than because he was not talented enough. Of course, with regards Dan in particular, his reputation for unreliability in later years may have harmed his chances somewhat in this sense, as I shall allude to in a moment.

In the subsequent season, 1892–93, Dan played an important role as Celtic Football Club won their first Scottish League Championship and, notably, opened the current Celtic Park for the first time. Initially, thanks partly to Willie Maley's well documented love of athletics, the ground's inaugural event was a sports day held on the thirteenth of August 1892, in which individuals from athletics and football clubs were invited to race over distances such as one hundred yards on foot, as well as longer stretches on bicycles, such as one and five miles respectively. By all accounts, the weather was horrendous that day, with thunder, strong winds and heavy rain affecting the times that were being set by competitors that afternoon, although the new stadium remained full of spectators to the end, regardless of the conditions.

One week later, on the twentieth, Celtic welcomed visitors Renton to the new Celtic Park for the first fixture to be held there. In a tetchy, hard fought affair, the match ended with only nineteen players on the field, as injury forced the retirement of Mathieson (Renton), and both Madden (Celtic) and Quigley (Renton) were sent off after the pair had **"came to blows"**. As the pair left the playing surface, the score stood at three goals each, and so the battle for the victory was on, as the relative lack of numbers lent itself to large pockets of space appearing on the field. With only moments left on the clock, **"Celtic, during a scrimmage, rushed the ball through"** and ended their first match at the place which would become known as **"Paradise"** with a dramatic victory.

It is perhaps also worthy of note that, only a matter of months later, Rangers would visit the new Celtic Park for the first time. A few hours on from their arrival, they left the stadium with their tails between their legs, having been definitively beaten by three goals to nil. Now, I have no doubts that, at some point in your life, you will have heard someone discuss the manner in which history often seems to repeat itself.

Well, with regards Rangers' first and last visits to the location of Celtic Park as we know it today, there are notable similarities – despite the fact the matches themselves were separated by exactly one hundred and nineteen years to the day. The final scores were identical (three-nil to the Celts), as were the half time scores (two-nil) and, on both occasions, it seems certain that the margins of victory could have been far higher. As for Dan's role in all of this, he is said to have **"repulsed"** Rangers **"when they got near the Celts' goal"** along with his defensive partner Michael Dunbar during the first tie.

While several players were rewarded with many plaudits from supporters and the media over the rest of the season's campaign, Dan Doyle continued his rise towards an almost God-like status. Celtic and Queen's Park met once again in the Scottish Cup Final in a game which is as infamous now as it was then, for this was the match where Queen's Park managed to score without actually putting the ball through the posts.

However, before that incident occurred, the teams met for the Scottish Cup Final proper – or so the crowd believed. As Celtic and Queen's Park ran out at Ibrox Park in front of fifty thousand spectators on the twenty-fifth of February 1893, the crowd (unsurprisingly) presumed they would be watching the long awaited Scottish Cup Final as scheduled, as no information to the contrary was made available to the gathering public. However, due to a frost on the ground, it was agreed prior to the match that it would be nothing other than a friendly.

Now, that wasn't a totally uncommon occurrence in those days, but what made this match strange was the fact that the Scottish Football Association chose not to tell anyone other than the Clubs about this decision prior to kick-off – therefore, as the spectators in attendance believed they were enjoying the Cup Final, they were actually watching a much hyped, half frozen, kick about. For the record, Celtic once again won by a single goal to nil, not that it matters. The following is an excerpt from "The Scotsman" on the following Monday, the twenty-seventh of February:

"Queen's Park v Celtic – Probably no match of the year arouses such widespread interest as the final tie in the Scottish National Cup competition when the combatants are well matched; but when, as is the case this year, the competing teams come together for the first time in the season, additional importance attaches to the game. The attraction afforded by the meeting of two such clubs as the Queen's Park and Celtic was fully attested last year on the occasion of the first meeting of the teams in the final of the same competition, when a record gate was established. In all respects, therefore, Saturday's game was looked forward to as one of the first magnitude."

"It was all the more to be regretted, therefore, in view of these circumstances, that the weather, as it has so often done this season with matches of interest, proved so unpropitious, more especially in the view of the large crowd which had turned out to witness the struggle. A hard frost setting in on Friday night, the ground at Ibrox Park, the scene of the contest, on the forenoon of Saturday was found to be as hard as iron and everything pointed to a postponement of the tie. Notwithstanding the ominous outlook, however, the officials, along with the referee, apparently did not deem it to be their duty to come to a prompt decision, and make that decision known to the public, but allowed the expectant spectators to make their way to and throng into the ground in their thousands in hope of the referee's decision, after an inspection just prior to the start, being favourable to the playing of the tie.

Naturally, once the ground was packed with a crowd numbering 50,000 people, it was deemed unwise, for fear of the consequences, to make it known that the inspection had shown it to be impossible to proceed with the tie, and those present, save a few in the inner circle, were kept in blissful ignorance of the fact that they were to witness only a friendly match."

"Still, once the teams took to the field, the difficulty which the players experienced in keeping control over the ball and maintaining their equilibrium on the hard and slippery ground – in spite of a liberal sprinkling of sand and hayseed over the greater part of its surface – could not escape notice, and with no official declaration on the subject having been made known, a feeling of doubt and uncertainty as to the nature of the contest prevailed, which was discreditable to the officials of the Association, inconsiderate to the members of the public, and detrimental to the best interests of the game...when this came to be fully known such expressions of dissatisfaction were heard on all hands at the actions of the officials in not making the fact known early in the day..."

Having just gone through the aforementioned rigmarole of the first attempted Cup Final, a new date was publicised, and once again, supporters of both sides trudged to Ibrox Park. However, as I mentioned earlier, this was to be a match filled with controversy. Until late in the nineteenth century, goal nets had not yet come into use, so it meant that when a goal was scored, the ball could fly far from the field, just as it continues to do in playgrounds and parks around the world. It also meant that, at times, it could be tricky to tell which side of the post the ball passed. Generally, this issue was avoided by good sportsmanship from the players and the help of vast numbers of spectators in the crowd. However, this wasn't the case in the 1893 Scottish Cup Final, after Dan Doyle blocked a shot and put the ball out for a corner, with the Celts already trailing one-nil. As the Celtic players prepared to defend the set piece, the referee awarded their opponents a goal. This sparked protests both on the field and on the terracing from those of a Celtic persuasion, but the referee was not going to change his mind, regardless of the irate comments coming from the players surrounding him.

Despite Celtic scoring late on through Jimmy Blessington to reduce the deficit and make the score two-one, Queen's Park held on to win the match. This must have been particularly disappointing for Dan Doyle, who had played well by all accounts, despite making one mistake which nearly led to a Queen's Park goal. Ironically, the match certainly left a bad taste in the mouth of Willie Maley, who had several teeth knocked out during the first half, forcing him to temporarily retire from proceedings, leaving Celtic chasing a deficit with only ten men for a period until he returned. Notably, several other injuries were suffered by Celtic players that day as Queen's Park took the naturally physical Scottish game to an extreme degree.

Sometime later, as the Scottish Football Association met for its Annual General Meeting, Celtic put forward a proposal that **"goal nets be used in the semi-finals and finals"** of the future, with the Club's representative claiming that **"they were a distinct advantage, and of great assistance to the referee"**. Nowadays, this may seem obvious, but in 1893, Celtic's proposal was only accepted after a vote of forty-one ayes to thirty nays. At the same meeting, Queen's Park, who were of course the eventual winners of the competition, suggested that it be made compulsory for pitch inspections to be carried out prior to the Cup Final in future, and described the first attempt this year as **"a farce"**.

In May though, as I previously mentioned, the Celtic supporters would have something to celebrate, regardless of their Cup Final defeat. As the team ran out against Leith Athletic on a Tuesday night at Celtic Park, they knew that a victory would hand the Club their first Scottish League Championship. Leith, whilst they weren't challenging for the title, were not bottom of the table cannon fodder either – in the end, they'd finish sixth of ten teams, so Celtic knew they wouldn't be a walkover. However, having worked so hard for this moment, the Celts weren't going to let it pass them by. By half time, they had taken a one-nil lead, and come full time, a three-one victory meant the League Title was theirs.

Remember the team – **"Joseph Cullen, Dan Doyle, Michael Dunbar, Willie Maley, James Kelly, John Curran, Jake Madden,**

James Blessington, Sandy McMahon, James Davidson, and Johnny Campbell" – for these men were the first Celtic eleven to become the Champions of Scotland. As forty-three titles became forty-four at the end of the 2012–13 season, and as forty-four will hopefully become forty-five at some point in the near future, we must never forget our roots. Less than six years after the decision was taken to form a Football Club in St Mary's Church, that same Club had proceeded to win the Scottish Cup one season and then the Scottish League Championship the next. These would have been incredible achievements for any Football Club at the time, let alone one of such a young age.

With the benefit of hindsight, we can see that the following campaign (that of 1893–94), had remarkably similar outcomes to the previous season. Celtic and Dan Doyle won the league comfortably, whilst losing in the Scottish Cup Final once more – this time to Rangers – as they won the tournament for the first time in their history. However, although the league would be won, the campaign didn't exactly get off to the sort of start Dan or his teammates would have desired. Having won two of their three matches in August, the Celts travelled to Ibrox on the second of September with some optimism. However, they were soon sent home despondent, having been beaten five-nil by the Ibrox side. Doyle, who had just returned from injury for the match, was utterly disconsolate about the result and this disappointment only hardened him and his teammates resolve to battle back over the remainder of the season, and so they did. From the second of September, they would not lose again in the league until March, including a dramatic victory by three goals to two over Rangers a week after the Scottish Cup Final defeat, in which Doyle was described as being in **"great form"**.

Whilst his reputation on the field had been rather stellar for a considerable amount of time, it was during the next few years of his life that Dan Doyle began to gain his reputation as a rather controversial figure in the world of football. The year after he had been given the honour of captaining Scotland in a tie against rivals England at the newly completed Celtic Park, he travelled with the international squad to Liverpool to face the English once more.

However, the night before the tie, Dan was nowhere to be found. It was widely presumed by the other players that he must have been otherwise engaged, perhaps with an old girlfriend from the area, or even at a local ale house. However, in the morning, Dan didn't appear as expected. The situation escalated to such a stage that Scotland had been forced to choose another left-back for the match before Dan, as if nothing out of the ordinary had happened, strolled into the changing rooms just before to kick-off, simply claiming he had spent the night with an old friend. As he was such an admired figure for the support, he was put straight back into the starting side, but went on to put in an uncharacteristically bad display, suggesting he may indeed have had a late night prior to the game.

As the years went by, and Celtic went through an 'up and down period' of some turbulence, Doyle developed a bit of a reputation for indulging in both alcohol and gambling. Of course, that is hardly a crime, but it most certainly affected him negatively at times. Celtic won nothing during their 1894–95 campaign, but proceeded to win the league and the two Glasgow trophies the following season. In 1897, Celtic became the first big Scottish side to lose to a minnow in the Scottish Cup, a tournament which was much more prestigious back then than it is often considered to be now.

Celtic were defeated by amateur side Arthurlie in the first round, in January, and had it happened nowadays, we would likely be hearing about it until the end of time itself. Even back then, without any form of instantaneous media, it haunted the Club for decades like a spectre, always there, but often not tangibly so. One of a catalogue of contributory factors to the defeat was the absence of a certain famous full-back. Once again, Dan had, inconveniently, disappeared off the face of the Earth, and to this day, no one is certain as to why. Rumours of player strikes and Doyle's new wage demands were flaunted as the most probable reasons, although it is possible he was simply otherwise engaged once more. Regardless, Celtic had not only been beaten, they had been embarrassed, and thus some of the responsibility must fall on Dan Doyle in this regard.

In an odd way though, this defeat helped to shape the future of Celtic Football Club, as the restructuring at team selection committee level which followed led to Willie Maley being appointed as the Club's manager in April 1897. One of his first acts, upon James Kelly's move from the playing squad to the boardroom, was to make Dan Doyle the new Club captain for 1897–98.

The following season, Celtic went on to win the League Championship again, without losing a single match along the way. They stuttered and stalled before being eventually eliminated from each of the cup competitions they took part in, but by coincidence they did meet Arthurlie once more in the Scottish Cup; this time putting wrongs of the past right and winning by seven goals to nil before losing to Third Lanark. Regardless, Dan Doyle, as captain, must take a tremendous amount of praise for the league win. Whilst he was aging, his performances that season were still largely exemplary, and the natural athleticism of youth had now morphed into experienced positioning on the field of play. Doyle, having seen so much of the game before, knew almost instinctively where to stand and where to run. He had become an expert at intercepting opposition passes and subsequently distributing the ball to his teammates, and this made him a formidable adversary to any given opponent.

Sadly though, by the time the next season came, the end of Doyle's footballing career was nigh. On his last international outing, a badly misplaced pass in front of seventy thousand spectators at Celtic Park topped off a victory for rivals England, signalling the end of his time as a Scotland player. In his final season at Celtic, Dan only featured occasionally, missing out on the team's Scottish Cup Final victory, but remaining proud of his teammates' success.

Dan officially retired from football in August 1899, ending an eight year spell with the Club he loved. In his later life, he owned a couple of off-licences, but he was not a successful businessman as his problems with alcohol meant he often drank both profit and product alike. It was a far from glorious ending to a life which had delivered so much to Dan and his almost endless array of adoring fans, but it did not diminish his stardom.

With only days of life remaining, as he suffered with the extremities of cancer, Dan was visited in hospital by his old manager and teammate, Willie Maley. In his later life, Maley would tell the world that Dan pulled down the blankets on his deathbed to show his friend how frail and weak the legs which had propelled him to stardom had become. The veracity of this story is debatable though, as Maley told it about more than one player over the years. There is an argument which suggests that Dan was the first to do this, and that in later years, other players would copy his actions in their final hours. Of course, the fact that Maley was a well known lover of symbolism and tales of poetic justice, combined with the passing of time and accounts being passed across the generations may well have contributed to this confusion.

On the eighth of April 1918, only months before the end of World War One, Daniel Doyle died at the age of fifty-three in the Glasgow Cancer Hospital. He had made one hundred and thirty-three appearances for Celtic, scoring six goals, and turning out nine times for his country. In all, he won four Scottish League Championship medals, and a single Scottish Cup medal (as well as his English Championship medal attained with Everton). He is buried in St Peter's Cemetery on London Road, Glasgow, only a few hundred yards from Celtic Park. In 2010, his previously unadorned grave became the first to be marked with a memorial and a service by the Celtic Graves Society, who continue their great work of remembering past Celtic players and bringing their burial sites up to an appropriate standard to this day.

Finally, whilst it is clear that Dan Doyle had personal issues, he continues to be known and remembered for his strength and determination above all else, and it is clear that his love of football stemmed from his strongly held philosophy on how the game should be played. As a man equally gifted with both feet himself, he once told a printed publication based in London:

"We have an endless supply of talent to draw on. A Scottish boy takes to football like a duck to water almost, and many of our cleverest players have not yet left school. Some little time ago I acted as a referee in the final stage of the Schools Cup competition,

and the play of some of the youngsters was a revelation to me. There was none of the old 'kick and rush' style of play, the passing being remarkably smart and effective. Given fair play, a team of boys could be found in our schools capable of beating an eleven twice their weight."

In my opinion, it is thanks to men like Dan Doyle that the style of football now widely regarded as **"The Celtic Way"** has always been, and shall continue to be, an integral part of Celtic Football Club, regardless of how other sides may play their own brands of the game. Our second Club captain may not have been perfect – far from it in fact – but no men truly are. A fantastically gifted player; what began as personal eccentricities became borderline addictions; but nonetheless the talents and achievements of the man are what people remember. Even in his later years, people in the street could be heard saying **"that's Dan Doyle"** whenever he wandered about near his home. Fathers told sons of seeing the great man play, and the fact he continues to be written about and remembered to this day speaks volumes for the man himself. Yes, he was a **"Wild Rover"** of sorts, but I doubt many supporters of his time would have traded him for anybody else.

"DOYLE – At Royal Cancer Hospital, on Monday 8th April, Daniel Doyle, late of Mossend and Celtic Football Club. R.I.P." – Glasgow Herald, Tuesday, 9th April, 1918."

"Not Men Against Boys, But Men Against Bhoys"

Expectation can be a terrible thing. Of course, we all harbour such feelings in our own unique ways, but when you allow yourself to embrace expectation, you risk dreadful disappointment. Late in the year 2002, one man, Graeme Souness, would learn the aforementioned lesson the hard way, when his Blackburn Rovers side were beaten by Martin O'Neill's Celtic. Having lost the first leg at Celtic Park by a single goal (despite being the better side on the night), Blackburn Rovers and their manager remained confident they could progress into the third round of the UEFA Cup with the second tie scheduled for Ewood Park. Continuing in this vein, Blackburn's captain, Garry Flitcroft, told the media after the first leg that Souness had said **"it was men against boys out there"** following the match, alluding to the fact he believed his side were far superior to the Celts.

Anyway, whilst Souness proceeded to deny all knowledge of the comment itself (which was not one I think his club captain would have created out of thin air, I hasten to add), he did come out with the following line in the build-up to the second leg: **"If Celtic score one then we can score three. Hopefully by 10pm tonight people will be saying "Bloody hell, that Blackburn are a good side""**.

Looking back on it, Blackburn were actually quite a good team at the point in time, boasting a squad which featured the likes of Brad Friedel, Damien Duff, Tugay, Andy Cole and Dwight Yorke. In fact, by the end of season, they would finish a very respectable sixth in the English Premier League. Regardless, they would be no match for Celtic, who dramatically improved on their first leg performance and strolled to a comfortable victory at Ewood Park, thanks to goals from Henrik Larsson and Chris Sutton.

Now, whilst that is the story of the football itself, there is far more to be said of the encounters between Celtic and Blackburn Rovers than that, as an almost endless amount of stories have surfaced about the events surrounding the two ties, but particularly that which took place in Lancashire. At this stage, allow me to introduce Marc Morrow. A lifelong Celtic supporter, Marc was only seventeen at the time of his trip to Blackburn, which was his first to follow the Hoops away in Europe, even if it was **"just down the road"** as he put it.

Normally a regular on the old **"Thornliebank Emerald Celtic Supporters Club"** bus, he was unable to secure a seat for the journey to England, despite his immediate decision to travel upon the pairing of the two sides: **"As soon as the draw was made I knew I was going, but the Thornliebank bus filled up virtually immediately, so I had to find alternative travel."**

Eventually, having searched through a local newspaper, he found a bus which still had room for more travelling supporters which was set to depart from Maryhill, so Marc and a couple of mates booked their places onboard.

And so, when the day of the game arrived, Marc and his pals presumed it would be a smooth journey to Blackburn – after all, they only had to make their way across Glasgow and then sit tight as their bus sped its way to England. However, due to a mix up regarding the time at which the bus was due to depart, the lads were running late, and it was left to one of their brothers to drive them across the city to Maryhill. Laughing as he did so, Marc said: **"It was ridiculous. We went from the Southside to Maryhill in what must have been a world record time. He absolutely floored it, and if it hadn't been for a bit of fortune regarding the traffic and some truly impressive driving, we would have missed the bus and I wouldn't have any stories to tell!"**

Anyway, having arrived just in time, the lads boarded the bus which was leaving from **"The Ram's Head"** pub in Maryhill. Coincidentally, this pub lies on the corner of one of the city's more memorable roads, which is aptly called **"Celtic Street"**, despite the fact it is situated only a few hundred yards away from the home of Partick Thistle Football Club. Marc told me that he **"thought**

it was a good omen" when he saw the street sign from the vehicle's window, and so it would turn out to be. A few hours later, the bus pulled up outside Ewood Park, one of the oldest football stadia on Earth, after a journey which was thoroughly enjoyed by all. According to Marc, the lads **"had an unbelievable time on that bus. To say it was bouncing would be an understatement."**

Upon disembarking, one of the first things which Marc noticed was a large marquee which had been set up adjacent to one of the pubs near the ground. Having had a quick look inside, he saw countless beer kegs being rolled behind a makeshift bar by staff, whilst big screens and projectors were being tested prior to the evening's match. **"It looked really impressive, and there was enough beer there to last most football supports for a week, so we made a note of where it was and headed into town,"** said Marc.

Upon reaching the centre of Blackburn, Marc heard there was a local off-licence selling bottles of Buckfast (the famous tonic wine) for one pound, fifty pence each. Unsurprisingly, with the prospect of such cheap alcohol being available, the lads went in search of the shop. In truth, it wasn't very difficult to find, as within a couple of seconds of turning a corner, Marc and his mates spotted a queue of green and white clad supporters stemming from the shop and trailing about thirty or forty yards down the street before disappearing around a bend. Undeterred, they joined the queue and, after a significant wait, they managed to buy a couple of the few remaining bottles inside.

Having been suitably watered, the trio then went in search of food. Soon, they came across a chip shop style cafe, and as Marc approached the counter, he asked for **"a roll and sausage"**. Now, you would be forgiven for thinking such an order would be a relatively common one, but that was apparently not the case in Blackburn, as Marc explained.

"So I approach the counter in this place, which is already half-full of Celtic supporters, and ask for a roll and sausage before turning away to check my phone or something. Anyway, a few seconds later, I look up to see the wee woman who took my order staring at me as if she hadn't heard me, so I repeated it, but to no avail. Now, obviously I'd had a few drinks by this point, so at first

I wondered if I was being really stupid or whether she just couldn't understand my accent. With that in mind, I spoke as slowly and clearly as I could – "a roll and sausage" I said – but she just wasn't getting it."

"Once a few seconds had passed, she asked "Do you want a teacake?" At this point, I had no idea that people from Lancashire use the word "teacake" as a slang word for bread rolls and stuff like that, so I ended up turning around and saying loudly: "Naw, I don't want a Tunnock's teacake! I want a roll and sausage!""

"At this stage, I could hear the laughter from the fans sitting behind me growing louder and louder, and I was becoming pretty exasperated. I mean, how hard is it to serve a roll and sausage to somebody? I just couldn't believe this had become an issue. In truth, I was tempted to order something else, but I was in one of those moods where I was being a bit stubborn, so I began to point to the ingredients one by one and take her through the process step by step: "Do you see those rolls over there? Naw, they're not called teacakes, they're called rolls. Aye, them. Take one of those, now open it up, and put two of those sausages inside it."

"We got there in the end, but my God, the wee woman still looked as if she still was clueless by the time I handed over my money. It was a struggle to say the least, but if nothing else, it gave all of the other fans in the cafe a good laugh – although I'll never look at a Tunnock's teacake in the same way."

Anyway, once Marc had overcome his language difficulty, he headed to the local shopping centre, where 'Charlie and the Bhoys' were due to play a set in a pub. However, he was turned away with his friends at the door because they did not have any form of identification to prove they were eighteen years of age or older. Despite this minor disappointment, the lads were not particularly despondent. As they proceeded to walk through the shopping centre, they tagged onto the back of a larger group of Celtic supporters who were now heading for the ground.

"Suddenly, we found ourselves strolling through these shops with the Hoops on and tricolours flying, belting out an array of Celtic songs, much to the local's amazement. It was fantastic, and to be honest, I think that's what away days in Europe are all

about – taking over someone's town or city for a day, but doing so in a respectful manner, making a lot of noise and enjoying yourselves, but leaving it just as it was before you arrived," said Marc.

Sometime later, the trio found themselves wandering up one of the main roads towards Ewood Park, which was now infinitely busier than it had been several hours earlier when the lads had headed in the opposite direction. "It was mega-busy. I knew we were going to bring a big away support, especially with all of the fake tickets that had been flying about, but I must admit, the number of Celtic supporters down there exceeded even my expectations."

Having heard talk of the large number of fake tickets available for this match, I proceeded to ask Marc for some more details regarding them. He said:

"Looking back on it now, it was crazy. There were more fake tickets in circulation for that game than I have even seen or heard of at any other tie – far, far more in fact. There were so many fake tickets that everybody who didn't have a real ticket had one of the fakes, if not several. I mean, they were being handed out on every supporters bus left, right and centre. I myself had three of them in my pocket, and my pals had some too! I've got no idea where they came from, but there must have been at least one thousand of them, if not more, and what made it even more ridiculous was the fact they were all copies of one real ticket, so they were all for the same seat inside the ground! Anyway, all joking aside, it meant that there were far more people trying to get through the turnstiles than there should have been that day, so it was packed."

Returning to Marc and his mates, they were still walking through the large crowd approaching the ground when they were met with a group of Blackburn Rovers' casuals. Incredibly, Marc still refers to this incident as "one of the funniest things he has ever seen," but the reasoning for this will become apparent in a moment, as he recalls his memories of the chaotic affair.

"We had been walking up towards the ground for quite a while, and we had gotten close enough to see it in the distance, only a few hundred yards down the road. It was one of those stereotypical streets which you find in the north of England, with narrow roads and huge stretches of terraced housing stretching off of it, but it was ridiculously busy – especially considering it was still about two hours until the game was due to start. Anyway, because of the buildings and the immense crowd, there was no way you could see up a side street unless you were right next to its entrance."

"All of a sudden, I looked down the road and saw a group of guys spilling out from one these side streets, and before I really had time to think about what was happening, bricks and bottles started landing all around us. I turned around and saw another bunch of these guys had come out from another street behind us, meaning we were stuck in the middle of it. Obviously, all hell broke loose, and despite the fact that there were only about forty casuals, things got pretty tasty."

"Almost immediately, folk of all ages were running in every direction imaginable, ourselves included. As I sprinted down the road trying to avoid the airborne missiles, I looked to my right and saw my mate, before glancing to my left and seeing two guys I recognised. In truth, it took a second for me to realise who they were, and I virtually had to look again to make sure I wasn't imagining things when I did, because here I was, running down a street away from Blackburn casuals, right next to Rob MacLean [a football commentator and regular on BBC television] and Sandy Clark [ex-footballer who has since worked as a football manager and within the media], both in their suits and ties. I couldn't help but laugh at this, even in amongst the chaos, and by the time we all stopped running, and I stopped laughing, we realised we were inside the gates at the edge of the stadium, next to the turnstiles."

"The police must have opened the gates when people started running that way in their desperation to avoid the fighting, and whilst it was great we had managed to bypass the security line which was previously set up to check fans for genuine tickets, we were all too aware of the fact that it was dangerously busy. In all seriousness, when you consider the size and speed of the crowd surge, it's amazing that nobody was badly hurt."

Regardless of the increasing mass of humanity outside the away end of Ewood Park, Marc told me that both him and his pals were buoyed by the fact they had avoided the police's ticket checks, and therefore they were **"almost certain"** that they were going to get into the game with their respective fakes. To be fair, it was nothing other than bad luck which prevented this, for countless other individuals managed to gain access to the ground using the counterfeit briefs. In fact, Marc was tantalisingly close to joining them, for he was only second in line for his turnstile when the man in front of him jumped over the small gate, causing the turnstile operator to close the automatic shutter over the doorway, leaving Marc staring at nothing other than blue, corrugated metal.

A few moments later, it was no longer a feeling of disappointment and a vision of steel which filled Marc's mind, but a searing pain at the back of his head and the sight of the underside of a police horse and the sky above it. Within seconds, long before he was aware of what was happening to him, he found himself being dragged out of the crowd by stewards and police, before being left sat against a wall on the pavement next to the main road. As Marc finally regained his senses a few minutes later, his mates were able to fill him in on what had just happened to him, as he now recalls:

"The guy who had been in front of me in the queue jumped over the wee turnstile as soon as he approached it, and a second or two later, down came the metal shutter. Apparently, this commotion attracted the attention of a mounted police officer who came trotting through the huge crowd and bundled into me, knocking me on my arse. Before I knew what was going on, I was staring at the sky, and these guys in high visibility jackets were dragging me out. At the same time, a lot of screaming and shouting was being directed at someone by other supporters, who I now know to be have been the cop on the horse. I was ok, but I must say I was gutted I didn't get into the ground. I was so close!"

Marc chuckled and continued, as he described what happened next: **"Once I'd reassured my mates I was ok, we decided that we could really do with a beer and, obviously, we had to find** somewhere to watch the game, so we headed for the marquee we'd spotted when we left the bus park at lunchtime. It was crammed full of people, but the atmosphere inside was already absolutely magnificent. There was still over an hour until kick-off, but the singing was already vocal and the drink was flowing."

"When the match finally started, the singing didn't die down either, it just kept going. Whenever Graeme Souness appeared on the big screens, you'd see loads of plastic pint glasses being hurled through the air towards them – it was hilarious. After all, Graeme has always been a favourite of the Celtic support. Anyway, when Henrik scored the first goal, the place erupted. Full pints flew, and because the tent was so full, we were actually forced forwards with the crowd. A couple of seconds later, people stopped celebrating and started screaming for folk to move back, because an old gentleman had been knocked over and a few people had ended up jumping on him essentially. However, a few seconds later, he was helped to his feet and brushed himself down, before shouting "It's alright folks! I'm fine! Carry on!""

And so, Celtic had done what Blackburn had failed to do in Glasgow, scoring a crucial away goal and meaning that, for the Lancashire side to progress, they would now need to score three times or more without conceding again – just as Souness had claimed they would do prior to the game. However, it was not to be, as midway through the second half, former Blackburn player Chris Sutton rose up to head home a Stiliyan Petrov free-kick and secure Celtic's place in the next round of the tournament.

"God," Marc said, "I thought when we scored the first goal that the place had gone nuts, but it was nothing in comparison to the celebrations which followed the second goal. It was utter pandemonium, with people falling all over the place, but it was just incredible. When the ball hit the back of the net, we all knew in that instant that we had done it. The "men against boys" line had been well and truly torn up, and we'd shown ourselves to be a far better side than many people south of the border seemed to believe. At this point, the bar ran out of beer, so the staff simply vacated the marquee and headed back to the relative calm of the pub itself, leaving us to our own devices."

"A few minutes later, someone started singing the Willie Maley song, and I'm not kidding, we all sang it for well over half an hour without stopping. Every time it began to die down, a few folk would really start to scream it, and the result was it just kept getting louder and louder, building to a crescendo that was just epic. In the excitement, a bunch of folk started climbing up on the temporary bar and continuing the singing and the dancing there. Me and my pals thought this was a great idea, and I can still remember standing there, looking out over an unbelievable number of away fans, all of whom were still singing, "and they gave us James McGrory and Paul McStay!" However, a few seconds later, I felt an odd sensation under my feet for a moment, and then the entire bar collapsed, sending people flying, but we were all fine and it was hysterical. It finally put an end to the singing of that one song though, and eventually people started heading back to their buses when closing time came, as did we."

Having returned to their coach, Marc and his mates sat down and relaxed for the first time in several hours. As the men and women from Maryhill discussed who was here and who had yet to arrive, the most common question being posed was simply "did you get into the game?" Due to the number of fake tickets in circulation, it transpired that many of those who had genuine briefs were turned away from the ground, as the away allocation was already full to, and perhaps beyond, capacity over an hour before the game began.

Anyway, as Marc sat there, he looked out of the window and recognised three of the lads who had been on the bus in the morning, although he didn't know any of them by name. To his puzzlement, one was in a wheelchair with a blanket thrown over his knees (despite the fact he had not seen him with a wheelchair earlier in the day), whilst one of the other lads was pushing him. Next to them, the third man was wearing a fluorescent yellow steward's jacket, and as they reached the steps of the bus, the man in the wheelchair leapt to his feet and bounded up the stairs without putting a foot wrong.

It then transpired that, somehow, the trio had used the wheelchair and the steward's jacket to blag their way into the game despite the fact they did not have tickets. One lad played the role of the wheelchair bound spectator, whilst another pretended to be his carer and the third, simply a steward tasked with accompanying the pair on their way in. Now, whilst I cannot officially sanction their actions, I must say that, if nothing else, there is a part of me which admires the ingenuity and guts it must have taken to pull off such a feat. Marc told me that he **"had always wondered where they had found the wheelchair and the steward's jacket!"**

Following that, the bus returned to Glasgow without any further incident. Regardless, Marc Morrow still considers his first European away day to be **"one of the best"**, despite the fact he was unable to gain access to the stadium itself.

"It was a mental trip," he told me in closing, **"but it was magnificent. The marquee is the best place I've ever watched a football match other than inside the ground. The only thing I could liken it to would be a concert at the Barrowlands when everybody in attendance is really, really up for it. It was ridiculously warm inside the tent, but that didn't seem to faze anyone, and the noise which we all generated was something special. At that stage, we were just delighted to have put Graeme Souness in his place. I don't think many people, if any, were seriously considering a run to the UEFA Cup Final itself, but that didn't take anything away from what was an amazing trip. If I could go back and do it all again I'd be there in a second!"**

And so, the team which many within the media presumed would emerge victorious in the first of two so-called **"Battles of Britain"** that season found their European campaign was over, whilst many people's underdogs continued onwards to the third round. In reality, it had not been **"men against boys, but men against Bhoys."** Expectation can be a terrible thing – isn't that right Mr Souness?

"This Is Truly A Family"

Séamus Cummins is a man whom I'm sure hundreds if not thousands of Celtic supporters will know, and yet many of those who consider him to be a friend have never met the man in person – I fall into this category myself. Born and raised in Philadelphia, a city of approximately four million people located on the eastern coast of the United States of America, Séamus is a proud Irish American. With his distinctive smile, the forty year old is instantly recognisable to his friends and family alike. Whilst his home city is famous for giving the world the **"Philly Cheesesteak"**, it has also given us the Cummins family; Séamus, his wife Jill, and their three boys, Liam, Ewen and Seán.

Like millions of people worldwide, Séamus would most likely not be where he is today if it hadn't been for **"An Gorta Mór"**, more regularly referred to as the **"Irish Potato Famine"** of the 1840's. Both sides of the family would struggle through the immense hardship the famine brought with it, but the two groups would take different routes to their eventual, modern day home. One half of Séamus' family headed directly for the United States in the early 1900's, whilst the others initially immigrated to Glasgow around 1880. Only forty years later, sometime around 1920, they would decide that the United States offered them and their family the chance of a better life and decided to move there.

Having passed through New York's famous Ellis Island before eventually settling in Philadelphia, they would coincidentally live within the same predominantly Irish neighbourhood the other half of the family had made their home many years previously. During their time in Glasgow however, Séamus' family saw the birth and rise of a new sporting side in the city's East End, as Celtic Football Club sprung into existence. Over the next thirty years, as Séamus' great grandfather – a man named William O'Neill – worked in the city's shipyards as a woodcutter, the love he developed for this football team was so strong that it would live with him, and his subsequently family, forever.

Such a love was demonstrated around a decade ago, when Séamus' mother's cousin, a woman named Pat Mallon (née O'Neill) who had spent a lengthy period living in Ohio, visited the family for the annual thanksgiving celebrations back in Philadelphia. As ever, Séamus wore his Celtic shirt that day without thinking too much about it. However, when Pat caught sight of the jersey, her eyes lit up and she became visibly excited – yes, there may have been many designs adopted over the decades, but the Hoops are still the Hoops, instantly recognisable across the globe – Pat then said, **"If only my father or grandfather could have seen this"**, and I feel that line speaks for itself.

To this day, Séamus remembers his grandparents and great grandparents speaking of **"the Celtic"** when he was a child, and singing not only Celtic songs, but also Irish pieces on a regular basis. He then told me that he never really began to truly appreciate his Irish identity until his teenage years, and as this occurred, his general interest in Celtic began to flourish, growing stronger with every passing year. While he has memories of older family members huddling (not in quite the same manner we do now) around radios in often vain attempts to find out the weekend's Celtic score, Séamus' first real encounters with the Club came via the American sporting network, ESPN. In the 1980's, soccer was less popular than it is today in America, and there was only one programme where he could see match highlights. Every week, during a round up of the matches from Ireland's Gaelic Football League, there would also be somewhat brief clips from any Celtic and/or Hibs matches which had been played.

As his love of Celtic grew into the 1990's and to what it is now, the introduction of televised matches in the United States markedly changed the way Celtic fans living there followed their side. Instead of having to wait for scores and highlights to be broadcast, games could now be watched in pubs throughout the country, live. However, matches weren't really available in home environments until the new millennium. This meant that if you wanted to watch Celtic, or any other team for that matter, you had to find a bar which showed the matches. At that point in time in Philadelphia, there was only one place which did so, "**The Dickens Inn**" (now known as "**The Dark Horse**"). Although this may seem like a contradiction in terms to many people, within the bar (which was owned by a Rangers supporter from Belfast), both the tricolour and the union flag hung side by side on the wall for years, as both Celtic and Rangers supporters from the Philadelphia area flocked there for their televised matches.

This arrangement worked rather well for several years, with light hearted banter and a bit of rivalry being the only results other than those of the games themselves. However, in 1996, with Rangers leading two-nil in a derby match, everything changed. As hundreds of supporters, predominantly those of Celtic, packed themselves inside the Philadelphia bar, the sounds of the Rangers support starting up "**The Sash**" was the spark that ignited the proverbial powder keg as, according to Séamus "**all hell broke loose**". During the resulting mayhem, television screens were smashed, the police were called and, symbolically, the Irish tricolour was torn down from the wall. Both sets of supporters claimed it was the other that had caused the incident, but when the owner (who Séamus, to his credit, still describes as a "**decent bloke**") eventually sided with his own supporters, it was clear the Celtic fans were no longer welcome, and therefore they needed to find somewhere else to watch their beloved Hoops.

In time, this would lead to the inception of Philadelphia's first Celtic Supporters Club, as the "**Molly Maguire C.S.C.**" was born in 1998, which would go on to be based at "**Paddy Rooney's**" pub in the city. In the coming years, as television coverage of live matches became more readily available stateside, Séamus would go on to be Vice President and then President of his C.S.C., positions which it is an honour for any man or woman to hold. As his family began to grow though, commitments at home meant that increasingly, he could no longer afford to disappear off to the pub in the city for hours a couple of times every week, and Séamus had to resign his role as President during the 2005–06 season.

Whilst part of him may have missed the atmosphere of the Supporters Club, Séamus realised that he was now entering a new stage in his life as he began to watch matches from the family home with his sons – in their Celtic themed basement no less – on **"Channel 67"**.

In February 2011, Séamus visited Glasgow (not for the first time) with his friend Brendan, having secured tickets for the upcoming derby match at Celtic Park. Once they arrived, they travelled out to Celtic Park to meet with Celtic employee and the legendary figure (at least on Twitter) that is Tony Hamilton for a guided tour of the stadium. Séamus still describes this as an **"almost spiritual experience"**.

Once the pair had left Tony and the ground behind them, Séamus tells a small story where he had to explain some basic facts about Glasgow to his compatriot. While Brendan was, perfectly innocently, willing to wander through the streets of the city dressed from head to toe in Celtic gear, Séamus had to encourage him to wear his normal winter scarf, and **"a sweater"**, when out and about on non match days. As I spoke with Séamus during our interview, he mused about the fact that he had previously been recognised and greeted whilst wearing the Hoops in Morocco, and yet felt he had to watch his back in areas of the city in which Celtic have played their football for over one hundred and twenty-five years.

When derby day arrived, Celtic produced a performance and a result befitting of the distance the two men had travelled to watch the team. As Celtic won three-nil, with two goals from Gary Hooper and one from Kris Commons, the Celtic support, led by the ever vocal Green Brigade, produced an astonishing atmosphere that will live long in the memory of many. Unfortunately, I did not meet Séamus during his last visit to Scotland, but he can rest assured that the next time he's in town, there will be many pints of his beloved Guinness waiting for him.

Once the two men had returned home, Celtic would go on to lose the league narrowly to Rangers. Like many of you reading this, the loss of a third league title in a row hurt our man from Philadelphia, but in the summer of 2011, a cruel twist of fate would put all of the things in his life, football included, into frighteningly stark perspective.

In early July, whilst Séamus and his young family slept soundly in their beds, a car with two people inside careered off of the street outside their home, crashing into the Cummins family car parked in the driveway and sparking an enormous fire. In the frantic moments following the incident, the entire family (including the dog) managed to escape to safety before the resulting fire engulfed the house with terrifying, unrelenting speed. Séamus and his family lost everything, as what remained of their house was demolished the next day. However, they felt incredibly humbled by the fact they still had each other, something that cannot be said for the two individuals who were in the car, both of whom were killed in the explosion which followed the impact.

Later that day, Séamus phoned Graham Wilson, the man who now hosts the **"Beyond the Waves"** radio show and the man Séamus regards as his brother, whom he had met outside a Celtic game held in Philadelphia a few years beforehand. With the help of Graham, members of the **"Lost Bhoys"**, Tony Hamilton and, in truth, too many other people to mention, help for the Cummins family soon started to flood in from members of the Celtic support across the globe. Séamus said: **"within three or four days of the accident, piles and piles of stuff started appearing for all of us, but particularly for the boys...shirts, scarves, badges, hats, memorabilia – you name it – it was there."**

It was only after that tragic event that Séamus' wife truly began to realise and appreciate what her and her family were a part of. She had been to Celtic games in the States before, as well as attending the annual convention in Las Vegas on occasion, but in her mind it was always just an extension of following a soccer team. Within days of the fire though, as she sat amongst the endless donations of money and items from people neither of them had ever met, she turned to her husband and said simply: **"This is truly a family."**

Upon the time of this book's publication, Séamus and his family will have been in their new home for a little over two years, having got back on their feet, with the help of their family, friends, and, perhaps most importantly, each other. The Bhoys in the family (and I don't just mean the kids) also have their Celtic basement back, as they have turned the bottom floor of their new home into a self-described **"Celtic shrine"**. With a large television at one end of the room and a ping-pong table in the middle, it may not look to be much different from many American basements in this regard. However, whenever anyone looks at the walls of the room, that impression changes quickly, for several Celtic tops adorn one side of the room, whilst flags and signed pictures covering the other. Poignantly, Séamus also had two of the family's Celtic tops which were damaged in the fire but were not wholly destroyed framed and mounted in their downstairs room also, serving as a constant reminder that whilst life may not always be easy, having the opportunity to live it for ourselves is a tremendous gift.

To this day, it is within their "**shrine**" that Séamus and his boys faithfully watch Celtic, wherever and whenever they may be playing. If the boys are at school, or Séamus is at work, then they will watch a recorded replay of the game later together. While I'm sure many of us will have watched Celtic alone at some point in our lives, I think we would all agree it is better to share the experience with others, especially those close to us. This is clearly something that is very important to Séamus and his family, and it is a privilege to write about.

Séamus is most likely best known within the Celtic fan base for one of two things; his mobile app or his musical exploits. Along with Matt Ansbro, Séamus' friend and head of the Philadelphia Union Supporters Club (the local Major League Soccer side which Séamus has a season ticket for, but little true emotional attachment to), he set about creating the first Celtic app for smart phones, specifically the iPhone. This led to the design and release of "**iCeltic**", an application now available on all platforms, which aims to keep users updated with the latest news coming out of Celtic Park and the online Celtic community.

The app was released in late 2010, around eighteen months before Celtic finally followed suit in February 2012 by releasing an official application themselves. In my mind, this is yet another example of the capability of the Celtic support to be both innovative and inventive. The application itself is designed primarily to bring together news and published items from several large unofficial Celtic sites, such as "**Celtic Quick News**" and the aforementioned "**Lost Bhoys**".

Whilst having a chat with Séamus, I asked him about where he believed the 'new' Celtic media had come from, since while most other clubs have an unofficial media presence; few if any can match that which surrounds Celtic Football Club. Perhaps unsurprisingly, he essentially agreed with the belief I have held for several years now, which says that the 'new' Celtic media has been driven forward because the Club's supporters feel they need their own voice in the world. Many either disregard or totally ignore most of what the mainstream media says in Scotland about Celtic and its fans, and it is this that has spurred the growth of our own media forward.

The movement that **"The Celtic View"** set in motion all those years ago is now exemplified by the fact there are countless unofficial forums and blogs, endless Twitter feeds and Facebook groups, several fanzines and independent authors, as well as (last but not least), several weekly Celtic radio shows, some of which Séamus is somewhat famous for his appearances on, as a fine singer with a deep love for Irish music and Celtic songs. It was only after a long pause that he decided **"The Celtic Symphony"** was his favourite Celtic song when I posed the question to him. Interestingly, he spent even longer considering his favourite Irish equivalent, which he eventually declared to be **"Four Green Fields"**, a song which he says reminds him of his grandparents and a piece of music of which I am a great fan of myself.

All in all, Séamus Cummins and his family are, in my mind, a credit not only to the city of Philadelphia, but to the Celtic support worldwide. Whilst tragedy has struck them in the past, they have bounced back admirably, and, according to Séamus, they now **"see what is truly important"**, considering themselves to **"be blessed on so many levels"**. Their unrelenting love of Celtic and the friendly, welcoming nature which they seem to exude (almost without end) are part of what makes our fan base so popular across the globe. Séamus is fiercely proud to be an American of Irish heritage, and he is also a true gentleman whom I always enjoy talking to massively. For those reasons, and countless more, I thoroughly look forward to meeting him one day in the future. He can be followed on Twitter – @iCeltic.

"The Icicle"

On Boxing Day 1883, in the small town of Bo'ness on the frigid shores of the Firth of Forth, a boy was born who is now a modern day unsung hero, of sorts, Alexander McNair. Alec, as he was generally known, would go on to become Celtic's longest continuously serving player, notching up a mammoth twenty-one year stint in the famous green and white jersey of the Parkhead Club. Now, being honest with yourself, have you ever heard of him? Do you know what position he played?

Up until relatively recently, (i.e. a couple of years ago when I really began to develop an interest in the early history of Celtic Football Club), I'll be honest and confess that I had not. With this in mind, as I read more and more about Alec and his achievements I became increasingly disappointed with myself. This man gave his all for the Club we all hold so dear and yet, for one reason or another, his story has been largely forgotten amongst the plethora of greats which the Celtic support have been fortunate enough to behold over the years.

Perhaps this was partly because he was a full-back, and partly because he played so long ago. In fact, he is forgotten to such an extent that, until relatively recently, he didn't even feature on Wikipedia's official list of the top ten players who made the most appearances for Celtic Football Club, despite the fact only five men have surpassed him in his feat of making six hundred and four outings as a Celtic player in all. As the aforementioned page on Wikipedia is locked for security reasons, one cannot simply edit it, and presumably it is only since someone contacted the Club directly that this error has been rectified. It is also worthy of mention that Alec only featured fifteen times for Scotland during his long and illustrious career.

Ironically, the following story is exactly the sort of tale which all Celtic supporters, young and old, can and should be proud of. Alec, you see, grew up supporting a team from Glasgow, but it was not Celtic – it was Rangers. Alec was, by his own admission, a "**thorough light blue**" in his younger years, whilst living in the town of Larbert near Falkirk. Whilst the religion of players has never been an issue at Celtic Park, unlike at another football ground in the city, it is perhaps worthy of note that Alec McNair was also a Protestant. And yet, even in the early part of the twentieth century, when religious divisions were deeply engrained in large parts of Scotland and those perceived to be Irish and/or Roman Catholic were treated as second class citizens by many, he was welcomed and loved by the Celtic support because the ethos of both the Club, it's founders, the management and it's ever growing fan base meant that people of all faiths were respected under the banner of one football team.

In 1904, whilst playing for local side Stenhousemuir, the young McNair had attracted interest from several clubs, including Celtic and his boyhood idols, Rangers. Perhaps his dream was to play for the Ibrox side, and personally, I wouldn't criticise any footballer for jumping at the chance to sign for the team they supported (regardless of who they may be), but whilst his aforementioned idols stuttered and stalled over a possible move, Celtic saw the potential the young full-back possessed and quickly made him an offer. Having looked things over and found they were to his satisfaction, he became a 'Bhoy' in May of 1904, and the Parkhead Club completed what would turn out to be one of their greatest transfers of all time.

In September of the same year, the opportunity came for the young man to make his Celtic debut, as he helped his side to a comfortable three-nil win in the first round of the season's Glasgow Cup competition against Queen's Park at Celtic Park. Interestingly, Alec was played as an outside right in this match, rather than as a full-back, and he was unfortunately denied a debut goal by a flag from the linesman in the first half. He would make his league debut a week later as Celtic travelled to Paisley to take on St Mirren and, once again playing as an outside right, Alec and Celtic came home with the victory they set out to attain, winning by two goals to one. A couple of days later, Alec would taste the first defeat of his Celtic career at the Hoops lost at Tynecastle.

Less than a month on from his first run-out in the same competition, Celtic picked up their first piece of silverware of McNair's time at the Club, by beating Rangers in the Glasgow Cup Final. Alec didn't play in the semi-final against Partick Thistle or the final against the aforementioned Rangers, but in time, he would force his way into the starting line-up with an efficient regularity.

Despite beginning his Celtic career as an attacking winger, Alec was called up for a more defensive role on his international debut in 1906 as Scotland prepared to take on Wales in the annual British Home Championship, only a couple of years on from his move to Parkhead. Alec played as a half-back that day, and despite a disappointing two-nil defeat at Tynecastle, it would be the first of several showings for Alec in the colours of his country. His next two appearances, in the spring of 1907 and 1908 respectively, would see him help Scotland to two victories, against Ireland and Wales. Prior to his first outing in a Scotland shirt, Celtic faced Bo'ness in the Scottish Cup in February 1906, but Alec was not given the chance to take on the club from the town of his birth, as the Hoops strode past their east coast opponents by three goals to nil.

As the years passed, Alec initially faded in and out of the Celtic team to some degree, until he finally stamped his mark on a new position in the side. Until that day in 1908, it is perhaps no wonder that Alec struggled to play with any real consistency. After all, as a forward, he was left to compete with the likes of the great Peter Somers and David Hamilton on the wings and, with the greatest respect in the world to him, although the athleticism of his youth may have suggested otherwise, Alec was never truly destined to be an outside forward of any great renown.

As 1907 became 1908, Alec spent some time as a centre-back, retreating from the forward line in doing so, thanks partly to the temporary absence of the injured Willie Loney. In February 1908, Celtic travelled to Ibrox for their second round Scottish Cup tie and Loney returned to the side, retaking his position from McNair. However, Alec's defensive performances, combined with his athleticism, had impressed Willie Maley enough that he moved Alec to full-back, replacing Donald McLeod for the match.

Donald, the man who had succeeded the great Barney Battles once upon a time, had been with the Club for many years, but his Celtic career was now coming to an end. Having had some issues with his weight, he was certainly not as quick and agile as he was in his prime, and Maley knew Rangers would attempt to target this defensive weakness should he play McLeod, and so he decided to gamble. And how his gamble paid off - with Alec McNair playing as a full-back, Celtic defeated their opponents by two goals to one, and they would go on to win the trophy a couple of months later, with McNair featuring in all of the remaining cup ties including the final. In March, the following quote appeared in **"The Glasgow Herald"** describing the vital role Alec had played at full-back in a narrow one-nil semi-final win against Aberdeen at Pittodrie:

"...twice Murray was dispossessed by McNair when he seemed clean through."

Such was the almost flawless nature of McNair's transition to a Celtic full-back, it took only a couple of months before he found himself filling that position in the Scotland side also – and not just any Scotland side, but the team that would face England at Hampden Park in April 1908. The game ended in a one-all draw, but Alec would not feature as an international full-back again for almost four years, instead being moved to half-back whenever his country called upon him. This decision frustrated many within the Celtic support, who felt that Alec, who was in their minds one of (if not the) best, full-back in the country, was being played out of position in order to accommodate the inclusion of other players.

As Celtic made it six League Championships in a row in 1910, **"McNair"** was fast becoming one of the first names on the team sheet every week. When the Hoops tried and failed to make it seven in a row, Alec joined the small band of Celts to have played in every single match throughout an entire season. This was the beginning of a transitional period for Celtic Football Club, as one great team began to fade away (with a few notable exceptions such as Alec who remained) whilst another crop of talented youngsters gradually began to progress into the first team. To fully understand the slump the team suffered, let me broaden your knowledge slightly. As Celtic won the last title of their famous six in a row in 1909–10, they were undefeated at home all season, and only lost four times all year. And yet, the following season, their record after the first four league matches read – **"One win and three defeats."**

Despite picking up some points as the campaign progressed, the Hoops continued to slump from time to time into winless runs and months where victories where hard to come by. Of course, the defence, and Alec, must take some responsibility for this, but I must say that, personally, I feel most of the blame should lie with the forwards of the time. Having scored sixty-three goals and conceded twenty-two when they won the league the previous season, you may be surprised to find that, as the Celts went on to finish a painful fifth in 1910–11, they conceded fewer goals than they had done in their league win of 1909–10, only eighteen – ten less than any other side, in fact. Critically though, Celtic scored fifteen less than they had done in the previous season; only forty-eight. The individual goals scored by great Celtic players throughout history which turn disappointing draws intro gritty victories and salvaged crucial single points in the face of impending defeats were sorely lacking – but they would come again, in time.

As Celtic set out on their Scottish Cup campaign that season, the situation on the pitch was still far from perfect. Having beaten St Mirren in the first round, Celtic found themselves with a home tie against non-league Ayrshire side Galston, who were then members of the Scottish Football Union. This tie set up the potential for a giant killing of sorts, as Galston had won their first round match by no less than eight goals to nil and, well, Celtic had been playing far from their best of late.

Thankfully though, Celtic managed to edge past their opponents by a single goal thanks to the aging Jimmy Quinn, but the newspaper reports of the day did hint at the ongoing trouble at Celtic Park:

"Celtic's form was too bad to be true. Galston never looked like winning, but Celtic never looked like scoring, and it was surely the most lamentable front line that ever misrepresented Celtic that only scored one goal after having practically nine-

tenths of the aggressive work. If the East-Enders are to go much further, changes are necessary, a new left wing and a half back imperative."

Interestingly, whilst a Club like Galston, who did make it to the 'proper' leagues in the mid-1920's for a time, faded out of existence with the outbreak of World War Two, other clubs who were members of the Scottish Football Union, such as Alloa Athletic and Stenhousemuir (whom, of course, Alec McNair played for), did not only thrive with time, but continue to operate and prosper to this day.

At the end of February, Celtic faced Clyde in the next round of the competition. This was, of course, the famous match in which nine and a half man Celtic managed to scrape past a rather good Clyde team at Celtic Park. Early on, Jimmy Quinn was **"rendered useless"** due to injury, and Willie Loney suffered a fractured arm. Despite the fact Willie tried his best to play on, he retired after only half an hour and, whilst Quinn was left hobbling about unable to offer much assistance to his colleagues, it was left to the nine fit Celtic men to rally – and so they did. One newspaper described **"McNair alone in his glory"** before continuing:

"Anything that was missed was left to be dealt with by McNair and Hay, and how well they performed their parts of the goalless record against Clyde, after 30 minutes pressure, shows. Altogether it was an exceptional victory..."

As the Scottish Cup run continued, Celtic faced Aberdeen in the semi-finals and, although he didn't have the best game of his career, Alec McNair not only saved the blushes of his goalkeeper Davie Adams, but potentially Celtic's season as a whole. Holding a slender one-nil lead, the ball came back to the Celtic goalkeeper on one occasion, who tried to kick it away and entirely missed the ball. As it rolled towards the Celtic net, the concession of an equalising goal looked to be seemingly unstoppable, but for Alec McNair, who sprinted towards the line and managed to clear the danger just before the ball crossed into the goal. Not only did this action help Celtic into the Scottish Cup Final, but it kept the Club's amazing record of not conceding a single goal in the tournament that season intact. This fact is reflected in the following newspaper quote, and McNair, along with his fellow defenders, as well as the goalkeeper Adams (who wasn't as prone to mistakes as the previous tale may suggest) deserve tremendous credit for their defensive achievements, which were an integral part of Celtic's success at the time:

"It may seem strange to term Celtic lucky when in their last two ties they have played with men more or less seriously crippled, but that they were fortunate admits of no doubt, and that in these three particular ties they have played poorly is just as certain. But in this season's competitions, not a goal has been scored against them, and there we have the real explanation of their position as finalists."

And so, in the final against Hamilton Academical, Celtic would maintain clean sheet once more, thanks in part again to the heroic defending of Alec McNair, as is described in the quote from **"The Glasgow Herald"** below:

"Very keen play took place afterwards, and McNeill was well on his way to Adams, when McNair effected a grand tackle and clearance."

In the same match, Alec was able to rekindle one of his old struggles on the field, as he came up against William 'Billy' Hunter, previously of Rangers. In a time where football coverage was fairly limited, with most normal domestic matches being described in a few lines or less, the following quote gives us a rare insight into McNair's ability to act as a tough tackling defender, ready to use physicality as well as finesse in his play when appropriate.

"The Academical wings continued to ply Hunter with the ball, but McNair anticipated the plan of campaign and, when McAteer was beaten, McNair did not spare the centre forward, charging him down repeatedly, the ex-Ranger more than once feeling the effects of his tussles with the Celtic back."

However, thanks to Celtic's inability to score themselves, a problem which I alluded to previously, the two sides would have to do it all again a week later. Of course, Celtic would go on to win the replayed Cup Final by two goals to nil, as is described in some detail in another section of the book. Whilst McNair's performance was competent and assured, Hamilton didn't attack particularly often during the match meaning little has been said of Alec specifically. However, one quote does say, **"They** [referring to two of the Hamilton players based on McNair's side of the field] **were twice rather easily beaten by McNair, who was not only tackling well but kicking with power and precision."**

It is also worthy of note that the Scottish Cup of 1911 would provide Davie Adams' final piece of silverware as a Celtic player. He had been the Club's goalkeeper for almost a decade, appearing in every match throughout several seasons, and as well as being the first Celtic goalkeeper to wear a different coloured goalkeeping jersey (due to a rule change), he was the last to wear the Hoops like the outfield players. It is thought that he never forgot about McNair's dramatic clearance off of the line against Aberdeen, and it is certain that there was a mutual respect shared by the two men. After all, Adams had saved Alec's blushes on a few occasions himself; such is the nature of a great defensive relationship built on trusting in each other's abilities wholeheartedly.

In time, Alec's consistency and reliability would come to earn him the nickname **"The Icicle"**, as due to the cool manner in which he conducted his business on the field of play, it was only on a very rare occasion he could be accused of making a mistake. He was immensely confident on the ball, and very little seemed to faze him.

Attributes such as these were, finally, rewarded with three call-ups to the Scotland squad in 1912, for each of the country's matches in the British Home Championship. Having defeated Wales by a goal to nil (thanks to a late winner from Jimmy Quinn at Tynecastle), the captaincy of the country was given to Alec McNair for the remaining two ties, a win against Ireland and a draw (to share the Championship title) with England at Hampden Park. At the time, the attendance of over one hundred and twenty-seven thousand spectators at the latter match set a new record for Scottish Football, and had the gates not been closed due to the incredible congestion, it would have undoubtedly been far higher. Of all of these throngs of Scotsmen and women, only one person had the honour of leading their country out on to the field of play, Alec McNair, and that must not be forgotten. Praised for his performance on the day, the newspapers of the time describe how Alec came close to scoring, saying he **"drove past after a short period of strong pressure from Scotland"**, as well as saying he **"tackled well"**, highlighting that Alec put in a performance fitting of any full-back, defending efficiently but also joining the attack when the opportunity presented itself.

Despite a defeat at Stamford Bridge in 1913 taking Alec's tally against England to two draws and two losses, he would finally be able to bask in the glow of a victory against the **"Auld Enemy"** in 1914, as Scotland recorded a famous three-one win at Hampden Park. This was the first triumph over England in four years, and it would be the last occasion on which the sides would meet until 1920. At a time when many footballer's careers, both those who were average players (a term I intensely dislike, but feel it is necessary to convey my point in this regard) and those who were exceptional, suffered badly in terms of longevity, it was remarkable that Alec was still regarded as a first choice full-back for his country at the age of thirty.

However, unlike many others, his fitness was never in doubt, nor could it have been for him to eventually continue on until the age of forty-one years old, and his work ethic set an example to his teammates around him. As a reflection of this fact, he was also given the opportunity to captain Celtic for a period towards the end of the 1910's but, to put it quite simply, he was often far too nice a man to be an effective Club captain. Whilst he would exhibit leadership in his style of play, he was never one to bark instructions at his teammates; he never swore; and was generally regarded as a quiet and polite man; and this may have contributed to his undoing in this regard.

Alec was never known for his goalscoring prowess, but he did chip in with eleven goals in twenty-one years. In fact, Celtic's defensive partnership were so well thought of during those glory years that Alec McNair became an integral part of a back line known colloquially as **"The Holy Trinity"** (along with goalkeeper Charlie Shaw and fellow full-back Joe Dodds).

Over the course of his career, McNair would go on to be part of Celtic sides which won no less than twelve Scottish League Championships (including the famous six in a row which was not bettered until the Jock Stein's sides managed nine in a row), six Scottish Cups, and nine Glasgow Cups.

And yet, in spite of all of these accolades, it could be said that his greatest achievement was attained off of the field of play. Tragically, in August 1915, Alec's wife Mary McNair (nee Nevin) died, leaving Alec with no less than five children to care for and support in the middle of World War One. He worked twelve hour shifts in a Bo'ness munitions factory for much of the war, whilst raising his children and playing for Celtic – a truly superhuman endeavour. Of course, incredible as such efforts were, they were somewhat commonplace in Scotland during wartime, regardless of whether they involved footballers or other citizens. One of his children, Jimmy, even inherited some of his father's ability when it came to the game of football, and in later years he would go on to make Alec proud by playing for both Falkirk and, like his father before him, Stenhousemuir.

Unsurprisingly, as Celtic kicked off the 1915–16 season at home to Motherwell, Alec would not feature in the side, having lost Mary only days earlier. At half time that day, hundreds of young Celtic supporting men were recruited for military service, thanks partly to the visit of a Victoria Cross winner, Corporal Luke (whom I believe to have been Corporal Frederick Luke V.C., a driver for the Royal Artillery who helped retrieve a large gun alongside two companions whilst under heavy enemy fire in France in 1914) to the ground.

Returning to the life of Alec McNair though, he first featured once again in a Celtic side at the end of September, as the Hoops eased past Clyde by the score of five goals to nil. It was only a little over a month on from the death of his wife, but, to Alec's credit, he continued to show a determination and drive with regards his football that few could match. When peace finally descended over Europe once more in 1918, Alec proved those who doubted the capabilities of a footballer in his late thirties by working his way back to his best, and helping Celtic to win the 1918–19 Scottish League title (his eleventh with the Club).

And, even at the age of thirty-six, Alec still had a few Scotland caps left in him, as 1920 signalled the beginning of the first British Home Championship since the start of World War One. Once again, Alec would feature in all three matches, and captain the latter two. A one-all draw with Wales in Cardiff gave the Scots a point going into their second match against Ireland. This would be Alec's final international appearance in Scotland and, with that in mind, it is perhaps fitting that he was not only able to captain his country that day, but to do so at Celtic Park, as the Scots beat Ireland by three goals to nil.

Sadly though, when it came to the day of the last international match of his career, Alec, along with all of those who loved Scottish Football, would be left somewhat disappointed. Knowing that a win or a draw would seal the Championship title, the Scots travelled to take on England in Sheffield, at Hillsborough. Once again, Alec was the captain and, with Scotland leading by four goals to two at half time, victory (or at worst a draw) looked rather likely. However, a phenomenal second half attacking display from the English, combined with some critical defensive errors from their opponents, allowed the home side to come back and win by five goals to four.

Whilst this was undoubtedly a sore defeat for the Scots to take, it remains the one of the second highest scoring clashes between the sides (there were several other examples where nine goals were scored, and once, in 1961, upon which no less than twelve were scored, as England won by nine goals to three at Wembley). **"The Glasgow Herald"** described the game as **"one of the fastest and most keenly contested ever witnessed between representative Scottish and English elevens."** Now, consider that, in 1920, without substitutions, a thirty-six year old was able to play without criticism in this match, on a **"quagmire"** of a surface, and then you may begin to realise just how special an athlete Alec McNair truly was.

On the fourth of January 1921, Alec had a tribute game held in his honour, as a **"Celtic and Rangers Select XI"** took on a **"Best of the Rest XI"**. The match attracted approximately thirty thousand spectators, and despite the fact Alec was forced to retire only minutes into the game (having been injured only days previously against Clyde) it was an occasion enjoyed tremendously by all, and most certainly by Alec himself. He was never a man to shout about his achievements or who he was, but this humbleness and humility only meant he appreciated and enjoyed the rapturous rounds of applause directed at him even more than many would, with a large smile spread across his face. For the record, the **"Best of the Rest"** Scottish League XI won by three goals to one.

Having enjoyed his benefit match, Alec continued on. Whilst he knew he was aging, he was still confident he had something to offer to the Club he had come to love, and clearly, Willie Maley must have agreed, as he would stay at Celtic Park for some time yet. In his few remaining years, he would win his twelfth title with Celtic as part of the 1921–22 league winning team, before winning his last major honour in 1923, as Celtic defeated Hibernian one-nil in the Scottish Cup Final at Hampden Park (whilst McNair was still a Celtic player when the Club won the same tournament in 1925, he did not feature in any Scottish Cup ties that season).

At the end of April, 1925, Alec McNair eventually hung up his boots, at the ripe old age of forty-one, having given a staggering twenty-one years of service to the rivals of the team he grew up supporting. He played his final match for Celtic in a one-all draw with Queen's Park, the team he had made his debut against over two decades earlier.

As I write this, I am, coincidentally, in my early twenties myself, and when I attempt to consider a length of service such as this, or, for example, the fifty-three years given to the Club by Willie Maley, I find it remarkably difficult to truly appreciate. In all, there were seven thousand, five hundred and twenty-five days between Alec McNair's first appearance for Celtic and his final match for the Club (not including a brief trial in 1903). To contextualise this somewhat, if a Celtic player such as Alec were to have retired in 2013, they would have began their time at Parkhead in 1992.

The Celtic line-up on his debut was – **"Davie Adams, Donald McLeod, Willie Orr, James Young, Willie Loney, James Hay, Findlay McLean, Jimmy McMenemy, Jimmy Quinn, Peter Somers**

and Alec McNair." Of this eleven, by the time McNair made his last appearance for Celtic, at least three of his old teammates (McLeod, Young and Somers) had since died, and, in truth, it is not known what happened to Findlay McLean, who was only at the Club for a short time and as such records regarding his later life are scarce.

Continuing on with this thought process, the Celtic team that ran out onto the park for Alec McNair's final match was as follows – **"Peter Shevlin, Alec McNair, Hugh Hilley, Jimmy McStay, Willie McStay, John McFarlane, Patrick Connolly, Peter Wilson, James McGrory, Alec Thomson and Adam McLean."** Of this side, Peter Shevlin and Peter Wilson hadn't even been born when Alec McNair signed for Celtic, and the great Jimmy McGrory was born only a week after Alec became a Celtic player. These facts, if nothing else, help to highlight the incredible length of Alec McNair's Celtic career, and that such longevity was truly special. With this in mind, I feel I should mention that, to this day, Alexander McNair remains the oldest man to ever play for Celtic Football Club in a competitive match. This record may never be beaten.

However, what made him a truly special Celtic player was not only the length of time he served the Club, but critically, the ability and attitude with which he did so. Despite the fact he began his time at the Club over a century ago, he remains a role model to aspiring footballers today.

Alec McNair's football story continued though, as he went on to become the manager of Dundee Football Club for a few years in the mid-1920's. In his later life, he worked at a stock brokerage in Falkirk, but still maintained some links to the game he loved by spending some of his time supervising Scottish referees.

Alec McNair, **"The Icicle"**, and one of the greatest servants Celtic Football Club has ever known, died a little over a month short of his sixty-eighth birthday, on the eighteenth of November 1951.

The following day, **"The Evening Times"** of Glasgow published the following article (which notably makes an error with regards his age), entitled simply **"The Greatest Of Them All"**:

"Alec McNair, who served Celtic for 20 years and was capped 15 times for Scotland, has died, aged 69. Along with Joe Dodds

he formed the most noted full-back partnership the Scottish game has ever known. Alec died yesterday in his Stenhousemuir home after a long illness. Willie Maley, one of the few remaining Celts of the Club's greatest days, has this to say of Alec McNair: - "He was a treasure and a gentleman in every sense of the word. In his 20 years' service I had never once reason to alter my first impression of him. Alec was the coolest and most intelligent and thoughtful player I have ever seen." The funeral is to Larbert Cemetery tomorrow at 3pm."

"We Felt We Could Mix It With the Big Boys"

Mark Sheffield, a thirty-nine year old gentleman who currently lives in Lancashire, England, spent most of his childhood in the small coastal town of Tywyn, Wales. By Mark's own admission, he was not a big fan of any particular football team in his early years, although one side of the family were nominal Southampton supporters. Whenever he watched live matches, he would do so at the town's playing fields, where a bag of extra footballs always had to be present in case the one in use flew over a perimeter wall and into the local river, never to be seen again.

In the early 1990's, Mark left the shores of Cardigan Bay behind him and headed for Heriot-Watt University in Edinburgh. Subsequently, as he was far from locally based, Mark found himself moving into the campus' student halls. There, he would be paired with another lad through nothing other than sheer chance, and in time, his new roommate, Paul, would change his life forever. According to Mark, **"one of the first questions he asked was which football team I supported, and he sort of shrugged his shoulders when I said that I "didn't have a particular club that I followed." He just laughed before telling me that he was "a lifelong Celtic supporter" and promising to get me involved with the Club. At first, I presumed it was nothing other than talk, but soon enough I found myself inside the away end at Easter Road."**

Yes, Easter Road. Granted it is not the most common place for one's love of Celtic to first take root, but with his rural upbringing, Mark isn't a man with a stereotypical history with regards his love of the Hoops. Of course, this is no bad thing, as our individual tales all add to the stature of the Football Club in their own particular way. As he recounted his memories of the trip to the home of Hibernian, Mark joked, **"well, considering how poor Celtic were back in the early nineties, nobody can accuse me of being a glory hunter – that's for sure!"** Critically though, he then told me that he remembered that **"the atmosphere was absolutely fantastic"** with **"such friendly people"** leaving him **"a little bit awestruck".**

And so, as the years passed and his love of Celtic began to flourish, Mark Sheffield joined the university's Celtic Supporters Club, following the team across Scotland and Europe in the process. For example, he was in attendance when Henrik Larsson suffered his horrible leg break in France, and sighed as he recounted how **"badly deflated everybody was when their worst fears were confirmed in the stands".**

Regardless, the Swede would recover from that injury as well we know, and as Celtic progressed past Blackburn Rovers in November 2002, the Hoops and their supporters were left with a tantalising possibility – they had a chance to retain their place in a European competition past Christmas for the first time in twenty-three years. With this in mind, as well as an attractive draw which paired the Celts with Spanish opposition Celta Vigo, Mark and his mates decided that this was a trip they could not afford to miss. Having seen a header from Henrik Larsson separate Celtic and their opponents in the first leg at Celtic Park, the lads touched down in the north of Spain a little under a fortnight later for the return fixture. However, they had not simply flown from Glasgow to the largest city in Galicia, but rather from Edinburgh to Heathrow, before going on to Madrid and then, finally, to Vigo itself.

Unlike the majority of the travelling support on that occasion, the lads arrived in the late afternoon on the day before the match, meaning they had more time than most to explore the city they were visiting. Having dropped off their belongings at a beach hotel some distance away from the city centre, they saw that the queue for taxis (predominantly made up of other Celtic fans) was somewhat lengthy, and therefore they decided to simply walk into town. After all, **"it couldn't be that far."** However, this would not be as simple a stroll as they had presumed. In fact, it turned out to be an extensive trek along a coastal road as evening turned to night and light turned to darkness.

Eventually, they began to re-enter some form of civilisation, as they continued to follow the tarmac road which would lead them to the old port area, around which many bars and restaurants were to be found. However, before they reached their destination, the university group had to make their way through the newer area of Vigo's large shipping port, which Mark described as **"a mildly scary place when it was dark and empty."**

With nobody in sight anywhere around them, in a city none of the lads had previously visited, this was, perhaps, not an unexpected view to hold. However, after some time, Mark spotted a woman standing next to a pedestrian crossing in the distance.

"She was a welcome sight initially. We hadn't seen anyone else on foot for about an hour, but I did think it was a little odd to see a girl dressed up to such an extent in an area without any bars or anything. A few seconds later, I began to ask myself why she hadn't crossed the road despite the fact there wasn't a car or lorry anywhere to be seen, and then the obvious struck me. I couldn't believe how naive I had been. I was actually a bit embarrassed as to how long it had taken me to twig."

"Anyway, over the course of the next ten or fifteen minutes, we wandered past more and more of these women, before we finally reached the old port and found a bar which was open. In all honesty, it was a massive relief. We were all tired and thirsty from our walk and so we approached the first pub we saw, only to notice several individuals wearing St Pauli shirts, sitting inside. It turned out to be a group of guys from Hamburg who had travelled to watch Celtic too, and what a night we had. It remains one of my favourite bars from all of my trips across Europe."

Having had a few drinks and recouped some of their energy, the lads then headed out in order to explore the rest of their surroundings. They enjoyed their wander, which included a couple of stops for some more drinks along the way, but increasingly Mark was beginning to appreciate that **"Galicia was not hugely affluent."** Of course, as he went on to point out, **"the recent oil spill off the coast had likely not helped matters for the people of Vigo."**

As they decided to head back to their hotel, the lads were adamant that they would not walk the same distance they had done previously, and therefore proceeded to hail a passing taxi. However, they had a change of heart (or stomach) soon after when they realised how hungry they were, and subsequently the driver dropped them off at one of the few bars which was still open in **"the wee, small hours."** There, Mark and the lads enjoyed some homemade hamburgers, a few more beers, and a couple of shots of the local liquor, **"Orujo".**

All in all, a great night was had by the group, and they eventually made it to their beds between 4am and 5am that morning. A few hours later, they were awoken when another member of the larger travelling party entered their room to enquire as to why they had missed breakfast. The **"Good Samaritan"** had retired much earlier the night before, but met his match when he immediately stepped in a small puddle of sick by the door. On the other side of the room, Mark's eyes opened, and he became starkly aware that all was not well, as he found himself lying in an expanse of **"Orujo"** inspired vomit, delightfully interspersed with remnants of Galician hamburgers – **"It wasn't one of my proudest moments"**, he said regretfully.

"Obviously, we then spent a good while cleaning all of that stuff up – as well as ourselves – before heading out onto the local beach. I should mention that I wasn't the only one who had been ill though. Anyway, as the morning became afternoon, we all recuperated to one degree or another, beginning by drinking coffee in the sun before eventually sampling some paella. It was only then that we returned to town and found thousands more Celtic fans had arrived on the charter flights which flew in that morning."

"As you would expect, the atmosphere was both loud and friendly. The locals, who had previously seemed somewhat dismayed about the aforementioned oil situation, appeared buoyed by the colourful party the Celtic support had brought to their city. Businesses did a roaring trade, and the dancing and singing really seemed to cheer up many of the city's residents, which was truly great to see. They really got into the spirit of things."

"Our group decided to head up towards the stadium fairly early, and as such we soon found ourselves inside a local bar which was covered in Celta Vigo memorabilia, as well as several pieces of

ultra merchandise. There were a lot of hardcore Vigo supporters there, but there was no trace of any animosity. Each group of fans took turns to sing one of their songs, before going quiet to listen to a number from the opposite support. It was fantastic."

Later, as they approached the Balaídos stadium, a few members of the away support commented on the dilapidated nature of the ground itself (although it is worthy of note it has since undergone some renovation). "It looked a bit rough to be honest," Mark said. "They had only opened two turnstiles, and with long lines and kick-off approaching, a few tempers began to get a little frayed. Of course, there were a lot of Celtic fans there who had missed out on entry to the Blackburn Rovers game at Ewood Park despite possessing valid tickets, and you could tell that a lot of them simply weren't going to let it happen again."

"Sometime later, only seconds after I had managed to pass through one of the gates, I heard a commotion behind me and I turned to see a policeman laying into people with a baton where I had been standing less than a minute before. Thankfully, the crowd didn't react much; otherwise it could have been quite nasty. In truth, even after the stand had filled up, it was only the emergence of the teams and the sounding of the first whistle which finally saw the tensions dissipate."

And so, Celtic set out to remain in Europe after Christmas for the first time in over two decades. However, the tie was thrown wide open a little over twenty minutes into the match when the Celta winger Jesuli gave the home side the lead on the night, levelling the aggregate scores. However, John Hartson would bully his way into the opposition box to score a few minutes before the break, regaining the aggregate lead and meaning that the home side would now need to score twice without reply in order to progress to the next round of the UEFA Cup. With this in mind, Mark said he was "relatively confident" at that point in time.

Despite this confidence, the emotions around the stadium were to shift dramatically only minutes into the second period as Benni McCarthy scored Vigo's second goal of the night, once again setting the tie on a proverbial knife-edge. Unsurprisingly, the home supporters were **"well up for it"** at this stage, as Celtic wobbled and their side pressed for the goal which would send them through. And, as some of you may recall, they very nearly managed it towards the end, when Jesuli missed a glaring opportunity to score his second of the night.

When the final whistle eventually sounded, the travelling supporters in the Celtic end erupted in celebrations which were born out of relief above all other emotions. People embraced each other and leapt around in delight, but Mark remained somewhat reserved. As he retold his story of his trip to Galicia, it was only at this stage that Mark enlightened me to the true meaning not only of his trip, but also that of many members of the group he was travelling with – for only a few weeks earlier, Mark had learned of the death of his old roommate, Paul, in a freak diving accident with the Royal Navy. He was only in his late twenties.

"It was quite a moment when the match ended and we knew that we were still in a European competition after Christmas," Mark said, **"but the true meaning of that moment, for us anyway, would have been lost on everybody else around us. As ecstasy filled the air, I couldn't help but think of the man who had helped to kindle my love of Celtic Football Club. He was at the forefront of my mind, and the combination of all the different emotions I was experiencing was certainly poignant. I just couldn't jump around like everyone else at that point, but obviously I was delighted with the result itself."**

Inevitably, as they lads returned to the nearby bar they had visited previously, their attentions returned to the night at hand to some degree, and, fittingly, they were determined to enjoy themselves. Once again the singing started, as countless other Celts passed the bar on the way back to their airport bound buses. **"We were so chuffed not to be one of them,"** Mark said, **"we were just happy to be able to have a beer and let some of the tension melt away. Sometime later, the Celta fans asked for silence, and this shy looking lad got up onto a stool and began to sing. In truth, it took a few seconds for us all to realise that he was belting out "A Soldier's Song" in Irish. Everybody stayed quiet until he had finished, but once the last word left his lips, the place went**

nuts! What a round of applause the lad received, and rightly so. God knows where he learned to sing like that though!"

Anyway, before they left the bar behind them, one of Mark's mates, Kevin, swapped shirts with a Celta Vigo fan – although he had to be forced into it. Essentially, whilst Kevin was wearing what Mark described as a **"cheap, 'Barras style' knock-off of the new Celtic kit,"** the Vigo fan wore a new shirt, with the name and number of a player on the back, as well as an accompanying signature in marker pen. Now, to his credit, Kevin was initially unwilling to make such a trade, as he tried to tell the local that he did not want him to part with his signed shirt. However, he was insistent, and to this day, it remains in the possession of Mark's mate, Kevin.

Moving on, the lads returned to the old port area, where they went for something to eat before revisiting the same bar in which they had found the St Pauli supporters the previous night. Once again, the group from Hamburg were already inside when Mark and his mates arrived, and upon their entrance, a cheer went up from the German group. As the night progressed, they all drank endless amounts of beer, as well as several shots of complimentary homemade liquor which the barman kept behind the bar in reused plastic lemonade bottles. To this day, Mark maintains that he has **"no idea what it was and no idea where it came from."**

As the night drew to a close, Mark and his pals wandered around in search of taxi, and as they did so, they happened to pass the bar which they had eaten in previously. It was now closed, but the barman was sitting on the kerb outside, enjoying a few long draws of a cigarette. They spoke to him for a few minutes, and after one of them joked about there being **"no more hamburgers,"** the barman proceeded to reopen the bar, serve them a few drinks and fire up the hotplate once more, catering for the group into the early hours of the morning when he really didn't have to. This show of hospitality has not been forgotten by the lads, and to this day they all wish they could make a return trip to Galicia with Celtic (although as Celta Vigo have only recently regained their place in La Liga, this remains somewhat unlikely to occur in the imminent future).

And so, the next morning, the lads returned to the airport and retraced their path to Edinburgh, flying via Madrid and Heathrow. They had seen Celtic progress to a European stage previously unknown to a generation of the Club's supporters, and as Mark recalls, it gave them confidence going forward: **"It was a big achievement for the team to progress to the fourth round, and to do so by beating a fairly good Celta Vigo team gave us all a bit of belief. Whilst nobody had any thoughts of going all the way to the final at that point, we felt we could mix it with the big boys and hold our own, so we couldn't wait for the next round. After all, we had nothing to lose and no fear. We just wanted to try to keep going and see what happened. It had been a wonderful trip to a city which is home to some truly lovely people, and I would do it again in a heartbeat."**

Around six months later, Mark Sheffield would travel to Spain once again, as he journeyed to Seville along with tens of thousands of other Celtic supporters, including many from the **"Heriot-Watt University Celtic Supporters Club"**. Despite Celtic's eventual extra time defeat, it remains one of the proudest days in the history of Celtic Football Club. In all likelihood, if it hadn't been for Mark's roommate, then he may never have been there to witness it – I'm sure Paul would have been very proud indeed.

"I Thank God for Football"

In the west of Kenya, the port city of Kisumu is home to around four hundred thousand people. It lies on the banks of Lake Victoria, and its name reflects what it is best known for, as Kisumu is derived from the Swahili **"Adhi Kisuma"**, which means **"I'm going to trade"**. The area around the city is known both for its agriculture and for the several types of exotic wildlife which you certainly wouldn't see strolling through the parks of Glasgow. Interestingly, Kisumu can be found less than forty miles from the village of Nyang'oma Kogelo, the home (and now the resting place) of Barack Obama Senior, the father of the first African American President of the United States, Barack Obama Junior. To this day, many of the President's relatives continue to live in village, which has become a tourist attraction of sorts in recent years.

And so, with this in mind, perhaps we should expect the unexpected with regards to Kenya, as we discuss the life and times of one of Kisumu's more intriguing residents, the Celtic mad sports journalist, Collins Okinyo (pronounced 'O-keen-yo', I am reliably informed). Born as the eldest of four siblings, Collins has one brother and two sisters. Whilst at school, he took part in several sports as he was considered to be a good athlete. Thanks largely to his height and strength, he enjoyed athletics, basketball and handball, but he admits himself that his true love has always been football.

Now in his mid-thirties, Collins writes about the African game extensively, particularly that played in Namibia, South Africa, Uganda, Zambia, Zimbabwe and, of course, Kenya, for the **"Super Sport"** website. However, prior to reaching one of his life's goals, that of being a football journalist, Collins worked in hire purchase and also owned a hardware store, selling tools, building materials and cement, before studying journalism at college in Nairobi, the capital of Kenya, around five hundred kilometres to the east of his home.

On a personal level, Collins is married to Eunice, his wife of eight years, and the couple have one young son, Prince Essien, who also shares his father's passion for football. The love which Collins possesses for his family is perhaps the only force in his life which is stronger than his aforementioned love of the beautiful game. The phrase **"Eat football. Sleep football. Live football."** is often used too lightly in modern times, but Mr Okinyo is someone whom I feel this phrase applies to rather well. **"There is always football on in the house"**, he told me. He continued, **"The family are all into it. They have to be – or else they would go mad."**

Before our discussions progressed on to modern football, both that played in Africa and much further north in Scotland, Collins explained to me how his love of Celtic had initially taken root:

"Everyone knew of the world's biggest derbies when I was young, even if we couldn't watch them, and the rivalry of Celtic and Rangers was famous in Kenya for the passion which was involved. Celtic were well known as the team that anyone could play for or could support, regardless of their cultural or ethnic background, so most Kenyans who took an interest adopted them as their favoured side in these matches."

"I have a large collection of old Celtic shirts, having bought my first when I was in my early twenties. As a young man, I would save up my money for weeks and then go to the local shop which sold second hand football jerseys from around the world. A lot of people would ask for Manchester United or Arsenal shirts, but I was always looking for anything Celtic."

"When I first began to follow the team seriously, there was not much internet coverage here. This meant that all I could do was wait and hope some short highlights would appear on the television or, more often than not, I would have to go through the back pages of the newspapers days after the games themselves to find the result and a brief match report. Whilst I read a lot about the likes of Henrik Larsson, I wish I could have watched him play live more often on the television, but such live broadcasts were very rare until fairly recently. Nowadays though, technology has revolutionised the way Africans intake their football and the

related news. Rather than waiting for newspapers to become available, people can go online and find everything they want about their chosen side. As I have more money in my pocket now than I have had in the past, I can afford to pay for cable television, and I can watch all of the live matches there. I am very happy about this."

As Collins grew older and began his career as a sports journalist, technological improvements (as I mentioned above) allowed his love of Celtic Football Club to flourish. Whilst he does not support a particular Kenyan side so as not to be considered biased from a professional point of view, Collins considers watching any upcoming Celtic match as **"a must."** He said, **"I will make time around my work to watch the matches as often as I can, and I enjoy nothing more than sitting down with my family and friends to enjoy a game."**

Consequently, Collins told me that he hopes Celtic will embark on a pre-season tour of Africa at sometime in the future: **"Obviously, Celtic are a massive Club. They have visited almost all of the corners of the globe over the years, and now visit the United States and Australia on a relatively regular basis. I would love to see them take a bold decision and visit Africa soon. The Club has so many fans here, and I think that many people back in Scotland do not truly grasp how many African supporters the Club has. After all, there are several examples of teams in Africa named after Celtic, such as Kibera Celtic in Kenya and Bloemfontein Celtic in South Africa. If and when Glasgow Celtic visit Africa, they will receive a welcome like no other."**

Having considered this idea on a personal level, I must say that I feel Collins makes a valid point. Celtic Football Club is well known and well supported worldwide, and whilst a trip to Africa may not produce as much income as a trip elsewhere, it would have the potential to capture an enormous amount of new fans and solidify the support which already exists there, especially if charity was at the heart of the trip. Imagine it for a moment, Glasgow Celtic, a Club formed to help the impoverished people of the East End of Glasgow, versus Kibera Celtic, a club born out of the slums of Nairobi.

The material and emotional difference which a match of such significance would generate would have the potential to be something very special indeed. For many Africans, tours such as these would be their only chance to see the Hoops in person, as, if we are brutally honest, millions on the continent struggle to afford to feed themselves and their families, so could never dream of having enough money to fund a trip over thousands of miles to Scotland. Maybe, just maybe, the Hoops will go to Africa one day, and I'm sure their supporters throughout the world would be proud to see them do so.

Until relatively recently, the most notable African player plying his trade in Scotland that Collins took an interest in was David Obua, previously of Hearts, who was born in Kampala, Uganda, only two hundred miles from Kisumu. However, with the arrival of Victor Wanyama in 2011, that changed and soon, so would the attitudes of many Kenyan people towards Scottish Football.

At this stage, it is critical to note that Collins has been covering African Football for several years now, at all levels. For this reason, whilst most Celtic fans had never heard of Victor Wanyama prior to his arrival, Mr Okinyo knew him rather well (albeit by a different name), having seen him play both as a youth and, latterly, for Nairobi City Stars in the top flight of the nation's football. From his earliest days watching the youngster, Collins recalls how **"he had something special in him...he was very, very strong on the ball – so much so that almost nobody could tackle him...his rapid progression surprised everyone, and we all felt he was destined for great things."**

However, after a few good performances for the City Stars, Victor moved to A.F.C. Leopards (the Club his father Noah played for around two decades previously - also of Nairobi) and then Helsingborgs of Sweden, before joining Germinal Beerschot in Belgium. At this point, Kenya largely forgot about him for a couple of years. **"He was not a big name when he was playing in Belgium – very few people here knew him, but that all changed when he moved to Glasgow."**

In fact, as Collins explained to me, "**Wanyama**" was not a big name at all when he left Beerschot, partly because nobody called him "**Wanyama**". Until his move to Celtic, Victor Wanyama was better known to many by the name Victor "**Mugabe**". According to Collins, Wanyama was the name of Victor's father, whereas Mugabe was that of his mother. For this reason, whilst he was a youth player in Kenya many knew him simply as Mugabe or Victor Mugabe. Similarly, it is important to note that Victor's brother, McDonald Mariga, who plays for Inter Milan, is rarely referred to by his full name, which is McDonald Mariga Wanyama.

Having signed for the Hoops for a little under a million pounds, Victor became the first Kenyan to play in the Scottish Premier League, and few could have predicted the monumental rise of the young man as a Celtic player. Upon his arrival at Parkhead, he selected the previously unused sixty-seven as his squad number as his own personal tribute to the Lisbon Lions, a choice which immediately endeared him to the millions of supporters of his new Club.

Collins laughed as he recalled his excitement upon hearing that Victor was being linked with Celtic. He said "**I wanted to phone him and shout, "You must sign for this Club! No matter what else you do in life, you must sign for this Club! They will not let you down!"**" before later reflecting on his reaction to the deal being done – "**I couldn't believe it,**" he said, "**It was just fantastic – a Kenyan, just like me, was now playing for one of the world's biggest Football Clubs – and I had a feeling things would continue to get better for him.**"

As we all know, Collins' prediction would turn out to be correct, as Victor's performances improved on an almost weekly basis, until we witnessed perhaps the greatest moment of his football career thus far, as he scored the opening goal in the famous victory over Barcelona at Celtic Park in November 2012. Collins continued, "**It is because of Celtic, and results like the beating of Barcelona, that the name of Wanyama has grown so big. He is a superstar now, not only in Kenya, but throughout all of Africa. For example, when I walked through the town yesterday, I saw at least twenty people wearing Celtic jerseys.**

They are almost as common here as Manchester United and Arsenal shirts, so the Club is very popular."

To contextualise this statement somewhat, I first spoke to Collins the day after the Kenyan national side had arrived in Nigeria for a qualifying match for the 2014 World Cup, and, according to him, **"there was almost a stampede at the airport in Nigeria, because everyone wanted to see Celtic's Wanyama, and everyone wanted pictures and autographs!"**

Critically though, Collins believes that Victor's success will be emulated by other Kenyan players in the relatively near future. **"Africa is producing more and more very talented players – in recent years we have seen the likes of Didier Drogba, Michael Essien and Samuel Eto'o - Victor Wanyama is just the most recent star to break through – what African Football really needs is experienced coaches from Europe and around the world to train our players, as well as better infrastructure. In the last few years, the broadcasting rights of television companies have meant that professional football is a sustainable career in Africa now, and that is very important, but we still need some of the expertise of coaches from Europe and around the world to truly help us to move forward."**

However, saying that is not to devalue the achievements or progress of Victor Wanyama, **"who has made the people of Kenya believe that they can do it, and that anything is possible. He is a role model for us all"** said Collins.

On one of Victor's visits to Kenya, Collins met him to discover that the young man had a surprise for him, or rather, two surprises. Subsequently, he presented Collins with a brand new Celtic shirt, as well as a full kit for his son, Prince Essien, with their names emblazoned on the back. Unsurprisingly, in a country where very few people can afford new football shirts, Collins and his son were soon the envy of their friends and family. Anybody who follows Collins on Twitter (@bedjosessien) will have undoubtedly seen the pair showing off these shirts in various pictures. The gesture meant a lot to Collins, and it is not something which he will forget any time soon.

As we all know, Victor Wanyama left Celtic in July 2013 for a fee believed to total approximately twelve and a half million pounds. When he finally put pen to paper and joined Southampton, he became the first Kenyan English Premier League player. Whilst Collins is tremendously proud of Victor's footballing progress, he acknowledged the fact that his move south was a risky one in certain aspects.

"Personally, I feel Celtic have lost a very good player. With any transfer such as this, there are potential positives and negatives attached to it. Yes, Victor will receive much higher wages in England, but I would have liked him to stay at Celtic for another year before moving on to a bigger club than Southampton at that point. Nobody knew of Victor Wanyama before he played with Celtic, and only time will tell whether it was the right decision to join Southampton – the grass isn't always greener on the other side, the move could backfire, but Victor is incredibly talented and I wholeheartedly hope he succeeds in the future."

Returning to football itself, the most expensive tickets to any league match in Kenya, which are designated for V.I.P.'s and executives, tend to cost around twenty United States dollars (the equivalent of about thirteen pounds sterling). As for the **"average"** supporters, they can generally gain access to one of the country's football grounds for around two or three dollars (between one and two pounds), although many of the dirt terraces these individuals stand on are uncovered, meaning they either have to wade through vast amounts of mud if it has been raining, or endure hours in the searing African sun if it is dry. Unsurprisingly, many of the current facilities in the country are **"not up to FIFA standards"**. However, massive investment from China in both new stadia and infrastructure is helping to change this, as a small part of a huge initiative known as **"Vision 2030"**, which aims to build Kenya into a **"globally competitive and prosperous nation"** by the year 2030.

As for Collins' future, the outlook is equally bright. He told me in depth about his dreams of a visit to Scotland, and even after my somewhat comical description of just how cold it can be here, he seemed unfazed. **"To experience the atmosphere of Celtic Park**

and to see the passion in the hearts of the fans would make me very proud – to watch a team like Celtic live would be incredible."

Interestingly, Collins also has a strong desire to visit Hampden, saying **"to see Celtic play at Hampden Park, the national stadium, would be...ah, I cannot even put it into words...I do not know when, but I believe it will happen for me...one day."**

Perhaps this should be no surprise – at one stage Hampden was the biggest football stadium on the face of the Earth, and undoubtedly it has been home to some magnificent matches over its long history. Fundamentally, Collins would love to visit Scotland and I have no doubt that, if and when he does, he will be welcomed with open arms by numerous Celtic supporters, including myself. When I last spoke to him, Collins told me: **"It is one of my life's dreams to visit Scotland and watch Celtic play, but the air fares are so expensive that it is impossible for me to consider such a trip at the moment. I have a family to support, and we do not have the sort of money that is required. The day when I step onto an aeroplane with my Hoops on knowing I am on my way to see Celtic will be the same day that I am the happiest man alive."**

All in all, it is always a privilege to speak to Collins Okinyo. He is a fantastically optimistic gentleman, whose attitudes and personality rarely fail to bring a smile to the faces of those around him. He told me that **"life in Africa is not easy, but I thank God for football, because my life wouldn't be the same without it."**

As I mentioned previously, Collins holds an integral belief that football can unite different groups of people like nothing else, and this is something we must all strive to make a reality around the world. As Kenya and many other developing countries progress into the future, football, sport as a whole, and people like Collins Okinyo will play large parts in their development. I wish him and his family all the very best for the future, and hope that one day, whether it is in Africa or Scotland, his dream of seeing the Celts in person will come true.

"From The Pits To Paradise"

In late May 2012, I climbed into my car in the knowledge that I was on my way to meet someone very special indeed. Running a little late, as is so often the case, I frantically headed along a windy 'B' road in the Scottish countryside. As some of you may recall, we had an unusually warm week of weather at that time (with temperatures reaching the mid-twenties daily), so I enjoyed the views of the hills and valleys as I travelled along in my little sauna, also known as my car.

Eventually, the road twisted its way into the Ayrshire village of Muirkirk, where I was set to visit the oldest living Celtic player, Mr William 'Bill' Boland. As I walked towards his house, I was met by his granddaughter, who was kind enough to have helped set up the meeting. I'll be honest, as I write this I do not consider myself to be a proper author by any means, having never published a book prior to this one, so I'll confess that I wasn't entirely sure what to expect. However, I was to be very pleasantly surprised.

The very limited online information regarding Bill Boland that I had seen prior to this visit told me fairly little about the man himself, except for the fact he had held a reputation as a big, square, burly forward player in his day. For this reason, I'd be lying if I didn't say I expected to see someone of a slightly larger stature when I strolled into his small and mercifully cool living room and met Bill for the first time.

I was greeted with a politeness and spirit that remains with me to this day, as Bill stood up from his armchair and shook my hand, before he invited me to sit down. He struck me initially as a fairly small individual (however, it is of note that I am a little over six feet and three inches in height myself), but nevertheless a man full of life, even at his age.

Born on the thirtieth of November 1919, Bill was ninety-two when I was fortunate enough to first meet him. Once he had commented on my height, he quickly informed me that he used to stand around five feet and nine inches tall, and weigh twelve stones, but that now he only stood five feet and five inches in height, and weighed a little over eight stones. As we sat in his living room, both Bill and his family's hospitality became apparent almost immediately, as seemingly endless cups of tea, glasses of orange juice, scones and biscuits began to make their way in and out of the room.

Once I had gulped down a sizable portion of a glass of icy cold liquid, I proceeded to tell Bill about both my plans for this book, and also about myself as a Celtic supporter. He then explained that I was not the first individual to have visited him to discuss his time at Celtic Park, saying he had spoke to two gentlemen, both significantly older than myself, a couple of years earlier. Regardless, this did not put me off, as I knew I was going to spend some time talking to a man who has followed Celtic for more than four times the length of my life as a whole thus far.

Mr Boland is, essentially, the definition of a hometown sort of guy. He grew up in Muirkirk, a village for which he holds a strong affection, and developed both a love of football and Celtic from a very early age. He quickly found himself as a part of his school's football team and yet, ironically, Bill claims he saw Rangers play live long before he ever saw Celtic play in the flesh.

I could see the proverbial cogwheels in Bill's head begin to turn, as he recalled his first trip to a professional football match, when his school's side were taken on a special trip to watch Motherwell take on Rangers at Fir Park in the early 1930's. Amazingly, Bill went on to then describe Motherwell's opening goal that day in some detail.

"Motherwell's outside right was called Stevenson, and he got the ball, beat his man, and then crossed the ball from the wing. Now, Rangers goalkeeper was a man called Dawson, and this goal would never have been allowed to stand nowadays. The ball looped through the air and Motherwell's centre forward, I forget his name, looked as if he was going to jump to contest the ball with the goalkeeper. Instead though, he waited for Dawson to collect the ball, and shouldered him just as his feet touched the ground again. The net bulged as the keeper fell into it, and although he was clever enough to try to throw the ball away before it crossed the line, a goal was given. I'll never forget that."

However, whilst Bill was able to describe this goal in such staggering detail, he admitted he was unable to remember his first Celtic game, saying **"it was a long, long time ago son, and I've been to so many of them that some seemed to have merged together in my head!"** Now, considering we're talking about football matches that took place almost eighty years ago, I think that's more than excusable. He does believe that it was sometime in the early to mid 1930's though, which is an impressive fact alone.

At the age of fifteen, Bill had a trial with local side Kilmarnock, but he was unsuccessful, and continued to play with his school side. He would later take part in trials for the international schoolboys team, and despite making the final stage of selections, he was once again thwarted in his footballing quest.

Only weeks before I first spoke to Bill, in the first half of May 2012, Celtic lifted their first Scottish Premier League title under manager Neil Lennon, having won it officially sometime earlier at Rugby Park, Kilmarnock. I, being a young man of course, decided to head out and celebrate this achievement after the final match of the season (a five-nil demolition of Hearts, with Gary Hooper scoring all five goals), and eventually found myself in the lounge of the famous **"Baird's Bar"** on the Gallowgate.

The pub was, unsurprisingly, incredibly busy as I fought my way to the bar along with a few friends. Once we had bought our rounds of drinks, the folk I was with moved away with their respective orders of cider and lager, as I waited on my pint of Guinness arriving. As my pint of the black stuff was handed to me, the little gentleman standing next to me (who also happened to be a Guinness drinker) began to talk to me.

Unfortunately, I never caught the old man's name with all of the music and the singing which was going on, but I did catch him saying **"I'm eighty-nine years old you know!"** Regardless, he began to tell me (as well as anyone else who would listen) about some of the players he'd seen and some of the matches he'd attended over the course of his lifetime. I was utterly amazed to find myself speaking to someone who had actually been at the 1937 Scottish Cup Final that day in **"Baird's"**, and so, while I sat in Mr Boland's living room, I felt I simply had to ask him whether or not he too had been there at Hampden in 1937.

Bill's eyes lit up as I posed the question to him, before he began to tell me what he could recall of that famous day in the history of Celtic Football Club. In other parts of this book, I discuss this match from the player's perspectives, down on the field of play. However, it is refreshing to consider how it felt to be on the surrounding terracing on days such as this.

In truth, perhaps it should not be too sizable a surprise to find that both men I asked had been there that day, as the match holds the record for the highest ever official attendance for a club tie at a European Football stadium. An incredible number – over one hundred and forty-six thousand people no less – were officially recorded as having passed through Hampden's gates that day. Now, when we consider the fact that thousands of boys were likely passed over the turnstiles, and that a fair number of people will have 'found another way in' (over the walls etc), the possible figure for the actual attendance becomes even more astronomical. As is described in another part of the book, it is not out of the realms of possibility that there were between one hundred and seventy, and one hundred and eighty thousand people at Hampden Park that day. For this reason, it is no wonder that Bill immediately recalled just how busy it was at that particular Scottish Cup Final.

Bill described the match itself as **"a very close game"**, before going on to say **"it was one of the best football matches I've ever seen!"** For those of you who may not recall, Celtic took the lead early on, before Aberdeen (playing in their old yellow and pink strips) equalised only moments later. Eventually though, the match which **"could have gone either way"** was won by Celtic, who scored a late winner and sent their supporters into rapturous celebration. Bill described the scenes as **"chaos, but friendly and good natured chaos."** While I think most of us will have tales of intense atmospheres and crazy goal celebrations, I don't think any of the younger generations (including myself), will ever be able to truly grasp what attending a match with approximately one hundred and eighty thousand other spectators must have been like.

As I continued to speak with Mr Boland, I was determined to attempt to achieve an insight not only into football's past, but also into football's present and its future. Therefore, when he said **"you had to make sure your hands weren't in your pockets when you went into the enclosure, otherwise they might end up stuck there for the entire match"**, I decided to ask him for his thoughts on the potential reintroduction of standing at Scottish Football matches. His answer would prove to be both interesting and heart-wrenching, but there'll be more on that later.

Only a couple of years after the triumph of the 1937 Scottish Cup Final, as Mr Boland continued to ply his footballing trade with junior side Muirkirk Hibs, the world was to change forever with the beginning of World War Two, an event ignited by the invasion of Poland by Nazi Germany in September 1939.

Soon, this affected virtually aspect of daily life in Scotland, and inevitably, it was to have a significant impact on Scottish Football. Soon, the professional game had been restricted massively to friendly cup competitions, and Mr Boland tells me that all junior football, at least in Ayrshire, was totally suspended, leaving him without a team to play for. Also, the maximum wages a professional footballer could take home was limited across the board to two pounds per week.

Bill Boland never travelled to the front lines of the world's battlefields during World War Two. Instead, he remained at home with thousands of other experienced coal miners, tasked with keeping the country's energy supplies stable in the face of growing adversity. Bill had worked in Kames Colliery since 1933, and along with many miners and shipbuilders, he was not automatically conscripted as the conflict with Nazi Germany began to gather pace.

As the war dragged on, Bill did his best to continue playing the game he loved so much. This led to Mr Boland and a group of other locals forming their own wartime 'boys and girls' junior team.

In 1944, Bill Boland would finally get his chance, as he was invited for a trial with Celtic Football Club, in which he was successful. And so, at the age of twenty-four, Bill signed for the

Club he had supported all of his life. He gleefully recalled the journey from Ayrshire that he took on a Wednesday evening, as he travelled to Celtic Park to **"put pen to paper"**.

Interestingly, Bill wholeheartedly believed for many years that he had signed for the Club on the same night as another youngster who would go on to become a Celtic great. Coincidentally, he too is featured in this book. However, after some time, Bill discovered that although he was joined by another lad (going by the name of Bobby Evans) on that summer's evening, he did not actually sign for the Club until the following week.

In time, Bill Boland and Bobby Evans would go on to become very good friends, and Bill still remembers the late Bobby fondly to this day, describing the lad with the famous crop of distinctive red hair as **"a true gentleman, and a great, great footballer."** Almost seventy years on from the footballing trial they both took part in, and from the time they spent together at the Club, Bill still maintains that Bobby was his favourite player that he ever had the chance to play alongside. However, if Bill (or anyone else reading this) thought that getting through his trial would be the biggest obstacle in Mr Boland's way with regards playing for Celtic, then they would be proven to be sadly mistaken.

As mentioned previously, Bill worked in an Ayrshire coal mine, and had done so for around a decade when he finally had the opportunity to sign for Celtic and play professional football. However, in case you'd forgotten, this did not happen during peacetime, so circumstances prevented Bill from having the so called **"life of a footballer"**. Bill had only been kept at home in Scotland (i.e. away from the armed forces) because he was a coal miner, and this wasn't just something he could abandon as several peacetime miners of old who went on to become footballing legends did. For the record, Bill **"didn't want to abandon"** his job. In fact, he wanted to continue doing his **"bit for the country"**, but he was determined to have his chance to play football too.

Sadly, even in modern times, we are often reminded just how dangerous working in a mine can be when we hear of individuals being trapped for extended periods of times by roof collapses or killed by gas explosions. Therefore, in a time when the words

"health" and **"safety"** were only found in dictionaries, working in a mine was an even more dangerous occupation than it is now. Bill told me he worked in something called a **"free pit"**, meaning the mine was meant to be free of gas accumulations, and thus free of any risk of explosion.

Bill worked in a role known as a **"mine deputy"** (previously known as mine **"firemen"**), which he described as **"one of the hardest jobs in the mine"**. In essence, Mr Boland was the human version of the stereotypical canary in a cage. Bill worked shifts covering **"his section"** of the mine, patrolling the area with a glass lamp with a small flame inside of it. Depending on the brightness and height of the flame, any accumulations of gas could be detected and that area of the mine evacuated before anyone was hurt – or that was the idea anyway. Thankfully, Bill never suffered any serious injuries, but he did tell me of one sad incident, where as a result of gas checks becoming less and less stringent at the colliery, a pocket of gas went undetected, and when it was ignited by a spark, nineteen young men lost their lives in the resulting blast.

With regards to Bill's footballing career though, his work at the mine became a hurdle that simply had to be overcome. Once Celtic had offered him a contract, Mr Boland went to ask the manager of his section in the mine for time off on days on which Celtic were scheduled to play, offering to do double shifts on surrounding days to accommodate for his absence. This request was denied, as his area manager told Bill **"mining is far more important than football."** This denial meant Bill had to think outside the box in order to find a way in which he could be granted access to play for the Club, and quickly, he would do just that.

During a discussion with one of his friends and colleagues in the mine, Bill remembered that his area manager and the general manager of the mine (the proverbial **"man at the top"**) did not get on particularly well with each other. In truth, this is probably a rather polite way of describing their fraught relationship. Regardless, this presented Bill with an opportunity, and critically, an idea.

Bill soon proceeded to walk a rare path for an 'average' worker, as he sought to speak directly to the general manager of the mine about his situation. Specifically highlighting the fact the area manager in question had turned down his request, Bill came to an arrangement whereby he would be allowed time off to play for his beloved Celtic. In saying this, it was still to be a less than ideal state of affairs, but Bill was delighted to finally have his chance and he certainly wasn't planning on complaining.

Bill was paid the standard weekly wartime salary during his stint at Celtic Park, as he took home the aforementioned sum of two pounds sterling plus travelling expenses for his efforts. Normally, his days consisted of early shifts in the mine, before he would take a bus to Glasgow for training in the evenings, returning home to Muirkirk thereafter. Incredibly, on match days, Bill would begin a shift in the mine at 11.30pm the previous evening, and work there until 7.30am on the morning of the game. He would then rush home for a couple of hours rest (at most) before boarding the public bus which would slowly wind its way from Ayrshire to Glasgow, where he was set to play at 3pm. Now, when we consider the regimes regarding fitness, nutrition and adequate rest in modern football, this is quite a thought and it must have required an incredible level of effort and determination from Bill.

Perhaps then, it is no surprise then that Bill Boland's first team debut ended with him being substituted with cramp. Bill made his first appearance for Celtic's senior side in a goalless draw against Clyde at Shawfield in early 1945. Of course, it is noteworthy that domestic campaigns were very different from their usual formats during World War Two.

The national game became more of a regional affair in most cases, as teams from the same geographic areas were grouped together to play each other in regional tournaments and divisions. Bill described how Celtic were grouped with three other teams in one particular competition during his time at the Club, which I have since ascertained to have been the 'Southern Scottish League Cup'. This was the only senior competition Bill would feature in, as he played twice against Clyde, once against Falkirk and once against Partick Thistle. In total, he appeared four times for Celtic as a part of the Hoops forward line. In doing so, Bill played twice at Celtic Park, scoring once there, and twice away from home, scoring once at Firhill in the north of Glasgow.

The enthusiasm and vigour with which Bill described both of his senior goals to me was indicative of a man who had the chance to play, and score, for the Football Club he had always loved, and continues to love, with all of his heart. He explained to me that these brief moments were virtually imprinted on his mind, and that he felt he could play, rewind, or fast forward each of them in his head at a moment's notice.

On the third of March 1945, Bill took to the field at his beloved Celtic Park for the first time in a senior match. Bill proceeded to describe the goal which he scored that day:

"We'd won a throw in just inside their half a few moments earlier. I felt the Falkirk player close behind me as the shy was taken, and I thought he was standing closer than he should have been, considering the shy was quite far down the wing. Anyway, when the ball came to me I turned and knocked it past him, and, because he was so close, I was able to drop my shoulder and get away from him. So as I ran towards the box, the defence backed off, giving me the chance to take a shot, which I did from the corner of the box. As luck would have it, in it went!" The match would, after a topsy-turvy style encounter, eventually finish with Celtic winning by three goals to two.

When Bill began to describe his second and final goal for Celtic, he reminded me a little bit of a small boy in the park or the back garden, shouting **"Did you see that? Did you see what I did there?"** to his mum or dad, and that is just how it should be – after all, the joy these moments brought to Bill were still clear to see when we discussed them. Mr Boland remains incredibly proud of his short time at Celtic Park, and although he is not the sort of man to brag about his achievements, it was clear to see just how proud he is of his **"best goal"**.

A few months after the previously discussed Falkirk match, Celtic travelled to Firhill to face local rivals Partick Thistle in the regional tournament, which was still at its group stage. The tenth of March 1945 may not have been an important date for many Celtic supporters, but it is undoubtedly a day that Bill Boland will never forget. On the same day, only hours before the football matches across Scotland kicked off, the United States Air Force launched **"Operation Meetinghouse",** an intense firebombing raid on Japan's capital city, Tokyo. This bombardment killed more than one hundred thousand people and flattened approximately a quarter of the entire settlement in the space of one night – it remains the deadliest air raid of World War Two, killing more people than either of the nuclear bombs which would subsequently be dropped on the cities of Hiroshima and Nagasaki. I suppose this only highlights the fact that the world was a very dark place at this point in human history.

However, on a football field in Scotland, there would be one small glimmer of light for those in attendance to enjoy. Before Bill began to tell me in detail about his goal, he likened it to a modern day 'Paddy McCourt style' goal, before jokingly saying, **"I hope you don't think I'm exaggerating this to make it sound better than it actually was."**

To be fair to Bill, if I had personally only scored one goal for Celtic, even from half a yard out when the ball bounced in off of my face, I would most likely spend the rest of my life telling people I went on a dazzling box to box run, beating the entire opposition team in the process, before somersaulting over the goalkeeper 'Patsy Gallacher style' into the net. However, while he undoubtedly remembers his goal fondly, the difference between the two previously referenced tales is that Bill isn't lying or exaggerating when he tells his.

That is unless, of course, ex-Rangers inside forward Bob McPhail, writing about the match in **"The Mail"** the next day, was exaggerating too. He is quoted as saying **"any young player that can forget his team mates and go on to score a goal like that is around to stay."** When we consider that this is an ex-Rangers great praising a Celtic player in the 1940's, we realise that it must have been a very impressive individual goal indeed, and therefore, I'll leave it to Mr Boland to describe it to you in all of its glory.

"The match was played at Firhill, and although the newspapers claimed there were twenty-five thousand people there, when I look back on it now it must have been a bit less than that. Otherwise, Firhill would have been packed, and it wasn't. Anyway, the game was still goalless, and our outside left had cut in from the wing with the ball and was running along the centre line whilst being chased by a defender. The two of them ran in one direction, as myself and another Thistle player ran towards them, after my teammate on the ball had taken a heavy touch."

"All four of us charged towards the ball and as the three others slid in I just managed to get my toe to it before anyone else. As they all lay there in a heap, I turned with the ball and started to head for goal. It was one of those runs where I didn't plan to beat three men initially, it just sort of happened. I went past the first man, then past the second, and then somehow past the third, and then I found myself on the edge of the box and struck a hard shot and scored."

The following day, **"The Glasgow Herald"** newspaper, which had been reduced to six pages per edition at that stage of the war, stated simply (albeit spelling Bill's surname incorrectly): **"Celtic too, maintained their long run of successes. In the usual hard game with Partick Thistle at Firhill, Bolland scored the only goal."**

During the coming season, the Football Club would see its second manager, Jimmy McStay, pass on the baton to the third man to take on the job, James 'Jimmy' McGrory. This managerial shift signalled the end of Boland's playing days at Celtic Park, but he still had time to feature once more for the Hoops, in a disappointing one-all home draw against Clyde. However, had it not been for a last gasp penalty from Jimmy Delaney to equalise for the home side, Bill would have tasted defeat as a Celtic player. Frustrated with a lack of any first team football, Bill eventually requested a transfer away from Parkhead and returned to junior football in late 1945 (once it restarted after the end of the war), rejoining his old local side, Muirkirk Hibs.

However, Bill's relationship with Scotland's national game did not end when his playing days eventually ended sometime later. As he continued to ply his trade in the local colliery, Mr Boland also continued to follow both Celtic and football as a whole. In May 1953, Bill attended the final of the Coronation Cup, and he was there at Hampden Park to witness Celtic defeat the **"Famous Five"** of Hibernian and win the one-off tournament in some style. One hundred and seventeen thousand people crammed inside the national stadium to see the match, and Bill watched the likes of Jock Stein, Charlie Tully, and his dear friend Bobby Evans contribute to a day in the history of Celtic Football Club that will continue to be spoken of for generations to come.

Obviously, the next question I posed Bill to was whether or not he had been at the 1957 League Cup Final demolition of Rangers, but sadly he said he was not able to attend that particular tie. However, he was at the 1956 League Cup Final, as Celtic defeated Partick Thistle to claim the Cup for the first time in their history.

In 1960 however, Mr Boland attended a match which would be the envy of any lover of the beautiful game, as Real Madrid took on Eintracht Frankfurt in the European Cup Final at Hampden Park. Real Madrid won the match seven-three (an incredible scoreline in itself), with the immortal Ferenc Puskás scoring four goals, and Alberto Di Stefano scoring a mere three. There have only been four hat-tricks ever scored in European Cup Finals, and Bill was lucky enough to witness two of them occur on the same day. For the record, Puskás repeated his feat only two years later against Benfica (Real Madrid lost by five goals to three on that occasion) and the only other man ever to add this achievement to his list of accolades was the great Pierino Prati in 1969, as his A.C. Milan side defeated Ajax by four goals to one.

Not only did Bill describe it as **"one of the greatest matches he had ever seen"**, this match is regarded by many as one of the finest spectacles the sport of football has ever created. Despite the fact there were almost one hundred and thirty thousand people in attendance on the eighteenth of May 1960, it is still fairly impressive when you find one of them sitting across from you, telling you all about it over a cup of tea.

The match itself had more than one connection to Glasgow, as Eintracht Frankfurt defeated Rangers over the two legs which made up one of the competition's semi-finals that year. In saying that, it wasn't as close an affair as some of you may fear, as the German side put the ball into the Rangers net twelve times in one hundred and eighty minutes of football, winning by twelve goals to four on aggregate. In the other semi-final, Real Madrid overcame fierce Catalan rivals Barcelona by six goals to two. Sadly, gone are the days when two semi-finals and a final (comprising five matches in total) would produce thirty-four goals between them!

Anyway, this was the day on which Bill Boland developed a love of Real Madrid and their football; a love that remains with him to this day. He recalled how over one hundred thousand Glaswegians applauded the Spanish side for their efforts, and thanked both teams for putting on such a memorable footballing display in their city. Bill described the match as having **"one of the most polite atmospheres"** he had ever witnessed. Once he had done this, Mr Boland rose from his chair and disappeared from his living room for a few moments, before returning with an item I could quickly tell was his pride and joy; an old encyclopaedia of all things Real Madrid, written largely in Spanish. While he was incredibly kind in offering to loan it to me, I had to decline (once I had spent five minutes looking at some of the remarkably rare old pictures within, that is) as I felt it could very easily become lost in the clutter that we all have in our homes.

In the following years, Bill would attend several more matches of note, as he travelled to Elland Road for the first of two mammoth ties (in all senses of the word) with Leeds United. There, he saw George Connelly (a lovely man whom I have had the pleasure of meeting briefly once) score the only goal of the game inside the first two minutes, in front of forty-six thousand spectators in West Yorkshire.

Only a fortnight later, Bill would make his way to Hampden Park, where a record was set for the highest attendance at any match in a UEFA competition, with over one hundred and thirty-six thousand people crammed inside Hampden on the fifteenth of April 1970. Bill, at the age of fifty at that time, saw Billy Bremner give the English side an early lead, before second half goals from John Hughes and Bobby Murdoch sent Celtic to their second European final.

Less than a year later, Bill would attend another famous game in the history of Scottish Football, but sadly it was a game written into the history books for all of the wrong reasons. On the second of January 1971, Celtic (and Bill) travelled to Ibrox Park for the customary New Year derby. With the match goalless and only a minute of regulation time remaining, Celtic took the lead through a Jimmy Johnstone goal. At this point, with the match seemingly over, many supporters began to head for home. Tragically, sixty-six Rangers supporters who attempted to leave the stadium via **"Stairway Thirteen"** never made it back home.

Bill left after the Celtic goal, as he **"always aimed to leave Ibrox a few minutes before the end"** in order to make the journey back to Ayrshire a lot easier. When Bill left, Celtic led by one goal to nil, and until the moment he walked into his house hours later, he had no idea of the horror which had unfolded on the now infamous stairway. With the final kick of the match, Colin Stein equalised for Rangers, but the result soon became irrelevant.

The loss of sixty-six lives at Ibrox that day shocked both ardent Scottish football supporters and those who never attended football matches alike. It was a truly horrific event, and one that will live long in the memory of the Scottish people. It was this story that Bill told me when I asked him early on in our discussions about his thoughts on the potential reintroduction of standing (through so called **"safe standing"**) at Scottish football stadia.

He told me that, personally at least, he prefers sitting at a football match. He admits his age may now have something to do with his view in that regard, but did highlight the fact that he had spent much of his younger days standing on the terraces of some of Scotland's most famous grounds. Bill always used to go to the enclosure at Celtic Park when he could, but now feels that a return to standing at football matches could be the start of **"a slippery road back to the old ways."** As Bill highlighted examples of being pushed along in football crowds unable to dictate the direction in which he was moving – he went on to say **"things are arranged much better now, as opposed to the way things were in the old enclosures. It's much safer nowadays"**.

Whilst I hold my own opinions on the potential reintroduction of standing at football matches, I have to say that Bill's views did strike a chord with me. It left me wondering whether people like myself, who were born after not only the Ibrox Disaster, but also the tragedy at Hillsborough in England, do not truly understand what the terracing of old was like. Of course, **"safe standing"** aims to nullify the risks associated with old terraces through strict control of numbers and high barriers at the front of every row. Nevertheless, that is an argument and a debate for another day, but one which must be had at some point in the future.

Before moving on to Bill's thoughts on the modern game in Scotland, and the individuals who currently find themselves at Celtic Park, Mr Boland proceeded to tell me of **"his favourite football match ever"**. Having already heard him discuss the likes of the Scottish Cup Final of 1937, the Coronation Cup Final in 1953, the European Cup Final in 1960, and the victories over Leeds United in 1970, I was intrigued to hear what he had to say. In truth, I was expecting him to say the twenty-fifth of May 1967, but this was not the match he chose.

To this day, Bill Boland still regards the two-nil win over St Johnstone in May 1998 as his favourite Celtic match. At the age of seventy-eight, Mr Boland was at Celtic Park that day to see the Bhoys lift their first league title in a decade, as Wim Jansen's men **"stopped the ten"**, thanks to goals from Henrik Larsson and Harald Brattbakk. In light of nine years of footballing agony, Bill said this **"was the game that gave him the most satisfaction when watching Celtic...to know we'd finally put things right, and brought the trophy home again."**

In 2009, Mr Boland was invited back to Celtic Park as the oldest living Celtic player, to watch a match and to draw the half time **"Paradise Windfall"** raffle, as the Hoops took on Queen's Park in the Scottish Cup. He was given a rousing round of applause by the Celtic supporters in attendance, and Bill was delighted to have had the chance to come back to Celtic Park once again. He was subsequently featured in an edition of the Celtic View, which he has framed and mounted in his home, open at his double page spread.

In saying that, it is not displayed in showy manner at all. The walls of Mr Boland's home are adorned with countless pictures of his family and friends, yet you could visit him (not knowing who he was) and have no idea of his past sporting achievements. In fact, the only hint of Celtic being a part of his life in his living room is a small, square alarm clock, made of bright green plastic with the Celtic crest featured on its face. Aside from this, his vast collections of Celtic and football books, as well as his pictures, are kept in other rooms.

As my visit began to draw to a close, I asked Mr Boland about his thoughts on the current Celtic team, and their manager, Neil Lennon. Bill lit up once more, as he started to praise the side which he sees as having **"great potential"**, which has already **"began to develop well"**. He struggled to select one favourite player currently at the club, but did say he feels that Kris Commons is **"incredibly talented, and should play more"**, before proceeding to praise both Charlie Mulgrew and Emilio Izaguirre very highly.

It was then Mr Boland began to talk about Neil Lennon. He started by saying that he feels **"very optimistic"** about the future for Celtic under Lennon, and feels that, while Jock Stein was **"the greatest"**, he could become a **"truly great manager"** himself. Bill told me how **"very few men could have withstood what Neil Lennon has had to go through, let alone thrive and succeed under the pressure it has brought along with it"**. Bill also said that he **"admired Lennon for having the guts to say what he feels, and be as straight forward as he can be,"** but did confess he felt **"Neil could learn to pick and choose his moments more"**. In saying that, Mr Boland did say that **"it was clear Neil had already learnt a lot since he took up his role, and that he was obviously continuing to learn his trade – doing so in an admirable manner"**.

Finally, I asked Bill about what it had meant to him to have the chance to both follow, and even play, for Celtic in his long life. Answering about his time as a supporter first, he told me **"that**

I have had a lot of pleasure following them...the ups, the downs and the excitement and fun of it all. In all my time following Celtic, I've only ever seen real trouble once, and when you consider how long I've been supporting Celtic, that tells you something about the Club's supporters".

I went on to ask Bill about what it meant to him to have played for his beloved Celtic, and this was the only question which I posed to Mr Boland all day which seemed to shake him a little. As he considered his answer, I could see how much it meant in the face of this old gentleman, before he had even said a word. People have said before that **"a picture speaks a thousand words"** and in this moment, I knew exactly what they had meant.

With what may just have been a small tear in his eye, Mr Boland simply said that **"playing for Celtic Football Club has always filled me with tremendous pride, and it will continue to do so as long as I live."**

I would just like to take this opportunity to say, in writing, that meeting Bill Boland was a magnificent honour for me. To have the chance to speak to someone with such experience of following Celtic Football Club was both incredibly humbling and unbelievably interesting. It only reinforced my belief that the older members of the Celtic support, who have seen so much in comparison to many of us younger fans, should be respected and revered. After all, we all start out as youngsters with the same passion for our team, and we all hope to still have the chance to follow the Club in our old age.

Bill played for Celtic four times, and whilst some modern footballers may view certain clubs as a **"stepping stone"** or regard only featuring on a few occasions for a team as **"a waste of time"**, it was clear that Mr Boland felt incredibly lucky to have had the chance he did. He is the embodiment of all the little Bhoys who grow up dreaming of playing in the famous green and white Hoops, and of all us adults, many of whom would give almost anything to have had that same chance.

Instead of feeling angry about not playing more often, Bill Boland is immensely thankful for having had the opportunity to play for Celtic at all. He lived his dream, and the dreams of countless others, as every Celtic player does when they take to the field. Bill may have only played four times, but that is four times more than most of us ever will, and to this day, he continues to take in every match from the comfort of his armchair at home.

As for Bill himself, all he said was **"I wouldn't change it for the world"**.

In my mind, he is an incredible man with an incredible story; one which I have been lucky enough to have been able to write about in some detail. I cannot thank Mr Boland and his family enough for allowing me that opportunity, and I, along with the rest of the Celtic support, can only wish them all the best for the future.

"Post-Script"

Since my initial penning of this piece (subject to edit after edit as is the case with writing a book) I have been lucky enough to visit Mr Boland on a few more occasions. Generally, these meetings have taken a similar form to the first, with most of the discussions surrounding Celtic and football in general. Having become good friends, in the autumn of 2012, I was aware that Mr Boland's ninety-third birthday was fast approaching, and I therefore decided to attempt to do something to mark the event. Soon, an idea had formulated in my head to see if we could arrange to frame a signed Celtic shirt for Bill's birthday.

With this in mind, I contacted the Football Club who, only after the interjection of Tony Hamilton, gifted us with a shirt previously signed by the first team to frame. To this day, I remain tremendously grateful to Tony for this, as delay after delay prior to his assistance meant we actually missed Mr Boland's birthday by a few months. Regardless, thanks to the support of the online Celtic fan base, I was soon able to raise the money to have the shirt professionally framed, with a small message placed below the shirt reading **"William Boland – Once A Player, Always A Supporter"** as well as referencing his relevant career statistics.

Upon presenting Mr Boland with his gift, which came as a total surprise to him, I can only say that he was absolutely delighted. Never before, and perhaps never again will I see a man in his nineties so excited about a present that one of his first thoughts was to invite his friends around to show it off. He could not thank the Celtic supporters enough for taking the trouble to do this for him – a gesture he appreciates to such an extent that it was almost beyond words.

To this end, I feel I can speak on behalf of my fellow supporters when I say that the pleasure was all ours, for the man who travelled **"From the Pits to Paradise"**.

"Post-Script II"

Bill Boland passed away on the twenty-third of September 2013, at the age of ninety-three. Whilst I remain saddened that Bill was not able to see the publication of this book, I am content in the knowledge that he did have the opportunity to read this chapter and that he thoroughly enjoyed it.

When I arrived at Mr Boland's funeral in the days following his death, all of the seats in the church were already filled more than half an hour before it was scheduled to begin. Therefore I stood, along with many other mourners, and perhaps that alone highlights the popularity of the man better than I ever could.

During the funeral Mass, Bill's son, a priest, recalled the following football chant from Bill's time playing with Muirkirk Hibs. I feel it is an apt manner in which to end a chapter dedicated to a good friend but, most importantly, to a great man (please note, Bill's mother was called Mary):

"Mary had a little lamb,
Its face was black as coal,
And every time it wagged its tail,
Bill Boland scored a goal."

"The Obliterator"

Born on the thirty-first of May 1879 in Denny, a town located a short distance from the larger settlement of Falkirk, Willie Loney would not have been known as **"The Obliterator"** as a child. In fact, nothing would likely have been further from the truth, as his famously quiet temperament would probably have been clear to see, even in his early years. In time though, he would become the most feared defender in Scottish Football, at least from any opponent's point of view, as everyone would have wanted a man like Willie alongside them on their team – a man of tremendous calibre, this is his story.

In the summer of 1900, just after the turn of the century, Celtic signed Willie from Denny Athletic, at the age of just twenty-one. Renowned mainly for his physicality and determination in his attempts to win the ball, many supporters would not have known of the other talents he possessed in abundance when he took to the field for his Celtic debut, at Tynecastle, on the seventeenth of September 1900. By all accounts, it was a dream start for Loney, as Celtic won by two goals to nil, with their defence keeping a clean sheet and our debutant grabbing his first goal for the Club. Prior to Willie's debut, Celtic had kept only one clean sheet in the six matches which had already been played that season. Despite a poor start from Hearts which allowed John Hodge and Willie Loney to add their names to the score-sheet, the Celts became subject to a barrage of attacks in the second half which often continued for long periods, and the fact they were able to keep a clean sheet despite such an onslaught from the home side was not lost on those with an interest in the sport at the time.

Now, whilst I referred to the name of **"Loney"** appearing on score-sheets previously, I feel it is worthy of mention that, until a significant period of his career had passed, the name **"Loney"** was not always spelt in the correct manner. For some time, in team line-ups and score-sheets printed in the Glasgow media, the wrong spelling, **"Lonie"**, was a relatively common sight. You would be forgiven for thinking this issue would have been dealt with quickly – after all more people read newspapers then than do so nowadays. However, the incorrect spelling continued to appear on and off, and if you ever look through some of the newspapers from the time you'll likely come across it somewhere.

Returning to the field of play itself, Willie did not reappear in the Celtic side for almost three months after his debut. However, he was eventually given his first serious chance midway through December and into the New Year, as Celtic took on the likes of St Mirren, Dundee, and Rangers in the league, before progressing through several rounds to reach the final of the Scottish Cup. During this period, whilst Willie impressed his manager enough to retain a starting place into the new season, the team faltered to a degree – two consecutive defeats in Glasgow to Dundee and Rangers soon ended any hopes they had of winning the league, whilst a disappointing defeat in what was widely regarded as a fantastic Scottish Cup Final (from the neutral's perspective at least) ended the season on a low-note.

As I have alluded to above, and contrary to what the nickname he would develop may suggest, Willie was not just a quiet man off the field, but often rather hushed on it as well. He rarely shouted or bawled at teammates or the referee, instead choosing to lead through his own actions, tackling as hard and fair as he possibly could, and accepting his errors when, on a rare occasion, he made them. Loney was, by all accounts, more talented with the ball at his feet than your average defender. With a great ability to control and distribute the ball, he even made a few appearances from time to time at outside right when the injury or suspension of others demanded it, and whilst he may not have sparkled in this position as more natural wingers did, he generally put in competent displays nonetheless.

In fact, Willie Loney would go on to do something few people have had the privilege of achieving during the history of the Football Club (and even less had at that time) and captain Celtic. As ever, he led by example, imposing himself as a quiet but strong figure the other players and fans could both respect and look to for inspiration. In truth he never asked to be the captain but was selected regardless, such were his footballing attributes. The captaincy is described as having **"fell into his lap"** by one writer on the fantastic **"Celtic Wiki"** website, rather than him ever aspiring or demanding he should hold it.

While Celtic did not win the league title until a few years into Loney's time at the Football Club, it was clear his presence was having an impact on the team's results from his first season there. In 1899–1900, Celtic lost the league to Rangers by seven points (in a time where victories only added two points to your tally). In 1900–01, this gap had narrowed to six points, and the season after that, to a mere two points. During the 1902–03 season however, both Celtic and Rangers fell down the table (to fifth and third respectively), as the new look league was won comfortably by Hibernian, with Dundee finishing as notable runners-up.

At the end of the following campaign, the League Championship had once again been won by a Glasgow side. However, the trophy did not belong to Celtic or Rangers, but to Third Lanark, a club with a long and illustrious, but sadly fundamentally finite history. The results of this season are worthy of mention though, as it was the first time Celtic had managed to finish on equal points with rivals Rangers (or above them in a league table) for six seasons, signalling a shift in the Club's fortunes was imminent.

At the end of 1904, Celtic won their first trophy in some time as they defeated Rangers by three goals to two in the Scottish Cup Final. Often known as **"Quinn's Scottish Cup Final"**, this was the day where Jimmy Quinn, part of a Celtic side losing two-nil, proceeded to score a hat-trick to win the famous trophy for the Celts. It is, of course, described in much more detail in the chapter devoted to the man himself. However, it is worthy of note that Willie also featured that day, and whilst the defence did allow their opponents to score twice in the first half, they organised themselves enough to withstand any further attacks on their goal, allowing the forwards the chance to try and turn the match in their favour which, of course, they obliged in doing.

Once again, in 1904–05, nothing could separate Celtic and Rangers in the league table at the end of the season. However, this time they were tied for first place. To be fair to them, Rangers had a far superior goal difference to that of Celtic, eighteen better to be precise, but at that point in time, this situation was still resolved by means of a **"League Championship Play-Off"** as opposed to goal difference. And so, on the sixth of May 1905, the two teams took to the field at Hampden Park, watched by over thirty thousand people.

When looking back on this tie, we must not underestimate how big a match this truly was, nor the part Willie Loney had played with regards to Celtic featuring in the match at all, for he had scored no less than six times over the course of that league season, the equivalent of almost ten percent of the Hoops' total goals (no mean feat for any player, let alone a defender). Also, Celtic had not won the League Championship since 1898, and the last time Rangers had done so had been in 1902. Therefore this was, at least debatably, the biggest Glasgow derby that had ever been scheduled at that point in time. The result itself would go on to become one of the most famous in the history of Celtic Football Club, and to this day, it is often virtually ignored by those of a different footballing persuasion.

With fears of bias surrounding the match, an English referee was specially brought in for the play-off, and the frantic tie began. Celtic lined up with a team of: Davie Adams, Hugh Watson, Willie Orr, Alec McNair, James Hay, Willie Loney, Alec Bennett, Jimmy McMenemy, Jimmy Quinn, Peter Somers and David Hamilton.

Rangers won the obligatory toss of the coin, and decided to play into the wind for the duration of the first half, so that a tired Celtic side (or so they hoped) would need to do so in the second half of the match, whilst they would have it at their backs, helping them to push forward. Most of the early pressure came from the men from the East End of the city, although both goalkeepers were forced into fairly simples saves early on, but nobody could make the breakthrough.

Newspaper reports state that the offside rule was enforced on several occasions, almost exclusively against Celtic, as their attackers attempted to break away from their opponent's defensive line over and over again. As half time approached, Celtic had a narrow escape as Rangers squandered a good chance as Jacky

Robertson, one of the Ibrox side's half-backs turned winger for the day, drove the ball over the top of the bar from an excellent goalscoring position.

At the interval, the match remained goalless, and as the second half began, the high tempo quickly returned as both teams strained and strove towards in search of the opening goal. Around fifteen minutes after the restart, the deadlock was broken by Jimmy McMenemy, Celtic's inside right, as he slotted the ball past Sinclair in the Rangers goal. Reports state that this strike sent the Celtic support gathered at Hampden into raptures, and as the game kicked off once more, the celebrations on the terracing at one end of the ground were still ongoing.

Less than a minute after the restart, following a Celtic corner, outside left David Hamilton hit a cross come shot which caught the goalkeeper out and looped into the Rangers net. Of course, if I was to state once again that the Celtic support were sent into raptures by the first goal from their team, then the second caused them to go absolutely barmy by all accounts, as one side of the stadium stood in stunned silence, having just watched their side concede two goals in as many minutes.

A few moments later, Rangers would claw one back through Robertson (who was never going to squander the second chance presented to him), but at the end of the match, with no more scoring forthcoming, the day belonged to Celtic. It is worth mentioning, I feel, that the man who scored the goal that turned out to be the winner that day, David Hamilton, was spoken to sternly by the referee in the match's dying moments, as it is said when the ball became dead at one stage, he proceeded to clear it high into the supporters gathered around the field, so as to waste some precious time. In a newspaper report the following day, which described the entire occasion (enormous as it was) in an article only a few inches in length, the author reflected, **"for the winners, Orr, Loney and Hay were very good."**

As the Celtic fans watched the team win their first title in eight seasons, it is noteworthy that the defence, with Willie Loney at its heart, only conceded one goal in a mammoth tie against a Rangers side which had scored no less than eighty-three goals in twenty-six league games that season (an average of over three per match). This day was to be the start of something very special for Celtic Football Club, as they went on to truly dominate Scottish Football for the first time in their history.

During the next season, with Celtic as defending Champions, the Bhoys went on to win the league by a sizable gap of six points from Heart of Midlothian. Loney and his defensive colleagues deserve tremendous praise for this, as they only conceded nineteen goals in the thirty matches that made up the league that year, and this led to the following famous quote circulating in the press at the time: **"Burglar proof, rain proof and wind proof."** Now, considering that this was an age where (largely) there were many goals scored, as I have alluded to, this was an incredible feat.

In the process of winning the title once again, the Celts, with Loney continuing to form an integral part of the defensive line, did not concede a goal in any competition from the fourth of November 1905, until the thirteenth of January 1906, save for one goal from St Mirren in a two-one victory on the twenty-fifth of November. The concession of only one goal in twelve matches around the turn of the year that season was undoubtedly a critical factor in the Hoops' retention of their league title. Come the start of the 1906–07 campaign, Celtic's defence and Willie Loney were at it again, this time not allowing a single goal to be scored against them in the first eight matches of the domestic season (whilst scoring twenty-seven themselves). With this sort of solid defending in mind, perhaps it is no wonder that the Hoops were able to go unbeaten throughout the first half of 1906–07, not losing until the first of January against Rangers (one of only two defeats throughout their entire campaign in all competitions, the other being against Third Lanark in mid-March).

Before we continue onwards, I would like to briefly highlight a short tale involving Willie which piqued my interest for no reason other than the fact that such oddities continue to this day. In December 1908, Celtic travelled to Fir Park to take on Motherwell in a league match. Going into the tie, the Hoops lay sixth in the table, thanks largely to the fact that they had played up to five matches less than some of the sides above them thus far. Anyway, with the match goalless, and Motherwell edging the play on the whole, Willie picked up the ball in the midfield. The following quote from **"The Glasgow Herald"** describes what happened next: **"Subsequently, Motherwell were, if anything, the better side, and it was a surprise when Loney, with a 35 yards drive, was adjudged to have scored. The ball came in very fast, struck the post and lay in the middle of the goal until Young cleared but the referee, who was in a good position, decreed that the ball had been over the line."**

Of course, with the continuing debate surrounding the potential (and increasingly likely) introduction of goal-line technology, it is interesting to consider the fact that such debates regarding whether or not the ball was over the line have been going on for almost as many years as the sport itself, as this example proves. Now, it would be ignorant of me to say whether or not the ball had indeed crossed the line on that particular occasion in 1908 as I was not there, and there is no conclusive evidence one way or the other. However, what is certain is that the goal which was awarded, combined with Celtic's defensive performance that day, were critical to the Parkhead Club's retention of their Scottish League Championship title.

Despite moving two-nil up soon after Willie opened the scoring, Motherwell regrouped in the second half, scoring one goal and very nearly equalising on several occasions. It was only a combination of good fortune and determined, resolute defending that helped Celtic to two points that day – two points that were absolutely crucial come the end of the season, as the Hoops edged the League Championship by a single point from Dundee. Some have said in the past that football is **"a game of fine margins"**, and on that winter day over one hundred years ago, they would have been right.

All in all, Celtic went on to win six league titles in a row as I have mentioned previously, and throughout this historic time, with Willie Loney at the heart of the Celtic defence, they never conceded more than thirty goals in a single season, even when the number of games involved in each campaign increased to thirty-four. Even in the 1910–1911 season, when Celtic came fifth, they still only conceded eighteen goals in thirty-four games, ten less than any other side in the league, as is discussed in the chapter regarding another defensive stalwart of the time, Alec McNair.

However, Loney was not an ever-present player throughout these years, as from time to time his bravery in tackles and physicality on the field of play resulted in injury. On different occasions, he suffered both fractures of the arm and wrist, which inevitably ruled him out for some time (despite him repeatedly attempting to run off such injuries in the matches). In saying this though, these injuries, and Willie's seemingly open attitude to the risk of incurring them, only added to his reputation as one of the toughest footballers in the country. Whether it was a conscious or subconscious decision is irrelevant – forwards genuinely thought twice about challenging Willie Loney for a fifty-fifty ball. He was not a dirty player though – far from it – he was simply a committed and clean sportsman.

In terms of his international career, Willie was often ignored by the selection committees in preference of other players. Despite playing over three hundred times for his Club, he only appeared twice for Scotland in the spring of 1910. He made his debut at Rugby Park, Kilmarnock, in a one-nil victory over Wales on the fifth of March. Whilst Scotland was the name of the team that ran out onto that Ayrshire field, you could have been forgiven for likening it to the Celtic side of the day, as Alec McNair, James Hay, Jimmy McMenemy and Jimmy Quinn lined up alongside Willie Loney. A fortnight later, a much changed Scotland side (without McNair or McMenemy) lost by a single goal to nil at Windsor Park, against Ireland. As you can see below, whilst **"The Glasgow Herald"** viewed Loney's first performance as impressive, his second and final showing in a Scotland jersey was not up to his usual high standards.

"Some reputations were shattered, others were damaged, and a few gilded. Brownlie, Mitchell, Loney, and Quinn gained in favour..."

"...and Loney never touched his real form."

Willie also played three times for the Scottish League during his career. International football aside, Celtic would go on to win four Scottish Cups during Loney's time at Celtic Park, in 1907, 1908, 1911, and 1912, although Willie didn't feature in the finals of 1907 and 1911. Only months after the Scottish Cup Final of 1911, in September, Loney was diagnosed with cholera, a disease which continues to kill people even in modern times, and unsurprisingly this kept him away from any competitive football for several months. Thankfully though, Willie battled through his illness and bounced back as he always did, to feature in the Scottish Cup Final of 1912, as Celtic defeated Clyde by two goals to nil at Ibrox. Unsurprisingly, as Celtic were the better side on the day, much of the talk in the newspapers of the time regards the Celts' attacking prowess, but one quote, from the one newspaper alluded to the vital role which Willie Loney did play that day, on the odd occasion he was called upon, as he broke up a dangerous attack only moments after Celtic's second goal: **"The Clyde responded pluckily, and but for Loney, Morrison might have tried Mulrooney from a header from Jackson."** Continuing in a similar vein, Edinburgh's **"The Scotsman"** newspaper said, **"The Celtic half-backs were a sound trio, with Loney outstanding..."**

All in all, Willie Loney finished his career with six League Championship medals, five Scottish Cup medals, and two international caps to his name. By the time he joined Motherwell in late 1913, Loney had made three hundred and five appearances for Celtic Football Club and scored an impressive twenty-nine goals.

He left the Club for Motherwell on the twenty-fourth of October 1913, the day before Celtic won two-nil at Ibrox in their pursuit of the 1913–14 League Championship title, as the following quote from **"The Glasgow Herald"** of the day outlines: **"Celtic Player For Motherwell – Yesterday forenoon Celtic transferred Willie Loney to Motherwell. The Lanarkshire club has been in difficulties for a centre-half owing to Hugh McNeill's regrettable injury and the Celtic directors readily acceded to the request for assistance. Loney has been capped by both Association and League."**

Willie had played his final match for Celtic on the twenty-seventh of September, in a Glasgow Cup semi-final. The match, which was a goalless draw against Third Lanark, would be the final time the word **"Loney"** would appear on a Celtic team sheet. It is perhaps apt that the team kept a clean sheet in the great man's final match.

Not a single individual from Willie's first ten teammates appeared in his final outing, and whilst players like Alec McNair would go on to play for some years yet, the contribution of Willie Loney to the great Celtic sides of that time must not be underestimated, nor forgotten. He was the rock upon which many a solid victory was built, but now his time had passed, and his position would be filled (as it was increasingly towards the end) by Peter Johnstone, another centre half with an abundance of talent. Tragically, Loney would outlive Johnstone, who was a decade his junior, by almost forty years. Peter, a member of the Seaforth Highlanders, service number 285520, was killed on the sixteenth of May 1917, at the Battle of Arras, France – another footballer and, much more importantly, another young man, lost to the horrors of war.

Without digressing too heavily, I feel I must mention that seven Celtic players in all died during the fighting of the Great War. Of course, there were countless Celtic supporters who also perished, many in the trenches of France and Belgium, but therein it mattered not if you were a footballer or a labourer – for therein, you were equals. In that sense, I would love to be able to name all of the supporters who died, but sadly that would be an almost impossible task. However, I will list the seven men to have played at some level for Celtic Football Club who died during World War One:

- Lance Corporal Leigh Richmond Roose - goalkeeper (Royal Fusiliers, PS/10898, awarded the Military Medal, as well as the Victory Medal and the British War Medal – died on the seventh of October 1916 in machine gun and artillery barrage - Somme)
- Sergeant Patrick Slavin – outside-right forward (Royal Scots, 20402, awarded the Victory Medal and the British War Medal – died on the thirteenth of November 1916 after being

caught in barbed wire whilst attacking an enemy position before being killed by gunfire – Somme)

- Private John McLaughlin – Position unknown due to the very scarce records of the man, who never actually made a first team appearance, and only spent a brief spell with the reserves (Highland Light Infantry, B/9377, awarded the Victory Medal and the British War Medal – died on the tenth of May 1917 after being injured by gunfire around a fortnight earlier – Arras)
- Private Peter Johnstone – half-back (Seaforth Highlanders, 285520, awarded the Victory Medal and the British War Medal – died on the sixteenth of May 1917, presumably through gunfire – Arras)
- Private Archie McMillan – outside-right forward (Argyll and Sutherland Highlanders, 202103, awarded the Victory Medal and the British War Medal – died on the twenty-third of November 1917 through gunfire after helping to successfully capture a village – Fontaine-Notre-Dame, Ainse)
- Gunner Donald McLeod – full-back (Royal Field Artillery, 201979, awarded the Victory Medal and the British War Medal – died on the sixth of October 1917 although the cause is unknown – thought to have died at the infamous Battle of Paschendale, Belgium)
- Private Robert Craig – full-back (South Wales Borderers, 30450, awarded the Victory Medal and the British War Medal – died on the nineteenth of April 1918 after being fatally injured defending the town of Mesen, Belgium around a week earlier)

At this juncture, I feel one more individual is worthy of mention, before we continue on with the life of Willie Loney – Lance Corporal William Angus V.C. – the first Scottish Territorial soldier to be awarded the Victoria Cross (the highest military decoration for valour within the United Kingdom's armed forces). Having been born in 1888 and raised in Carluke, South Lanarkshire, he joined the war effort along with another man from the town, James Martin, who would go on to become a Lieutenant. Having gone to war, both men saw action in the trenches, before Angus was injured by gunfire and had to retreat for medical assistance at one stage, separating the two men for a time. Not long after Angus' return, a section of his colleagues mounted a night attack on an area of German trench opposite their own which was to go catastrophically wrong. Having quickly seen the error of their ways, all of the men returned except a few, including Lieutenant Martin.

Presumed dead, it was not until dawn that the men caught sight of Martin, lying motionless only feet away from the enemy lines. A moment later, the Lieutenant stirred, moving slightly, indicating that he was still alive. This led to calls from Angus for a rescue attempt of some sort, which was initially denied by his superiors. However, he was insistent, and soon agreed to volunteer himself. William, who was a Celtic player for two seasons between 1912 and 1914 but never featured in the senior side, slowly crawled on his belly across no-man's land, before eventually reaching his stricken friend undetected.

He then carried Martin, who had laid in the hot sun for hours injured and very weak, back towards their own lines. However, when the German soldiers opposite noticed what was going on, they unleashed a hail of bullets and small bomblets towards the pair. Angus received several injuries whilst shielding Martin with his body, and despite falling on several occasions due to these impacts, he somehow rose to his feet time and time again until they were safely back in their own trench. Incredibly, both men survived, and whilst Martin suffered three wounds, Angus endured over forty, losing his eye and a section of one foot in the process. Described by one Lieutenant Colonel as **"the bravest deed done in the history of the British Army"**, the rescue of the twelfth of June 1915 has been admired by many.

Upon his return and the reception of his medal from the King, he was given standing ovations at both Parkhead and Ibrox on the same day for his heroism, and went on to take up a role as the President of his old side, Carluke Rovers Football Club. With such tales and tragedy in mind, I would urge you all to remember this story whenever anybody tries to talk down Celtic Football

Club and those who follow it, branding us as **"foreigners"** or telling us to **"go home"**, for when it really mattered, countless Celtic fans and several players fought and died for the land they call home.

Returning to the tale of Willie Loney, throughout the rest of his life, he was a man who was never too far away from Celtic Park. Less than week before Christmas in 1913, less than two months after he had officially left Celtic for Motherwell, he visited his old stomping ground with his new side, and, remarkably, came away with a point and a clean sheet after a goalless draw, after Motherwell had put on a **"good defensive show"**.

Only a few weeks later, Motherwell would travel to Glasgow once more to take on Rangers at Ibrox. Having defeated the league contenders by a single goal a couple of months previously, the Lanarkshire side were confident and composed, eventually coming away with a goalless draw like that they had achieved at Parkhead. However, it could have been a day to remember for Loney, as he uncharacteristically missed a penalty kick which could well have given Motherwell the points and allowed them to complete the domestic double over the second best side in the country – but it simply wasn't to be. Regardless of the penalty miss, the fact that Motherwell were able to travel to Glasgow twice in quick succession and to come away with two clean sheets speaks wonders for what Loney's experience and talent added to his new side defensively. Ultimately though, Willie's footballing days were numbered, and he retired in 1917, after spells with the aforementioned Steel Men, as well as Partick Thistle and Clydebank. As a shareholder of Celtic Football Club, he was always interested in the Club's progress and hopes for the future, and helped his old manager by doing the odd piece of unofficial scouting around the country from time to time.

In 1953, at Willie Maley's testimonial, two men who had once been his protégés, Willie Loney and Jimmy McMenemy, helped the aging Maley out onto the field at Celtic Park one last time. Maley then received a rapturous round of applause from supporters and colleagues of all ages which he thoroughly deserved. However, the old man would outlive one of his protégés by over two years, as on the sixth of March 1956, Willie Loney died at the age of seventy-seven. Make no mistake about it, Loney was a hugely talented, brave, physical footballer in his day, but he was also a quiet and inspirational figure throughout his life as a whole. Rest assured, **"The Obliterator"** will never be forgotten by the Celtic support.

EVENING TIMES TRIBUTE

"Willie Loney Dead" – front page

"Willie Loney, the famous Celtic player, has died at his home.

Loney joined Celtic from Denny Hibs, and from 1904–11 he was centre half in the famous Celtic team – Shaw; McNair and Dodds; Young, Loney and Hay; Bennett and McMenemy; Quinn; Somers and Hamilton.

Although Loney was a distinguished player, his honours were limited to three Scottish League appearances (v. Irish League 1909, 1911 and v. English League 1910). He played in full internationals for Scotland against both Wales and Ireland in 1910."

"Willie Maley's tribute – page 14"

"Willie Maley's Tribute to a Great Celt"

"Loney's Play Was A Treat"

"Willie Loney was a member of one of Celtic's most famous teams, that of 1904–11. The team can still be rattled off by many fans – Shaw; McNair and Dodds; Young, Loney and Hay; Bennett and McMenemy; Quinn; Somers and Hamilton.

With Loney's passing, only one of that team is still living – Joe Dodds, who, I am happy to say, is still hale and hearty. Joe is the man who, on one occasion, played two league games in one day. He was at full back in one game and centre half in the other – and Celtic won both games.

Loney came from Denny Hibs, who gave three world-beating half-backs to the game – Matt Busby and Jimmy McMullan were the others.

Willie Loney was at all times the real footballer, playing the game at its highest pitch and with that love of a club which I think was a big feature of his time.

Although he did not gain many international honours as a centre half, he was a treat to watch. And he carried in his make up a magnificent shot which scored many memorable goals.

Willie Loney didn't earn a lot in football, but he did earn a place in the hearts of all who loved pure football."

"How Is This Possible?"

As Celtic travelled to Germany towards the end of February 2003, it is fair to say that history stood against them to some degree. The Club had not reached the quarter finals of a European competition since 1980, and, having played thirteen competitive matches against German opposition over the years (including the home tie against VfB Stuttgart in the first leg in Glasgow), the Hoops' record read as follows: **"Thirteen played – three wins, two draws, and eight defeats"**. Of their six trips to the country, the Celts had only managed to come away with a solitary draw and, of their six two-legged European ties against sides from Germany, Celtic had only progressed on one occasion. However, with a three-one lead from the first tie at Celtic Park, many would have felt that this was one of the best chances Celtic were going to have to better their poor record against German opposition, and book themselves a place in the quarter finals of the UEFA Cup.

On the twentieth of February, Christopher Burke, a twenty-two year old originally from Milngavie, watched strikes from Paul Lambert, Shaun Maloney and Stiliyan Petrov overshadow Kevin Kuranyi's early headed goal for their visitors. Less than a week later, he found himself stepping off of a plane at Stuttgart International Airport along with several friends, a couple of days before Celtic were set to play in the city. Only months previously, Chris had attended his first away match in Europe as the Celts eased past Blackburn Rovers. However, this was to be the first trip he truly considered to be a European adventure, in a foreign country against formidable opposition.

"I was thoroughly looking forward to it," said Chris. **"We were all fairly confident going over because of our two goal lead, despite our past record. There was always the thought the European run might not go on forever, especially with so many good teams left in the competition and a hard game in Germany facing us, but we were determined to enjoy ourselves regardless of what happened on the park."**

Having travelled into the city, which is purported to have been where the automobile was invented by Gottlieb Daimler and Wilhelm Maybach, the group retired to bed. Now, whilst some of you may not have heard of these two famous residents of the city in question, I would presume that all of you will know another one of Stuttgart's sons, football manager Jürgen Klopp.

Anyway, Chris and his pals ventured out the following day, searching for the predominant gathering place of Celtic supporters, the number of whom rose notably by the hour: **"I'd never been to Germany before, and looking back on it I suppose I had some preconceived images of the country as being super efficient and immaculately clean, and whilst it was to an extent, it was no different from many of the places I've visited over the years. It wasn't as picturesque as some cities, but it was nice, and we soon discovered that many of the locals had taking a liking to us."**

And so, when the lads found the city's main square, they found the vast majority of the Celtic supporters who had already arrived in Stuttgart. **"It was funny,"** Chris said, **"In a lot of cities, big streets lead into the main squares and you can see them from quite a distance away, but in Stuttgart, it seemed as if you happened to turn a corner and all of a sudden there it was. There were hundreds, if not thousands, of Celtic fans already camped out there, with carry-outs and food, drinking, dancing and singing. Anyway, because of the fact you couldn't really see the square before you reached its edges, a lot of the locals seemed surprised at first to see us. A lot of them stood on street corners staring, and they appeared to be amazed by the volume of the singing that was going on."**

Anyway, having located the square and the main body of the travelling support, Chris and his mates decided to go in search of some beer. Having noticed the fact there was a supermarket right next to the square, similar to a **"Tesco Metro"** in size. They then crossed the road and headed inside, as other Celtic supporters came and went from the premises. However, when they reached the aisle which was meant to be filled with beer, they found it to be almost completely empty, much to their disappointment. Clearly, the shop had not realised there would be such a demand for this precious commodity and their stocks had dwindled, but it seemed that all was not lost as one of Chris' mates rushed down the aisle and grabbed one of the few remaining crates. However, having inspected the packaging, the lads noticed the prominent use of the word **"Frei"**, meaning the only remaining beer on sale was the alcohol free variety. Whilst they had spotted this before making a purchase and parting with their cash, many fans had not, and for hours to come, Chris saw other people glugging the stuff down in the square, seemingly bemoaning the unexplained lack of effect it was having, but he didn't have the heart to tell them.

Now, as many of you would expect, Chris and his mates were not ones to give up easily in their search for a cold beer (or several in fact). Having decided that they were not going to find any near the square itself, they decided to choose a street and walk away from the majority of the Celtic support. Soon, they realised that all of the supermarkets and smaller shops nearby were indeed sold out of beer, although some wine and other drinks were still available. At this point, Chris purchased a bottle of wine from one vendor, but it was only when he attempted to open it that he realised he required a corkscrew – not something he had brought with him from Scotland. However, after an extensive battle with said cork, the lads managed to open the bottle and have a small drink, before continuing on their quest for beer.

Eventually, just as they were all beginning to give up hope, one member of the group caught sight of a Turkish kebab shop a short distance off of the street they were on, in what appeared to be little more than an alley, and decided to wander over towards it for a further inspection. The shop was below street level, situated in the basement of a building, with a flight of stairs leading down to the front door. In Chris' own words: **"It was the sort of place you would have normally walked past, that is unless you were drunk or, in our case, wanting to get drunk."**

Having spotted a couple of bottles of beer through the window, he gestured wildly to the other lads as if he had just seen an oasis in the desert, who then descended on the shop and approached the till with the small number of bottles which had previously been inside a fridge. Chris then proceeded to ask the owner, who appeared to be in his thirties, whether or not he had any more beer which he would be willing to sell to the group. Subsequently, he nodded and disappeared down a narrow staircase. Sometime later, he emerged from the shop's cellar with two of the dustiest, most aged crates of beer one can feasibly imagine, before heaving them up onto the countertop.

"They were clearly his entire stock, and by the looks of things, they'd be in the cellar for a good while," said Chris. **"There were spider webs all over them, and you could have written your name in the dust piled on the top. Still though, the bottles inside looked ok when we had a peek, and once we had wiped them half clean and carried them back to the square, we decided to open them up. There was certainly a bit of trepidation at first, with us all looking at each other as if none of us wanted to take the first gulp, but the beer actually turned out to be remarkably good. The cellar must have been quite cold as it seemed to have chilled them, and after the walk we'd had, a couple of cold beers went down a treat. Looking back, it was a win-win situation, we got our beer and the kebab shop owner made himself a nice wee profit."**

Later that same day, once the crowd of supporters in the square had dissipated, Chris and his pals headed for a local bar. Now, as I'm sure you can imagine, the pub in question was **"absolutely rammed"** with Celtic fans, despite the fact it was a simple, traditional German establishment. According to Chris: **"Initially, there wasn't a single person in the pub who wasn't a Celtic supporter – well, other than the staff, of course, but at some point, two businessmen walked in wearing smart shirts and trousers. I caught sight of them and presumed they would immediately turn around and head off to find somewhere else, but instead they bought a couple of drinks and began to search for somewhere to sit."**

"We had some space at our table, and as they passed us, we gestured towards them and they came and sat down. For my sins, I can't remember their names, but I do know they were in their late forties or early fifties, and worked in the automobile industry. They were in the city on business, having travelled down from

Frankfurt. They weren't big football supporters, or so they told us, but they seemed to be amazed by the sights and sounds surrounding them in the pub."

"In fact, after a couple of hours, one of them asked: "You have all been singing for two hours now and you haven't sung the same song twice, how is this possible? How does everybody know the words?"

Now, as you will all know, the Celtic support have an extensive catalogue of music to pick from, ranging from fan's chants to lengthy ballads to adaptations of famous pieces of pop music, but it is perhaps something that we do not think about very often. After all, it is what it is, and it is what it has always been. However, the two German men in question were very impressed with this, and I have heard similar views aired elsewhere, so I feel compliments such as this should remind us just how special our support truly is. Continuing onwards, Chris said:

"At first they had said they would only stay for one drink, but that soon changed, and in the end they stayed with us until closing time, and when I last saw them they were suitably merry, wandering off into the Stuttgart night. I know one thing for sure though; they would definitely have been cheering on Celtic the following night!"

And so, the lads travelled back to their hotels and somehow found their way into bed, although few of them can actually remember very much about how exactly they did it. They had several rooms booked at differing hotels, each sleeping two or three, while Chris himself shared with two friends, Brian and Martin. However, when Martin woke Chris on the morning of the match, a little before 9am, he told him that Brian was nowhere to be found. Initially, this didn't particularly worry Chris, who was still shaking off the remnants of sleep and suffering from a substantial hangover. Presuming Brian was simply in another room or even another hotel, he went to the toilet, poured himself a glass of water, and proceeded to quench his thirst.

In time though, the pair found out that Brian was not in any of the other rooms or indeed any of the other hotels after making a few phone calls, and had therefore all but disappeared. Unsurprisingly, considering the amount of drink that had been consumed the previous day, this did actually worry the lads somewhat. Well, that is until Brian appeared a couple of hours later as if nothing had happened, nonchalantly strolling into the room around 11am. Of course, this was far from the true story, for Brian had spent the night in one of Stuttgart's finest police cells – without being guilty of any crime.

Amazingly, I'm not simply trying to save Brian's blushes, he had genuinely done nothing wrong nor had he been arrested. In fact, it transpired that, somehow or another, he had become separated from his mates once they had left the pub, and this resulted in him ending up somewhat lost. With no idea of where he was meant to be going, and clearly suffering from the effects of a few too many beers, he caught the attention of a pair of local police officers who offered to drive him to his hotel. When he told them he could not remember which hotel this was, they simply took him to the local police station and offered him a glass of water and an empty cell in which to sleep off his hazy state of mind, and he duly accepted. The next morning, Brian awoke with absolutely no idea where he was, or how he had gotten there, until a policewoman appeared with a cup of tea, and explained what had gone on previously. They then drove him back to his hotel as he could now communicate where it was located, and that was the end of that – well, for now, anyway.

Reunited once more, the lads headed for the main square once again, which was now packed to previously unforeseen levels, as virtually every Celtic fan making the journey to Germany had now arrived in the city. However, even amongst the jovial atmosphere which was being created by a number purported to be as high as ten thousand fans by the local media, all was not well. In fact, put simply, Chris was not well, for he had made the mistake of consuming the tap water in his hotel room which was not deemed as suitable drinking water earlier that day:

"We stayed in a high-rise hotel and it turned out that the tap water was pumped from a storage tank on the roof, so a couple of hours after I had drank it, it began to play havoc with my insides. In truth, I ended up having to take several trips to the toilet and for a while I felt distinctly dodgy, but after a few beers

had masked those feelings somewhat, I was ok. It's funny to look back on it now, and at the time I must admit I felt awful, but it was never going to stop me going to the game."

And so, as the afternoon became evening, Chris and the lads jumped into several taxis and headed for the Gottlier-Daimler-Stadion, a stadium with a somewhat chequered past. Upon its construction in the 1930's, it was originally known as the Adolf-Hitler-Kampfbahn. However, after the end of World War Two, it hosted Germany's first international match in 1950 (when it marked its highest attendance ever as almost one hundred thousand people packed the terracing), as a nation which was no longer ruled by a fascist dictatorship began to find its feet in the world once more. In more modern times, the stadium has taken on the name of one of Stuttgart's greatest residents, who was mentioned earlier in this chapter (no, not Jürgen Klopp), and it is now known as the Mercedes-Benz Arena.

Anyway, having arrived at the ground, the lads made their way inside the bowl-shaped stadium. **"I was actually surprised at the number of away fans at the game,"** said Chris. **"Obviously I knew the city was full of us, but to see our allocation behind the goal, as well as various other wee spots of green dotted around the ground was really impressive."**

Once the match finally began, Celtic opened the scoring through Alan Thompson a little over ten minutes into the tie. Obviously, this sparked celebrations amongst the Celtic supporters, as they moved four-one ahead on aggregate: **"Everyone thought we were home and dry when the first goal went in,"** reflected Chris. Only a few minutes later, Chris Sutton extended the Hoops' lead, and suddenly Celtic, the team with a fairly poor record against German sides, appeared to be easing to their first victory in the country: **"When we scored our second goal, we were all thinking "this is perfect" and "this is meant to be". After all, we were five-one up on aggregate, but typically Celtic don't like to do things the easy way very often."**

Just before half time, Stuttgart clawed a goal back whilst Celtic were temporarily down to ten men as Alan Thompson received treatment for an injury on the sidelines. However, this didn't affect the continuous celebrations ongoing amongst the Celtic supporters, as Chris recalls: **"To be honest, we hardly even registered Stuttgart's first goal because we thought we were so far ahead that we couldn't be caught. The away end was in party mode, and one goal wasn't going to change that."**

Around the seventy-five minute mark, Alyaksandr (Alexander) Hleb levelled the scores on the night, snatching away the prospect of a first win in Germany from Celtic, but still not causing too much distress to the away supporters in the ground: **"Once they scored their second goal, the general feeling seemed to be that because there wasn't too much time left, we'd be ok. However, I remember looking at the Stuttgart fans, who had been remarkably quiet all night and feeling a little nervous because they'd woken up all of a sudden. Every time Stuttgart gained possession of the ball from that point onwards, they roared their team forward, and wave after wave of attack followed."**

And so, with only a couple of minutes left, Stuttgart took the lead on the night, and drew the aggregate scores back to five-four in Celtic's favour, causing much consternation within the away support. **"We were caving in,"** said Chris. **"Suddenly we were surrounded by arguments about how many goals Stuttgart needed to score to put us out. The home fans were going mental, and the stoppage time at the end of the match seemed to take an eternity, but we got there – just. Obviously, scenes of joy followed, but the feeling of relief was palpable. It was great to get through, but most felt that it had been far too close for comfort. Anyway, it was soon forgotten about as we all headed back into the city for a few more beers."**

The next day, Chris and his mates flew home from Germany. During the flight, they discussed the events of the previous days, and, of course, they looked ahead to the next round of the UEFA Cup: **"For people my age, it was surreal simply to remain in Europe after Christmas. However, for us to reach the quarter finals of a European competition was magnificent. Of course, we would go all the way to the final, but we didn't know that at that time. We didn't fancy drawing Lazio, Liverpool or Porto, but we knew that the next round was going to be huge, regardless of who we faced or how we played."**

And so, another European trip came to an end – well, almost. As some of you may remember, I hinted earlier that there was a little bit more to the story of Brian and his encounter with the Stuttgart police. Now, sometime after he had arrived home, Chris and several other lads were over at Brian's house watching a Celtic match on the television, discussing the trip which had taken place a few weeks earlier. Subsequently, Brian told the group that his mother had since sent a letter to the chief of the Stuttgart police thanking them for looking after her son, much to the embarrassment of Brian and the hilarity of everybody else, who all fell about laughing for several minutes.

As for Chris, he moved to Australia in the summer of 2013, and therefore the chances of him attending too many games in the near future are somewhat slim. However, having made contact with the **"Perth Celtic Supporters Club"**, he continues to follow the Hoops avidly from **"down under"**.

"They Used to Call Me Larsson"

In Denmark's second largest city, Aarhus, lives our next Celt, Kresten Andersen. At the age of nineteen years old, Kresten (pronounced 'Cry-sten') is an avid football fan. With a love of both Celtic Football Club, and his local team, A.G.F. Aarhus, he must be a member of a relatively rare footballing breed, as I doubt many other people hold a passion for both of the aforementioned sides. Anyway, whilst Celtic won the Scottish Premier League and the Scottish Cup in the 2012–13 season, as well as battling their way into the knockout stages of the UEFA Champions League, A.G.F. ended their second season back in the Danish Superliga with a seventh place finish, after an encouraging start saw them rise as high as third before they dropped away towards the end of the campaign.

According to Kresten, Aarhus had their best years in the 1950's and 1960's, as they won the Danish Superliga three times in a row and also made some relatively significant strides in European competitions (where they have actually come across Celtic on a couple of occasions). In 1961, the club reached the quarter finals of the European Cup. Kresten told me that A.G.F. Aarhus have some similarities with Celtic, as both clubs were formed in the 1880's, and both boast strongly held traditions and values. In truth, considering the size of the city they play in, A.G.F. should perhaps be a bigger footballing force than they have been for some time. However, things certainly seem to be on the up for the **"De Hviie"** (**"The Whites"**), as they have now stabilised their position in Denmark's top league once more.

Kresten was introduced to Celtic by his brother Janus, seven years his senior, who in turn had his interest in the Football Club strengthened by a friend. Janus played football and worked politically for a time with a lad who was half Danish and half Scottish, with a deeply held love of his favourite football team, Celtic. As Janus became more and more friendly with his footballing companion, his love of the Hoops continued to develop, and the rest, they say, is history.

Convinced by his brother, Kresten started to watch Celtic around the age of twelve, and soon found himself developing a stronger and stronger interest in the goings on across the North Sea in Scotland. He currently watches most Celtic matches with a small group of like-minded individuals in an Irish bar in Aarhus called **"Tir Na Nog"**. Despite the fact there is a bar with the same name in Glasgow, I must confess until recently I had absolutely no idea what the name meant. According to the website of Aarhus bar, it is named after the fabled island of perpetual youth off the west coast of Ireland. This means that the concept of **"Tir Na Nog"** becomes **"The Bar of Eternal Youth"**.

Whilst Kresten has grown rather fond of the aforementioned bar, he did highlight the fact that there isn't a tremendous amount of choice with regards finding a place to watch Scottish Football in Aarhus: **"A lot of pubs and clubs are located down by the river, which is only about five minutes walk from "Tir Na Nog". There is an English pub in that direction, called "The Golden Lion", and that was one of the first places I saw Celtic. However, because it is an English pub you have to ask the bar staff to see whether or not they will put any Celtic game on the television screens for you, whereas up at "Tir Na Nog" all of the games are on without question. There is also a huge sports bar called "Bridgewater", but often they'll choose to show almost anything else over the games from Scotland – lower division German matches often get precedence for example, and I don't like that."**

Returning to their pub of choice then, Kresten explained to me that Aarhus' premier Irish bar is rather large on the inside: **"Tir Na Nog is quite big, but often when Celtic are playing during the day then you will only find Scottish and Irish people in it – as well as me and my brother, of course. Most of the staff don't speak any Danish, so English is certainly the predominant language used inside the pub. They have four big screens that the matches are shown on, which is great, but it can be quite expensive. A pint of beer will cost you between four and five pounds depending on whether the match is before or after 7pm our time."**

Anyway, Kresten's life is not totally devoted to Celtic, and nor should it be. He is currently studying English, Spanish, and social studies at college, although he did mention to me that the Danes do have a bizarre educational structure, at least when it is compared with those employed in other countries around the world. For example, in Scotland, a child will spend seven years at primary school, before continuing on to secondary school for between four and six years. However, in Denmark, all children spend nine years in their first schools, before moving on to colleges where they can specialise their studies to some degree to meet their individual interests, whether they may be literary, scientific, technical, or whatever else. Critically, after their nine initial years as a student, teenagers in Denmark are allowed to take a gap year of sorts before moving to a college. As you would expect, many use this as an excuse to travel the world, volunteer, or even pursue a sport such as football.

As Kresten's year out approached, he applied to spend this time as an exchange student in several countries (including Scotland), before he eventually decided to head for New Zealand, a country which he had visited a few years earlier with his family and loved with all of his heart. **"It was a big culture shock,"** he told me. **"Upon my arrival, I went to a campsite where they spent two weeks introducing myself and the other exchange students from around the world to the culture of New Zealand – which seemed to involve a lot of cricket and, of course, rugby."**

During his time there, Kresten played on his school's football team, and his coach (who happened to be Irish) decided to nickname him **"Larsson"** because he was Danish, and therefore Scandinavian. Of course, the fact the Kresten regularly wore a Celtic jersey whilst training contributed to this somewhat also. Now, obviously Henrik was Swedish, but I suppose Denmark is a lot closer to Sweden than New Zealand is, or that would have been his coach's reasoning at least. With regards the popularity of football itself though in the country, Kresten said:

"When we played our home matches on the school grounds, we would be lucky if more than ten people showed up to watch us, but when the school's rugby team played, the average attendances were between one and two thousand people – for a school game – the country is rugby mad. It flows in their blood,

and I must confess that after spending a year of my life there, I have developed a bit of a liking for the sport. It is almost infectious in fact."

Reflecting on his time in the Southern Hemisphere, Kresten did chuckle a little when he recalled watching Celtic games and catching up on any news during school time, because apparently his teachers didn't seem to care much about what exchange students such as him got up to:

"Obviously I wasn't allowed to do it all the time, but whenever I was in a class and we were told to study something individually, whether I was doing so on my personal laptop or on a school computer, I would take the chance to check out what was going on or watch a stream of the game if one happened to be on. I still did my schoolwork, but it was clear to see that the teachers were less strict with us exchange students than they were with the locals. Of course, I had to look over my shoulder from time to time to make sure I wasn't going to get into too much trouble, but it was almost always fine."

Now, while this may seem like a dream trip to many of you, it is worth remembering that Kresten was only fifteen when he left his home in Aarhus behind him for a year to live with a **"host family"**. Whilst he told me that **"it was very hard at times"**, Kresten went on to say that **"it was the best thing I could have done with that year. It was very rewarding, I got so much out of it, and I would definitely do it again given the opportunity. I arrived in the country without knowing anyone, and left a year later with friends whom I shall stay in touch with for the rest of my life."**

Nowadays, Kresten is back at home in Denmark. Aside from studying, he also works as a telemarketer, having lost his job in **"Blockbuster"** (a DVD rental store) because he turned eighteen and therefore they would have had to pay him the wages of an adult. Despite the fact he is a bit short of money, Kresten is absolutely itching to visit Glasgow and attend a Celtic game at some point in the future with his brother – something he hopes to do during the coming season or two.

As our chat progressed, Kresten began to happily recall some of his favourite memories of supporting Celtic – Robbie Keane's hat-trick against Kilmarnock sticks in the mind of many, as does Shunsuke Nakamura's free kick against Manchester United at Celtic Park, and these were just two of the recollections Kresten described as his favourite moments. Obviously, in more recent times, watching his side beat Barcelona was **"certainly up there"** also.

Considering the future, Kresten is looking forward to seeing how Celtic can continue to perform on the European stage, and feels that we have the right manager in Neil Lennon, and the right captain in Scott Brown, for our Club to continue to progress. However, having recently lost Victor Wanyama and Gary Hooper, he hopes to see Celtic invest in strengthening the playing squad, so that the aforementioned progression can continue.

Regarding Kresten's future, he hopes to attend university in the coming years and eventually find himself working within the world of journalism: **"I've always enjoyed writing and travelling, as well as current affairs. A job as a journalist could allow me to combine all three of these things, and I would absolutely love that."**

During my final conversation with Kresten prior to the publication of this book, we discussed the nature of football around the world but particularly that played in Denmark, and when notable parallels to current issues within the Scottish game were highlighted, I could not help but become engrossed in the matter. In the early part of the conversation, Kresten explained the negative impact which money is having on Danish Football:

"When I was a teenager, I first started to watch Aarhus play live both home and away with some regularity. At this point in time, many home matches had an attendance of about twenty-one thousand, with the stadium essentially full to capacity. Nowadays though, it is a rare event when more than ten thousand people watch A.G.F. I myself no longer go as often as I used to, as I simply cannot afford it – a single ticket can cost the equivalent of twenty-five pounds, and that doesn't include travel or other associated costs."

He then continued on to talk about Danish football in general, as well as its overall place in the world: **"Football is our national sport. Denmark is not a country like New Zealand wherein football is overshadowed by another game. Almost everybody plays football to some level as a child in this country, and, with a combination of investment and youth development, we are continuing to produce many good players as a nation. However, despite the fact our clubs have a great record of developing home-grown players, any of them with any serious level of talent can, and usually will, be picked off by teams from other European nations simply because they can afford to pay them more money than we can. It's one thing to lose players to Ajax, but it's something quite different to lose them to lower to mid-table English sides like Aston Villa."**

At this stage, I posed the following question to Kresten, as whilst I agreed with what he was saying, something sprung to my mind: **"Denmark has a population of just under six million people, a not wholly dissimilar figure to that of Scotland, which is around the five million mark, so why do you think Denmark continually outperform Scotland on the international stage?"**

To this, Kresten replied, **"From the point of view of the international side, we are lucky to produce good players in Denmark that then go elsewhere to play in the leagues of the highest quality. In this regard, they gain a lot of experience from testing themselves against the best players in the world, and undoubtedly this helps them when they come together to play for Denmark. However, whilst it may help to improve the image of Danish Football, it cannot actually help football in Denmark – only a change to the way money dictates modern football can change that."**

Finally, Kresten told me that other Danish people often find it slightly odd when he tells them he supports Celtic, but that it doesn't perturb him. On several occasions, he has been asked who his favourite English team are, before being told **"you must support one of them,"** after he has said that he has no significant interest in the English game.

Throughout my discussions with the individuals I have interviewed for this book, I could not help but notice that there appears to be a stigma attached to the image of Scottish Football not only in Denmark, but around the world. The competitiveness and quality of our competition appear to regularly be the subjects of scrutiny, and whilst I feel that these claims are not totally ungrounded, they certainly appear to be vastly exaggerated in most cases. Perhaps if our national sport is to progress in the future, we must seriously attempt to address this stigma and talk the Scottish game up more often.

Regardless of such stereotypes, Kresten remains proud to be a Celtic supporter and a fan of A.G.F. Aarhus. In conclusion, he said: **"Both clubs have long and detailed histories, and it is a privilege to follow each of them."**

"Celtic's Bayard"

Born in the town of Birkenhead, directly across the River Mersey from the city of Liverpool, on the seventh of March 1912 (a day which fell between two Celtic victories at the time – both of which typically ended with clean sheets for the Hoops), William King Lyon moved to Scotland at an early age. He grew up here, and as a young and aspiring footballer, he found a place with Kirkintilloch Rob Roy, before moving on to Queen's Park.

In April 1935, Willie signed for Celtic, making his debut at the start of the next season in a three-one league defeat to the rising power of Aberdeen. Newspaper reports regarding the match state that Celtic actually started rather brightly under the oddly warm August sun at Pittodrie, but it would not last. Debutant Lyon, playing at centre-half, had pressure exerted upon him from the earliest moments of the match, as Aberdeen attempted to exploit what they saw as a potentially rewarding weakness in Celtic's defensive line.

Approximately fifteen minutes into the tie, a mix-up between the Celtic defence and their goalkeeper, James 'Joe' Kennaway, allowed Aberdeen's new left winger, Johnny Lang, to sneak in and open the scoring. In the process, as a result of both Lang and Kennaway charging towards the ball with all of their might, they collided heavily, with the latter suffering an injury to his back. Of course, at this point in time, injured goalkeepers had no choice but to persevere as best they could, or leave the field of play and force an outfield player to take their place.

Joe bravely carried on, but reports state that the injury suffered by their goalkeeper shook the Celtic team, who had only lost the young John Thomson to a similar collision less than four years earlier. For those of you who may not know, Joe Kennaway was born in Canada in 1905, and actually faced John Thomson in the opposite goal on one occasion in 1931. Whilst playing for Fall River, a football team based in Massachusetts, Kennaway and his teammates defeated the touring Glasgow Celtic by a single goal to nil. Joe's performance on that day impressed Willie Maley, who was always on the lookout for talent, even during summer tours when most of the other people associated with the Club considered themselves to be on a holiday of sorts. Having tragically lost Thomson in early September of that same year, Maley signed Kennaway at the end of October, and he would remain at Celtic Park until 1939.

Returning to the match at Pittodrie, around fifteen minutes after the opening goal, at the half hour mark, Johnny Lang found himself in room within yards of goal and fired home a shot which was described in a local newspaper as **"unstoppable"**. Celtic went in two-nil down at break, and things went from bad to worse early in the second half, as Aberdeen's centre forward, Matt Armstrong, added another for the home side. Kennaway was again involved in a collision moments later, this time with the Aberdeen winger Jackie Benyon, who was subsequently forced to take leave of the match with concussion for a trip to hospital. Late on, Jimmy McGrory scored for Celtic with his head as he so often did, but in truth it was never going to be enough to save a rattled Celtic side from defeat. Willie was **"not of great success"** in the match according to one journalist, whilst another stated, **"Lyon had a tremendous amount of work thrown upon him, and if he was unable to hold the inside forwards of Aberdeen it was no discredit and it would be unfair to judge his real value on this first game."**

Regardless of his debut resulting in a loss, Willie would go on to prove just how talented and resilient a footballer he really was. Never the sort of character to simply accept defeat, he was handed the role of the Club's captaincy during his first season. One week after Celtic's opening defeat, Hamilton Academicals visited the East End of Glasgow, with the Celts, and Willie, determined to set the record straight.

Lyon made his home debut in the match, which was decided by a late winner from goalscorer extraordinaire Jimmy McGrory. However, as the home supporters welcomed their new captain, they also applauded the return of one of Lyon's predecessors, Jimmy McStay (now a Hamilton player), who had led Celtic throughout the majority of the 1930's thus far, and would, only a few years later, become the second manager of Celtic Football Club upon Willie Maley's retirement. One newspaper report said: **"A contrast of old and new was provided by Lyon, who was making his first home appearance for Celtic at centre half, and McStay, who, after occupying the position in the Celtic team for many years, is now in the Hamilton side. McStay was more prominent, but Lyon, after a shaky start, gave a promising display."**

Indeed, a few weeks later, as Celtic continued their winning streak, Queen's Park were beaten by three goals to nil at Parkhead, with Lyon being hailed as one of the best performers on the day: **"Lyon's display against his old club was critically watched, and it can be said with confidence that he successfully survived the ordeal. He never indulged in the spectacular, but went about his work in a quiet manner and showed resource and a cool head in trying situations".**

It is also of note that Lyon led Celtic to their first victory over Rangers at Ibrox since 1920–21 only weeks later, a feat that neither Jimmy McStay nor his brother Willie managed to achieve. In the chapter devoted to the life and times of Bobby Evans, I mentioned the fact that, in 1957, only a month or so before the legendary League Cup Final of the 1957–58 season, Celtic had travelled to Ibrox and won there for the first time in twenty-two years. This, of course, was that last victory, all the way back in 1935, as goals from Frank Murphy and Johnny Crum, coupled with a fine penalty save from Joe Kennaway gave Celtic the points, and, according to another newspaper, caused a celebratory pitch invasion from the away supporters at full time.

"Seldom does a football match end amidst such tense excitement as this one did at Ibrox Park. And how the closing minutes flew for the home supporters and dragged for the visitors! Celtic were fighting to retain a goal lead which would give them their first victory at Ibrox since 1920–21, and Rangers forgot weariness in their attempts to secure the equalising goal."

"Celtic had slightly the better of matters in the first half, but both teams were goalless when the interval arrived. Four minutes after the resumption Smith scored a grand goal for Rangers.

Hardly had Ibrox cheers died down, however, when Murphy ran in and headed a clever goal for Celtic following a corner kick by Delaney."

"Then Celtic went ahead 15 minutes from the end, when a McDonald move outwitted the home defence and Crum was presented with an easy chance to score what proved to be the winning goal."

"Thereafter Rangers were seen at their best, Meiklejohn and Simpson discarding defence and throwing all of their activities into attack. Kennaway gathered a high ball and clung to it. Smith charged him twice, but the goalkeeper evaded the centre, only to find Meiklejohn rushing in, and he shot out his hand at the home captain."

"Such sanction might have been allowed as a hand-off in Rugby but it is not part of the "soccer" code, and a penalty kick was granted. In an almost unnatural stillness, and with five minutes to go, Meiklejohn stepped forward and placed the ball to the right of Kennaway. The goalkeeper dropped to his knee and turned the ball out with his hand. Rangers last hope had gone."

"Celtic were the sprightlier team and deserved their success, in which Kennaway, Lyon, Geatons, and Delaney played a big part."

With that notable victory under his belt, Willie scored his first goal for the Club in mid-November, as Celtic hammered Arbroath by five goals to nil in the East End of Glasgow. **"The Scotsman"** described the events which led to Lyon establishing his role as Celtic's main penalty taker as follows: **"The second half had a sensational opening. Delaney was going strongly when brought down in the penalty area. From the resultant award Lyon gave the visiting goalkeeper no chance. That was the Celtic captain's first goal for the Glasgow Club."**

As the season progressed, the plaudits began to fly in from all directions for Celtic's new captain. Whether reports were describing Lyon as **"outstanding"**, **"grand"**, **"heroic"** or even as **"a tower of strength"**, Willie was establishing himself not only as the on-field leader of a football team on the rise, but also as one of the great talents in the Scottish game. He became recognised as not only an intimidating physical presence, but also as a cultured footballer. Calm under pressure with the remarkable ability to often find a teammate even in the most difficult of circumstances, he was the envy of many managers and supporters alike who would have loved to have him on their side.

Having spent a significant amount of time researching the endeavours of Willie Lyon throughout the 1935–36 season, I must say that it was only on the odd occasion that I ever found any sort of negative comments regarding his performances in the press. Most of the time, even when the Hoops lost, he was still being praised by individuals within the media, with Celtic's Scottish Cup defeat to St Johnstone being the cause of one of the few pieces of negativity: **"Beattie was the man of the moment in the visiting attack and Lyon was never comfortable against the elusive centre."**

Generally though, quotes such as **"The best of all was Lyon. The centre-half covered the ground in remarkable manner, and assisted in ever so many little affairs not strictly his concern"** gave a more accurate reflection of the captain's conventional standards of play. Critically, Willie always paid great attention to his opponents, especially those such as the aforementioned Beattie whom he had significant trouble with, in an attempt to continually learn from his mistakes and better himself as a footballer.

As the season wore on, Lyon found his shooting range once again and struck home a couple of goals from free kicks, the first of which opened the scoring in a four-nil league triumph over Kilmarnock in February: **"Celtic's opening goal was the result of a free kick, and rather against the run of play. Lyon drove hard for the goal, and Delaney, who had taken up his position in the barricading line, ducked to allow the ball free passage into the net."**

In the second to last game of the league campaign, Celtic faced Ayr United at Celtic Park, knowing that any victory would all but secure them their first League Championship title in a decade (theoretically, Rangers could have still snatched it had they won all of their three remaining matches, and Celtic lost their final one, but the Ibrox side would have had to score a barrel-load of goals and then some to overturn Celtic's vastly superior goal difference). However, this was not all that was on the mind of the green and white supporters in attendance that day, as they turned out to see Jimmy McGrory attempt to break Willie MacFadyen's record of fifty-two league goals in a single season.

Midway through the second half, McGrory had scored a hat-trick already, taking his current total to fifty goals in the 1935–36 campaign. And so, when Celtic were awarded a penalty, it showed the true character of Willie Lyon as he invited McGrory to take the kick, despite the fact Lyon had only had one penalty saved all season: **"Delaney had a solo run, and was brought down, and to the loud approval of the crowd, Lyon called on McGrory to take the penalty."**

However, McGrory sent his penalty kick wide, and an injury he would later sustain would rule him out of the final match of the season at Firhill the following week, meaning he wasn't able to break MacFadyen's record, which still stands to this day. In all likelihood, it may never be beaten, and this is testament to the Motherwell player's performances upon setting the record. For the sake of clarity, it is noteworthy that only moments after McGrory's miss, **"Lyon put Celtic further ahead with a glorious free-kick from twenty five yards out"**, as Celtic won six-nil, and all but officially became the Champions of Scotland once again.

And so, in Willie's first season as Celtic captain, his side would only lose four times in the league, as well as twice in cup competitions. The Celts topped the table by five points from Rangers and Aberdeen after the Hoops' final match (a three-one win at Firhill, in which Willie scored again), as they formally secured the League Championship for the first time in a decade. Critically, not only had Willie led his side that season, but he had also battled alongside them, through every high and every low. He did not miss a single match in any competition that season and, in fact, it would be over one year, one month, and one week after Lyon's first appearance in a Celtic shirt that he would miss his first game, which happened to be a one-all draw with Rangers at Celtic Park. Interestingly, the opening goal of that match, which went Rangers' way, was the subject of much controversy. Prior to a forward converting a cross, the linesman raised his flag high into the air, as if signalling that the player about to deliver the ball was offside, but this was ignored by the referee and the goal was allowed to stand, much to the bemusement of the Celtic players and the fans in attendance.

Lyon then returned to the side for consecutive trips to Tynecastle (a one-nil win) and Ibrox (a two-one defeat), where he was described as **"a power of strength in defence"**. As the season progressed, despite Celtic's relative unpredictability, Lyon continued to lead by example, chipping in with the occasional goal and consistently being referred to as one of the team's top performers. Even after a disappointing league defeat at home to Dundee, Lyon's versatility came in for significant praise from one newspaper reporter: **"Lyon and Geatons were auxiliary forwards for Celtic in the second half, the thrust of their forward play being equal almost to anything demonstrated by McGrory."**

On St Patrick's Day 1937, Celtic were set to face Motherwell, one of the most dangerous attacking sides in the country, in the quarter finals of the Scottish Cup at Parkhead. With Celtic losing four-two, Motherwell conceded a penalty early in the second half, and up stepped Willie. With a significant amount of pressure on his shoulders, the captain held his nerve and showed the way, scoring from the spot. The momentum this goal provided drove Celtic forwards, and with less than ten minutes left, Willie Buchan scored to earn the Hoops an unlikely replay. This was a crucial day in Celtic's Scottish Cup triumph that season, and had Lyon succumbed to the pressure upon his shoulders and missed his penalty kick as many men have done before and since, things may have been very, very different for Celtic Football Club.

A week later, the Celts travelled to Fir Park, which was filled to, and perhaps even beyond capacity for the replay, such was the public demand to see the fixture. Previously, I referred to Motherwell as **"one of the most dangerous attacking sides in the country"**, and with good reason. Comparatively, they were a high scoring team in Scotland at that time, and this was emphasised by the fact that, at the end of the season, despite finishing fourth, they had scored more league goals than all of the sides above them – including Celtic. Having conceded four times at Celtic Park, the Hoops, with Willie

Lyon as their protective cornerstone, knew that they simply couldn't afford to be so defensively lax this time around.

As one of the most heavily anticipated matches of the season so far, **"The Glasgow Herald"** reported how **"many spectators found accommodation in the trees overlooking the ground."**

Whilst the same newspaper would go on to describe Lyon repulsing a **"dangerous movement"** from Motherwell, **"The Scotsman"** would state that Lyon provided a **"splendid service"** to his team, as Celtic edged past their host by two goals to one.

Having defeated Clyde by two goals to nil in the resulting semi-final, Celtic, who were no longer contenders for the League Championship, made sure they would still have something to play for as the season drew to a close. Of course, the epic that was the 1937 Scottish Cup Final is described in significant detail in a later part of this book, so I shall not repeat myself in that regard. However, it should not be forgotten that Celtic's captain, who led them to that famous victory was none other than Willie Lyon, who exorcised any remaining demons of his debut defeat at Pittodrie as he laid his hands on the famous old trophy after his side had defeated Aberdeen at Hampden in front of an immense crowd. In all, Willie only missed three competitive matches all season and therefore only three games in his first two years at the Football Club – an impressive record for any player, let alone a tough tackling half-back from the 1930's.

Having said that, only a week later Celtic suffered the worst defeat in the entire history of the Football Club, as they lost by eight goals to nil at Fir Park against Motherwell in the final league fixture of the season. To their credit, Motherwell were four goals up early on, and clearly the superior side, but injuries to two Celtic players, including goalkeeper Joe Kennaway, meant Motherwell played a Celtic team made up of nine men with forward Willie Buchan in goal for the majority of the match. Undoubtedly, it was a disappointing end to the season, but it didn't take any shine away from the Scottish Cup glory of the previous week. Considering the enormity of the tie at Hampden Park, I am confident that the vast majority of Celtic supporters who stood on the terracing one week prior to the trip to Fir Park would have accepted such a defeat in an exchange for victory in the final, had it been offered to them beforehand.

If the freak result at Fir Park at the end of the 1936–37 season was unexpected, it is safe to say that the start of the 1937–38 season was equally so – in fact, Celtic missed it. Due to being caught amongst heavy traffic on match day, Celtic's opening league match against Queen of the South was delayed until the visitors eventually arrived late, changed into their kits, and immediately ran onto the field for a two-each draw, without so much as a warm up or a tactical discussion prior to kick-off.

In a similar manner, the season itself got off to a stuttering start for the Parkhead Club, as wins against Hamilton (twice) and Morton, another two-all draw with Queen of the South, and defeats at both Rugby Park and Ibrox left the Celts desperately seeking a bit of consistency as their league campaign entered its second month. With this in mind, it is notable that Lyon was played at left-back a couple of times as Maley sought to address the defensive issues his side were currently facing. However, the few games in which this experiment were carried out were some of the worst in Lyon's career, as the captain was swiftly returned to his usual position at centre-half following an injury which saw him absent from the side for a couple of games, and his performances returned to their usual **"outstanding"** standards.

Having lost to Arbroath in the tie which saw Lyon's injury occur (Delaney was also hurt in the same match, and despite Willie battling on hurt, Jimmy could not finish the match, essentially leaving Celtic with nine and a half men on the field come full time), the Hoops went on to defeat St Johnstone six-nil at the end of October, before repeating the feat a week later against Partick Thistle, as their season finally began to gather pace. Incredibly, from the disappointment of the loss to Arbroath in early October, the Hoops would not lose another league match until the start of April. This run, which included massive victories over the likes of Kilmarnock (with Celtic the eight-nil victors for a change), Clyde and St Mirren, also saw an emphatic three-nil defeat of Rangers on New Year's Day, as Celtic adapted to life without Jimmy McGrory for the first time in fifteen years.

Interestingly, "**It was the first New Year's Day success against their rivals in 10 years**" according to "**The Glasgow Herald**", before the article continued: "**With Rangers beaten and Hearts losing another point in a two-goal draw, Celtic now hold the leadership on points basis.**"

The same newspaper reflected: "**It was a pity, considering the occasion and the splendid crowd, that only occasionally did Rangers rally their forces and threaten to break down an indomitable Celtic defence at Parkhead. For the most part they were lamentably lax and stereotyped in movement, and were excelled almost in every position by a grand Celtic side. Steadfast in defence, mobile and thrustful at half-back, fast and daring in attack, Celtic reduced Rangers to a sad plight indeed, and in doing so impressed everyone by their wonderful team spirit and apparently endless reserve of stamina...Celtic's half-back line can scarcely have played a better game this season...Smith found Lyon almost impassable.**"

Throughout the unbeaten run, Willie Lyon led his side not only through his role as captain, but, once again, through his actions. Only two days after the derby victory, Celtic faced Queen's Park at Hampden and, in light of a three-nil win, one newspaper journalist said this of Lyon's performance: "**Lyon, facing his former clubmates, was a dominating personality, not only shackling Martin, but spreading the play with intelligence.**"

This small quote alludes to what helped to make Willie Lyon such a special footballer, for not only was he capable of tough tackling and the winning of aerial duals, but he was really rather talented with the ball at his feet too. He was comfortable in possession, a trait which was only consistently displayed by the very best centre halves, and his ability not only to spot a pass, but to deliver it expertly, were major factors in my personal decision to include him in my fictional team.

As the season continued, Celtic were truly a force to be reckoned with. Despite a disappointing Scottish Cup exit at home to Kilmarnock, and the aforementioned defeat to Falkirk ending an almost six month long unbeaten league run, the Hoops were the proving themselves to be the best team in Scotland overall.

In late April, Celtic faced Dundee twice consecutively, beating them on both occasions. During the second of the two meetings, Willie Lyon took and scored two penalty kicks in a three-nil victory. However, it was a nasty affair, with some overly zealous tackling keeping not only the referee, but also the Celtic captain rather busy. One reporter wrote the following of Lyon's actions and how the referee, bizarrely, found it worthwhile to book the Celtic player: **"That he found occasion to reprimand Lyon when Coats fell after jumping for the ball seemed mysterious to most, for the Celtic captain has continually tried to pacify the "hot-heads" on his side and had not had an infringement against him previously."**

Regardless of that relatively minor incident, by the end of the domestic campaign, Lyon had led the team to a second Scottish League Championship in three seasons, and maintained his impressive record of appearances, missing only a couple of games throughout 1937–38. It is perhaps no wonder then that Willie Maley referred to his captain as **"Celtic's Bayard"**, a reference to Pierre Terrail, a French soldier who fought in the late thirteenth and early fourteenth centuries respectively, more commonly known as **"Chevalier de Bayard"**, or **"the knight without fear and beyond reproach"**. Famed for not only his toughness, but his intellect and quick thinking in the face of adversity, this was a massive and wholly intentional compliment being handed out by Maley (who was a fan of such symbolism), especially when one considers the number of captains who played under him during his time at Celtic Park.

In truth, the mid to late 1930's were to be the best times that Celtic fans would experience for many a year. With the prospect of World War Two looking increasingly likely, Celtic won the 1937–38 League Championship by three points from Hearts, their nineteenth in fifty years of existence. At the end of the season, Celtic were set to take part in a one-off tournament, the Empire Exhibition Trophy, to commemorate a truly massive event showing off the wealth and size of the British Empire, which covered Bellahouston Park for the summer months.

The top teams from both Scotland and England were invited to attend, and so Aberdeen, Brentford, Celtic, Chelsea, Everton, Hearts, Rangers and Sunderland began to play their relevant matches. Celtic met Sunderland in the quarter finals of the knockout competition, and after they had been reduced to nine men through injuries, managed to cling on for one hundred and twenty minutes for a goalless draw. This earned them a replay the following day which they won by three goals to one, setting up a semi-final tie with Hearts in the process. A single goal from Johnny Crum soon booked Celtic's place in the final, where Everton, the slayers of both Rangers and Aberdeen, awaited them.

The next weekend, Celtic lined up with the following eleven men: Joe Kennaway, Bobby Hogg, John Morrison, Charles Geatons, Willie Lyon, George Paterson, Jimmy Delaney, Malcolm McDonald, Johnny Crum, John Divers and Frank Murphy.

And so, the tenth of June 1938 was to be one of the great days in the history of Celtic Football Club. As the supporters had only just celebrated the fiftieth anniversary of their side's first match, this was a chance for Celtic and their aforementioned fans to show that they truly were the best in the land. In the fifth minute of extra time, with the score still goalless, Johnny Crum once again grabbed the only goal of the game and Celtic were crowned as the winners of the Empire Exhibition Trophy, but most importantly as the best football team in Britain and its empire, at Ibrox Park, Glasgow. The trophy, which was a stunning model of a tower, was presented to Willie Lyon and his side on the field that day. It still sits proudly inside Celtic Park, never to belong to any other team. Five decades on from the formation of the Football Club to feed and clothe the starving and impoverished people of the East End of Glasgow, that same team, upon whom much disdain had already been voiced by a sizeable section of society, had (for the lack of more succinct phrase) **"stuck it right to the establishment"**, and did so in a manner which was simply exemplary.

Sadly though, as I mentioned earlier, this was to be the final piece of footballing glory for Willie Lyon and Celtic. Rangers won the league title over the course of the 1938–39 season by eleven points from second placed Celtic, despite the fact the Hoops recorded an incredible victory over the Ibrox side only weeks into the new season, defeating their rivals by six goals to two (a very good scoreline, I know), with Willie Lyon scoring a brace and later being described by **"The Scotsman"** as **"an inspiration"**. Only months later, Germany, ruled by the National Socialist Party and Adolf Hitler, declared war on Europe and invaded Poland on the first day of September. This meant an end to competitive football for many years, and with it, signalled the end to the careers of so many footballers.

Willie Lyon soon enlisted as a soldier in the Scots Guards, featuring very occasionally in friendly football matches back home, which were scheduled in an attempt to keep people's morale up rather than to be taken as any form of serious competition. Willie served with anti-tank regiments in North Africa and Sicily, before he suffered a serious leg injury in 1944. His actions in North Africa led to him being awarded the Military Cross, an inspirational honour for an inspirational man. In a similar manner to his footballing career, where Willie arrived at Celtic as a young debutant and left as a famous and successful captain, William King Lyon joined the war effort as an undecorated Private and retired as a Military Cross winning Major. To this day, it is thought that there were only around ten thousand such medals awarded to British and Commonwealth soldiers during World War Two, highlighting the prestigious nature of the decoration.

In total, Willie played one hundred and sixty-three times for Celtic competitively (one hundred and eighty-seven if you include wartime friendlies), scoring seventeen goals in his time with the Club. When he died in Manchester at the tender age of just fifty years old, on the fifth of December 1962, his death was met by unbridled grief and sadness from the Celtic supporters who had loved him so. He will forever be remembered for his bravery and cool head, attributes which helped him to succeed in all walks of his life, not only on the football field but on the battlefield also, and for being the man who captained Celtic Football Club in 1938 – the greatest side in the British Empire.

The following article was printed in "The Evening Times" following Willie's death:

"WILLIE LYON – A GREAT CELT"

"Willie Lyon, Celtic's centre half in their great Exhibition Cup winning side of 1938, died yesterday in Salford Royal Infirmary," write Gair Henderson.

Mr Lyon, who was 50 years of age, began his football career with Clydebank Juniors and was a Queen's Park player before moving to Parkhead, where he became Celtic's captain and one of the greatest centre half-backs in the history of the Club.

Although born in England, he was "capped" for the Scottish Football League against the English League and the Irish League in 1938, but his football career ended when, after winning the M.C., he was wounded in Italy during the war."

"I'll Do The Talking"

In recent years, the term **"Celtic Family"** has become both erratically prevalent and somewhat maligned in its usage – especially within the online world. I'm sure that any Twitter user reading this will have seen some of the various spin-offs regarding this phrase, ranging from serious examples such as **"#CelticNorwichFamily"** to one which I created during the summer months of this year myself, **"#CelticBorussiaMonchengladbachFamily"** – bit of a mouthful, eh? Of course, I am being purely facetious, but I'm sure you get the idea. Essentially, many people felt that, whilst the Celtic support largely make friends wherever they travel across Britain and Europe, and such sentiments are undoubtedly well meant, the use of such terms has now become somewhat ridiculous.

Regardless, whilst it can be all too easy to write about a family of such a size as the **"Celtic Family"** (cringeworthy or not as you may consider the term to be), I have discovered that it is significantly more difficult to write about the members of my real family – especially when the chapter in question regards my father Frank and one of my older cousins, John, who managed to watch the UEFA Cup quarter final between Liverpool and Celtic at Anfield for free, without being gifted tickets or winning any sort of fancy competition.

"How did they manage that?" I hear you ask, well, I'd invite you to read on and discover that for yourselves. However, I would highlight that, as I know both of this story's protagonists very well, I regard this as a sequence of events which could ever only happen to them. So if you're sitting comfortably, I shall begin.

One week prior to the return leg on Merseyside, Liverpool had travelled to Glasgow and admirably managed a one-all draw with their hosts. Despite an improvised finish from Henrik Larsson giving Celtic the lead less than two minutes after the first whistle, Liverpool equalised through Emile Heskey around fifteen minutes later, ending the evening's scoring. The night began with Gerry Marsden, famous for his rendition of **"You'll Never Walk**

Alone", leading the singing as fans of both clubs belted out their beloved anthem. In the aftermath of the match, the BBC described how **"the decibel level at Celtic Park reached a deafening intensity"** on the night.

However, the actions of one moronic individual risked souring the generally friendly relationship between the two clubs and their respective supporters, as a Liverpool player, whose name I shall not include in this book out of principle, spat at members of the home crowd residing in the front of Celtic Park's South Stand. Unsurprisingly, the individual in question was almost lynched for his disgusting behaviour, before being swiftly substituted. Thankfully, this incident did little to sour relationships between the supporters or their clubs, as the incident was roundly condemned, and the offender banned for two weeks meaning he would not feature at Anfield seven days later.

And so, knowing that Celtic would have to travel to Liverpool and score to have any chance of progressing, our two aforementioned protagonists, Frank and John, decided to travel to the city without any tickets, in the hope that one of John's friends may have been able to help them out. Having driven down early on the day of the game and dropped their things off at a local boarding house on the outskirts of Liverpool, the pair travelled into the city in search of John's mate, a couple of tickets, and a few pints (after all, travel often works up a mighty thirst).

Soon, they found themselves within sight of Goodison Park, the home of Everton Football Club and, the pair squeezed their way into a pub which was already near to bursting with a large number of supporters of both Celtic and Liverpool inside the premises. Eventually, after a bit of a search, John spotted his mate, who was, according to John, already thoroughly enjoying himself. However, a drunken shake of the head across a crowded room meant just the same as the sober equivalent would have, as the friend in question indicated that he had not managed to track down a pair of tickets for John and his uncle. Whilst this was a disappointment, it was not wholly unexpected, and so the pair set about the task at hand of having a few beers and keeping their eyes and ears open for any spare tickets.

Once some time had passed, they were informed that someone was selling two tickets behind the bar, and despite them hurriedly expressing an interest in buying them, they were beaten to the proverbial punch by another pair of supporters by all of thirty seconds. At this point, as it seemed as if fate was against them. They discussed whether or not to walk to the ground to see if anyone was selling spares there, or whether to simply head back into the city centre and find somewhere to watch the match on television. The fact they hadn't managed to find tickets thus far was not massively bothering the pair, who described them as being like **"gold dust"** in the city that day. However, it was clear that they were a little disappointed to have missed out on those which were behind the bar.

With the benefit of hindsight, their decision to leave the pub and head to Anfield was to prove crucial, as fate finally smiled down upon them for the first time on that day in March 2003. For those of you who may not know, Goodison Park and Anfield are only a few hundred metres apart, on opposite sides of Liverpool's Stanley Park. According to my father, the approach to Anfield was a strange one, as you seem to stumble across the stadium after following crowds through narrow rows of Victorian terraced houses, many of which have fallen into a state of disrepair, which block your view of the ground from any distance. With these streets laid out in a grid-iron system, hundreds of supporters stream out of the perpendicular side streets onto the main roads, with more and more people joining the throng as you approach the ground itself.

It was amongst this crowd that my dad, who was in his mid-forties at the time, noticed that his nephew, a couple of decades his junior, had stopped behind him next to a bus stop and bent down. Presuming John was tying his shoe laces or simply picking up something that he had dropped, Frank continued on, before an excited John rushed up from behind him, virtually dragging him into an alley just off of the main road. It was then that John revealed what he had found, and began to examine his discovery in detail.

"I know they were tickets as soon as I saw them", recalled John, "but obviously I couldn't just stand there gawking at them. I quickly looked about to make sure no one was visibly looking for them and then went to catch up with Frank. I presumed they must have been used tickets from an old match at first, but when we had a look in the alley we realised they were for our game, but we didn't know if they were forgeries or not."

At this stage, my father interjected and continued the story: "I couldn't believe our luck, but as John said, we didn't know if they were real or not. Also, we were aware that there must have been two people somewhere looking for these tickets, so we went back out to where we found them and stood there for quite a while, looking for anyone searching the area and shouting to see if anybody had lost tickets."

"Well, I don't know if we were quite shouting..." joked John.

"In all seriousness though, we knew that if they were real they must have belonged to someone, so we did try to find them", continued Frank, "Eventually we headed down to the ground and stood at the first of two police cordons for a while, waiting to see if anyone was visibly looking for lost tickets, but with fifteen minutes until kick-off, no one was making themselves known, so we decided to chance it – keep in mind we didn't know with any certainty that they were real."

Having passed through the two cordons without any issues, the pair stood again for a few minutes outside the relevant turnstile, before John bought a programme and they headed inside the ground. "We half expected the seats' rightful owners to already to be in place", John said, "but once we got out onto the tier and found our row, we could see they were empty. The folk around us gave us a few funny looks, as we clearly weren't the people they had expected to fill those two seats, but they were friendly enough. Nobody gave us any bother."

The pair had heard great things about Anfield prior to their visit. After all, it's often described by those interested in English Football as a ground famous for its incredible atmosphere, especially that which is generated on European nights. With this in mind, they expected to experience something fairly special, but according to Frank, **"it wasn't even a patch on Celtic Park. I was expecting to be really impressed, but it was...alright, I suppose."**

And so, the teams emerged and the match began, with Celtic starting fairly brightly, encouraging all of the Hooped supporters inside Anfield, the majority of which were located only a short distance to Frank and John's right hand side in the away section. However, to say that my relatives were the only Celtic fans in amongst the home supporters that night would be a lie, as small pockets of green were clearly visible in amongst the vast expanses of red all around the stadium.

However, whilst with around fifteen minutes gone things were looking hopeful for Celtic, they were looking decidedly less so for Frank and John, as the latter spotted the high visibility jacket of a steward on the stairwell adjacent to them, with two Liverpool supporters noticeably pointing towards the him and his uncle. At this stage, the two men rose from their seats and Frank, being the eldest, told his nephew, **"I'll do the talking"**, before they exited the row and began the following discussion with the steward and Liverpool supporters.

"Excuse me gents, can I just ask where you got these tickets?" enquired the steward, **"because they've been reported as stolen"**, gesturing towards the couple who were the seats' rightful owners.

In all honesty, my father and cousin had been expecting that this may happen, but in fear of being ejected from the stadium, the pair made an effort to be as polite and apologetic as possible, ignoring the manner in which they had truly acquired the tickets. My father began: **"Stolen? I'm really sorry! We bought them from a tout outside and had no idea that was the case. Please, take your seats, we're sorry again."**

With the benefit of hindsight, it is fair to reflect that it was not only quick thinking on the pair's part, but critically their apologetic demeanour, which influenced the steward's actions following the aforementioned discussion. As the Liverpool supporters took their seats, Frank and John were led off of the tier itself and into the internal concourse of the Anfield Road end. Had they been even remotely confrontational, it is reasonable to presume they would have been ejected without a second thought at this stage, but as the three men stopped and the steward continued to seek further details from the pair, Frank expanded on his initial story: **"We paid fifty pounds each for those tickets on the road leading to the ground. We're sorry, as we said we had no idea they were stolen. We just wanted to see the game, after all we travelled all the way down from Glasgow this morning and we were willing to buy tickets off of a tout to do so – it's not normally something we'd do."**

Having heard this tale, unaware of the fact it was partially fictional, the steward told the pair to wait where they were and that he **"would see what he could do"**, before disappearing for a few minutes. During this time, Frank and John considered whether or not their luck had run out, as time began to pass and their situation looked increasingly bleak. However, when the steward returned, he gestured to them as if to say **"follow me"** before leading them back out onto the tier once more. Having followed him down a set of stairs, the steward, whom both of my family members remain eternally grateful towards to this day, pointed towards two vacant seats – in the second row from the front of the lower tier – only yards away from the goals which Celtic were currently defending, next to some of Liverpool's fans with special needs.

Understandably, the realisation that they would be able to watch the remainder of the match inside the stadium was a great relief to the my father and cousin, who became even more jubilant a minute or so before the half time interval as Alan Thompson drove his free kick under the leaping Liverpool wall into the bottom corner of Jerzy Dudek's net. Late in the second half, with Celtic still leading one-nil (therefore two-one up on aggregate), John Hartson received the ball and passed to his striking partner, Henrik Larsson. As he did so many times over the years, Henrik then slid the ball perfectly back to the Welshman, who went past one man before unleashing a fearsome shot which was destined for the top corner of the Liverpool net.

"Time slowed down", recalled John, **"it was one of those times when you knew the ball was only headed for one place, but it seemed to take an eternity to get there. When it did, we were**

close enough that we heard the ball connecting with the back of the net, and that's a sound which will probably stay with both of us for the rest of our lives."

And so, as John Hartson wheeled away towards the section housing the majority of the Celtic support inside Anfield, my father and cousin leapt around like lunatics (and they weren't the only ones). In fact, if you were to watch the television coverage of Hartson's goal that night, you would see the two men leaping out of their seats as the ball flew into the net, alongside another group of Celtic supporters sitting behind the goal. In that regard, they will forever be linked, in their own small way, to an integral moment in the Club's history. Barely anyone who watches the goal in years to come will know who they are (or perhaps even care), but as long as the replay of that goal exists, as generations to come remember a historic night at Anfield, there they will be, immortalised in a moment of sheer ecstasy.

Around ten minutes later, the final whistle sounded through the Merseyside night air, and Celtic found themselves in their first European semi-final in almost thirty years. Whilst the main body of the support continued to celebrate after Hartson's goal, Frank and John sat down in an attempt to show some respect for their hosts.

"To be fair to the Liverpool fans, they were great. Here we were, sitting smugly struggling to hide our huge smiles, having just given their side a bit of a doing on their own turf, and they didn't give us any grief. Let's put it this way, there are several grounds around the world that I wouldn't take a risk like that in, but Anfield isn't one of them. They were lovely people", recalled Frank.

Once the match was over and they had exited the stadium, celebratory drinks were, inevitably, prominent in the minds of uncle and nephew alike. Having leapt into a taxi, the pair headed for **"The Cavern Club"** on Mathew Street, the nightclub which has been graced over the years by the likes of Elton John, Queen, The Rolling Stones and The Who, but which will forever be synonymous with one act above all others, The Beatles.

However, on that famous night in 2003, **"The Cavern Club"** did not rock to the sounds of an electric guitar or a rhythmic baseline, but to the sounds of countless voices celebrating a historic Celtic victory. This continued long into the night, and whilst I would like to briefly sum up the rest of the night and the journey back to the boarding house, neither my father nor my cousin can actually remember any of it, so I see no need to do so. It's safe to say they enjoyed themselves anyway, along with countless other members of the support, and that's the most important thing.

Nowadays, whenever the pair reflects on their trip as a whole, a few themes seem to recur time and time again. Firstly, the people of Liverpool were very friendly, even in defeat. Secondly, Anfield didn't live up to the hype that often surrounds it in the English media, and thirdly, and most importantly, luck smiled down upon them that night on several occasions. With this in mind, I feel I must take this opportunity to thank the steward for his actions, and also the two Liverpool supporters for dropping their tickets in the first place – you made two Glaswegian Celtic supporters very happy, and gave our family a story which will be told for generations to come.

"I Don't Regret A Minute of It"

My father has always possessed an almost entirely unique sense of humour – well, I say **"almost"**, as I am one of only a few individuals who seem to hold something similar. Anyway, after a late night prior to this incident, I strolled into his work one morning to drop off some medication which he had forgotten to take prior to leaving the house only a couple of hours earlier. In all honesty, I was expecting to be in and out of there within a matter of seconds. After all, it was a quick drop off, nothing more. However, as I opened the door to reception, he appeared from an adjoining room and made the following announcement to a couple of his colleagues: **"This one was up most of the night talking to a woman in Chile on Skype!"**

Now, as you can imagine, that's the sort of sentence which has several connotations – especially when people don't know you're writing a book which requires you to speak to people living all around the world at ungodly hours of the morning. Anyway, once the ensuing laughter had died down and I had attempted to provide a half-hearted explanation for such a late night discussion, I made my excuses and left, thoroughly looking forward to returning to my bed once I arrived home again.

Regardless of his comedic reference, my father's previous statement had, in fact, been correct – I had been up until the early hours speaking to a woman in Chile on Skype, although I feel that I should perhaps stop being rude by referring to her as a random woman and from here on in simply use her name, Rachel Kennedy. In fact, I must highlight that I owe Rachel rather a lot, for even in the late stages of this book's production, I had not yet managed to find a Celtic supporter based in South America to speak to me when, thankfully, she got in touch. Before our discussion on Skype, I knew very little about her in truth, other than her name and her current location, the capital city of Chile, Santiago.

With this in mind, as the dialling tone sounded out from the laptop and an electronic pulse zipped across the world, I must confess that the last thing I expected to hear was an accent from the north east of England on the other end of the line saying **"hello"**, and yet there it was. I soon discovered that Rachel, originally of Middlesbrough (hence the accent) was, in fact, a little bit of a globetrotter, as opposed to a Chilean or a simple 'A to B' style ex-pat.

Returning to her early life, Rachel was born into a Catholic family who supported their local side and had no interest whatsoever in football north of the border. Midway through her childhood, the family moved to the town of Cramlington, around ten miles from Newcastle, and there she would continue her school career, before progressing to study physics at the University of Manchester. And so, in 1987, Rachel accepted a job offer from the Met Office (that's the abbreviated term for the Meteorological Office, the U.K.'s national weather service, for any of you living elsewhere who happen to be unfamiliar with the term) and moved to London. A little over a year later, she was asked to transfer to Glasgow by her employers, and so the seeds of a sporting love story were sown.

On the twenty-second of August 1989, Rachel wandered up towards Celtic Park for the first time in her life and paid at the gate for access to the old Jungle, as the Hoops took on Queen of the South in the Skol Cup. During the match, Jacki Dziekanowski scored his first competitive goal for Celtic, as the Celts eased themselves to a two-nil victory in front of a little over twenty-one thousand spectators. As she left the stadium and made her way back home through a few of the rather rundown areas around the ground, Rachel recalls considering how much she had enjoyed herself. She'd seen Middlesbrough, Manchester City and Arsenal (amongst a few other sides) in the past, but the match just gone had **"felt different"**. Ironically, whilst she honestly cannot remember what drove her to visit Parkhead on that day in August, the woman from Middlesbrough soon found herself travelling to both home and away games regularly, before purchasing her first season ticket for the following campaign. Within a couple of years, Rachel would also find herself travelling to European away games, such as those against Neuchatel Xamax and Paris St Germain in the early 1990's.

However, before she could do so, there was the little matter of a Scottish Cup Final against Aberdeen to deal with. Unable to find a ticket for the Celtic end for love nor money, Rachel found herself standing amongst tens of thousands of other people from the north east at Hampden that day, although these folks were from the north east of Scotland! To their credit, Rachel told me that she never felt threatened or intimidated amongst the Don's supporters, but she did recall struggling to look happy when Celtic lost the tie after a penalty shootout. Having been one of thousands who thought **"Oh no, it must be Anton up next"** prior to Anton Rogan failing to score his penalty kick and handing Aberdeen the Scottish Cup in the process, Rachel told me that she has never been able to watch such a shoot-out involving Celtic since, despite the fact it is now more than two decades on from the event.

Regardless of disappointments such as these, Rachel stuck by the Celts throughout the entirety of the 1990's, when successes were few and far between and often all too short lived when they did arrive. Having endured such barren years, Rachel travelled with thousands of others to East End Park on the third of May 1998, knowing that a win would be enough for Celtic to **"stop the ten"**. However, despite an early goal from Simon Donnelly, a combination of misfortune and nerves conspired to see Celtic concede an equaliser with only minutes remaining before the tie finished in a one-all draw. With only one week remaining in the season, it meant that everything would come down to the final home match against St Johnstone. With this in mind, it is perhaps no surprise that Rachel told me she **"felt sick"** after the aforementioned draw. **"It was a horrible feeling"**, she said, **"We were all so disappointed, and although nobody voiced it, everyone was thinking the same thing – we can't lose this now, we just can't."**

Thankfully though, as we all know, the Hoops won their final match of the season and stopped Rangers from winning ten league titles in a row. Rachel described it as **"her most amazing moment as a Celtic supporter up until that point"**, as she rushed onto the playing surface in celebration alongside countless others. **"I just felt overwhelmed, it was such a happy feeling. I'd made some very**

good friends already as a Celtic supporter, and to see everyone so happy was just amazing. To be honest, the final day that season is a bit of a blur. I can't really remember the goals, but what I can remember is the feeling of relief that we had finally done it and nobody could take it away from us."

Five years later, Celtic would book their place in the UEFA Cup Final, and soon Rachel Kennedy, the woman who had little to no interest in Scottish football (let alone Celtic) as a girl soon found herself travelling to Spain. Whilst the resulting extra time defeat was a difficult one to stomach, Rachel told me that she **"couldn't have been more proud of her team that night"** and I'm sure these sentiments would be echoed by thousands of others, even to this day.

In the year or so following her trip to Seville, Rachel began to wonder whether it was time for a change in her life. She had spent well over a decade in Glasgow by this point, and despite the fact her love for nothing more than a particular Football Club had stopped her from moving on several occasions beforehand, the thought continued to linger. Eventually, as the members of that team began to go their separate ways, Rachel decided it was indeed time for her to follow, and soon found herself teaching in an English speaking school in Cordoba, Spain, a city around ninety minutes drive to the east of Seville.

"I absolutely adored my time in Glasgow", she told me. **"I'd spent sixteen years there and loved every minute of it, but I felt it was time for a change. As I'm sure you can imagine, I hated the weather, but more than anything, I had to force myself to walk away from Celtic to a degree. It's funny – it was like an addiction in a way. My week's consisted of thinking about the last match and looking forward to the coming tie at the weekend, and then my weekend's were structured around going to the game itself. It's not like I thought about it, I just did it. My reluctance to leave Celtic behind had forced me to turn down job offers in the past, but when the opportunity to go to Spain came I just felt it was right for me. I'd seen my team reach a European Final, and I'd saw the game for myself – that was the pinnacle, and it was a good time to move on to greater things on a personal level."**

Looking back on it, it was perhaps a blessing in disguise that when Rachel's move south came, it did so quickly. She saw her last Celtic match as a season ticket holder only days before Christmas 2004, as Celtic beat a Dundee United side which included the likes of Mark Wilson and Barry Robson by a single goal to nil. When Rachel left the ground that day, there was no emotional goodbye or reluctance to leave upon the final whistle, no tears and no regret – she simply left as she had done so many times before, perhaps more concerned with the injuries to Alan Thompson and Joos Valgaeren than anything else.

"I was very fortunate in that regard", she recalled, **"If I had known that was to be my last game I would have been distraught. The experience would have made me doubt the move I eventually made, so I feel lucky that I didn't have to go through that "goodbye" moment. Before I left, I gave my season ticket to a friend, who eventually changed the name on it and that was that. I do still have one link to the Club though, I'm a shareholder! I bought the minimum amount applicable during Fergus McCann's share issue and I still have them to this day, although I don't think I'll be popping over for the A.G.M. any time soon!"**

Anyway, upon her arrival in Cordoba, Rachel was buoyed by the fact that the local football side also happened to play in green and white, although she never developed any sort of emotional attachment to them. A couple of years later, in fact, Rachel would find herself on the move again, as she headed to Malaga, a little under two hours south of Cordoba on the sunny coast of the Mediterranean Sea. Here, Rachel Kennedy would spend the next six years of her life, again teaching in a school and checking the news from Celtic Park via the internet from time to time: **"I watched the occasional stream online at that stage, but when you're largely cut off from the daily football news that you used to digest in Glasgow, the players and faces at the Club change very quickly and it becomes less difficult to deal with the lack of live matches."**

Early in 2013, Rachel left Malaga and Spain (her home for the last eight years) behind her to live in South America. Having cited her love for travel and her belief that following your gut instinct is often a good idea, Rachel felt that a move was once again necessary in her life and, after considering her options, eventually chose Santiago as her destination.

"I didn't know much about it as a country or a city to be honest. I'd seen the advert for the job and looked online for information. I saw snowy mountains and amazing scenery – it just looked like a lovely place to live. By all accounts Santiago was a very European city in many regards, and this suggested that it wouldn't be too difficult to settle in there, and so eventually, I just went for it. I must confess that I miss the heat of Spain, but I'm happy I made the move."

Once Rachel had told me a little bit about Chilean Football, and, notably, about how much the local people love the game, she began to discuss the public transport system in the city. Now, that may seem a little random at first, and in a sense, it seemed that way to me too, as Rachel described how busy the metro trains can be. However, when she finished off her story by telling me that one day as she travelled on the subway, another passenger's tattoo caught her eye, it all made sense. For here, as she stood crammed inside a metal can speeding through a dark tunnel underneath the Chilean capital, Rachel, a woman from the north east of England who happened to stumble across Celtic and develop a love for them, found herself standing looking at a commuter with the crest of Celtic Football Club inked onto his neck.

"I couldn't believe my eyes. I'd only been in the city for a month or so, and I had to check myself once or twice to make sure I wasn't imagining things. The train was so busy that I didn't speak to the man, and as we reached his stop, he disappeared off never to be seen again, but it did reassure me of one thing – there's at least one other Celt in Chile!" she said.

As our conversation drew to a close, I asked Rachel three questions. First of all, I enquired as to whether she had any plans to return to Scotland or the United Kingdom in general at some point in the future. To this, she said **"I can't imagine living in the U.K. again at the moment – I mean I'd never say "never", but I can't see it happening any time in the foreseeable future."** Secondly, I asked her where her favourite place was, expecting her to say **"Spain"** or something to that effect, but instead she simply joked, **"Do you mean apart from Celtic Park?"**

Finally, I posed a question which can often be very difficult to answer for anyone, regardless of their history or situation: **"What does it mean to you to follow Celtic?"**

I was so impressed with Rachel's answer that I shall end this chapter with her reply, and take this opportunity to thank her for coming to my proverbial rescue, all the way from the city wedged between the Andes Mountains in the east and the Chilean Coastal Range in the west.

"Now that's a tricky question", said Rachel, pausing for a moment as she considered her answer, before continuing: **"I don't know how to define it. It's something very special, I know that much. I don't think I could explain it to someone who didn't feel it themselves. Celtic's not just about Glasgow or the Scots-Irish, or even religion or nationality, it's more than that – it's a feeling and attitude which personifies openness, completely opposed to racism in every regard. Everybody seems to see the difference between right and wrong in this sense, and there seems to be a particular type of person drawn to Celtic as a Football Club and as a family. Personally, I don't regret a minute of it. I saw the likes of Henrik Larsson and Lubomir Moravcik in their prime; I saw us reach a European Final and stop ten in a row; I saw us win, lose and draw, and I couldn't help myself from coming back for more. Call it the "Celtic Family" if you like; there is certainly something which bonds people together at Celtic even though they aren't blood relatives. It's more than a Club, it's a way of looking at life, and I absolutely love it."**

"His Middle Name Should Be Consistency"

Robert 'Bobby' Evans was born in Glasgow on the sixteenth of July 1927. Typically, the man who would go on to make a name for himself playing football was born on a Saturday, and only one day prior to his birth, another Robert, 'Bobby' Jones, wowed the Scottish public by successfully defending his Open Championship title from the previous year. Whilst Jones would co-design the Augusta National Golf Course, and play an integral part in founding **"The Masters"** golf tournament itself, Bobby Evans would master another game – football.

Bobby signed for Celtic in July 1944 from youth side St Anthony's, and that is where he would remain until May 1960, becoming not only a Celtic player, but a Celtic great. Although he had a brief spell in an attacking role, Celtic's third manager, James McGrory, soon realised the defensive potential young Evans held and decided to start playing him as a half-back. Perhaps McGrory knew that, having been a forward himself, he would have viewed Evans as a formidable opponent had he been playing against him, and for this reason, he may have seen the promise Bobby possessed in this regard before many others.

Evans made his debut for Celtic in a one-nil win over Albion Rovers in August 1944. He was widely regarded as the best player in a Celtic jersey that day and Bobby, with his fiery red hair, was one of the earliest (if not the first) professional footballers to play with his shirt untucked.

He was a quiet, humble man away from football, but on the field of play he was a force to be reckoned with. Renowned for his fitness, work ethic, and strength, you could be forgiven for thinking Bobby Evans was more of a brute than a ballerina. However, he is still known to this day for his ability to select and deliver the correct pass to a player further up the field when the situation required he did so. In fact, some would say that this was one of his greatest attributes, as he almost always looked to play the ball forward rather than sideways or backwards. This meant that his presence on the field drove his side onwards as he encouraged them to progress towards the opposition goal.

Unlike many Celtic greats though, Bobby was not fortunate enough to win a plethora of trophies and medals during his time at the Club. In the years after the end of World War Two, Celtic were not the force they had been previously in Scottish Football. Evans was undoubtedly one of their best players and one of the side's most consistent performers at the time, but regardless, things were grim in the late 1940's. In the 1950's, things would improve to some degree at Celtic Park, but before that could happen, Bobby would play a critical role in simply keeping Celtic Football Club in the top flight of Scottish Football, as well as making his first strides in the international arena.

In 1947–48, the Hoops would come perilously close to relegation to Division 'B' – something which had never happened before and, thankfully, has not occurred to this day either. Having only won three of their thirteen league matches since the turn of the year, Celtic were due to travel to Dens Park for their final fixture of the domestic season. Whilst Celtic lay twelfth in the delicately poised sixteen team league table; their hosts sat fourth, having won ten of their previous fourteen league matches at Dens that season. Celtic, on the other hand, had only won four times in fourteen attempts away from home.

In all, the visitors had only scored thirty-eight times in twenty-nine league matches, conceding fifty-four, whilst Dundee had scored sixty-five, conceding only forty-nine. Therefore, on the face of it, Dundee were rightly viewed as the favourites for the match, but incredibly, Celtic pulled off a typically dramatic victory to save themselves from the looming threat of lower league football.

Celtic lined up as follows: Willie Miller, Bobby Hogg, Jimmy Mallan, Bobby Evans, William Corbett, Patrick McAuley, Jock Weir, John McPhail, Dan Lavery, William Gallacher and John Paton.

Critically, this was to be one of the first matches where, upon the instructions of his manager Jimmy McGrory, Bobby Evans would feature as a half-back, rather than as a forward. To put this change in context, Bobby had played up front in each of the Celts' last three league matches, all of which had resulted in defeat. McGrory felt that Evans' physical strength, as well as his natural passing ability, could be just what the team needed to bolster their midfield. After all, Third Lanark, who were fighting for their top flight survival just as Celtic were, had scored eight times in two games against Celtic in the aforementioned three match losing streak, highlighting an obvious weakness within the Celtic team at that time, as the Hoops seemed to haemorrhage goals.

And so, with Bobby Evans at half-back, Celtic ran out on the seventeenth of April 1948, at a thirty thousand strong Dens Park. Less than fifteen minutes into the match, Jock Weir, whom Celtic had only signed in February that year from Blackburn Rovers, opened the scoring. However, just before half time, the hosts equalised, before taking the lead with around half an hour left not only of the tie itself, but of the season. Whilst I can only speculate, I think it is fair to suggest that when Dundee scored their second goal, more than a few Celtic supporters were left thinking **"oh no"**.

Soon though, Jock Weir would grab a second goal, equalising for Celtic and sending a pulsating match into a frenetic finish, as Celtic pushed for a vital winner whilst Dundee attempted to catch Celtic's still rather unpredictable defence unawares. As the minutes ticked on, a miskick here or a bad pass there really could have spelled disaster for the Celts, but it wasn't to be. With less than two minutes of their season remaining, Jock Weir became the first Celtic player all year to score a hat-trick and secure an incredible, invaluable win for his new Club as he did so. Interestingly, on the same day, one of Celtic's first forwards, John Madden, died in Prague, at the age of eighty-three. Perhaps the spirit of one striker shone down on another in Dundee that day, or perhaps it was merely a somewhat romantic coincidence.

In the end, Celtic would avoid relegation by four points. However, it is worthy of note the sides below Celtic had games in hand going into the Hoops' last fixture of the season, and so, from our point of view at least, we simply had to win – and so we did. Jock Weir should not be forgotten for his services to the

Football Club that day, and neither should any of his teammates. Regardless, it would be days like this which would help to shape the then twenty year old Evans into an eventual Club captain, and the great he is fondly remembered as today.

In September of that same year, Bobby would feature in a three-one victory over Third Lanark in the Glasgow Cup Final. A month later, Bobby made his international debut, as Scotland recorded their first post-war victory against any home nation, defeating Wales by three goals to one at Ninian Park, Cardiff. This would be the first of many appearances in the blue of Scotland for Evans, whose fantastic performances in a Celtic jersey soon made him an international regular. In fact, it is worthy of note that Scotland won seven of the first eight matches Bobby appeared in, drawing the other, before finally losing to Austria by a single goal over two years after his international debut, indicating the almost wholly positive effect he had when playing alongside his fellow countrymen.

However, it would take another three years for Bobby to secure the first major silverware of his professional career, as Celtic won the 1951 Scottish Cup Final in front of almost one hundred and thirty-two thousand people at Hampden Park. The game itself was decided by a single goal from forward John McPhail, as Celtic, who would finish seventh in the league table, defeated Motherwell (who would end their campaign two places below the Hoops) by a single goal to nil.

A couple of months later, a one-off tournament, not dissimilar to the event which accompanied the Empire Exhibition in 1938, was held to celebrate **"The Festival of Britain"**. Sixteen Scottish sides competed for the Saint Mungo Cup and, after victories over Hearts, Clyde (through a replay) and Raith Rovers, Celtic found themselves in the final where they would face Aberdeen.

And so, on a sunny day at Hampden Park, the teams walked out in front of over eighty thousand expectant supporters. Celtic started poorly, and within fifteen minutes they found themselves a goal down. Twenty minutes later, it was two-nil, as ex-Celt Tommy Bogan gave Aberdeen a seemingly comfortable lead. In the process of trying to stop Bogan's goal bound effort, Celtic's goalkeeper, George 'Sonny' Hunter, clattered his head off of the post and was forced to leave the field of play for treatment.

In the days before substitutions, this meant that Celtic would have to play an outside player in goal for a time. Subsequently, Bobby Evans took up the challenge and, with the help of the defence he himself was usually an integral part of, Celtic managed to endure twelve minutes without the concession of a third goal until Hunter was able to resume his duties between the posts.

During that period of time, Sean Fallon, a man whom I seriously considered for inclusion within this fictional eleven, scored to narrow the half time deficit to only a single goal. As is often customary with Celtic matches, the events leading up to this goal were to be remembered as moments of some controversy. On the wing, down by the corner flag, the ball went out of play for a throw-in to Celtic. As an Aberdeen player picked up the ball and handed it to Charlie Tully (a character discussed at much greater length in a later chapter), he grabbed it and threw it off of the opposing players back as he turned away, resulting in a corner to Celtic. Seconds later, Fallon headed home the resulting corner kick.

A week later, the incident would be referred to in **"The Evening Times"**, as a journalist discussed the potential results of an imminent rule change regarding what we now refer to in the game as obstruction. In the article, the gentleman discusses whether the fears of many that this rule will lead to endless **"non-scoring free kicks"** as well as debating the potential for cheap goals to be scored from quickly taken free kicks. Whilst, nowadays, these fears may seem to be somewhat unfounded, it is interesting to consider which of the concerns discussed at the time came to any sort of fruition. For example, the writer asks how the referee will be able to inform the players as to whether infringements inside the penalty area are to result in an indirect free kick or a penalty if the players wish to continue play as quickly as possible. Of course, nothing has come of that concern, although many of us still find occasions upon which to berate referees and their decisions (myself included).

However, he then asks **"What action will be taken if a player deliberately stands holding the ball until his colleagues are in a defensive position, thus making a quick free impossible?"** Now, whilst this is far from a massive issue in the modern game, we do find ourselves discussing it from time to time, when a player purposely holds on to the ball (or kicks it away, for example) in order to either waste time or allow his teammates a chance to reorganise. At times, this is seen as nothing other than gamesmanship, but on occasion it is punished with a yellow card. Regardless, such debates rage on, over sixty years after they first started.

Returning to the matter at hand, as the Cup Final continued, Evans acted as a **"most efficient"** teammate by **"keeping Tully out of trouble when the Irishman took exception to a foul by Yorston on Peacock"**. Celtic then equalised through Fallon, who scored once again early in the second half, before Tully crossed for Walsh to score the winner sometime later. Following the final, one newspaper journalist said that **"The second half was Celtic's, and none did more to bring it about than Evans..."**

Upon being presented with the trophy, the Celtic players and staff found that it was adorned with mermaids and lifebelts. In time, the Club would discover that their prize, which one would have presumed to be a new piece, was actually previously awarded as a yachting trophy in 1894, before being slightly remodelled and first awarded as a football prize in 1912 and, once again, in 1951. Despite initial complaints from the Club, it still retains a place within the walls of Celtic Park to this day, a relic of a lost time, with an interesting story attached to it, as well as the aforementioned sea themed regalia.

Despite their victory in the Saint Mungo Cup prior to the start of the new season, Celtic would once again struggle to produce a memorable league campaign, let alone mount a serious challenge for the Championship itself. They would go on to win only ten of their thirty league matches in 1951–52, and only eleven the following year, leading to a sinking feeling within the support that any sort of notable success may not be forthcoming for a long time yet.

Before continuing on to such victories, I would like to briefly mention a story which I happened to stumble across not long after a minority of idiotic individuals online accused members of the Celtic support of smuggling **"a fake gun"** into Parkhead for the final derby match against Rangers. For those of you who may not know, these allegations came about when a photo of the Green Brigade's section 111 included a silhouette of a lad with a rolled up flag – of course, to anyone with even a modicum of common sense, it was clearly that, a flag – however, some people, incredibly, saw what they believed to be a replica firearm and reported it to Strathclyde Police as well several media organisations, all of which told them, unsurprisingly, that it was just a flag.

Regardless, during Bobby Evan's playing career, someone did actually take a firearm to the football, and not only that, he pulled it from his pocket and started to wave it about on the terracing. This may sound incredible, but I assure you that it is true. With the year of 1953 only hours old, thousands travelled to Ibrox Park for the heavily anticipated New Year derby match. The encounter a year to the day beforehand at Celtic Park had ended, literally, in a riot, and with tensions between the two sets of support and the police at an all-time high, appeals for calm were made prior to the 1953 clash.

Notably, these requests were heeded and there was to be no serious incidences of violence at the match in question, which Rangers won by a single goal to nil. Other than the occasional report of drunkenness, and one Celtic supporter being arrested for intentionally knocking a police officer's helmet from his head, there was nothing major for the newspapers of the following day to cover – other than the actions of Robert Carr, that is.

At the end of the match, Mr Carr, who was standing on the eastern terracing at the Copland Road end of Ibrox Park, brandished a pistol from his coat for some unknown reason (presumably he was in the midst of some altercation) and began to wave it around, screaming and shouting angrily. As police officers attempted to reach him, they were unable to do so as the masses of supporters trying to put some significant distance between themselves and the gun wielding Carr blocked their path.

Eventually, he was detained outside the ground (having attempted to flee) and found to be in possession of a firearm and ammunition.

During his court appearance the following day, the judge said: **"Of course, there is always an idiot like yourself who is liable to start a riot, and I can think of nothing more likely to cause a riot than the production of a weapon of this sort. It is a deadly weapon – a weapon that could kill. You were well warned, and now you are going to prison for 30 days."**

Moving on, in May of 1953, Glasgow hosted the famous Coronation Cup to celebrate, as the name suggests, the coronation of the new monarch. Four teams from England and four from Scotland took part, in a one-off knockout tournament to be played over a period of a few weeks. This was, of course, in the days before the inception of continental competition, so it was a rare chance for the teams involved to seriously compete against sides from another country. Celtic went on to win the trophy, defeating Arsenal, Manchester United, and Hibernian along the way.

In the first round of the tournament, as is mentioned previously, Celtic were set to face the English Champions, Arsenal, at Hampden Park. During the league campaign which had just ended, Arsenal had scored no less than ninety-seven times, and yet Celtic, who had conceded more goals than they had scored in the Scottish League, proceeded to defeat them by one goal to nil. At this point, you may be thinking, **"maybe it was a lucky goal or a penalty?"** Well, I'm afraid you're about to be just as bamboozled as the Celtic supporters in attendance were that day, for one newspaper journalist said after the match: **"Had Arsenal lost by five or six goals they could have had no valid complaint."** Incredibly, Celtic had simply dominated their opponents, much to everyone's surprise and delight.

The same individual later continues this theme in his article [referring to John McPhail initially]: **"Arsenal did not have a single player comparable with him last night; nor for that matter had they one of the calibre of Evans, with whom McPhail has evolved magnificent understanding."**

He then continues to discuss some of the tactics employed by Celtic, whilst describing one occasion upon which John McPhail strode forward with the ball: **"The ground pass that he had**

frequently given to Peacock or Tully was the orthodox move, but with an eye to Evans running into an open space 30 yards away on the other side of the field he despatched the ball shrewdly to his accomplice. Evans was gleefully on to the ball and once again Arsenal expected the start of a wing advance, this time on the right. McPhail was now running into a zone of his choice, however, and just as intelligently the cross-field pass was repeated. The ruse was employed again and again with comparable success...as English tongues hung out."

The short passage above only goes to demonstrate the offensive abilities of Bobby Evans (as well as those of John McPhail), and this is a trait for which, alongside defending, I'm sure he will be continue to be renowned for. However, not all of Evans' behaviour on the field of play was perfect. For example, in the very same match, Evans stole the ball from Arsenal forward Don Roper, who proceeded to say something which enraged Bobby. As the referee sprinted over towards Roper, whom he believed to be the guilty party, Evans reached him first, and according to newspaper reports: **"a minute elapsed before peace was restored."** Interestingly, the two men who crossed each other that day, both of whom continue to be revered by their respective Football Clubs, died less than two months apart in 2001, almost five decades later.

Returning to 1953, having out-gunned Arsenal, Celtic were set to face Manchester United in the semi-final of the competition. Once again, the Hoops were set to play at Hampden Park, albeit on this day the beautiful sunshine of the first round had been replaced with strong, swirling winds and blackening cloud. The match finished with the score-line of two-one to Celtic, thanks to goals from Bertie Peacock and Neil Mochan, but Evans too was to be praised very highly in newspaper pages across Britain. One read: **"Once again Evans and McPhail, these wing halves of contrasting styles, inspired their sides to victory. So fine a player Evans has been – and for so long – that anything but a distinguished display from him would be a matter for wonderment. Consistency should be his middle name."**

Interestingly, in the same article, the author makes a reference to the much maligned attempt to stop Celtic Football Club from flying the Irish tricolour in the early 1950's. You wonder what reaction the scene in Seville would have conjured from this journalist, who said of the semi-final **"...he had spooned his shot grotesquely high in the direction of several Eire flags, the reappearance of which amongst a section of the Celtic following is inopportune to say the least."**

In the final against Hibernian (who had won two of the previous three League Championships and only lost this season's to Rangers on goal average), much of the credit for the victory must go to the defenders and, in particular, to the Celtic goalkeeper, Johnny Bonnar, who had, by all accounts, a truly tremendous game. Only a few weeks earlier, Celtic had made an offer for a goalkeeper from Morton named Jimmy Cowan, but he had turned them down, and so it was left to Bonnar to play in this tournament – and what a tournament he had. As the final whistle blew, he was mobbed by both his teammates and the coaching staff, who congratulated him on a truly magnificent performance.

Whilst much of the coverage in the press discussed the sterling showing of Bonnar, there was, once again, large amounts of praise being directed towards Bobby Evans also: **"Perhaps, too, fortune might have decreed that the magnificent Evans be a little less magnificent against them** [Hibernian]**. In all of his career for Celtic and Scotland, Evans has never served a side better. When the speed of Smith and Johnstone threatened to engulf the slower-moving McPhail, Evans was a left half as well as a right half, and it was he who, after he had tackled Smith, as the outside right tried to gain the long-awaited equalising goal, set his forwards in motion for the score that would settle the tie. All in all, over one hundred and seventeen thousand supporters saw the Hoops prove that "no team in Britain can conquer this Celtic side on level terms.""**

This triumph, which came as another blow to many within the establishment across the United Kingdom, seemed to spur Celtic on. In the coming season, they would win both the Scottish League Championship (for the first time in sixteen years) and the Scottish Cup, defeating Aberdeen by two goals to one in the final in front of more than one hundred and thirty thousand spectators once again. It is of note that this Aberdeen side were no pushovers either, having beaten Rangers by an incredible score of six goals to nil in the semi-final. The Dons had also beaten Celtic on three of the four occasions on which they had played them domestically that season, in both the League and League Cup. And so, on that day in April, it took a sixty-fourth minute winner from Sean Fallon to bring the trophy back to Celtic Park.

Regardless, the achievements of 1953 and 1954 should perhaps be remembered as greatest of Bobby Evans' footballing career. Whilst there were still some memorable victories to come for Bobby, he had played a truly integral part in a side which had won the Scottish League Championship for the first time since 1938, and a domestic double for the first time in forty years. Imagine it for a moment – that is the equivalent of Celtic not winning the league again until 2029, and not repeating last season's double success until 2053! It's almost unthinkable by modern standards, but nevertheless, it reminds us that we must enjoy our successes when we are fortunate enough to achieve them, for nothing lasts forever.

Even after the disappointment of the Scottish Cup Final defeat of 1955 against Clyde, Evans continued to be praised by the Scottish media. Following a replay against the Shawfield side, one newspaper said: **"Evans and Peacock were their usual inspiring selves, but theirs was a thankless task. Far too often for their piece of mind the ball was back upon them through their colleagues' failure to respond."**

However, a year later, as Celtic lost the Scottish Cup Final of 1956 to Hearts, Bobby would become the recipient of significant criticism for one of the few times in his entire career, having made a couple of uncustomary mistakes which led to goals for the Edinburgh side. This is not to say that the defeat was his solely fault – far from it in fact – as many of the Celts on show had a distinctly off-day, but nonetheless, those who make the most obvious errors can often be considered as scapegoats of sorts in the sporting world. One newspaper said:

"I cannot recall an occasion on which Celtic have played in which Evans was not one of their outstanding men. Here again he was prominent but not a successful centre half. Before Crawford scored the first goal in 20 minutes Evans lost the ball to Bauld through overcarrying it, and before Bauld swung over the cross which led to the outside left scoring his second goal three minutes after half time. Evans was not nearly decisive enough in his tackle of the centre forward."

I suppose that this result proved that no footballer, however good they may be, can always play well. Evans was renowned throughout his career as a "**Mr Consistency**" of sorts, but he was not superhuman, nor was he infallible. It is also of note that Bobby took over the role of Club captain from Jock Stein at the start of the 1955–56 season, and therefore the Scottish Cup Final against Hearts was his first experience of a major final as the captain of Celtic. Whether nerves were an issue, or whether he simply had one of those days where everything seems to go against you, we may never know. However, what is critical is that Evans clearly learnt from not only his personal mistakes of that day, but the errors of the side he was tasked with leading on the field of play.

A little over six months later, Celtic would win the Scottish League Cup for the first time against Partick Thistle. In the replayed final, Celtic won by three goals to nil, and for the latter portion of the match, Evans was moved to inside right as he had suffered an injury which severely limited his movements. However, he played on, and even managed to register an assist for the third goal, which was scored by another Bobby – Bobby Collins. Only a few days later, Collins would join Evans on the injured list, as he suffered the pain of a broken ankle away at Dundee.

In 1957, Celtic once again progressed through the League Cup competition, but before they could face Clyde in the semi-final, they faced a trip to Ibrox as part of their league campaign. Incredibly, it was to be the first occasion upon which the Celts had won a league match at Ibrox in twenty-two years (as referenced in the chapter dedicated to the life of Willie Lyon). Bobby put in a sterling performance and, being back to his personal best in many regards, he helped Celtic to emerge the victors by three goals to two, as the following newspaper report dictates:

"The result did not unduly favour Celtic. Theirs was a victory of superior football. Rangers almost certainly lost the match in the first half, in which with the wind at their backs they were frequently remiss in attack. Perhaps the backs and half-backs conceived the idea that strong, bustling inside forwards could provoke errors in the Celtic defence as the long, high ball sailed into goal, but on almost every occasion this unattractive if potentially dangerous form of thrust was attempted, Evans, of superb heading ability and sound judgement in anticipation baulked them, or the ball, driven ahead with insufficient thought for the power of the wind, passed over the bye-line far ahead of the pursuing forwards."

The article concluded: **"Celtic had the best full-back afield in Fallon, a clearly superior half-back line, and as obvious an advantage in skill and shrewdness in the forward line. Perhaps their disadvantage in physique was to their advantage; in any event they gained the reward of devoting more attention to the arts and crafts of the game."**

Please note the pattern of the game described previously as well as the styles of play employed by both sides also – I suppose it was yet another example of **"plus ça change"** in the Glasgow derbies of old, whereby the more things change, the more things stay the same.

One week later, Celtic edged past Clyde in the aforementioned League Cup semi-final. Bobby had just recovered from a bout of flu to play that day, which undoubtedly helped Celtic to triumph over their opponents. However, it is also noteworthy that, as the strain of influenza spread around the city and its population, three of Clyde's first choice eleven were unable to play due to contracting the illness. Regardless, Celtic won by four goals to two, and set up a mammoth final tie against Rangers in the process.

With this in mind, the Celtic victory at Ibrox less than a month prior to League Cup Final day only added to the anticipation within the ranks of the Parkhead Club's support. Generally, in my experience, Celtic fans like myself are fairly optimistic people – at least when it comes to football. We've spent far too many years as the underdogs of both sport and society not to be. However, I doubt even the most optimistic Celtic supporter could have predicted the events of the nineteenth of October 1957, as Celtic faced their fiercest rivals in the League Cup Final at Hampden. This was to be Celtic's finest hour against Rangers, at least in terms of the scoreline, as the Hooped underdogs scored no less than seven goals against their heavily fancied opponents, who were many people's pre-match favourites for the League Cup, having finished almost twenty points ahead of Celtic in the previous league season.

Bobby Evans was one of the few players dressed in green and white that didn't score that day, but perhaps the result alone displays how well Celtic played more succinctly than any single match report. For the first time in thirty years, Celtic met Rangers in a domestic final and not only did Celtic dominate their opponents – they annihilated them. This result remains as not only the biggest margin of victory in a Glasgow derby, but also the biggest win in any major U.K. Cup Final. Writing for **"The Glasgow Herald"**, Cyril Horne describes how Bobby blocked an early Rangers shot through a **"shrewd intervention"**, prior to describing him as **"throughout a centre half of absolute competence."** However, Mr Horne does not stop there, as later in his article he states, **"Never have I seen Rangers so out-classed in half back play; Fernie, Evans, and Peacock were, each in his own distinguished way, tremendous players in everything but bulk and brawn."** Sadly though, this was to be the last piece of silverware Evans was to win with Celtic, but what a triumph it had been.

In 1958, Bobby featured in all three of Scotland's matches in the World Cup in Sweden. In truth, it was to be a disappointing campaign for the Scots, who lost two of their three ties, finishing bottom of their group in the process. However, they did manage a point against Yugoslavia in their first outing, the side that eventually went on to finish third in the tournament after reaching the semi-final stage. Bobby captained Scotland in their final match against group winners France, one of twelve occasions upon which he led his country over his long and illustrious international career.

And so, after sixteen years, three hundred and eighty-four appearances, and ten goals in the green and white Hoops, Bobby Evans left Celtic in May 1960 to join Chelsea for a fee of twelve and a half thousand pounds. In truth, it was a less than harmonious end to his Celtic career for Evans. For years, he had been increasingly angered by the mismanagement he believed to be going on at the Club, as the board of directors and then chairman Robert Kelly continuously meddled with team affairs. In time, one of Bobby's former teammates, Jock Stein, would banish the spectre of interference from Celtic Park for the foreseeable future, but, in footballing terms at least, it was too late for Bobby. Upon his departure in 1960, Evans is quoted as saying the following:

"He [referring to the Celtic captain] **has no decisions to take about team changes or tactical changes. The answers to these problems come from the directors' box to the track, and they are passed to the field by the trainer."**

In all honesty, it was most likely this frustration with regards to the way the Club was run, combined with his own gradual decrease in form (largely down to age slowing his pace and affecting his fitness somewhat) that influenced Bobby's final decision to leave the Club he adored. While he was undoubtedly angry at the board, he never felt any ill feeling towards the Club or its supporters, and he dearly held many fond memories of his time there for the rest of his life.

After a less than impressive spell at Stamford Bridge, Bobby would go on to play with Newport County, Greenock Morton, Third Lanark and finally, Raith Rovers, where he retired at the age of thirty-nine in 1968, after a monumental twenty-four years in the professional game. I must confess that it surprised me when I first discovered Bobby Evans was still playing competitive football after his former Club's journey to Lisbon in 1967. It is also worthy of note that during his time at Newport County and Third Lanark, Bobby managed both sides, the latter of which sadly ceased to exist a couple of only years after his departure.

In his later life, he would, regrettably, go on to suffer badly with the effects of Parkinson's disease. Robert 'Bobby' Evans died of pneumonia on the second of September 2001, at the age of seventy-four years old. He is still fondly remembered as one of Celtic Football Club's greatest players, and was posthumously inducted into the Scottish Football Hall of Fame in 2008. He still holds a place within the top ten Scottish internationals to have played for Celtic in terms of international caps, and upon his retirement, he was the second most capped Scotland player of all time. Not only did he earn his title as Celtic's **"Mr Consistency"**, he conducted himself impeccably away from the football field, and I can say with certainty that he will be both spoken of and loved by both the fans of Celtic Football Club and Scotland for many, many generations to come.

Below, you will find the article published online by the B.B.C. in the days following Bobby's death, entitled **"Celtic Mourn Bobby Evans"**:

"Bobby Evans, who enjoyed a long and distinguished career with Celtic and Scotland, has died of pneumonia aged 74. Evans, who had been suffering from Parkinson's Disease, died on Saturday at Darroch nursing home in Cumbernauld. He leaves a daughter, Margaret, and son, Robert.

Evans' career spanned the 1940's and 50's, during which time he played 535 times for Celtic and collected 48 international caps. He joined Celtic in July 1944 and made his debut in the wartime Regional League on 19 August. He captained Celtic when they won the League Cup for the first time with a win over Partick Thistle in 1956. The highlight of his career was surely the following year's 7–1 League Cup win over arch-rivals Rangers.

Another Celtic great, Bertie Auld, signed for Celtic as Evans' time at the club was nearing an end and he told Celtic's official website of his memories of the man: "I'm shattered by the news. He was a tremendous Celtic player, and there was no badness in him. He was very warm-hearted and was always happy to help the younger

players. He was very good to me when I first joined Celtic. No-one ever had a bad word to say about Bobby."

Celtic chief executive Ian McLeod told the website: "It was with great sadness that I learned of the death of Bobby Evans. Bobby played for the club for 16 years, making over 500 appearances and is rightly remembered as a Celtic great. The thoughts of everyone at Celtic Football Club are with his daughter Margaret and son Robert at this sad time."

One minute's silence will be observed prior to kick-off in Celtic's home match with Dunfermline on Saturday in memory of Evans."

"It Will Live With Me Forever"

And so, a little over seven months after Celtic's first foray into the 2002–03 UEFA Cup, it would all come down to this – a trip to the north of Portugal and the city of Oporto. Having just knocked out Liverpool (one of the most successful sides in the history of European competition) in the quarter finals, only one match now stood between Celtic and the promised land of a European Final. Having only managed a one-all draw with their opponents Boavista in the first leg in Glasgow, the tie was delicately poised going into the return fixture, and the potential prize of a trip to Seville was now tantalisingly close.

With Celtic's impressive away record in Europe that season firmly in mind, the Club's supporters around the globe felt that the prospect of their first European Final in over three decades was a very real possibility. Unsurprisingly, a huge number of men, women and children followed the team to northern Portugal for the second leg of the semi-final and, of course, one of them was individual this chapter revolves around, Jim Kerr.

Now in his fiftieth year, Jim was a little short of forty when he made that memorable trip to Europe. This was something he had done several times before when following his beloved Hoops, taking in cities such as Amsterdam, Dortmund, Madrid, Turin and even Mostar in the past, as well as every away day of the Seville run with the exception of Suduva, but this was to be the biggest of them all. Whilst there were many obvious similarities with other journeys, such as thousands of Celtic fans descending on an unsuspecting European city centre, this trip was to be notably different with such a prize at stake. Incredibly, the whole excursion would last less than twenty-four hours, with Jim arriving in the city on the morning of the game and flying home only hours after the final whistle, but what a trip it would be regardless.

In light of Celtic's quarter final success, Jim hastily booked his place on a chartered flight with **"67 Travel"** to Portugal alongside twelve friends, at a time when they had only three tickets between them (clearly they are not people who believe that thirteen is an unlucky number). Now, as Jim had one ticket himself, the lads held a ballot for the other two on the bus home from the first leg. All of those involved had known about the draw before the first leg had kicked off, and so, when the time finally came, excitement was almost at fever pitch. Within a matter of minutes, two men were very happy, leaving the others hoping and praying they would be able to turn up a ticket for the match some other way. In fact, according to Jim, one of the unlucky men, Gary, had tears in his eyes as he got off the bus sometime later, such was his disappointment.

Thankfully, by the time the day of the game dawned, Jim had worked his magic and managed to find a ticket for each member of the group, as well as actually being in possession of a few spares. Having gone in search of a pub they considered to be an old favourite from previous trips to the city when they arrived in the morning, Jim and his mates settled in for the day, enjoying the chance to have a few beers, meet the locals and warm up their vocal chords for what was to come, before eventually heading to the stadium itself.

And so, as Jim and the rest of the group set about draining what remained in their pint glasses before leaving the pub, one of his mates, Rab, ventured outside to check the details of the local bus service to the ground. Unbeknown to those still inside, he proceeded to befriend a tiny homeless man, giving him a few coins and trading his mint green dress shirt for the man's bedraggled and somewhat whiffy equivalent so he that could surprise his friends.

According to Jim: **"When Rab came back into the pub, it looked like someone had taken a packet of "Refreshers"** [sweets with a distinctive multicoloured packaging sold in Scotland] **and used it as inspiration for this shirt. It was unlike anything I'd ever seen before! The shirt was skin-tight on him, and the smell of stale sweat coming off of it was awful."**

He then elaborated: **"Rab told us that he had borrowed it from a homeless guy outside, and we all had a good laugh at the sight of him in this monstrosity, but that paled in comparison to**

what happened next. When we all left the pub two minutes later, the homeless lad was nowhere to be seen – he'd done a runner with Rab's shirt! We were howling with laughter and the tears were running down our faces, but to be fair that might have been because of the stench which was coming from Rab!"

In Jim's mind, it wouldn't have been totally unreasonable for his mate to have thrown away his 'new' top after they had left the pub but, to his credit, he wore it with pride and tied his hoody around his waist as they travelled out to Boavista's Estádio de Bessa.

Many of you may recall that, at the time of this match, the stadium in question was still in the process of being built in parts. As part of a wider construction effort for the upcoming European Championships of 2004, Boavista's old ground was being demolished and rebuilt on a stand by stand basis, meaning that, although the Club were never forced to vacate the site, construction was ongoing in and around the stadium area for a couple of years.

Even with this in mind, you may have been surprised if you had found yourself outside the stadium, like Jim, watching none other than Dermot Desmond – Celtic's billionaire owner – trudging through one of these building sites irately, all whilst his entourage scuttled around him and supporters of both sides looked on. I must confess that I chuckled to myself upon hearing this brief story, which began with Mr Desmond being refused entry to the stadium's main stand as the security staff on the door clearly did not believe him when he claimed to own Celtic Football Club. Obviously, this perturbed Mr Desmond (to say the least), and he set off in search of another way in, leading to his impromptu crossing of a Portuguese building site, muddy shoes and all, before he proceeded to march over a section of grass behind a nearby house. As an increasing number of supporters gathered to observe this pantomime, Mr Desmond returned to the main stand once more (having been turned around by the owner of the house after he had found Celtic's owner casually walking through what turned out to be his back garden) and was finally spotted by a member of Celtic's staff inside and, after a lot of hassle, he was allowed into the stadium.

As for Jim, he found himself with a couple of spare tickets to one of the most important Celtic matches in decades, and eventually proceeded to simply give them away to two of his fellow supporters, much to their delight. Having entered the ground with his mate, Jim found that they were not sat with the main body of the Celtic supporters, but in a smaller section in the main stand alongside several of the team's friends and families. Unsurprisingly, this area was a little more sedate that of the main away allocation, but in time, the atmosphere would improve dramatically.

Prior to the match starting however, far away on the other side of the ground where the majority of the Celtic support was housed, Rab and his shirt were making a big impression on those around him. Jim said: **"In the hours after the game my mates told me Rab had got pelters because of the smell. It was so bad that folk were purposely trying to stand as far away from him as possible, but then it got worse. By chance, the guys from "Still Game", Greg Hemphill (Victor) and Paul Riley (Winston), happened to be in the row behind Rab and apparently they let Rab know in no uncertain terms that the stench was truly eye-watering. Funnily enough, sometime later, Paul Reilly happened to walk past Rab again outside another Celtic match back in Scotland, and upon seeing him again, Paul shouted: "Alright big man, you still stinking?""**

Returning to that night in Portugal, and the smaller section of Celtic supporters in the main stand as the teams finally appeared on the field of play, Jim told me that his nerves began to take hold of him, before explaining the faith he held that Celtic would, somehow, find a way to progress to the final.

"Normally, I get pretty nervous before big games. I'll think about the game all day, but once I leave the house, I seem to go through a bit of a hiatus on my journey to the ground, until I'm inside the stadium and the teams come out – and that's exactly what happened in Portugal that night. The magnitude of an occasion such as that would get to most people, and I had my heart in my mouth several times over the course of ninety minutes, but equally well, the belief was always there."

"When we were due to play Suduva and Blackburn Rovers all those months ago, most people thought we could beat them, and so we did. However, when we drew Liverpool, I think a lot of folk were less sure of victory against them, and yet we beat them anyway. And so, we found ourselves set to face Boavista. I was nervous, as I'm sure a lot of supporters were, but every victory so far that season had instilled a confidence in us, especially that over Liverpool, and I thought that we would find a way to progress. With Henrik in the team, I felt anything was possible because he always seemed to conjure something up when we really needed him to, and so the game began."

Midway through the match, with the score still goalless and the tie on a knife edge, a metal sign fell from the top of Jim's section and landed on the stairwell next to him. Fearing the risk it posed to other fans, Jim picked it up and carried it to the front of the seating area, laying it down and quickly returning his attention to the match itself. Minutes later, Henrik Larsson, one of the greatest players ever to pull on the green and white of Celtic, stabbed the ball past Ricardo in the Boavista goal and sent the Celtic fans in attendance into truly mad celebrations rarely seen before or since.

According to Jim, countless grown men, including himself, began to cry soon after the goal, as it began to dawn on them that Celtic were going to a European Final once more, whilst a small woman began to kiss the multitude of Holy Medals which were hanging around her neck. At this point, Jim's mate Malky, who was awaiting a stomach operation at the time, began to vomit violently, as that potent mixture of excitement, nerves and alcohol took its toll.

"Thank God the camera didn't pan over us," recalled Jim, **"What a sight we must have been, in with all these executives in suits and family members, with me crying my eyes out and my pal bent over chucking his guts up!"**

And so, as the final whistle sounded, the global family of Celtic supporters rejoiced, in homes, bars, restaurants and, of course, inside the Estádio de Bessa. Tears continued to flow, as people hugged each other and leapt around, all as the little woman kissed her Holy Medals once more, clearly offering thanks to the footballing Gods above for Celtic's victory. However, ecstasy would soon turn to terror for Jim, as a delighted Rab Douglas ran towards his small section of the crowd.

No, it wasn't the fact that Rab Douglas was running over which terrified him, but what was to follow. As the rest of the team approached the main group of Celtic supporters, Douglas, who had been defending his goal at the other end of the field, turned to those closest to him in celebration. Delirious, Jim ran down the stairs towards the front of the section, forgetting about the metal sign which he had laid down there earlier in the evening. Upon stepping onto the sign, Jim's feet slipped out from underneath him, propelling him into the air. In the process, he very nearly went over the glass barrier at the front of the section, which had a forty foot drop on to cold, hard concrete steps on the other side of it.

Later, his mate would describe how he **"couldn't believe he didn't go over...his feet were so far off of the ground I could see their soles."** Incredibly, Jim was fine, suffering only a couple of bumps and bruises having somehow landed back on his feet, but he still considers it to have been a **"near death experience"** to this day – **"If I had gone over that barrier I would have probably been dead. The support would have been celebrating reaching the UEFA Cup Final while the media told the story of how a fan had died at the Boavista game."**

Having thanked his lucky stars not only for Celtic's progression, but more importantly for his own good health, Jim joined his mates at the makeshift bus park behind the stadium where they would await the bus back to the airport for their flight home.

"Once we left the ground, we found a woman selling individual cans of beer for one Euro each, so we got all of our leftover coins together and bought about thirty beers. We sat down on the steps of a library opposite the bus park, and began to take it all in. It was weird, there were periods when the singing and shouting would stop for a few minutes at a time, as if everyone was in a stunned silence of sorts. I mean, we'd actually done it! We were in a European Final! Personally, I couldn't believe it."

Later, once Jim had reached the airport, he spotted a few well known faces – Gordon Smith, Sandy Clark, and Murdo MacLeod – who had presumably been there working with the media. I doubt that too many of you will be surprised to hear that only the latter appeared to be happy about Celtic's result that night. Before departing for Glasgow, Jim still had time to be caught by a camera filming the multitude of Celtic's supporters that night, meaning he does appear in the background of Celtic's official Seville DVD for a few seconds, but neither of these relatively minor events compare to Jim's main memory of his time in the airport that night.

"We had sat in the departure lounge for a wee while and nothing much was happening. I'd bumped into an old friend and managed to buy one of the spare copies of the match programmes that he had with him, and just as I returned to my seat, I spotted someone in a grey Celtic kit through the darkened glass partition which separated the various lounges. It was the kit the staff wore, and whilst I didn't recognise the man himself, I gestured over to my mates who came and had a look for themselves. When a bus pulled up at the door below that lounge a moment later, we realised that the Celtic team were about to come through and travel out to their plane on the tarmac."

"Anyway, there was a corridor which was sort of 'L' shaped that bent along the edge of our lounge that led towards the exit doors next to the bus, so we thought, "right, the team will have to pass through here, and it's only a few feet wide, so we should get a great view", and so we stood. A few minutes later, the team appeared in the lounge next door, heading towards the wee corridor we were next to and everyone started going mental. With us making so much noise, it attracted the attention of all the other fans and before the players had reached the corridor, everybody had run over and pressed themselves up against the glass trying to get a decent view."

"When the players got closer, we started to bang the glass and shout and scream, and as soon as they saw us, they all started to do the same thing. The glass partition didn't go all the way to the roof – it was probably only about twelve feet high – so the noise

passed over from the other side easily enough. You could hear the players shouting and stuff, it was fantastic. Folk like Bobo Balde and Alan Thompson were going absolutely mental! In fact, Big Bobo saw us and actually leapt up onto the partition screaming. They were all hugging each other and jumping about, even once they'd left the terminal and boarded the bus. As they drove away, we all moved over to the windows overlooking the tarmac and began to bang the glass again whilst the team waved back. You could tell how much it meant to them, and that only added to how much it meant to us. I've got goose pimples just talking about it now. It was euphoric."

Once the team departed, Jim, as well as the hundreds of other fans still waiting on their flights simply sat down again, drained once more by the physical and mental exertions of the day. A stunned silence descended, as the fans awaited their flights home, and that was that.

Finally, I shall finish with a few words from the man himself, Jim Kerr:

"I don't remember Lisbon because I was too young. I can still recall a few bits of the 1970 European Cup Final but not much and, well, parts of that night aren't really worth remembering in all honesty. I'd followed Celtic all over the place and all I'd ever wanted; all I'd ever dreamed of; was to see them reach again European Final in my lifetime – and they'd done it. It was the most amazing feeling ever, and although we didn't win in Seville, I was still fiercely proud of the team and what they'd achieved. The spirit they'd shown to reach that stage was magnificent, and I'll never forget that night against Boavista. It was the greatest event of my time supporting Celtic thus far, and it will live with me forever."

"It Was An Offer I Couldn't Refuse"

Singapore, one of the five sovereign city states on Earth and one of the icons of global trade and prosperity, lies at the southern tip of the Malaysian Peninsula. With a relatively steady and predictable climate, the temperature in Singapore tends to stay in the high twenties or low thirties (Celsius) for most of the year, with heavy and regular rainstorms meaning approximately twice as much rain falls there annually than as in Glasgow. In amongst all of this urbanisation, which has seen Singapore become one of the world's leading financial centres, almost nineteen thousand people inhabit every square mile of the city on average.

Whilst the majority of Singaporeans are of Chinese or Malaysian ethnicities, there are also a significant number of foreign workers to be found there, one of which goes by the name of John Cassidy, originally of Arden, Glasgow, a housing estate located well over six thousand miles away from his current home. Having been born in Thornliebank in 1959, John lived in Arden and attended St Louise Primary School before he moved to Stewarton with his family in the early 1970's.

When I spoke to John, he explained to me that while there were some very poor people in Arden when he lived there, his family were fortunate enough not to find themselves in that particular financial bracket. **"The sense of community in Arden and Thornliebank was greater than anything I've ever experienced"**, he said, **"There was an external perception that the housing estate was worse than it actually was."**

From an early age, John embraced his father's passion not only for football, but for a particular team, Celtic. To this day, he can recall being passed over the turnstiles as a small boy at Celtic Park. Whilst he thoroughly enjoyed the experience of watching the Hoops, John did admit to feeling vulnerable at times in amongst the large crowds, remembering an occasion upon which he almost fell under a police horse during a crush outside the ground. However, the presence of his father at his side always reassured the young John, who would go on attend countless games.

Whilst some of his early life as a Celtic supporter is, by his own admission, a blur, the memories of the twenty-fifth of May 1967, when John was only eight years old, will be forever imprinted on his mind. As kick-off time approached in the early evening, he joined his parents, as well as his older brother and sister, in the living room of their top floor flat in Arden and huddled around their television. Upon each of Celtic's goal bound strikes connecting with the back of Giuliano Sarti's net, **"the roof almost came off of the house"** according to John, as the family's nerves turned to delirious joy. Although he was an avid football supporter, John only had some grasp of the European Cup's place at the pinnacle of European Club football prior to that night. He told me how Celtic's achievement had only truly begun to hit home after the match was over, as **"supporters filled the streets, dancing and singing as if they didn't have a care in the world."**

When I considered in which manner I should approach this chapter, a thought crossed my mind. If, during the 1950's, when (other than the occasional highlight) Celtic were far from at their best, someone was to have asked John's father Eddie, a postman by trade, **"Do you think there's more chance of Celtic winning the European Cup or one of your children travelling to Asia and settling there?"** – I wonder what his answer would have been. In all honesty, he may well have thought that both of them were unlikely to happen anytime soon, with Celtic's seemingly endless inconsistency and the financial reality in Scotland at that stage, and yet he would see both occur during his lifetime.

Whilst John cannot remember which Celtic match was his first, he believes it was sometime in 1965 or 1966 – not exactly a bad period to begin watching the Club. One of John's first clear memories of attending a match actually came several years later, when he travelled with his father to Hampden to see Celtic take on Aberdeen in the Scottish Cup Final of 1970. Sadly, John would leave the national stadium disappointed as Celtic slumped to a three-one defeat that day, with the Dons winning the trophy for only the second time.

"The size of the crowd absolutely stunned me", reflected John, **"I'd never attended a derby match at that point in my life, so this was far and above anything I'd ever seen previously. I couldn't believe how busy it was, but to the majority of supporters there it was just another big tie at Hampden. They were used to it. I remember Bobby Lennox scoring to narrow the deficit, but Aberdeen scored again soon after and that was that. I don't think I'll ever forget the feeling of disappointment. We were leading from the first leg of the European Cup semi-final, and cantering away with the league, whereas Aberdeen were stuck in the middle of the table, so everyone expected us to win – especially a young boy like myself. Sadly that wouldn't be the final disappointment that season either with the loss to Feyenoord taking place only weeks later."**

A couple of years onwards, John would find himself at Hampden Park for the Scottish Cup Final once more and, this time, he would see his side emerge victorious. On the sixth of May 1972, Celtic hammered Hibernian by six goals to one in front of approximately one hundred and six thousand people – two of which were John and his father.

"In all honesty, I can't remember too much about the game itself, but I do remember a bit about the day as a whole. Once again, I was in awe of the crowd, as well as the scoreline and Dixie Deans' hat-trick, but nothing beats the memory of seeing the team lift the Scottish Cup. I don't know why, but me and my father were sat only a couple of rows behind where the Cup was presented in the stand, so we had a perfect view of that moment. I can still remember Jock Stein walking along and saying "hello" to people. It was a very special moment in my life."

Having left school at the age of sixteen without pursuing any form of higher education, John found work in the National Savings Bank at Cowglen (he did complete a banking qualification in later years thanks to the nature of his employment), along with several thousand other men and women like him. Around this time, as he suddenly had a bit of money in his pocket, he began to attend away matches seriously, following the team to every domestic match they played in the 1976–77 season.

Returning to the matter of his work, John considered the possibility of a long career as a civil servant and, having decided it was not for him, he began to look elsewhere. With the opportunity to cash in on a lump sum given to bank employees every five years, John went against his family's advice and used the cash to fund a move to Jersey where he had a friend. Until he found work with the **"Hong Kong and Shanghai Banking Corporation"** on the island in 1980, John had made ends meet by delivering furniture, something he had no problems with on a short term basis.

Now, many of you may (or equally well may not) have realised that the aforementioned Hong Kong and Shanghai Banking Corporation is actually a regular sight on high streets across the country and the world today, although most branches of the bank abbreviate their titles to just **"H.S.B.C."**. Having started at the bottom tier of the company as a bookkeeper, John worked hard, and began to progress up the proverbial ladder in the coming years. The potential of further progression appealed to John as a young man as he felt it gave him something to aim and work towards, as well as a chance to broaden his horizons and travel the world.

In 1987, John was asked to travel to Hong Kong with only two days notice. Without a wife or children at that stage in his life, such short notice was not an issue, and soon John Cassidy, the boy from the Arden, was on his way to Asia. Several hours later, he touched down at Hong Kong's Kai Tak International Airport, a facility located unusually close to the heart of the city itself.

"I flew in and out of Kai Tak countless times over the years", recalls John, **"it was a technical, challenging landing. Nowadays a lot of airports are so well designed that the autopilots could virtually land most planes, but Kai Tak put the pilots to the test, and I actually think a lot of them enjoyed it. I remember you could see people's washing hanging out to dry on the surrounding buildings as you flew into the airport. It was remarkable really. Looking back on it, I think I'd be a lot more frightened if I had to do it now than I was then, although there were very few**

accidents during my time, probably because pilots' minds were so concentrated on the task before them when they landed there."

Kai Tak eventually closed its doors in 1998 as it was simply deemed to be far too small to handle the boom in passenger numbers which was going on and now sees over fifty million pass through the new Hong Kong airport every year.

Regardless, John spent a few weeks in Hong Kong on his first visit, and despite certain culture shocks, like some of the food and the weather, he loved the overall experience. Yes, some things took a bit of getting used to, such as the heat, humidity and periods of intense rainfall, but these did not put the young John off. Neither did the grub, as whilst some of it was a little strange, the vast majority was exciting and delicious. In the late summer of that same year, his employers asked him whether he would be interested in accepting a permanent post on the island, and in his own words: **"It was an offer I couldn't refuse."**

Whilst he still resided in Hong Kong, John first met his future wife, a Malaysian, and in time they would have two boys together, Sean and Michael. However, by John's own admission, neither of his sons have taken any great interest in the goings on at Parkhead – **"I consider it to be one of my great failures in life"**, John joked. However, I shall return to this point.

To continue, despite the fact that neither of his sons are big Celtic fans as yet, I think it's safe to assume that they are aware of the love their father holds for the Football Club. Not only does John watch matches on the other side of the globe, shouting at the television and dancing around the living room in the dead of night on occasion (see John Hartson scoring at Anfield for a notable example) but he always makes an effort to take in a game or two whenever he returns to Scotland.

In 2008, John travelled to Japan's capital, Tokyo, and was amazed to see the presence that Celtic, particularly through Shunsuke Nakamura, seemed to have in the city. Previously, John had told me about the manner in which many Asian people treat their football – which is seriously – very seriously. He said that: **"Liverpool and Manchester United are the most popular teams on the whole, and it's always a good laugh to go to a sports**

bar when the two teams play each other and not only watch the match itself, but the fans also. Some of their celebrations are fairly hysterical in their nature, but I suppose it just goes to prove that people who have never even set foot in a particular country, whether it's Scotland, England or anywhere else can care about the football which is played there tremendously."

Returning to the subject of his time in Tokyo though, John said: **"It was a bit bizarre in truth. I passed sports shops and saw mannequins of Shunsuke Nakamura dressed in a full, new Celtic kit, and I even saw several locals in the shirts themselves. At first I thought I shouldn't have been too surprised. After all, Nakamura is worshipped over there, but I must admit I was stunned when I discovered that the hotel I was staying in was screening one of Celtic's Scottish Premier League matches live. There was a genuine interest in the Hoops over there when Nakamura was a Celtic player, and I feel it simply underlines the marketing opportunities which can become available with the signing of foreign talents."**

As 2010 became 2011, John enjoyed the New Year celebrations with his family in Stewarton. However, his brother Eddie, a season ticket holder who lives in the East Midlands of England and travels back up to Scotland for almost every Celtic match, was unable to join them due to the horrendous weather making unnecessary travelling unadvisable at best. For this reason, he asked John to use his ticket for the derby match at Ibrox on the second of January, the day Georgios Samaras **"dined in hell"** (as the Green Brigade dubbed it the following weekend), and scored a match-winning double.

At this stage, it is noteworthy that John Cassidy had not attended a Glasgow derby since November 1976 (when Joe Craig scored the only goal in a one-nil Celtic victory at Ibrox). Therefore, I felt it was reasonable to ask John what differences and similarities he noticed with regards the latter modern games and those of decades gone by. John said: **"Well, for a start, Ibrox is an all-seater stadium now, so that was one noticeable difference. The fans are also segregated far better than they were in the past, but in terms of the singing and chanting, it was mostly the same old stuff.**

Whilst supporters in the ground are safer than they were once upon a time, the vitriol was certainly still there. Most importantly though, the feeling of winning at Ibrox was just as good as it used to be, that's for sure!"

Nowadays, it is easier for John to watch Celtic in Asia than ever before: **"Whenever we reach the Champions League proper, all of the matches are broadcast live, so they're never difficult to find. However, for a time domestic games were somewhat less predictable with regards their coverage, but since 'Goal TV' began to cover Scottish matches, that has all changed, and I can watch the games pretty much whenever I like now, except when timing and work dictate otherwise."**

Two of the last occasions on which John saw the Bhoys live were when Juventus visited Celtic Park in 2013, and then the subsequent victory over Dundee United the following weekend. The last time that John watched the Hoops in person though, was when Elfsborg came to town, in late July 2013. Prior to this match, I was fortunate enough to meet John and one of his sons, Sean, outside the ground. Granted, we only spoke for about five minutes as the Glaswegian rain fell and kick-off approached, but I valued the chat nonetheless. Of course, it is always enjoyable to speak to Celtic supporters living around the world on the internet, but to have the opportunity to meet them in person and shake their hand is something special. As for the game itself, John and Sean witnessed a slim one-nil victory, with Sean particularly enjoying experiencing the huddle for the first time. Now, as time progresses and his sons gradually grow older, John has noticed that they are beginning to take an increasing interest in all things Celtic, and it gives him hope that he may not have **"failed"** (as he joked earlier) in this regard after all.

Having moved to Singapore in 2009, John continues to enjoy life in the Far East. Whilst he travels to Scotland to visit family and friends (as well as watch some football) on a roughly annual basis, he has no plans to return to the country permanently at this stage. This means that John Cassidy will continue to follow Celtic from afar for now, and I feel that Scotland's loss in this regard is most certainly Singapore's gain.

"Who Is That With Charlie Tully?"

There are few more recognisable names associated with Celtic Football Club than that of Charles Patrick Tully. Charlie, as he was widely known, was an inside forward, born in Belfast on the eleventh of July 1924. In his early years, it was clear that he possessed a natural talent for football, and as such, he joined local side Belfast Celtic in 1942 whilst he was still a teenager. As he learned his footballing trade in his home city, it took the young Charlie more than a little while to really stamp his own personal footprint on the destiny of Belfast Celtic. At the end of a brief loan spell to Cliftonville in 1944, Tully returned to his parent team and prospered, scoring the winning goal against Glentoran in the Irish Cup Final of 1947, securing the Irish Cup for his club for the final time in their ultimately finite existence.

As Tully left the club in June 1948, he replaced his fame in Belfast with almost wholly unmitigated stardom in Glasgow. It is evident that Celtic (Glasgow) saw Charlie's potential, as they paid a fair price to get their man. After all, eight thousand pounds was a significant sum of money in post-war Britain. Charlie made his debut for his new team on the fourteenth of August that same year, in a goalless draw against Morton at Celtic Park. Whilst the result wasn't ideal, the performance appeared to be an improvement on those seen by the supporters the previous season, when the Hoops came within only a few points of relegation as is discussed in the chapter devoted to Bobby Evans. And so, as Charlie Tully took to the field for the first time at Celtic Park, his new side had not won a piece of major silverware for over a decade. Thankfully though, the young man from Belfast with both incredible skill and an infamous personality would help to change all of that. Weeks later, he was rewarded with his first full international cap, as Northern Ireland lost by six goals to two against England in Belfast.

However, even with Charlie's wonderful talent in the side, it would be a lie to say that Celtic's fortunes were turned round almost instantaneously by his arrival. At the end of his first season at Celtic Park, Tully was part of a team which won only twelve of their thirty league matches and finished sixth in the league table, behind the likes of East Fife, Falkirk, and the Champions, Rangers, who became the first side to lift a domestic treble at the end of the 1948–49 season. To put this into context, it wasn't until the thirtieth of October 1948, the eighth match of the league campaign, that Celtic and Tully would win their first league match together at Easter Road in Edinburgh.

Weeks prior to this, Tully began to make his first notable impact as a Celtic player, scoring a wonderful goal in a three-all draw with Albion Rovers in early September. This was recalled by one football correspondent in **"The Glasgow Herald"** the following Monday, as follows. It is interesting to note that this would be the last match played by Tommy Bogan for Celtic Football Club before he completed his transfer to Preston North End (he would play for both Manchester United and Aberdeen in the future also, amongst a few other sides).

"Five minutes later Milne, also at midfield glided the ball inside to Evans when the usual punt upfield was expected. A goal in a thousand resulted. Evans passed on to Bogan, and the latter continued the movement on the ground by squaring it to Tully. Out came the home defence to indulge in offside tactics that had already proved successful if irritating. But the quick-witted Tully was not to be caught in the trap, dribbled through, and, drawing the goalkeeper out, finished a perfect move with a perfect shot."

A few weeks later, Tully would face his Club's biggest rivals, Rangers, for the first time in a League Cup match at Celtic Park. The Hoops would triumph somewhat unexpectedly by three goals to one that day, and despite the fact he didn't score himself, there was one man above all others who came in for mountains of praise from all and sundry following the game, as this newspaper report highlights:

"The person who must take most of the blame or credit [clearly the journalist who penned this piece felt that you could delete one of the previous words as appropriate depending on who you supported!] **was Tully, undoubtedly the cleverest forward**

in the last 10 years of Scottish Football. There were occasions on Saturday on which the Irishman beat three would-be tacklers in the space of as many yards – and each time by a different manoeuvre. His artistry was almost tantalising, though that did not excuse several of the lunges made at him."

Although I am aware that I have largely criticised their start to the league campaign thus far, it is worthy of recall that the Hoops did pick up their first piece of silverware since the end of World War Two in late September that year, even if it was only the Glasgow Cup. However, having used the word **"only"** above, it is unlikely that many of the eighty-seven thousand strong crowd (yes, eighty-seven thousand) in attendance would have felt that the trophy was only of minor importance. At that stage, Celtic hadn't won the Glasgow Cup since 1940, and their opponents hadn't done so for several decades. For a time, it looked like Third Lanark would be the winners, as they were awarded a penalty whilst one-nil to the good.

Thankfully for Celtic, the ball hit the post and rolled tantalisingly along the goal line as both spectators and players alike held their breath. Eventually, it struck the other post and bounced out, as time returned to a seemingly normal pace and the match continued. Thanks to an equalising goal from William Gallacher (Patsy's son) and a brace from Jock Weir, the Hoops would be victorious, and, whilst this victory did not ignite their season fully, it seemed to bolster their confidence levels and help them along towards their first league victories of the campaign as mentioned above. Charlie did play, but the man who was already being described as **"the darling of the Celtic crowd"** was not quite as impressive as he had been previously against Rangers.

The next season, 1949–50, Celtic improved to fourteen wins from thirty matches and secured a fifth place finish, but once again Rangers dominated, winning both the Scottish League Championship and the Scottish Cup. Despite this, Charlie Tully continued to impress both Celtic and non-Celtic supporters alike with his talent and ingenuity. However, controversy would find him only weeks into the new season, as an incident between himself and Rangers defender Sammy Cox caused chaos on the terracing at Ibrox Park in late August, 1949.

For the sake of brevity, I shall attempt to summarise the events of that day without going into extensive detail (after all, one could virtually write a short chapter on this affair alone). For the third consecutive season, Celtic had been drawn alongside Rangers in the group stages of the Scottish League Cup, and having lost to Celtic in the first group match at Parkhead, Rangers were out for revenge a few weeks later in the return tie. It was one of those days where the Ibrox side seemed to have every refereeing decision go in their favour, and regardless of whether you're young or old, I'm sure you must have some experience of what I'm talking about.

With this in mind, allow me to describe the following turn of events. With the match goalless, Charlie Tully and Sammy Cox chased a ball back towards the Rangers goal around half an hour into the game. Cox won the footrace by the slightest of margins, allowing the Rangers goalkeeper, Bobby Brown (who would go on to manage Scotland in the future) to gather the ball. However, as Brown did so, Cox swung his foot around wildly and kicked Tully in the stomach, causing him to drop to the ground in significant pain. Incredibly, and yet all too familiarly, the referee waved play on as if nothing had happened, leaving the great Tully rolling around in the mud, winded.

This decision was seen as blatantly biased by the Celtic supporters gathered behind the goal and they were so incensed by what they had just witnessed that a riot erupted. Bottles flew through the Glasgow air and fights broke out across the large terrace, as the police battled to gain control of proceedings. Supporters spilled onto the running track next to the pitch and play was suspended for a time. Ironically, this stoppage allowed Tully, who was still down, to finally receive some form of treatment, and he was eventually able to play on when the match restarted.

As I continue this tale, I shouldn't laugh – but I must be honest and say that if I didn't chuckle slightly, I'd probably cry, because the parallels which can be drawn with this match, played over sixty years ago, with even the final encounters with Rangers before their ultimate demise are striking. Prior to the borderline assault on Tully, Celtic had been the better team according to most reports; hitting the bar, missing another good chance and generally dominating the majority of the match thus far. However, moments after the restart (post-riot, the embers of which had not been fully extinguished in the stands) Rangers took the lead.

Ten minutes into the second half, Rangers, now shooting towards the goal which the Celtic supporters were housed behind, were awarded a somewhat dubious penalty by the referee, sparking another invasion of the running track (the initial riot on the terracing had never really ceased entirely, it had just petered out to a large degree before reigniting within moments of this latest decision in the home side's favour). Playing the role of the 'Devil's Advocate' though, one newspaper reporter for **"The Glasgow Herald"** stated he thought the decision was correct, **"although Waddell would not have regained control, even unimpeded"**, but nonetheless, the Celtic fans, as well as several players (Mr Tully included), were far from impressed with the referee.

As the quality of the football on display began to deteriorate rapidly, so did the quality of the tackling, as certain players, clearly antagonised by the increasingly vitriolic atmosphere at Ibrox flew into challenge after challenge. One Rangers player, the striker Willie Thornton, even had a bone in his foot broken by a tackle from Celtic's Alec Boden. The match finished two-nil to the hosts, and **"The Glasgow Herald"** reflected on the encounter as follows.

"Rangers were not the better footballing side, but they did accept the few chances that the opposing defence allowed. Celtic have recovered much of their traditional poise, and in the first half particularly were far superior in passing and running into open space. But they sorely need a finisher."

Despite the fact the match was over, the story of the incident involving Cox and Tully was to continue for some time, until the Scottish Football Association, in their infinite wisdom, decided it would be best to punish both Sammy Cox for kicking Charlie Tully, and Charlie Tully for having, well, the audacity to be kicked by Sammy Cox. This farcical outcome was challenged by Robert

Kelly at an S.F.A. Council Meeting only weeks later, who demanded that Tully's name be cleared as he was the innocent victim in all of this. However, his motion was defeated by twenty five votes to five, with the Council officially stating that **"Tully had simulated any slight injury he had received."**

At the end of May, Celtic would travel to Rome for the first of two friendly matches between themselves and Lazio (who were celebrating their fiftieth anniversary that year), with the latter due to be played in Glasgow in September. However, the first encounter turned out to be anything but friendly, as both John McPhail and Leandro Remondini were sent off for fighting in front of an angry, hostile crowd. The match itself ended goalless, but that is not why I am recalling this story to you, for not only did Celtic play a football match in Rome, they grasped their opportunity to see many of the city's famous sights.

Charlie Tully, who was of course a Roman Catholic, recounts some of his thoughts and feelings regarding the visit below, in an excerpt from his book **"Passed To You"**, which has been out of print for several years by all accounts and is therefore somewhat difficult to procure a copy of:

"The team stayed in a plush hotel in Rome. Believe me, until you've seen the Holy City you haven't lived. At least that's the way I feel about it. We saw the sights, the wonderful buildings and the fountains and we were all very much impressed, including the non-Catholics. Whatever religion you may be, Rome is a sight worth seeing."

"We visited St Peter's Basilica where the Pope gave an audience to 80,000 people. He read out many messages to pilgrims in many languages and it was wonderful for us to hear him announce that "the Glasgow Celtic from Scotland" were with us today."

"No matter what kind of hard face I put on things while I'm playing, I'm really sentimental at heart. And I could have cried when I heard His Holiness mention us. I wished that my mother and father and my wife could have been with me. I wished, too, that we could have had a private audience. I've won a lot of medals and international caps since joining Glasgow Celtic, but

this was the most exciting and satisfying moment of them all. No prize or honour could ever be greater than this."

Now, so high was the esteem in which the Celtic support held Tully that this visit to Rome spawned one of the many famous jokes (or funny stories, I suppose you could call them) regarding the great man. Essentially, the tale said that two pilgrims were together in St Peter's Square, awaiting the emergence of the Pope high above the plaza where they standing. However, as proceedings began, two men strolled out onto the Papal balcony, rather than one. Having paused and strained his (or her) eyes for a moment, one of the pilgrims turned to the other and said: **"Who's that with Charlie Tully?"**

Moving on, with that event confined to the history books (such as this one), the next campaign was to be thoroughly more enjoyable for those who followed the Hoops. Early in the 1950–51 season, Celtic defeated Lazio (who had finished fourth in the previous season's Serie A table) by four goals to nil in the second of their two 'friendly' ties, with all of the goals coming from striker John McPhail, the man who had been sent off a few months earlier in Rome.

This was to be a sign of things to come, as Celtic once again won the Glasgow Cup, in a three-two replay triumph against Partick Thistle, only twenty-four hours after they had previously drawn one-all at Hampden Park. Whilst the Celts once again slipped into mid-table mediocrity in the league (finishing seventh as Hibernian won the title by a large margin from Rangers), they did manage to summon up a gutsy performance to defeat the eventual league runners-up in September, banishing the demons of their meeting a year earlier. Once again, Tully played an integral role in Celtic's forward line, helping his side to a three-two victory.

"Tully gobbled up the excellent pass and, drawing Young, crossed meticulously for the newcomer Weir to head a perfect goal."

"The man who made most of the difference to Celtic was, however, Tully. Sometimes his trickery ends in the deception only of himself and his team-mates, but when he uses the ball he really uses it. As he prepares to cross or pass he seems to say, "Put your

head or foot in the scoring position and I'll not be an inch out with the ball.""

Regardless, by the turn of the year the Hoops' main focus was not on the league, but on the Scottish Cup, as they began to quietly progress through the rounds, defeating formidable opponents in such as East Fife, Hearts, and Raith Rovers on their way to the final. They also played amateur village team Duns from the borders, as well as dominating Aberdeen at Celtic Park in the quarter finals. One goal separated Celtic from each of their opponents throughout several rounds of the tournament, and while this may show they did not emphatically defeat all of the sides they faced along the way, it does highlight some of the steely determination which all of the Celtic players must have possessed in order for them to continually emerge victorious.

Tully, as was so often the case, grabbed the limelight in the three-two semi-final victory against the aforementioned Raith Rovers, despite the best efforts of the Kirkcaldy side to ruin the day for the Hoops.

"Tully has been a brilliant player in the past, and his lapses from grace, say the critics of his critics, have to some extent been the result of the praise lavished upon him. All who watched the Irishman on Saturday will be excused for running the risk of gilding the Tully lily. Practically the only orthodox item Tully contributed to the game was his straightforward swing at the ball when he scored the winning goal barely nine minutes from time; on almost every other occasion on which he was in possession – and his team mates wisely plied him with the ball as often as possible – he provided some delightful titbit of football. Yet each caress of the ball, each sway and swerve, was calculated to bring about his opponents' downfall – there was no artistry for the mere sake of artistry. Tully was indeed so masterly that one anticipated his indulging just for a moment – and just for the devilment of it – in one of the tricks that have not been to his credit in games gone by. Of them however, there was nary a sign, which is to the advantage of Tully and all the rest of us."

And so, for the first time since the Scottish Cup triumph of 1937, Celtic had a chance to win the famous old trophy once more. The last occasion upon which they had faced Motherwell in the final was in 1933, and the score from that day at Hampden was to be repeated eighteen years later, as an early goal from John McPhail was enough to win the Scottish Cup for the Celts. Although Charlie Tully played in Scottish Cup Final of 1951, the plaudits from the press and the crowd of almost one hundred and thirty-two thousand people were mainly directed at one man, Celtic's goalkeeper, George Hunter. He had made his debut for the Hoops only months earlier in the Scottish Cup, and has been since been described as critical to the success of that campaign. Sadly, in the months to come, Hunter would be struck down by tuberculosis, and while he returned to Celtic in 1952, he would never truly be the same again.

Now, it is worth remembering that at this point, Charlie Tully had just won the first of only six major honours he would have to his name by the end of his time at Parkhead, and whilst Celtic were far from fantastic at this stage in their history, I am sure we can all appreciate how sweet some sort of success must have tasted for the Celtic supporters of the day, especially after such an extensive trophy doubt. I suppose, to many, the only comparisons they could hope to draw would be with the barren years of the 1990's, but I digress.

During the course of the next two seasons, Celtic would again slip down the league table, this time falling into disappointingly poor ninth and eighth place finishes respectively. However, as is so often the case in football, a truly great moment which will be spoken of by generations to come can occur even in the some of the darkest times in a Club's history. Step forward, Mr Tully!

In February 1953, Celtic played Falkirk away from home in the Scottish Cup, having defeated Eyemouth United and Stirling Albion in the previous rounds. Celtic won the match by three goals to two, but one of the strikes was truly special. Charlie Tully, a skilful passer of the ball, was assigned the duty of delivering any corners into the opposition's box, as ever. Celtic trailed by two goals to nil at half time, and to say they faced an uphill battle would have been an understatement. However, around ten minutes into the second half, they won a corner kick, and Charlie Tully strode over to the corner flag and placed the ball on the turf at his feet.

He whipped a fearsome ball into the box, which arced high through the air and flew inside the far post (as Charlie saw it) for a goal for Celtic. However, whilst players and fans alike began to celebrate such a feat, the referee saw things a little differently (not an unusual occurrence in Scottish Football). He insisted that Tully must have placed the ball outside of the 'D' at the corner flag and disallowed the goal, asking Charlie to retake the corner...so he did, repeating the process of placing the ball on the ground and calmly taking a few steps back, before he struck it and scored again!

This was far from a fluke as some would claim, as not only did Tully repeat the feat twice in the space of a few moments, but he had also done so previously in an international match against England for his native Northern Ireland in 1952. The initial disallowed goal caused a minor invasion of the running track by Celtic supporters, who had been forced out of the terracing by the brief celebrations which had ensued before the referee's decision became apparent. However, upon Tully's repeat performance, the Celtic fans in attendance went absolutely ballistic, having seen Charlie overcome what they perceived to be a biased referee through nothing other than sheer pluck and almost terrifying ability, causing a somewhat larger invasion, and a slight delay of proceedings.

Around five minutes later, Willie Fernie equalised, and this resulted in an even more significant incursion of supporters onto the track and field. The Celtic players, concerned that the referee may see fit to abandon the game if things became notably out of hand, urged the away fans back onto the terracing which, to be fair to those in attendance, was fitted with poorly maintained crush barriers not fit to safely accommodate that size of a travelling support, as was discussed in sections of the press in the days after the match.

And, as you can perhaps imagine, when John McGrory (a forward who faded in and out of the starting line-up over the years) shot and scored what turned out to be the winning goal to complete the dramatic comeback and give the Hoops the lead, Celtic supporters swarmed out onto the field yet again. They surrounded McGrory, and in their delirious attempts to celebrate with their new found hero, they proceeded to crush him somewhat, forcing him to receive treatment from the Club's trainer before returning to the field for the final minutes of the match.

At the end of the 1952–53 season, Celtic became the unlikely winners of the Coronation Cup, defeating both English and Scottish heavyweight opposition along the way, although Tully did not play in the final due to injury. Many have said that without his performances in the earlier rounds, particularly the semi-final against Manchester United, then Celtic would perhaps not have reached the final nor won the trophy. Before suffering an injury in the match against the Old Trafford outfit, he created two wonderful opportunities for his teammates to score, as well as several which they did not manage to convert, including a chance from which Bobby Collins struck the bar:

"No Celtic player was, however, more shrewd in the first hour of the match than Tully. In the twenty fourth minute when, with Crompton looking into the sun and groping for a high ball, Collins headed across goal, Tully must have been tempted to shoot even though his angle was acute. The neat side step with which he outwitted McNulty and the chipped back pass to Peacock were worthy of the great goal that Peacock shot in his stride from just inside the penalty area."

"In the fifty third minute Tully controlled a Rollo pass and as Mochan accelerated down the centre lofted the ball over Chilton's head; the timing was perfect and the centre forward placed his right-foot shot into the corner of the net as Crompton advanced from his goal."

"It might have been an even greater day for Tully had he not been injured. When in the dying seconds he pulled a muscle and kicked the ball indiscriminately towards the corner flag only he knew that he had damaged a muscle; the throng are so used to his peculiarities when he is hurt no one pays a great deal of attention."

Undoubtedly, Tully was one of the stars of the show as Celtic, far from the pre-tournament favourites, went on to win the competition. In the following days, the Celtic team posed for an official picture with the Coronation Cup at Celtic Park. Three members of the team I have chosen for this book – Bobby Evans, Charlie Tully, and Jimmy McGrory – all stand directly next to each other in this photograph which, with the benefit of hindsight, captures some of the greatest men in the Football Club's history. In the front row, with the Coronation Cup placed on the ground between them, are sat Jock Stein and Sean Fallon, the pair who would go on to lead Celtic to their greatest triumph of all, less than fifteen years later, under the Lisbon sun.

The following season, 1953–54, was a mixed affair for Tully. Whilst he continued to impress with some magnificent displays of natural ability, he suffered **"ligament damage"** in early November through a poor tackle in a match against Hibernian, which kept him out of competitive action until February. And so, Celtic, without the great Charlie, were left to carry on, as Tully spent a couple of months with his leg in plaster. This damage also stopped Tully from appearing against England at Goodison Park only days after the aforementioned Hibernian fixture.

Several weeks prior to his injury, Tully travelled to Ibrox for the first Glasgow derby of the league campaign. The two sides had drawn one-each there a little over a fortnight earlier in the Glasgow Cup, before Rangers hammered Celtic by four goals to nil at Parkhead in the subsequent replay. However, having put that heavy defeat behind them, Celtic managed to leave Ibrox with a respectable point after another one-all draw, although in truth, the Hoops could well have won the match yet again, had their finishing been of a better quality.

By all accounts, Tully was incredible that day, in that typically Glaswegian type of driving, unrelenting and seemingly horizontal rain. Whilst several players struggled to adapt to such difficult conditions, Charlie seemed to revel in them, knowing that his trickery combined with such a slippery surface would allow him the opportunity to put several opposition players onto their backsides as he dribbled around them. To say that this remarkable performance was related to the fact that the relevant international selectors had travelled over to watch the match would be entirely speculative, but it is likely that Tully was aware of their presence there. The following quote, taken from one newspaper article written in the aftermath of the match, not only alludes to the incredible display of one Charlie Tully, but also to the two differing footballing styles employed by the sides at the time:

"Tully made an auspicious return to the Celtic team, and from the inside left position frequently baffled his immediate opponent, McColl, with dexterous footwork and sprayed inviting passes all around. McPhail in particular cooperated and the result was some delightful football on the ground. There was however, as in the recent past, little indication that Celtic have recovered the art of shooting accurately and strongly."

"Rangers for their part were far from idle in attack, though their methods of threatening the Celtic goal were entirely different. Rangers, indeed, had only one forward of note for almost all of the 90 minutes – but what a forward he was. Waddell has rarely played a better part for his side. Almost invariably he had the beating of an injudicious Fallon, who seemed short of match practice, and his crossing with either foot was superb. Bell, Haughney and Stein were alive to the danger of these far-flung crosses, however, and the most unenterprising other Rangers forwards did little to relieve Waddell of the burden of attack he carried in so distinguished a manner throughout."

However, even after all of that, this match was not one that was remembered for the action on the field, but the events which occurred on the surrounding terracing. Unusually, this derby match was not an all ticket affair, and even in the horrendous weather, over sixty thousand spectators made their way to Ibrox Park to take in the afternoon's proceedings. Half an hour before kick-off, the ground was essentially as full as it was going to become, and as the fans awaited the beginning of the game itself, a large orange banner appeared in the Rangers end. Perhaps unsurprisingly, some Celtic supporters soon produced a large green and white flag which they displayed at the other end of the ground.

Whilst the orange banner was allowed, at least initially, to be displayed unchallenged, the police soon moved into the Celtic end in an attempt to remove the aforementioned green and white flag, which they did, arresting two men in the process. Midway through the first half, officers once again waded into the away support to remove another flag, this time having to avoid several bottles being thrown in their direction as they did so. Of course, the supposed censorship of one group of supporters over another only added to the tension and bad feeling within the stadium, but upon the arrival of the half time break, it became clear the police intended to enter the Rangers end of the ground.

When they did so, in an attempt to recover the orange banner (which had disappeared briefly after the Celtic fans flag had been seized) as well as some of the other **"blue favours"** on show, **"fighting and bottle throwing seemed to be going on at various spots"** according to one newspaper. As the violence intensified, thousands of innocent Rangers supporters spilled out of the terracing and onto the field in an attempt to escape the chaotic scenes unfolding behind them. This led to many being led away by ambulance workers with injuries, whilst the remainder were eventually ushered back into the stand for the second half (which was delayed by several minutes) by mounted police. The aforementioned newspaper report later reflected: **"Nothing on the field justified the trouble. It looked as if the Rangers element resented the police taking action similar to that at the Celtic end."**

Returning to the football itself, regardless of the relative madness in the stands that day, the international selectors were clearly impressed enough by the performance of Charlie Tully to include him in the squad for Northern Ireland's upcoming World Cup qualifier against Scotland at Windsor Park, Belfast. Whilst Scotland would run out the victors by three goals to one, it is noteworthy that the home side were rather unfortunate not to take anything from the game, with a mixture of bad luck and incredible goalkeeping damaging their chances. As the following quote from **"The Glasgow Herald"** dictates, Charlie was magnificent for a large part of the match, before an injury seriously affected his playing capability and forced him to leave the field for ten minutes of treatment. However, upon his return, he terrorised Scotland once again as they **"held grimly on to the ridiculous lead"**.

"Then there was Tully, a Tully of infinite grace and delightful craft, a Tully who for 45 minutes baffled Evans and others of the Scots as easily as he would have flicked on or off his bow tie, and set the Irish attack in motion with passes of superb judgement. In one minute Tully was more of an inside forward than Fleming and Watson combined in ninety."

As you may have gathered, it was becoming clear by this stage that whilst Tully's talents were incredible, his body was beginning to suffer the tolls of the consistent kicks and knocks which he received over the years. In light of the aforementioned serious injury he would suffer in the following weeks, Charlie Tully would not return until February. However, upon doing so, he helped Celtic to their first league title in sixteen years (which they had all but officially sealed at Easter Road in a three-nil over Hibernian). Therefore, with the Championship in the bag, Celtic and Tully travelled to Hampden for the Scottish Cup Final against Aberdeen a week later. The Hoops edged past Aberdeen by two goals to one, although Tully was not quite as prominent as he had been on big occasions in the past.

The match itself would be remembered again, by one journalist at least, mainly for the off-field disorder rather than the course of the play. **"The Glasgow Herald's Football Correspondent"** began his article the following Monday by saying: **"...for many the spectacle of the final was seriously affected by the deplorable behaviour of a section of spectators who may believe that they are Celtic supporters but who are nothing of the kind and are indeed a disgrace to the club."**

He continued, after praising the Football Club and the players themselves: **"Celtic are, however, cursed with a section of hooligans whose conduct is an outrage to every decent, reasonable person. Even in the knowledge that the club which they profess to support disapprove of the flying of flags or banners other than of the club colours, this shocking minority continue to flaunt the flag of Eire."**

Finally, he states: **"I seriously suggest that Celtic and the police so arrange for the future that we never again see a tricolour on the terracing. What the Aberdeen players, officials and supporters must think of Glasgow is easy to imagine. A fortnight ago they had the Union Jack thrust in their faces with the accompanying barrage of allegedly patriotic noise and now they get the tricolour and comparable inanity."**

Returning once again to the story of Charlie Tully, as was mentioned previously in this book, Celtic would go on to win the League Cup for the first time in 1956, defeating Partick Thistle by three goals to nil in a replay. Charlie, who featured on the right wing rather than on the left where he could usually be found, had a magnificent game, as the following excerpt shows:

"Nevertheless during spells in which Tully was brought into the scheme of Celtic's attack there was an obvious menace to Thistle; sooner or later, one felt, this mercurial player who was having one of his best days of dexterous ball control, astute passing and intelligent crossing and corner kicking would contrive such a scoring chance as not even his finicky colleagues could squander. In the event it was Tully more than any other player who won the cup for his side."

In 1957, Celtic defended the trophy in remarkable fashion by beating Rangers by the now infamous scoreline of seven goals to one. While Tully did not score that day, he came remarkably close in a match which, in all honesty, could have ended in an even heavier defeat for the Ibrox side, who were completely and utterly outclassed by a Celtic side who had not played to such a level **"since their Coronation Cup days"** according to one newspaper report.

"Not one Celt, however, but did not contribute handsomely to the team's glorious day. The effect of the now restrained but clever as ever Tully should not be minimised. Perhaps only Fernie of all footballers in Scotland could have emulated Tully's first-half feat of ball manipulation which enabled him to outwit Baird, Davis, Valentine and Caldow. Then as his team mates poised themselves for the chip back from the goal line Tully struck like lightning with his right foot and the ball cannoned off the very edge of the near post, passed between Nevin and the goal line, and

out of play beyond the far post. The goal of the century had been within a fraction of an inch of achievement."

High praise indeed, and an indication that whilst Tully may not have been as athletically able as he was in his younger days, he still possessed that innate ability to control a football, as if by some form of black magic, beating players before they even possessed a grasp of what he was attempting. To this day, Charlie Tully is remembered in the first verse of the Celtic support's song about that famous victory:

"I see Tully running down the line,
He slips the ball past Valentine,
It's nodded down by 'Teazy Weazy',
And Sammy Wilson makes it look so easy!"

In 1958, as Charlie Tully's Celtic career entered its final season, the Hoops ran out two-nil winners against Clyde in the early stages of League Cup. In what was a rather pass remarkable game in certain aspects, Tully was praised yet again for dancing through the defence with a **"ballet effort"**. However, the same match will also be remembered as the competitive debut of a Celtic youngster, one Billy McNeill, who replaced the injured Bobby Evans in defence. Interestingly, Bertie Auld scored a magnificent goal that day too, as the embers of one Celtic side began to slowly fizzle out and a new flame of youth was kindled, as has been so often the case at Parkhead.

In October of the same year, Charlie Tully found himself strolling along Sauchiehall Street, minding his own business. As he approached a newspaper stand, he saw a headline attached to the side which stated that Pope Pius XII had been given the Last Rites, having suffered a serious deterioration in his health during the night. As Charlie rushed towards the stall in order to purchase a paper and discover what had happened to the Pontiff, he caught sight of the headline attached to another side of stall, which read something along the lines of **"Tully Handed International Call-Up"**. Considering that he hadn't been selected for international duty since 1954, it is said that Charlie was unsure as to which news headline had shocked him more. Regardless, Charlie Tully would appear for his country one last time, in front of over one hundred and twenty thousand people in a six-two loss to Spain at the Bernabeu in Madrid (the same score as his debut a decade earlier).

On the thirty-first of January 1959, Charlie Tully made his final appearance for Celtic, although nobody at the time thought it would the last time he would feature for the side. The Hoops faced Albion Rovers at Celtic Park in the Scottish Cup and, despite his age, Tully shone brightly one last time. On a terrible pitch, which was still frozen in large parts: **"Charlie Tully came prancing into the game, with vintage footwork...Tully was emerging as the Celtic mastermind. One right wing wiggle and waggle took him past three Rovers before he passed."**

"The 50th minute brought Tully trouble as he went down heavily in a raid with a leg knock. To a cheer from thousands of relieved Celtic fans, Tully came back two minutes later."

However, that seemingly innocuous **"leg-knock"** would spell the end at Celtic for Charlie. He had been appearing less and less often as time had passed, and whilst he recovered from the injury within weeks, he was struck down with a bout of flu upon his return to training (as so many of his colleagues were too). As the season ended, there was to be no last cameo for Charlie Tully. He was released by the Club only weeks into the new season and, in November, was given a final send off at the Celtic Supporters Rally by approximately three thousand people, all of whom were sad to see him go, but immensely proud of all he had helped the Club to achieve during his time there.

Charlie then went on to become player manager of Cork Hibernians in Ireland, before he spent time in purely managerial roles at Bangor and Portadown. He would return to Bangor in 1968 and lead them to their first senior trophy. Unsurprisingly, he was a somewhat controversial manager, regularly clashing with referees and criticising decisions which he felt to be unjust. However, he remained a tremendously popular figure and a regular at Celtic Park whenever he returned to Scotland. This was reflected famously through two incidents which took place in

1970 when the Hoops faced Fiorentina in the quarter finals of the European Cup at Celtic Park and, subsequently upon the visit of Leeds United to Hampden Park in the following semi-final six weeks later.

On both occasions, Charlie found himself in the press boxes pretending to be a reporter of some type, with a jacket and trilby style hat to match such an appearance. Now, I'd hope that you would know by now that Charlie was a lively character, and not one who tended to hide his emotions. With this in mind, it is perhaps no surprise that, whilst in the act of celebrating a Celtic goal on each of the two nights previously discussed, Tully threw his hat into the air. Each time, it landed in amongst the true pressmen and he drew attention to himself when, by all accounts, he wasn't strictly supposed to. Interestingly, against Fiorentina, the hat landed on an Italian journalist who turned around angrily, recognised the man celebrating, and proceeded to totally alter his demeanour, returning the hat to its rightful owner and asking for an autograph whilst doing so.

A little over a year later, having spent the night in his local pub discussing football and other business with a good friend as he so often did, Charlie Tully died in his sleep on the twenty-seventh of July 1971, at the age of only forty-seven. Despite fears for their safety, Jock Stein lead an official party from Celtic Football Club to Belfast for the funeral, and watched Billy McNeill, the European Cup winning Celtic captain (who had played with Tully on his debut), help to carry the great man to his grave, along with Charlie's teammate and friend, Bertie Peacock. Charles Patrick Tully is buried in Milltown Cemetery, Belfast, and will forever be remembered as one of the greatest players and one of the most vibrant personalities ever to have worn the famous green and white Hoops.

He is a Celtic legend.

"Charlie Tully Dead"

"Charlie Tully, one of the greatest personalities ever to play for Celtic, died of a heart attack in his Belfast home today. He was 47."

"Tully, 'Laughing Cavalier' of Celtic"

"Charles Patrick Tully, laughing cavalier of the great Celtic teams of the late forties and fifties died early today in his sleep at his Belfast home. Tully, who was 47, had a heart complaint."

"The remarkable Tully was a gifted footballer and a knowledgeable one, but most of all he was a "character".

"Tully, born on July 13 ("I just missed the Twelfth"), 1924, was a great Celt and a great Irishman."

"When Tully joined Celtic in the close season of 1948–49 they were at a low ebb. The previous season they had just escaped the humiliation of dropping down to the Second Division."

"But Tully's arrival helped to change Celtic's fortunes."

"In 1951 they won the Scottish Cup; in 1953 the Coronation Cup; and in 1954 the Scottish League Championship and Scottish Cup."

"Then, in 1957 came, perhaps, Tully's greatest moment – when Celtic beat Rangers 7–1 in the League Cup Final."

"Good Times"

"Charlie was one of the very first big-money players in Britain – but he had to go to Southern Ireland to get it. Celtic freed Tully with great reluctance, and he signed for Cork Hibs for the princely sum of £40 a week."

"I saw his first match in Dundalk where, after the splendour of Hampden, Parkhead and Ibrox, he had to change in an old railway carriage."

"I remember him telling his buddies John McPhail and Sean Fallon later how he scored the only goal of the game – "I beat two leprechauns, dribbled through a cabbage patch and tricked the keeper with a body swerve.""

"Tully seldom missed a mid-week game at Parkhead, though it meant travelling from Belfast. Always a wisecracker, Tully could read more out of a game than almost anyone I ever knew."

"The Celtic team and everyone at Parkhead were shocked when they heard the news."

"Tully played in the same team as manager Jock Stein and was championed by former chairman Sir Robert Kelly, who always reckoned Charlie was something of a card."

"Tully leaves a wife, son, and daughter."

The first ever Celtic team - 1888

Dan Doyle

Willie Loney

Jimmy Quinn

Jimmy McMenemy

Alec McNair

Celtic win every competition they enter - 1908

Hampden burns - 1909

Patsy Gallagher

Jimmy McGrory

John Thomson

The funeral of John Thomson - 1931

Willie Lyon

Maley, McGrory and the rest celebrate their Scottish Cup triumph - 1937

Bobby Evans

Charlie Tully

Coronation Cup winners - 1953

Bill Boland and his birthday gift from myself and the Celtic support - 2013

"Son, Look Around"

Prior to the UEFA Cup run of 2002–03, Seville was nothing more than a place name you saw on a map to many Celtic supporters, including myself. Equally, to the seven hundred thousand residents of the Spanish city, Celtic were simply one of European football's famous Clubs, albeit one which had not made any serious inroads in Europe for over twenty years. However, by the end of May 2003, the capital of Andalucía would forever be intertwined with the history of Celtic Football Club, and the stories of that week under the Spanish sun will likely outlive us all.

My own tale of Seville most likely began unlike any other, with a trip to a dry ski slope outside Edinburgh. The previous week, Henrik Larsson's late goal in Portugal had sent our family, as well as countless others across the globe, into a state of unbridled ecstasy. If I'm honest, I don't remember too much about the return leg against Boavista itself, for it was all a bit of a blur, but I do remember two things clearly; the nerves, and consequently, the celebrations.

To clarify the next part of this story somewhat, let me say that, whilst my father is an ardent Celtic supporter, he is relatively good at keeping calm, both with regards celebrations and anxious countdowns. Normally, if we are watching a match on television, my dad may celebrate a goal by shouting out, punching the air and clapping his hands, but that's generally about it. Whilst he would leap around like a lunatic as a younger man, he'd be the first to admit that, in the house anyway, it takes a fairly important goal to cause him to actively jump about. However, when Henrik managed to put the ball in the back of the net that night, not only did he leap up, but he ran away down the hall of our house screaming like a madman. To my mum's delight, I continued a family tradition by jumping up and down on top of our new sofa (my grandfather did the same upon Stevie Chalmers' winner in Lisbon, causing my grandmother to tell him off, although he couldn't have cared less at the time).

Regarding the nerves we often experience at matches, whilst I sit there with sweaty palms, anxiously looking at the clock every five seconds, my father will tap his fingers and offer the occasional word of advice to the players. However, in our living room that night, myself, my father, and a well loved family friend, Clare McCourt, kicked every ball and hurled ourselves into every tackle. When the final whistle went, it was I who shot away down the hall screaming and shouting for my mother. My dad, on the other hand, simply sank to his knees with a tear in his eye.

At this stage, I'll be honest and admit I simply couldn't believe it. In all seriousness, I struggled to get my head around it – Celtic, in a European Final. Remember, I had grown up in the 1990's when, with respect to those who gave their all for the Club during that time, Celtic won virtually nothing. I had lived though the pendulum swinging back and forth in Glasgow in more recent times, but I could quantify that, for I sort of expected it. In Scotland, it was largely a two horse race in my early years. However, in Europe, it was more like the Grand National, with fences coming in the form of European giants and difficult away ties. I'd learned all about the glory days of the 1960's and 1970's, yes, but at that time it as thirty-three years since our extra time defeat to Feyenoord and, to a twelve year old at least, that might as well have been the dawn of time itself.

And now, you may be wondering where the aforementioned dry ski slope comes into the equation. Well, having battled past Boavista, it was only a matter of minutes before the rush was on to secure travel to, and accommodation in, Seville. To my knowledge, my father and one of my older cousins were planning on going, but being twelve, I had school, and to be honest with you, I had simply presumed that I would be staying at home because no one had told me any differently.

About a week before the final, I was due to go on a school trip to a dry ski slope outside Edinburgh. However, the night before, my parents called me into the kitchen and told me sternly, **"make sure you don't hurt myself or break any bones tomorrow."** Obviously, my first question was **"why?"**, although I must admit that I was not expecting the answer that followed, which was

"because you're coming to Seville." Obviously, I was ecstatic, and inevitably I became the envy of my friends. However, before the ecstasy could truly begin I had the small task of making sure I didn't end up in casualty the following day, and as a result I was certainly one of the more cautious skiers on the hill. Coincidentally, someone in my class did manage to break their arm during our trip, but thankfully it wasn't me.

In later years, I would discover that my father's initial plan was to wait until the family (including me and my younger sister Cecilia) were dropping him off at Glasgow Airport for his flight to Spain before telling me I would be accompanying him. I must confess that I've never been a tremendous fan of big surprises, and in hindsight I'm pleased he found a reason to inform me in advance. Otherwise, I'm not entirely sure that I could have coped with the excitement of the whole affair. Regardless, on the day before the UEFA Cup Final, ten years ago to the day as I write this, I climbed out of the car with my dad at Glasgow International Airport and waved goodbye to my mother and sister. It was so busy that the queues stretched out of the main terminal building, down the road, and into a second, smaller structure. Television cameras and journalists buzzed about, whilst more and more Hooped individuals clambered out of cars, buses and taxis.

It was the morning, perhaps a little before rush hour, and yet Glasgow Airport was not only busy, but packed to an incredible extent. When I consider my various visits abroad, both as a Celtic supporter and as a holidaymaker, I cannot think of any other time when the terminal has been even half as busy as it was on that day in 2003. For those of you who know the building itself, the first pub, which was just up the old stairs from the check-in desks, had a queue about twice its length filling most of the concourse. Around the corner, we managed to squeeze into another pub (above where the Celtic shop is now located) and, amazingly, we found two seats together through nothing other than sheer good luck.

Having sat down, I finally began to put the scale of the scene in front of me into perspective. Men, women and children,

Celtic supporters of all ages in fact, were everywhere – and I mean, everywhere. Kids who were too young to grasp what was happening were propped alongside the elderly and infirm, some of whom were almost certainly not strictly well enough for travel, and yet there they were. I glanced up at a television in the corner of the bar which displayed the outgoing flights, and almost all of them were destined for Seville. Even those which were not were bound for the Andalucían capital were set to fly to cities in the same general area; Madrid, Faro and Barcelona being notable examples. In truth, a direct flight to Seville was something of a rarity, and I was somewhat impressed by the fact me and my dad were to be on one – or so we thought.

Sometime later, we boarded one of countless Boeing 747's, the planes more commonly known as **"jumbo jets"**, and our trip to Seville began. However, for a couple of reasons, things wouldn't turn out to be quite as smooth as we envisaged. I've never been too keen on flying, but things were fine. Well, that was until our pilot decided to make a little announcement, which went as follows: **"Ladies and gentlemen, I regret to inform you that due to severe air traffic congestion in Seville, they cannot accommodate a plane of our size at present, and therefore we shall be diverting to Faro, where you will be met by a fleet of buses which will transport you to your destination."** Now, for those of you who may not know, Faro is in Portugal, so we had essentially just been told that we'd be landing in the wrong country.

Amazingly, despite a few moans and groans, this didn't really dampen the spirits of the support too much. After all, we were on our way to see Celtic in a European Final. The mood on the plane remained jovial to say the least, with singing filtering through the compartments and bright sunshine shimmering through the windows. As we passed over the Alps, our pilot's voice came through the intercom (amidst the singing of **"Over and Over"** ironically) and came out with the usual line about looking of out one side of the plane if you wanted to see a particular mountain. Being a jumbo jet, about seventy percent of the passengers either weren't next to a window, or were located on the wrong side of the plane, but by chance, me and my dad found ourselves in an ideal position to see the famous mountain range. And so, without a second thought, we gazed outside at the snowy peaks below us, as did another gentleman who was sat alongside us.

A few moments later, without warning, our plane pulled strongly to one side, as a small, private aircraft, which looked like a **"Learjet"**, flew past our windows heading in the opposite direction. Whilst I'm sure the distances involved were significantly larger than they appeared, to all of the Celtic fans on the plane that saw the smaller jet, it was far, far too close for comfort. As the plane tilted, a cacophony of exclamations, ranging from **"Jesus Christ"** to other's beginning with the word **"Holy"** (you can fill in the blank yourself there) erupted from our side of the cabin, as the other passengers attempted to work out what was going on. Perhaps the incident itself had something to do with our reroute to Portugal, or perhaps not, but either way, it gave a lot of people a serious fright which they would not forget quickly.

Anyway, having survived that scare, we touched down in Faro later that afternoon. As soon as the doors were opened, a wall of heat hit us all, and we knew that the next couple of days were going to be markedly different from their equivalents back in Scotland. Having passed through passport control with our hand luggage, a line of officials piled us onto coaches, all of which were bound for Seville. Even in Portugal, the Hoops were a common sight, as planeload after planeload of Celtic supporters disembarked in Faro. After some discussion, me and my father decided that we weren't quite sure how far away Seville actually was. With this in mind, he left the line of passengers being led to the buses and wandered off in search of **"a few cans of juice for the bus journey."**

Now, his quest for some cold carbonated drinks didn't particularly concern me at that stage. After all, I thought it would be some time before the buses left, and prior to departure, I presumed there would be checks made to make sure everyone was onboard. However, I was soon to be proved wrong as I clambered aboard one of countless buses marked **"Seville"** and found a window seat. As the bus began to fill up, and the minutes passed, I began to feel a little nervous. Soon, I found myself actively looking over my shoulder towards the terminal building hoping my father would appear, but to no avail.

As one bus after another pulled away, I realised ours would soon follow, and my anxiety levels grew accordingly. Honestly, when I look back on the incident now, I cannot recall with any certainty whether the driver shouted **"Ok to go?"** or whether the bus just began to move off without warning, but I do remember jumping up and loudly telling the other supporters around me that my dad wasn't onboard yet. Thankfully, they conveyed this message (in one way or another) to the driver, who proceeded to wait. A few minutes later, my father appeared somewhat nonchalantly, with a six pack of Coca Cola, and a story about how he'd managed to get lost after finding that the first shop he'd seen was closed, before deciding to wander off in search of another.

Regardless, I was delighted to see my dad sat alongside me once again, safe in the knowledge that I wasn't about to be left alone in a cross border bus trip to a city I'd never visited with people I didn't know. And so, the bus pulled out of the airport car park, and as we accelerated down the slip road onto the motorway, local music began to emanate from the internal speakers. I'm not an expert with regards which type of music it actually was, but I do remember it was a rather upbeat Latin number, with what sounded like a trumpet player being given a prominent role.

Of course, with a significant bus ride facing us, one of my fellow supporters pulled a cassette tape from his bag, and marched purposefully down the central aisle towards the driver. Having tapped him on the shoulder and smiled, he pressed the eject button, removed the driver's cassette, and clicked his version into place. Within seconds, the distinctive voices of what I would later find out to be Wolfe Tones began to blare around the bus and, accordingly, the singing began. Being twelve years old, I had no idea as to the words, and I can still recall asking my father about what each of the songs meant.

Regardless, the journey itself turned out to be fairly pleasant. As we powered along the motorway, we passed into Spain, and spotted countless buses and cars decked out in both the green of Celtic and the blue of Porto, with their regalia streaming along the road. By nightfall, we reached Seville but skirted the city, heading for our hotel which was situated about an hour's drive from the centre and, by the time we arrived, I was knackered. The adults however, tired as they may have been, were thirsty, and seemed somewhat bemused when they discovered that the earlier buses to arrive at the hotel had literally drank the bar dry. And so, my dad and I retired to our room, knowing that Celtic would play in a European Final for the first time in thirty-three years only the next day.

I don't remember much about waking up the next morning. I can recall the anticipatory excitement coursing through my veins, but surprisingly little more than that. As we left the hotel, my father asked me to pose for a photo in my new Hoops (which I was immensely proud of) with an inflatable finger in the design of a tricolour – despite the fact I have no idea where I got it from. And so, after another stifling hour on a coach, we stepped out into the sunshine outside the Estadio de La Cartuja (more commonly referred to as the Estadio Olímpico).

Even at this point, in what was still the mid-morning, there were hundreds if not thousands of supporters milling about. All of the UEFA Cup decorations were in place, with a huge billboard which read **"Welcome to the UEFA Cup Final"** being a notable backdrop for many a photograph. Having never travelled to the continent for a football match before, I was immediately struck by the differences in the area around the stadium. In Glasgow, the inner city has, well, it's less desirable areas to say the least. However, in Seville, small trees lined long avenues, and the stadium's light stone exterior was unlike anything I had seen before.

Next, we went in search of tickets, having been two of the tens of thousands who travelled to Spain without any. There were several people selling them, particularly Porto fans who had realised just how sought after their thirty Euro tickets had become. Having looked at a couple without success, my father began conversing with a small Portuguese man who said he had two for sale. Within a few moments, he produced a couple of tickets from his pocket, and allowed us to look at them. Not being experts, and not having seen a real UEFA Cup Final ticket in the flesh, we weren't entirely sure if they were genuine or not.

With this in mind, I wandered over to the stadium cordon, about twenty yards away, and gesticulated at the police officer standing there to come and offer his opinion, and he duly obliged. However, with little grasp of English, he struggled to be of much assistance. As time passed, our discussion attracted the attention of several Irish Celts who happened to be strolling by, some of whom had real tickets which we proceeded to compare our prospective purchases with. Therefore, by this stage, two Scots, several Irishmen, a Spanish police officer and a Portuguese seller were attempting to have a discussion, which involved three different tongues, a lot of hand signs and people attempting to make some use of their basic foreign language classes from their schooldays.

Eventually, my father agreed a price (which I shall not specify in case my mother decides to kill him all these years later) and therefore, moments later, my dad prepared to pay the gentleman. Now, this was not to be as simple as you may imagine, and hilarity would soon ensue as a result of it. To contextualise this story, I should mention that, for several years prior to this trip, my dad had always worn a money belt when travelling abroad and carrying relatively large sums of cash, as both he and my mother believed it was the safest manner in which to do so. For those of you who may not know, these belts are worn under a set of trousers or shorts around your waist, in order to make it almost impossible for thieves to steal from you without alerting you to their presence.

This meant that when my father prepared to pay the man in Seville, he began to unzip his trousers. Unsurprisingly, the poor Portuguese man, perhaps somewhat concerned that something had been lost through the language barrier, looked decidedly terrified by this. Inevitably, all of the Irish lads (and the policeman), fell about laughing when they realised what was happening. However, the Portuguese man simply looked like he wanted to take his money and get away from us – which he did, two UEFA Cup Final tickets lighter, several Euros richer, and possessing an intense phobia of Scotsmen and their money belts.

Anyway, with almost all of the afternoon left, we found ourselves with several hours of spare time to kill, and decided to head into the city centre. The main square had been a much spoken about meeting place prior to our trip, but in the days before Twitter and other equivalent forms of social media, we had not seen any photographs which would enable us to know what to expect. Upon reaching the square, Celtic fans appeared to be everywhere, and once again, I mean everywhere. Not only were they standing about, dancing and singing, but they were also on benches, atop statues, up lampposts and perched on window ledges. On the odd occasion I spotted anyone without a Celtic shirt, it was a rare sight – and even then it was mostly because they simply had taken it off to enjoy the sunshine. Ironically, the few locals mingling around looked somewhat out of place in their own city, without the Hoops on their backs or a Celtic scarf around their necks.

At this stage, we were set to meet my older cousin John, who you will remember from the chapter regarding the trip to Anfield for the return leg of the quarter final. My father had spoken to him on his mobile phone earlier in the day and we had arranged to meet in the square. Many of you will remember the famous double-decker bus, sponsored by one Scottish tabloid newspaper, which was emblazoned with **"V for Victory"** insignia (at the time, this was a reference to the fact that every side Celtic had faced in the tournament thus far had the letter "V" somewhere in their names). Having once again managed to contact John on the phone, the following is the side of the conversation which ensued between my father and him that I overheard.

"Hello! Hi John! Where are you? Aye, we're in the square. Next to the bus? Alright we'll head over there and see if we can spot you...what? Ah well, that'll be a lot of help finding you won't it?! See you in a bit."

This resulted in my dad laughing loudly, so presumably something amusing must have been said. Having ended the call, we set off across the crowd towards the bus. It was only as we approached the double-decker, which featured a massive picture of Henrik Larsson on the side, that my dad told me what John had said on the other end of the phone: **"Hi Frank, yeah I'm in the square, next to the bus. No worries, I've got my Hoops on. Haha, aye, right enough, bye."**

Anyway, having eventually met up with John, we headed out towards the ground once again. Despite the fact we'd just came from there, it was left to twelve year old me to lead the way, as neither of the other two, smart men though they are, have been blessed with any natural sense of direction. Somewhere along the way, the heat really began to hit us. Shade was a much sought-after commodity, and we made use of it as often as we could. We were provided a short respite when, having allowed one particularly red looking Celtic supporter and his family to use some of our sun cream, they repaid the favour by giving us a can of cold beer each (Irn-Bru in my case).

By the time we eventually reached the stadium, in the early evening, there was no let up with regards the temperature. It was simply incredible, with the electronic thermometers that you found situated on billboards still reading well over thirty degrees Celsius only an hour or two before kick-off. Once we had helped John to buy a ticket (with us using our tickets as comparisons on this occasion, and without a repeat of the money belt incident) we set off on our separate ways towards the turnstiles. Having purchased tickets from a Porto fan, it was not a surprise when we found ourselves queuing in amongst thousands of supporters clad in blue and white outside the Estadio Olímpico. However, to say we were the only Celtic fans in these queues would be a lie, as hundreds of others joined us as we made it past the first police cordon before approaching the ground itself.

Soon, we found ourselves at the turnstiles. Well, I call them turnstiles now, but in truth they were the sort of small three-pronged gates you often see at railway stations. They were only hip high for adults, and even in the short time that we were stood there waiting, we saw one Celtic supporter simply hurdle over them and sprint away into the crowd. Laughably, a police officer began to give chase before stopping, shrugging his shoulders and returning to his post without any further action. Thankfully, we didn't have to attempt such a feat ourselves, but nonetheless we still had to hope and pray that our tickets were genuine and that they would be accepted by the ticket machine.

To gain access to the ground, supporters had to slide their tickets into a small slot in the gate with a little light above it, in a not dissimilar style to the system currently in use at Celtic Park. A green light, of course, meant the ticket was good and you were granted access. However, a red light meant the opposite, and as we queued, we saw one or two fake tickets being rejected by the machines. And so, with more than a few nerves within me, I slid my ticket into the machine – a moment later, the light went green, and I was in, followed by my father after a few seconds.

However, as we climbed the stairs onto the tier, before we even had the chance to look for our respective seats, several police officers saw we were Celtic supporters and quickly ushered us through a large glass partition which ran directly down the tier dividing the two sets of supporters. Now, on the face of it, this was excellent. Whilst we had no concerns about the prospect of sitting with the Porto fans (after all, those who we had met previously were very friendly), we would have preferred to sit with our own supporters if possible, and this move had solved that issue – or so we thought. As time passed, we watched countless Celtic fans appear from the entrance we had walked through, only to be met by police and pushed through the glass partition. Even with kick-off some time away, it quickly became clear that overcrowding in our area was going to become an issue, as so many extra supporters had been pushed through from the Porto end but, as ever, the mood within the support was as friendly and accommodating as could be.

Sometime later, as the stadium continued to fill up and the noise emanating from the Celtic support continued to increase in volume, my father turned to me and said something which will stay with me for as long as I live: **"Son, look around. This sort of thing only happens once in a generation. You're about to see Celtic in a European Final, and you'll remember this day for the**

rest of your life. You'll tell your kids and grandkids about it. Enjoy it, no matter what the score is, just enjoy it."

To say the atmosphere was incredible would, again, be an understatement on my part. As **"You'll Never Walk Alone"** rang out through the Spanish evening air, I saw more than a couple of teary eyes around me, and this was before the match had even started. Everyone sang – everyone – men, women and children alike. Pensioners found the voices from their younger days, and children like me did our best to sound intimidating. With all of the scarves held aloft, it was truly a sight to behold, and also a sight that I firmly believe I will see again in the future.

In truth, I don't actually remember too much about the match itself, such was the frenetic nature in which it was played. When Porto scored their first goal, I recall watching their supporters celebrating and hugging each other through the glass partition, as the rallying cry went up from our own fans. As the Portuguese leapt up and down, we could all feel the stand shaking beneath our feet, and as I gazed out towards the back of their end of the stadium, where several large openings between the pillars at the back of the stand allowed me a glimpse of the outside world, it seemed as if the motorway off in the distance was moving up and down (whereas in reality it was, of course, the stadium itself which was moving). As the teams on the park prepared to resume play, my dad said: **"If we score, this place is going to fall down."**

Now, to contextualise this statement somewhat, I should highlight that, by now, the overcrowding around us was rather significant. Whilst there were little gaps in other parts of the ground, our section was absolutely packed, with people sitting on all of the stairs and sharing seats. Even at the age of twelve, I found myself sitting on my father's knee for the majority of the game, and perched on the very edge of a seat shared by another adult for a few minutes here and there.

Thankfully, as Henrik Larsson headed home the first of two Celtic equalisers, the stand didn't fall down, but I have to say that it didn't feel like it was too far away from it, as the travelling Celtic support were sent into delirium. Only six years earlier, I had leapt about as if Celtic had scored a goal of great importance in a virtually meaningless game against Aberdeen, and yet now, I was witnessing the real thing, a truly historic goal. As the ball nestled in the net and the crowd erupted in celebration, my father pulled me close to him and held me tightly, as jubilant fans began to tumble over the rows, such was the nature of the overcrowding combined with the excitement which the goal had caused.

Having equalised again midway through the second half, the celebrations were even more chaotic than they had been previously. In the seconds following the goal, a woman landed on top of us, as well as a couple of other people. Moments later, she looked back up the tier towards where she had come from and declared something along the lines of: **"I'm so sorry! Oh my God, that's me come down three or four rows!"**

As the regulation ninety minutes ended, the heat was almost unbearable in the stands, so who knows what it must have been like to play football in it. The vendors inside the ground had run out of water and juice long before half time, and so by this point, energy levels were beginning to wane all around us. I can still recall standing in the large, stifling toilets before extra time began, staring at the dull orange tiles on the wall and feeling distinctly unwell. Of course, it was simply a combination of the unrelenting heat and the excitement attending a European Final, but still, I felt awful. And so, as Celtic battled through extra time, I sat there in the stand battling my nerves and emotions.

Had Celtic managed to find a winner, all of my ills would likely have disappeared in the absolute bedlam which would have inevitably ensued. However, when Derlei put the ball past Robert Douglas with only a few minutes remaining, my heart sank, and the feelings of anxiety drifted away, only to be replaced by those of utter despair. I knew that the dream was likely over now, and this was a crushing realisation for anyone, let alone a twelve year old. In Glasgow Airport, when I had been asked by a newspaper reporter for a score prediction, I said **"three-two to Celtic!"** and the fact that I had got the score right but not the winners sickened me. In fact, it still does.

In all honesty, I felt that Celtic had done all that could have been asked of them. Yes, mistakes had been made and yes, there had been varying levels of performances from our players in testing conditions but regardless, I believed the team had given their all, and that is all anyone could have asked of them beforehand. However, in my mind, I couldn't help but wonder whether we had been cheated. The playacting of many Porto players, as well as the lack of consistency from the referee troubled me and, to this day, I cannot help but wonder whether things could have been very different.

And so, both mentally and physically exhausted, I stood there and watched the Celtic team file past the UEFA Cup on the pitch below. Even from a distance, it was notable that whilst some players barely gave the trophy a glance as they passed, others could not help but glimpse the prize which they had come so close to possessing. Henrik Larsson was one of the men who looked at the UEFA Cup, and I doubt mine was the only cheek which a tear or two ran down when met with such a sight. As Porto lifted the trophy, and blue and white confetti erupted through the air, the sound of a defiant version of **"You'll Never Walk Alone"** rang around the stadium. Hopes and dreams were left unrealised, but a burning pride within us all remained, as me and my father turned onto the stairwell and exited the ground. As we did so, grown men sat around us in tears, and outside, countless people could be seen simply staring blankly into space, as if they were in a state of shock.

As I trudged through the sandy red soil towards our bus, I had an encounter which I shall never forget. A small Portuguese woman, decked out in blue and white, approached me and presented me with a Porto scarf. She spoke no English, and I only caught the words **"Celtic"** and **"okay"** in amongst those of her native language, but her sentiments were clear and well intentioned. Whilst I still dislike Porto as a team, I cannot express any such ill-feeling towards their supporters, who were lovely people in my experience of them. To this day, the scarf still resides in my wardrobe, and I shall never throw it away because that little woman, who was only a part of my life for a matter of seconds, felt it appropriate to give it to me as a present. It was a symbolic gesture, and one which still brings a bittersweet smile to my face.

Sometime later, having clambered onto our bus which was parked directly beneath the motorway a little distance away from the stadium, our driver informed us that we would not be returning to our hotel, as the addition of extra time (as well as the post match celebrations and commiserations) meant that there was not sufficient time to reach the hotel and then return the airport. For this reason, we would wait where we were for an hour or two, before heading directly back to the airport. As everyone's luggage was already onboard the bus in preparation for such a scenario, nobody was too annoyed to hear this news. Due to the sweltering heat inside the vehicle, which had no functioning air conditioning, many of us instead headed outside into the marginally cooler night air.

Exhausted, having had a day and night that will live with us all forever, many supporters, including myself, lay our heads on the sandy soil in an attempt to catch some sleep. Whilst many great works of fiction portray romantic notions of sleeping under a starry night sky, our reality involved a view of the underside of a Spanish motorway that night. However, I must say that it was actually a fairly comfortable place to relax, and after the chaotic nature of the previous day or two, the dull whirr of engines passing above us was somewhat soothing.

And so, early in the morning, we headed for the airport. Having checked in amongst thousands of other Celtic supporters, I couldn't help but notice the way in which different people had, and were continuing to, react to the defeat. Some dragged their feet as they walked, suffering from horrendous hangovers whilst others simply continued drinking. Some people sat quietly, as if their brains had simply overloaded the night before, awaiting a reboot upon a return to Glasgow, whilst others showed a defiant stand against defeat, singing as loudly and proudly as they had done on their journey to Seville (albeit with slightly creakier voices). Many laughed, a few continued to cry, and countless slept, but we did so as one big family.

Having battled my way through an airport meal which, despite the fact it was labelled as pork, didn't look, smell or taste anything like any pork I have known previously or since, we awaited our flight home. Almost every plane was bound for Glasgow (or another city nearby) and as there were only a few airlines operating that day, all of these planes had very similar flight numbers. These factors, combined with the fact that the terminal was very loud and that the Spaniard operating the tannoy system had an accent which was difficult to decipher, led to many people missing their flights, or ending up on the wrong one. Eventually, we heard something along the lines of the following emanate from an overhead speaker:

"Thomas Cook flight, TC1888, to Glasgow at 11.30am, last call for passengers Adams, Aitken, Andrews, Collins...[this continued for some time, as countless supporters had clearly not heard the previous tannoy calls]**...O'Neill, Peacock, Rafters, Roberts..."**

Having heard our names, we leapt from our seats outside an airport bar and began to frantically search for the appropriate gate. Unsurprisingly, we were not the only people to jump up and start running about. In truth, perhaps we should have foreseen this eventuality, as we had already witnessed it happen to other people on several different occasions as we awaited our flight. Having run to the gate, concerned our plane was set to leave without us, we arrived to find a large queue of supporters waiting to board the aircraft. Even once we were onboard, the plane did not leave for some time due to the business of the runway. However, the air conditioning was a blessed relief from what had been a remarkably warm journey to Andalucía (and, of course, Portugal).

Anyway, after a blissfully uneventful flight home, we touched down on Scottish soil once more and began to make our way through the airport's arrivals hall, mingling with countless Celtic fans arriving home from airports all over Europe, as their trips home from Seville had taken some of them via weird and wonderful destinations. Tired but fiercely proud renditions of **"The Celtic Song"** rang through the terminal building, as some fans announced their returns home, beaten, but most definitely unbroken. For us, a lift home from my mother awaited us, and as we walked towards the car through the cold Scottish wind, I realised that, despite the fact we lost, I had been incredibly fortunate enough to witness a special moment in the history of Celtic Football Club in the flesh. As I write this, nothing has matched it, but I have no doubt in my mind that one day, whether it is in the near or the distant future, I shall see Celtic play in another European Final – and win.

"I'll Leave You To Draw Your Own Conclusions"

Throughout the generations, there have been numerous Celtic supporters who have firmly held the belief that the Club's players have not always been rewarded with the international call-ups that their abilities and achievements have warranted. Various theories regarding potential reasons, as well as an almost endless plethora of examples of such treatment have been cited in this regard. In this chapter, I will consider these issues, aiming to use facts, statistics and, yes, numerous examples, in an attempt to allow you to come to your own conclusions on the issue. Of course, I have my own views on the matter, but in an attempt to remain as objective as possible, I shall refrain from expanding upon them, hoping instead to broaden your own knowledge and allow you to make up your own minds. And so, without further ado, allow me to take you on what I hope will be a rather interesting trip through time.

Formed on the sixth of November 1887, Celtic took to the field for the first time on the twenty-eighth of May 1888, a couple of months after that year's British Home Championship, the only source of international football at that point in history. For this reason, the first opportunity for a Celtic player to receive an international cap for the Scotland would come the following spring, in the March of 1889. On the ninth day of that month, the Scots were set to face Ireland at Ibrox Park. Whilst no Rangers players were chosen to represent their country on their home field, two of the men currently plying their trade with Glasgow's newest Club, Celtic (which had played less than fifty matches thus far), were selected to wear the blue of Scotland.

In this sense, the names of Michael McKeown, a full-back from Ayrshire, and Willie Groves, a forward from Leith, retain a special place in the history of the Football Club. They were the first two Celts to be given the opportunity to represent Scotland, as the Irish were heavily defeated by seven goals to nil just south of the River Clyde. Whilst McKeown made his international debut that day, it was the second such outing for Groves, who had been capped almost a year to the day earlier whilst playing for Hibernian. Willie had scored against Wales that day in 1888, and he would go two better against Ireland in 1889, scoring only the eighth Scottish hat-trick ever at that point in time (to this day, only thirty-six have been scored).

In April 1889, a Scottish party travelled to London to indulge once more in their increasingly famous rivalry with England. The Scots team, which included Celtic players James Kelly and James McLaren, won by three goals to two, as the latter scored the deciding goal with only moments remaining. Having lost by five goals to nil to the Englishmen at Hampden in 1888, and having been two-nil down at half time on this occasion, the victory of **"the Scotch"** that day, thanks in part to the two Celts representatives was not to be overlooked, as Scotland went on to reclaim their British Home Championship title from their English foes.

A little over a year later, in April 1890, as Scotland drew one-all with England at Hampden Park, the international careers of Michael McKeown and Willie Groves would end, with the grand total of five caps between them. Now, it would be very easy, particularly in relation to Groves and his hat-trick to question why he was not picked for either of the remaining two international matches in 1889, but it is worthy of note that only one man, Francis Watt, a forward playing for Kilbirnie, featured in more than one match that year. This was not a time when virtually the same eleven men would run out to represent their country time and time again, although at least one or two people within the game did mention it as an idea.

Regardless, James McLaren joined the aforementioned pairing in bowing out of the international game, but not before he became the first Celtic player to captain Scotland on that very day. James Kelly also played on that occasion, as the Celts were the most heavily represented domestic team in an international side for the first time in history. Kelly however, would go on to have a more successful international career, racking up eight caps (the cumulative total of his three compatriots) by the time he made his last appearance for the country in 1896.

In 1891, no Celtic player was chosen to play for Scotland, despite the fact the Parkhead side was beginning to establish itself, slowly but surely, as a rising force in the domestic game. This was met with great disappointment by many, as not one Celtic player was given the chance to represent their country in the first international match to be held at Celtic Park.

However, in 1892, Peter Dowds, the first Celt to play in every match throughout a domestic season, was awarded his one and only international cap in a three-two win against Ireland at Solitude in Belfast. A couple of weeks later, Dan Doyle and Sandy McMahon made their international debuts alongside the increasingly experienced James Kelly, as England eased to a four-one victory at Ibrox Park. In 1893, with Celtic as the reigning Scottish League Champions for the first time, the Club saw its first continued representation in the national side, as Willie Maley, James Kelly, Sandy McMahon and John Campbell all featured in two consecutive international matches. Prior to this, Celts' centre-forward John Madden became only the third man to score four goals for Scotland in a single match. Despite this, he would be awarded with only one more cap in 1895. To this day, he is one of only ten Scotsmen to achieve such a goalscoring feat. For the record, the last time that anyone scored four times (or even three times for that matter) in a Scotland jersey was May 1969 – a little over twenty-one years before I was even born.

Returning to the earliest days of Celtic Football Club, whilst Maley would only be capped once more, and McMahon on a few future occasions, Campbell would go on to become the first Celtic player to appear ten times for his national side, eventually leaving the international game with an impressive twelve outings to his name in 1903. Having scored twelve times in a reserve match at Parkhead, his striking talents had been clear to see for some time, but they were only truly rewarded by the international selectors around the turn of the century. Regardless, after the first five seasons upon which Celtic players could have been selected for international duty, ten Celts had turned out for their country at one stage or another, making a grand total of twenty-two appearances between them. In comparison to other Clubs at the time, only Queen's Park players racked up more international outings, with thirty-six. The men from Ibrox only managed ten, and Hearts thirteen – but it is worth remembering that Queen's Park remained the club of choice for the establishment at that time.

And so, as the twentieth century dawned and Celtic's strength grew, so too did the number of caps awarded to their players. As the 1900's became the 1910's, men such as Jimmy Quinn (eleven caps), Jimmy Hay (eleven caps) and yet another Jimmy, McMenemy (twelve caps) became regular names in Scotland line-ups. In fact, during the famous **"six in a row years"**, Celtic were the most represented Club in the Scottish national team over the period as a whole (although only in two of those six individual seasons).

However, this should come as no surprise, as those of you who possess even a basic knowledge of those great days will appreciate that Celtic were almost unstoppable at that time. They were certainly the best side in Scotland, and the debate continues to rage as to whether, truly, they were actually the best team on Earth. Nevertheless, my point is that it should be no surprise our players were capped more than any other Club's players at that time, because they were undoubtedly the best. And yet, even with this confirmation, several oddities continue to puzzle the minds of many supporters more than a century later.

Yes, almost one in five international caps during the period were awarded to Celtic players, with many others going to players from Rangers, Hearts and even Newcastle United; and yes, players such as the three Jimmy's listed above were capped with some regularity; but still, the aforementioned oddities remain. Starting from the back, Davie Adams, Celtic's stalwart goalkeeper for almost a decade (and the last keeper to wear the Hoops before the introduction of different coloured goalkeeping jerseys), was not even capped once by his country, despite ending his career with one hundred clean sheets (a notably high number for a time when lots of goals were scored). With this in mind, one may wonder why, in the latter years of the **"six in a row"** run,

Third Lanark's Jimmy Brownlie was called upon almost constantly to be Scotland's goalkeeper, despite the fact that he was regularly conceding twice as many domestic goals as Adams.

"Ah, but Adams' defence were better" think many of you – and you would be right – but the point stands. Celtic were famed not only for their attacking prowess but for their defensive abilities in those days, but therein too lies a couple of odd statistics. For example, despite their impeccable partnership at half-back, only the latter member of the famous trio of 'Sunny Jim' Young, Willie Loney and James Hay was capped seriously by Scotland. Whilst he received eleven caps, Loney only managed two, and Young only a solitary cap. One of the three available half-back slots was regularly handed to Hearts captain Charlie Thomson (latterly of Sunderland), and I feel no one can quibble with this too strongly, as Thomson was regarded as one of the great talents of the Scottish game at the time. However, whilst Charlie was an almost ever present face for virtually a decade, Hay, the most capped Celtic half-back at the time, had to wait for almost four years after his international debut to receive his second call-up, despite consistently forming an integral part of the best defence in the country.

Moving on to the forward line, we come to the slightly curious case of Alec Bennett, an outside forward who regularly fed Jimmy Quinn with the crosses from which he would score for years on end. Despite being a Rangers supporter, he won four league titles and two Scottish Cups with Celtic before, eventually, he succumbed to temptation and signed for the Ibrox Club in 1908. For this, I cannot and will not personally criticise him. After all, footballers have forever dreamt of playing for the Club they support.

In his five years at Celtic, Alec was capped three times for his country in 1904, 1907 and 1908 (essentially receiving three call-ups from a potential fifteen, or twenty percent of those which were possible). However, having moved to Rangers, he immediately found himself involved in seven of Scotland's next nine matches (or a little under seventy-eight percent of those which he could have been). Speculation remains as to whether this was because it enabled the country to benefit from his partnership with Quinn and McMenemy, or whether any other reasoning was involved.

In the following years, the continued favouritism with regards to Third Lanark's goalkeeper Brownlie would conspire with the outbreak of World War One to snatch any prospect of an international career away from another one of Celtic's greatest goalkeepers, Charlie Shaw. With a clean sheet rate of over fifty percent from almost four hundred and fifty appearances, it is a tragedy that he was never able to appear on the international stage. Having wholly established himself as the best goalkeeper in Scotland during his first season at Parkhead (conceding only fourteen times and keeping twenty-six clean sheets), and helping Celtic to go on the longest undefeated run in the history of the British game, we can only wonder whether he would have been awarded for his endeavours with international call-ups had the international game not been suspended upon the outbreak of the Great War. At that time, Jimmy Brownlie was aging, and despite continuing into the 1920's with Third Lanark, one can only speculate as to whether Shaw would have managed to snatch his place away from him. In all likelihood, somebody would have, but sadly we shall never know for certain whether it would have been Charlie or not.

As the 1920's wore on, it was clear that Celtic were no longer the best side in the country, as Rangers romped to title after title whilst Willie Maley attempted to build another great side. In time, he would be somewhat successful in this regard, thanks partly to the extraordinary talents of men such as Jimmy McGrory. As is described in more detail in the chapter regarding the man himself, McGrory was a truly exceptional goalscorer, scoring five hundred and fifty goals in five hundred and forty-seven outings as a professional footballer. Upon his return from a loan spell at Clydebank, he began to set Parkhead alight as goal after goal flew in thanks to his head or boot.

In order to emphasise my point with regards to his incredible record, allow me to break it down to some degree. Whilst in his prime, McGrory's goalscoring record read as follows – thirty goals in thirty-six appearances (1924–25), forty-nine goals in fifty-two appearances (1925–26), fifty-nine goals in forty-one appearances (1926–27) and sixty-two goals in forty-six appearances (1927–28).

Throughout these four seasons, Jimmy scored two hundred goals in one hundred and seventy-five appearances – more than many strikers score over the course of their entire careers. Nowadays, that is the sort of record which would make somebody a global superstar, with a truly enormous price tag attached to them. And yet, during that period, Jimmy was rewarded with only one international cap, as the Scots lost by one goal to nil against Ireland in February 1928. Granted, he did not have the best of debuts, and by all accounts he looked nervous. After all, representing your country was an even bigger deal then than it is now, and at the age of only twenty-three, it is not surprising that he would have required time to settle, especially as he had never played with many of his new teammates before. However, Jimmy would not be allowed such an opportunity and he would not feature again for Scotland until three years had passed.

During the aforementioned three year spell, his goalscoring tally read as follows – forty-two goals in thirty-four appearances (1928–29), forty-one goals in thirty-five appearances (1929–30) and forty-seven goals in thirty-eight appearances (1930–31). When a more experienced Jimmy was finally given his chance again in 1931, he grasped it with both hands, scoring his first international goal. In fact, he would go on to score five goals in his next four Scotland outings, including a double against England at Hampden in 1933 as Scotland recorded a historic two-one victory. However, having failed to score in his seventh appearance for Scotland, only a few months after that triumph over the English (thanks partly to a lack of quality service according to newspaper reports), Jimmy's international career ended. He would not feature in a Scotland jersey again, despite topping the fifty goal mark at the end of the 1935–36 season once again.

And so, not only the most successful British goalscorer of all time, but one of the ten highest goalscorers in the history of football (alongside the likes of Pelé, Ferenc Puskás, Zico and Gerd Müller no less), ended his career with a measly seven international caps. Yes, seven. In contrast, the four men listed above represented their respective countries over three hundred and thirty times between them (although I appreciate more international matches were scheduled in later eras), and therefore we are left asking the obvious question: **"Why wasn't Jimmy McGrory capped more often?"**

Well, I feel that the following two words are a good place to start – **"Hughie Gallacher".** Born a little over a year prior to McGrory, Gallacher was another Scottish forward with a reputation for goals, goals, and more goals. Having begun his career with Queen of the South, impressive stints with Airdrieonians, Newcastle United, and Chelsea helped him to an admirable goalscoring record. Interestingly, he finished his career having made only seven more appearances than Jimmy, with five hundred and fifty-four outings to his name. In this time, he scored four hundred and six goals which, I'm sure, we would all agree is magnificent. However, it is notable that such a total remains one hundred and forty-one goals less than Jimmy McGrory scored in almost an identical number of matches.

Now, it would be easy for me to sit and here say that: **"McGrory was a better player than Gallacher and that therefore deserved to be capped more often."** However, having not seen either of the two men play first hand, I feel that would be a foolish assumption to make. Both men were fantastic goalscorers – that much is certain. However, what is also certain is that Gallacher was picked over McGrory time and time again by Scotland's international selection committee, and one is left to wonder why. At this stage, it is also worth remembering that, in 1928, Arsenal (the side which would soon dominate English football for years to come), did everything in their power to sign Jimmy McGrory, not Hughie Gallacher, as they looked for a striker to propel the club to success.

In many senses, the two men appear to have been fairly similar in what they offered on the field of play also. They were both around the same height, each with broad shoulders and the ability to score in almost every way imaginable. They could head the ball, hassle opposition players, and strike shots with incredible power and precision. However, it was clear that, for whatever reason, Gallacher remained the favourite of the selectors, although he did fade latterly, allowing other men to compete with Jimmy for the centre forward position. Although these individuals, such as Neil Dewar of Third Lanark, were undoubtedly good goalscorers, most people would concur (with the greatest respect), that they were not a patch on McGrory. Personally, I am left rather disheartened by the lack of international recognition that our greatest goalscorer received. Tragically, in later years, only months before McGrory tasted immortal success as manager of the Celtic side which beat Rangers by seven goals to one, Hughie Gallacher threw himself in front of an oncoming train – a sad end to an illustrious life.

Focusing our attention on the aforementioned selection committees, I feel it is worth highlighting that there was no such thing as a Scotland manager between 1872 and 1953. Over the course of eight decades, the job of picking the next Scotland team fell to the members of the Scottish Football Association's prestigious **"International Selection Committee"**. These groups generally numbered just under ten individuals, drawn from across Scottish Football, with not only 'big' teams being represented, but often smaller sides also. For example, whilst the committee of 1899–1900 included a representative from Celtic, it also included members from second division and lower league outfits, such as Douglas Wanderers, Ayr Parkhouse and Mossend Swifts. Members were then elected via a vote at the end of every season, and therefore many of them appeared on these committees for long periods of time. These men alone held the power of who played in a Scotland jersey and who did not, as they travelled the country taking in domestic matches with some regularity in order to broaden their knowledge of the game.

Anyway, only a year after the end of Jimmy McGrory's playing career, Europe was once again plunged into the depths of war, along with large parts of Africa and Asia, cancelling international football once more. Upon its resumption came the emergence of the first Celtic player to be recognised by Scotland in earnest – Bobby Evans. The talented, strong, and consistent half-back eventually retired with an incredible forty-eight caps to his name, as Scotland's second most decorated player at that time.

To contextualise this achievement somewhat, I should point out that Bobby became the first Celtic player to gain a twentieth international cap in May 1955. The first man to reach this figure was Robert Walker of Hearts all the way back in 1908, before the first Rangers player to do so, Alex Smith, achieved the feat in 1911. In all, fourteen men would reach the twenty cap mark before Bobby, including representatives of Newcastle United, Liverpool, Dundee, Morton and Hibernian. In fact, Rangers had five men achieve this before Celtic even had one, as the fifth, Sammy Cox, passed the mark in 1952. Of course, Rangers had been the dominant domestic force at times, but so had Celtic at others, and it is statistics such as this which may lend credence to the view that Celtic players have not always been chosen for international duty as often as their respective talents have warranted.

However, returning to Bobby Evans, he represented his country at both the 1954 and 1958 World Cups, captaining the side twelve times during his lengthy stay at Celtic Park. Whilst he remains one of only twenty-two men to captain Scotland whilst a Celtic player, he was the first Celt in almost twenty-five years to receive the honour when he was first awarded it in 1958 (the previous Parkhead recipient being Peter McGonagle in 1933). Comparing this with our rivals, Rangers had twenty-eight men awarded the honour of captaining Scotland, and their longest barren spell in this regard was a little over a decade encompassing all of the 1980's.

To this day, Bobby Evans remains tied in fifteenth place (along with Christian Dailly), in terms of the number of Scotland matches he captained. In top position, we find George Young (Rangers, forty-eight), who is followed by Billy Bremner (Leeds, thirty-nine), Gary McAllister (predominantly of Leicester and Leeds, thirty-two), and Barry Ferguson (Rangers, twenty-eight), before reaching Graeme Souness (Rangers) and Roy Aitken (Celtic) tied on twenty-seven appearances as the captain of Scotland each. **"The Bear"** remains the most honoured Celtic player in this regard, and this record looks unlikely to be beaten at any time in the foreseeable future.

Fast forwarding your minds to Celtic's glory years from the mid-1960's through to the mid-1970's, allow me to rhyme off a short list – **"Ronnie Simpson, Jim Craig, Tommy Gemmell, Bobby Murdoch, Billy McNeill, John Clark, Jimmy Johnstone, Willie Wallace, Stevie Chalmers, Bertie Auld and Bobby Lennox."**

Every Celtic supporter will know these to be the names of the men who took to the field on the twenty-fifth of May 1967, and retired from that same pitch at the end of proceedings as immortals. Each Lion was born within a thirty mile radius of Celtic Park in Glasgow and, led by the one and only Jock Stein, they were a team which the Celtic supporters believed were capable of just about anything.

After all, not only had they become the first non-Latin team to win the European Cup; not only had they become the first British team to win the European Cup; and not only had they became the first (and only) Scottish team to win the European Cup; but they had also brought Europe's premier footballing prize home to one of the most deprived parts of one of the poorest cities in Europe. Gleaming silver shone through a grey and dreary neighbourhood, as Celtic supporters lined London Road and packed Celtic Park to see their heroes and to catch a glimpse of the trophy for themselves.

In the minds of many, this remains the greatest sporting achievement in Scotland's history and yet, few of the players mentioned above would make any significant impact in the national team. To emphasise this point, allow me to cite another list of eleven Scottish footballers – **"David Marshall, Robbie Neilson, Tosh McKinlay, Maurice Ross, Andy Webster, Kirk Broadfoot, Pat Nevin, Craig Mackail-Smith, Scott Dobie, David Goodwillie, and Gary Teale."**

The eleven men whom I have just named have all either won the same number of Scotland caps (or more), than that of the equivalent Lion who won the day in Lisbon, 1967. Each has a closely corresponding number to their predecessor in the list above, which I will briefly discuss in order to illustrate my point that many of the Lisbon Lions were notably under-capped. For the record, I am aware that the eleven men listed above played more recently than the Lisbon Lions, and therefore more international matches were played but please, stay with me. There is a point to this thought process, bizarre as it may seem.

Ronnie Simpson, goalkeeper with Celtic for six years (as well as that of Newcastle United and Hibernian amongst other clubs for over a decade), was only capped five times for his country. **"Faither"**, as he was affectionately known due to his comparative old age, was voted Celtic's greatest goalkeeper in 2002, ahead of stiff opposition and yet, he has one less Scotland cap than David Marshall to show for his efforts. Of course, Marshall was impressive in his time at Celtic, and many would agree that he has not had the career his talent and potential may have promised. In saying that, the famous clean sheet in the Camp Nou with the young David between the sticks will undoubtedly live long in the memory of many Celtic fans, including myself. However, as Simpson was first capped in 1967, at the age of thirty-six, his relatively small number of caps can be attributed somewhat to his age.

Jim Craig, European Cup winner (amongst fourteen major honours in total), was rewarded for his career with a single cap for his native Scotland. An academic man, who originally joined Celtic as an amateur in order to allow him to finish his dental studies, Jim was a fantastic right full-back and yet he has the same number of Scotland caps as one Robbie Neilson, most recently of Falkirk, a player who has been the winner of only a single Scottish Challenge Cup and, more recently, one Scottish Cup.

Tommy Gemmell, scorer in both the 1967 and 1970 European Cup finals, played for Celtic almost two hundred and fifty times, scoring thirty-seven goals. Famously, Tommy remains one of only two British players to score in different European Cup finals (the other being Phil Neal of Liverpool), and he was one of only five Lions to achieve double figures in terms of Scotland caps as he reached a total of eighteen, four behind future Celtic defender Tosh McKinlay.

Bobby Murdoch, the first Lion to lose his life at only fifty-six years of age in 2001, played almost five hundred times for the

Hoops, scoring over one hundred goals in the process. The midfielder, known for his incredible passing as well as his honesty both on and off the field was capped twelve times for his national side, the same number of occasions as Maurice Ross. Helenio Herrera, the man regarded as one of the finest managers in the history of Italian Football (also the manager of Inter Milan throughout most of the 1960's), described Murdoch as **"my complete footballer"** after the European Cup final in 1967. Teammate Bertie Auld was quoted as saying the following about Bobby: **"The phrase "world class" is a bit overused, but he was that and a little bit more. Sometimes people forget that."** Maurice Ross, on the other hand, has rarely played twenty times in any single domestic season, scoring only three goals in over two hundred career appearances thus far.

Unsurprisingly, Billy McNeill – the captain of the Lisbon Lions – racked up the most Scotland appearances of any member of the famous side, representing his country twenty-nine times in total. The man who holds the esteemed honour of making the highest number of appearances in the history of Celtic Football Club, having played seven hundred and eighty-nine times for the Hoops, was rewarded with a similar number of Scotland caps as those awarded to Andy Webster. Yes, Andy Webster – the Hearts player who featured three times in four years for Rangers. As Andy is still an active international player, he is likely to surpass McNeill's total in the near future, requiring only one more cap to equal **"Cesar"** in this regard.

John Clark, winner of both the European Cup and several domestic honours to boot, received only four international caps for his troubles. The modern day Parkhead kit-man is a passionately proud Celt, and someone I personally admire hugely. However, as I write this, Kirk Broadfoot has the same number of international caps as John. Whilst this may bewilder some of you, others will find it all too unsurprising as they have noticed the path which this chapter is following. If I am honest, the sarcastic side of me would like to make a joke about Kirk's culinary skills after he famously landed himself in hospital whilst using his microwave, but I'd be too concerned about the prospect of ending up with egg on my face – just like he did.

And so, all joking aside, we reach Jimmy Johnstone, the red haired man many regard as the greatest Celt there has ever been. Famed for his incredible skill and flamboyant style, he was renowned for his talents on the football field. Incidentally, he was also well known for his actions off of it, spending time with supporters and generally being one of the nicest men anyone could hope to meet. In total, he made twenty-three appearances for Scotland, five less than fellow winger Pat Nevin. In the near future, Steven Naismith, who has twenty-two caps at present, may well overtake the great Jinky too. Whilst I mean no disrespect to Mr Naismith, if this doesn't highlight the decline in the overall quality of the Scottish international side, then I don't know what does.

Continuing on through the line-up, we come to Willie Wallace, the man Jock Stein believed was capable of playing in any of the five forward positions. He scored twice against Dukla Prague in the European Cup semi-final of 1967, and despite impressive stints with Hearts and then Celtic, he was only awarded with seven caps for his country. Currently, Craig Mackail-Smith, previously of Peterborough United and presently playing with Brighton & Hove Albion, has the same number of Scotland caps to his name.

Next, allow me to draw your attention to the man who fired home the goal which won the European Cup for Celtic, Stevie Chalmers. He scored over two hundred goals for Celtic, at all levels of the game, and for this he was awarded with only five Scotland caps. Scott Dobie, who played most prominently with Carlisle United and West Bromwich Albion was capped six times by Scotland in 2002 alone – one more than Stevie received in his entire career. At the time of writing, Scott had made over four hundred career appearances as a striker, scoring less than eighty times.

Bertie Auld, one of the eternal favourites of the Celtic support, is well known not only for his abilities with a football, but his traits as a quick-witted comedian. It's a rare occasion when you don't see Bertie Auld with a huge grin across his face, even now, and his sense of humour is the stuff of legend. After all, it was

Auld who posed the following questions to the infamous referee, Tiny Wharton:

"If I call you an arsehole, Mr Wharton, will I get booked?"
"Yes Mr Auld, you'd be in trouble."
"What if I just thought you were an arsehole? What would happen then?"
"If you just thought it? Nothing would happen."
"Alright. Well, Mr Wharton, I think you're an arsehole!"

In all seriousness though, Bertie Auld was a magnificent footballer, and that fact must not be forgotten. Outwith his two spells at Parkhead, he played for Birmingham City and Hibernian, and also spent a time on loan at Dumbarton. He formed a vital part of the European Cup winning Celtic side, not only on the field but in the dressing room too, helping to ease the nerves of his teammates. He received the grand total of three Scotland caps in all, the same number currently held by David Goodwillie.

Finally, allow me to briefly mention Bobby Lennox, the second highest goalscorer in the long history of Celtic Football Club. Not only did Bobby win a plethora of medals in his time at Celtic Park, but he also impressed many of those he played against. One notable admirer was none other than one of the greatest players of all time, Alfredo Di Stefano, who praised the Ayrshire man greatly after he scored the only goal of his testimonial match at the Bernabeu in 1967. Bobby has ten Scotland caps to his name, despite winning the European bronze boot (awarded to the third highest goalscorer on the continent) one season – an accolade which I cannot see another recipient of twelve caps, Gary Teale, adding to his collection any time soon.

Now, the previous eleven comparisons are, of course, somewhat farcical, but that is the point. My intent in discussing those figures was purely to highlight how few caps, relatively speaking, many of Celtic's greatest ever side received, as well as highlighting the gradual decline in the quality of our national team. However, perhaps some more accurate, reasonable comparisons would help to hammer my point regarding the lines home. Speaking of home, let us look quickly at a couple of domestic comparisons, which I shall expand upon in a moment. In 1967, it was not only Celtic that reached a European Final, but Rangers too, who lost to Bayern Munich in extra time of the European Cup Winners' Cup Final in Italy.

The Rangers side which played that day consisted of ten Scots and one Dane, Kai Johansen, who received twenty caps for his native Denmark. Ignoring him for a moment, we find that of the ten Scots, only seven ever represented their country. These seven men finished their careers with a grand total of one hundred and sixty-seven Scotland caps between them – a cumulative total of fifty more than the eleven Scotsmen who defeated the great Internazionale in Lisbon that same year. Continuing on from this, Rangers' European Cup Winners' Cup victors of 1972 also received more caps in total than those which were awarded to the Celtic team which lost the European Cup Final of 1970.

And now, having seen a couple of these inconsistencies on the 'home front', let us widen our gaze across Europe. Only twice in the history of Europe's premier competition (European Cup/Champions League) have the winners of the tournament been awarded less caps by the end of their careers than those the Lisbon Lions received. The first of these were the inaugural Champions of Europe, Real Madrid, who would finish off their respective footballing stints with a total of one hundred and twelve caps between them – five less than the Lisbon Lions.

However, by the following year, when Real Madrid won the tournament for the second of five times in a row, a couple of transfers had been made and this figure shot up to one hundred and sixty-three. Regardless, this pales into insignificance when compared the international records of the 1982 winners of the European Cup, Aston Villa. Remarkably, the side who started that match would only achieve a cumulative total of thirty-three caps by the end of their careers, which is truly staggering to consider for any group of European Champions.

Returning to 1960, the eleven men who won the Cup for the fifth time for Madrid had over three hundred caps between them – the sort of figure which became the relative 'norm' for such a side. In fact, European Cup winning sides have only ended their careers with less than two hundred caps on a few occasions. Feyenoord for example, who beat Celtic in 1970, had three hundred and forty, whilst 1967 runners-up Internazionale had three hundred and thirty-five. Now, some of these figures can be attributed partly to the fact that sides such as The Netherlands were relatively successful on the international stage (and thus played more matches at knockout competitions), but nonetheless, the point stands once again.

Finally, I would like to bring one final band of statistics to your attention, before proceeding to the obvious question. According to the records, a little over one thousand, three hundred and fifty Scotland caps have been awarded to players whilst they were plying their trade with Rangers. However, a little less than one thousand two hundred caps have been awarded to men playing with Celtic as of the time of writing. Now, some would say that this fifteen percent difference could be placed down to Rangers being the more successful Club for a lengthier portion of time than Celtic but, personally, I would disagree.

Of course, it is undoubtedly an argument that would arise if the question was posed to someone with blue tinted spectacles, and I would expect no less. After all, Rangers Football Club won fifty-four Scottish League titles (without gaining any **"unfair competitive advantage"** of course – you'll have to forgive my cynicism there). Statistically speaking, there is a notable symmetry to be observed when one discovers that, throughout the history of Scottish international football, Rangers have also been the most represented Club in the national side during fifty-four seasons. Nice eh?

However, this idea of symmetry falls apart when you take a look at Celtic's record. The Celts have been Champions of Scotland forty-four times, and so, if things were consistent, you would presume that the corresponding number of seasons our players have dominated the Scottish national side would closely correlate to that of our number of Championship wins, but it does not. Despite proving ourselves to be the best team in the land on forty-four occasions, our players have only made the most international appearances twenty-nine times, a third less than the equivalent Ibrox ratio (although five of these took place during wartime, when international football was suspended).

And so, after several pages, a tonne of statistics, and a little bit of suspicion, we come to the ultimate question, **"Why?"**

Through the extensive research which has gone into not only this chapter, but this book as a whole, I have come to the conclusion that yes, there may well be significant substance to the view that Celtic players have often been overlooked for the Scotland caps their talents warranted. However, to examine that and highlight it is relatively simple, but to accurately answer the question of why such inconsistencies exist is remarkably difficult.

It would be very easy for me to simply say that bigotry, and/or a hatred of everything associated with Celtic Football Club and its support is the root cause of the problem. However, it is not an accusation that I, personally, would be willing to make without concrete proof. In saying that, considering the socio-religious problems which have scarred Scotland (and particularly the west and central areas of the country) in the past, it is likely that, at some point in history at least, it has played some part in the aforementioned footballing issue. However, I could not pin it on any particular individuals with any certainty, and would therefore be unwilling to attempt to do so.

Another factor, as I discussed at some length earlier, was talent. Whilst massively talented Celtic players were often overlooked, those who chose to ignore them were often able to fill their respective positions with another very talented player, thus giving those making the decisions an excuse of sorts and not affecting the potential outcomes of matches too dramatically. For example, as long as Hughie Gallacher scored goals (which he did regularly) and Scotland were successful; many Scots supporters were not too fussed about the fact that Jimmy McGrory did not feature as often as he undoubtedly should have, even though many Celtic supporters were angered by the lack of recognition for the great man.

The final factor which I shall mention is one which, in all likelihood, I feel has played a significant role in the history of Scottish international football – favouritism. Regardless of which era you look at, you will find that certain players were chosen more often than not, sometimes making a number of consecutive appearances as if they are almost **"undroppable"**. In certain sense, this is no bad thing, as consistency of selection can result in consistency of performance. If a player is familiar with those playing around him, he is more likely to be comfortable in his role. However, this does not always guarantee positive performances or results, as footballers are not infallible, and they are prone to make errors from time to time, just as all humans are.

For example, at points during the 2012–13 season, I heard people refer to Charlie Mulgrew as Celtic's **"undroppable man"**, in light of a few less than perfect performances from the generally reliable Scotsman. Clearly, such supposed favouritism can be found at domestic level too then. However, if we were all to sit back and think about it, we would all find that, on a personal level, we are all guilty of favouritism to some degree or another. We all have favourite players, men whom we would like to see in a particular position instead of another man, for example. However, we are not charged with picking the team (as much as we might like to be) and, unlike at Club level, where the number of choices available to us is rather finite, the options available for international selection are significantly more numerous in their nature.

Fundamentally, football managers (and members of international selection committees) are human. They will be subject to preconceived perceptions regarding some players, and these will continue to be broken apart or reinforced by the actions of the men in question. For example, whether a manager gets on well with a player or not will, undoubtedly, have repercussions in terms of the player's potential international call-ups in the future (see the Steven Fletcher and Craig Levein affair for a recent, public display of this).

In the same manner, if a player gets his chance and seizes it, performing well when called upon, it will make the manager more likely to recall that player in the future, because he will feel he has already proven his capabilities. And lastly, in the same vein, if a manager or selection committee do not like a player, for whatever reason that may be, warranted or not, it will seriously harm his chances of being rewarded with the number of caps he perhaps should be. Of course, that does not make it right, but it is, I feel, a fair reflection on the situation as a whole.

And so, ladies and gentlemen, I'll leave you to draw your own conclusions – firstly, as to whether there has been some anti-Celtic biased within past international selection processes and, secondly, for those of you believe there has been, to make up your own minds as to why that may have been the case.

I will say this though – for one reason or another, the quality of Scottish international football has plummeted over the last few decades. Men such as Craig Beattie now hold the same number of caps as Jimmy McGrory, and whilst a trip to Hampden was once feared by opposition the world over, it is now considered by many to be the potential source of three points. Many factors are likely to blame for this, but I feel that many of those men who have held the power in Scottish game for the last few decades must shoulder much of the blame, as our country has fallen far behind many of its competitors.

"A Guy With Dreadlocks And Another Guy Called Backpack Scored"

Falls Church, Virginia, is an independent city of approximately twelve thousand people which lies within the suburbs of Washington D.C. Geographically speaking, it lies only seven miles away from the official residence of the most powerful person in the world, the President of the United States of America.

Born in Philadelphia to American parents with Irish heritage but no interest whatsoever in football (or **"soccer"**), the man who now hosts one of the numerous flourishing Celtic internet radio shows grew up with virtually no knowledge of the sport, let alone the Club, which he now loves. In fact, even for a man who works in the optical trade, he himself jokes that he could never have seen this coming in his early life.

"Now, to really get your head around all of this, you have to understand the way Americans tend to view sports" said Graham, as he began to explain how his love of a team playing on the other side of the world's second largest ocean took root.

"In America, most people tend to support their local teams. Now, that's fine, but if, for example, the individual in question moves to another city or state, many of them proceed to simply change their allegiances and support their new local guys. Some people even have favourite players and will simply support whoever they happen to be playing for at that time! Obviously, there are a fair number of people who are loyal to one team, but the kind of tribalism you tend to find in European sports is totally different from what you see over here."

And so, as a result of being a resident of Philadelphia for most of his life, Graham supports the local sides from that area, namely the baseball team, the Philadelphia Phillies; the basketball side, the Philadelphia 76ers and American football franchise, the Philadelphia Eagles, despite the fact he now lives in Washington D.C.

While he was at college in the 1990's, Graham laments that the Eagles, in particular, **"totally sucked"**. Now, it is not uncommon in some cities in the United States for one, or several, of their sports teams to go through long spells of poor form, and this is largely accepted. Whilst some cities seem to produce success after success, others seem to struggle to find anything remotely resembling it for decades at a time, and yet the fans still turn out in their numbers.

For example, whilst the Eagles last won the old National Football League Championship in 1960, they didn't reach their first modern day **"Super Bowl"** until 1981, before losing heavily on that occasion. They repeated the feat in 2005, but once again they came away as losers. In fact, the only recent success the city has enjoyed came courtesy of the Phillies, who won the **"World Series"** in 2008. To contextualise this somewhat, the city's previous triumph came in 1983, when Graham was just four.

Anyway, despite all of this, it is safe to say that the American people absolutely love their home-grown sports. Graham told me he found it odd though when he heard the manner in which a friend at college spoke about American sport. Born in Glasgow, Scotland, the man in question spent his days not only talking down the Eagles (which was a fairly common pastime as I alluded to earlier) but also talking down the National Football League and other competitions in general.

"He had absolutely no interest in American sport whatsoever. All he kept talking about was this team from Scotland called "Celtic", continually mentioning scores against teams I'd never heard of and discussing rules I didn't understand" said Graham.

With the coverage of soccer in America in the 1990's being virtually non-existent (one MLS game each month was shown on television and, even then, it had Spanish commentary), Graham had no idea who Celtic were, but surprisingly he initially recalls disliking them.

"I'd never seen them play, I didn't know where they played, who any of their players were or even what kits they wore... but in Philadelphia, the city's basketball team have one big rival in particular, the Boston Celtics. Now, I used to hate the

Celtics – everyone did – so I'll admit that I was a little sceptical at first when I heard this guy from Glasgow constantly going on about Celtic."

However, as those who have heard Graham speak about Celtic will know, his opinions have changed dramatically. In his fairly brief conversations with his friend from Glasgow, Graham began to learn not just of the history of Celtic and their supporters, but also of their fiercest rivals and those who followed them. In the United States, hatred based on religious or ethnic grounds virtually never defines a sporting rivalry, so this idea did come as a bit of a shock when Graham first began to discover it. He admits he couldn't really grasp why one group of people would hold such disdain for Catholics and/or people of Irish descent. Anyway, having learned a little about the football rivalry in Glasgow and of how much it meant to people, Graham decided to **"go and check it out"** as he put it.

Typically, as if it was destiny, the first Celtic match Graham Wilson ever saw just happened to be one of the greatest days in the Club's history, when he was invited to watch the game at the local Celtic Supporters Club on the ninth of May 1998. Celtic Football Club stood on the verge of Scottish League Championship glory, something which they had not tasted for nine agonising years. To stop Rangers surpassing Celtic's record of nine league titles in a row, Celtic had to beat St Johnstone. If they were successful in that regard, whatever Rangers did that day would be irrelevant.

Of course, at the time, Graham didn't really understand any of this. He confesses to feeling slightly intimidated due to his American accent in a bar predominantly filled with Scottish and Irish people. Watching the game **"from the edges"** of the pub, with no real idea as to the intricacies of the sport at that stage, Graham saw Celtic **"stop the ten"**, witnessing fully grown adults hug people they had met only hours before as if they were siblings, often whilst tears streamed from their eyes.

The atmosphere and passion he observed that day struck something deep within him, and it would lead him to research the history of Celtic Football Club in some detail, as well as the sport itself.

"I remember standing there at the St Johnstone game thinking: "Oh my God. I want this team to win so badly. If they lose, I'll be so pissed. I don't even know where they play; I need to learn more about these guys.""

I have to say that I did chuckle (as does Graham) when he recalled talking to someone about the game in the coming days and producing the unforgettable line: **"A guy with dreadlocks, and a guy called Backpack scored."** However, it just shows you how someone can go from knowing almost nothing about a subject to becoming a full-on enthusiast when they kindle an interest in something they genuinely love.

By the time his twenty-first birthday came and went, Graham was regularly checking the scores on the internet to see how the Club he was already describing as **"my team"** were doing, but with the lack of coverage in America, he still rarely saw anything of Celtic themselves. It was only after he left college and returned to Philadelphia that Graham asked a friend from Belfast if he supported Celtic. Despite being a little taken aback by the question, his friend told him that he was indeed a huge Celtic fan, and invited Graham to the still fairly new **"Philadelphia Fado C.S.C."**.

Once again, by his own admission, Graham was wary at first. He only knew a few members of the Supporters Club, one of which was Séamus Cummins (also the subject of a chapter in this book). Séamus was one of the others in the Club with an American accent, but Graham didn't speak to him much as he considered him to be of the more senior figures within the group. Perhaps naively, he didn't feel that it was his place to do so at first. However, as time went on, his interest continued to grow, and he fondly tells me of the moment he knew he was hooked:

"I was young, and as young people do, I used to go out drinking a lot. Initially, if you'd asked me whether I would have rather gone out for the night or got up at 6am the next morning to watch a football game I know what I would have said, but over time I found myself thinking "Celtic are playing on Sunday, so I'll be sure to go out on Friday night, not Saturday." Maybe it was the passion growing within me, or maybe I was just getting bored of

the endless hangovers, but it certainly changed my approach to the weekends."

In 2002, with the introduction of "**Channel 67**" online, Graham began to feel more confident and comfortable supporting Celtic. The continuing research which he had been doing now meant he understood a lot more about the game of football as well as the Club itself than he had done initially. This work, combined with a move with his wife to Washington D.C. (and, perhaps more importantly to the Washington D.C. C.S.C. that was based there), had a huge impact on his life with regards to Celtic. The supporters in D.C. welcomed him with open arms, and this only spurred on his desire to follow the Hoops. In several ways, this development was a labour of love for Graham. The more he learned about Celtic, particularly about proud, unshakable figures like Martin O'Neill and Neil Lennon, it simply reinforced his growing love for the Football Club. This, coupled with his increasing knowledge of his own connection to the Irish Diaspora, with family originating from Armagh and Cork, added a personal touch to it all.

In amongst all of this was Graham's wife, Elizabeth, who actually has more of an Irish connection in her family than he does in his. However, whilst she has an interest in American sports, she doesn't view "**soccer**" in the same manner as Graham, who said: **"I would be sitting there listening to the Celtic Underground podcast, and she'd come in and ask, "How can you understand what those people are saying? It sounds like a totally different language to me!""** Little did they know then that one day, Graham would go on to host his own Celtic show.

In the coming years, Celtic would make several trips to the United States of America, and these visits would provide Graham with his first opportunities to see the Bhoys in person. He happily told me about the run-up to one fixture, where his hometown team Philadelphia Union were set to take on Celtic: **"I could barely contain my excitement. It was all I'd been thinking about for weeks, regardless of whether I was driving, working, eating, or just lying in bed. To see Celtic play in my home city was something very special indeed, although it was a little surreal as I wanted**

to see this side from thousands of miles away hammer the local team."

However, at the match itself, he told me about receiving some verbal abuse from certain individuals supporting Philadelphia (who supported Chelsea as their **"British team"**) about the Pope and Catholicism simply because he had **"the cheek"** to support Celtic and have an American accent. I'm sure I don't need to go into the specifics of what was said, as you'll get the gist, no doubt. Anyway, this troubled Graham greatly and, as a result, he admits to losing much of the love he once held for the Philadelphia support. He still attends matches on occasion, as he wants to see Major League Soccer continue to progress and the sport of football develop in the States, but he confesses it is just not the same as it was.

In the spring of 2011, Graham travelled around Ireland on holiday. Whilst in Dublin, he visited the pub owned by Anthony Stokes' father. He spoke of how amazed the locals were to see someone, with a noticeable accent, who was so enthusiastic about Celtic. In fact, he claims he had similar experiences all over the country, with one man even saying he was **"stunned at his tactical knowledge".** Graham adored the people of Ireland, but it did trouble him slightly that some of them seemed to presume an American could not, or perhaps simply would not, have a clue about football.

Once he was back in the United States, Graham developed a bond with fellow Celtic supporters (and future presenters on the show), Jim McGuigan and **"The Rev"**. This led to them meeting up to watch the Scottish Cup Final of 2011 against Motherwell, where they continued to **"hit it off"**. In amongst the fairly large quantities of beer, Graham suggested that the three should do a Celtic radio show or podcast, following in the footsteps of **"Over and Over"** and the **"Home Bhoys"**, in order to let people around the world know that there are indeed United States born Celtic supporters who love and follow the Club just the same as anyone else.

For a while though, the idea remained as just that, an idea. However, one day that would all change when they finally organised themselves and aired the first edition of the **"Beyond the Waves"** Celtic radio show which went live on **"UStream"**, winning endless plaudits in doing so. When I first heard the show, I recall that I was heartened by the fact there were so many people who were not only based in America, but were born in America, who absolutely adored Celtic. It was something I had always known to be true in the back of my mind, but that, coupled with my own personal experiences as I began to play a part in the online world which surrounds Celtic Football Club simply hammered this fact home. Fundamentally, I believe these supporters are just as important to the Club as someone born within sight of the stadium, and they should be treated as such.

Graham regrets that the supporters in North America were, in their minds, provided with a poor service by the Club in the early years. **"Setanta"** (which became **"Premium Sports"** latterly) charged Supporters Clubs three hundred dollars per game in broadcast fees, meaning that even at ten dollars a head, C.S.C.'s needed to draw at least thirty people every week just to break even. Now, that might seem like a small number of people for a pub on the face of it, but we have to remember that the east coast of America is five hours behind us in terms of time, meaning games are generally either in the early morning or the middle of the working day.

Anyway, the Club were roundly criticised by the North American support for refusing to speak to the C.S.C.'s or the broadcaster about this issue, which sadly forced some Supporters Clubs to cease to exist. In more recent times though, Graham cannot praise Celtic enough for the improvements they have made. The introduction of **"Celtic TV"** has brought the prices for watching Celtic games abroad down significantly, and this cost saving (coupled with an increase in the standard of football it must be said) has people who have not been regulars at C.S.C.'s for years coming back again. This move, together with the relatively recent birth of Celtic's official presence on Twitter, has Graham complimenting the Club on the efforts they have made, although he still bemoans the amount of time it takes for items bought from Celtic's online store to be shipped to the United States.

Moving back on to the subject of this chapter, as those of you who regularly tune into **"Beyond the Waves"** will know, Graham has a fairly unique style of broadcasting. As a well spoken man, he can, and often does, speak his mind for a several minutes at a time in an eloquent manner. At times, he does this to fill time between calls or to introduce the new topic they are set to discuss, but, on occasion, Graham has one of his increasingly famous rants. Now, you must understand that if something Celtic related vexes Graham, he is generally more than happy to say why. These rants can go on for several minutes at time, seemingly without the host pausing to draw breath, and they make for interesting listening if nothing else. Anyway, as **"Beyond the Waves"** continues to grow from strength to strength as part of the **"Hail Hail Media"** group, with weekly downloads of the show in the thousands, Graham does admit that he was originally a little concerned people would laugh at him in the show's earliest days.

However, the determination he possessed to succeed and prove to people that anyone can develop a love of something and, as a result, amass a significant knowledge regarding it drove him, his counterparts, and therefore their show onwards. In the coming months, he would show this sort of spirit once again, but this time it would affect people much closer to home.

One morning in the summer of 2011, Graham received a phone call from Séamus Cummins to tell him about the blaze which engulfed his family's house. Despite the fact Séamus reassured Graham that everyone was ok, Graham told me he felt compelled to do something – even though at that stage, he didn't know what it would be. He recalls driving straight to the nearest football store, and buying all the Celtic shirts and footballs he could afford, before sending them onwards to Séamus' sons.

As the news of the events of the previous night began to circulate around the internet and consequently the world, Graham spent much of his time over the coming days telling people that the family were all safe and sound. Such was the desire within the support to help the Cummins family, Graham set up a PayPal fund where Celtic supporters could donate some money if they wished to do so. In only a short space of time, a staggering four figure sum was raised. Without repeating myself with regards to the chapter about Séamus, this event had a big impact on Graham. It reminded him firstly of the fragility of our lives, but also of the good in the hearts of so many members of the Celtic support. Thankfully, Graham and Séamus still feature together regularly on the show, and keep in touch most days.

In more recent times, as Celtic reached the last sixteen of the UEFA Champions League in 2012–13, Graham Wilson finally did what he had dreamt of doing for over a decade, and came home to Celtic Park. I'll allow him to finish off this chapter with his own words, describing his hopes and fears for his trip to Glasgow, as well as what the reality was like:

"I had only pictures and video to give me my perspective of Celtic Park previously, but as I set my eyes on it for the first time whilst walking up the Gallowgate, it took my breath away. It was as if I'd seen a phoenix rising up out of the East End of Glasgow - the tangible product of the vision and determination possessed by the wee man with the bunnet, Fergus McCann. I welled up with emotion and the only thing I could say was "wow". As I walked closer to the stadium, I was almost speechless and I needed a few moments so that I could to attempt to take it all in. As I rounded the corner and saw the statues of Brother Walfrid, Jock Stein and Jimmy Johnstone, I nearly sobbed tears of joy."

"I'd finally made it after years of dreaming about that moment, and having wondered, at times, if the day itself would ever actually come. I'd seen Celtic six times in the flesh before, but only in the United States. To see Celtic play at their home ground in a Champions League tie was utterly surreal, and to be surrounded by another sixty thousand Celtic supporters singing "You'll Never Walk Alone" was something I will never forget. Of course, the result against Juventus was very disappointing, but it didn't ruin a thing for me. I was lucky enough to see a second game on the following Saturday as well, as Celtic thumped Dundee United by a margin of six goals to two."

"Afterwards, I was joined by a dozen or so of the show's supporters [including the author] for a few pints on Sauchiehall Street, and in spite of suffering badly with the flu, I had a brilliant time. More importantly, I attained a sense of just what it means to support Celtic. To have such a close network of folks who have your back and are excited to meet you was an incredibly humbling and proud moment for me. Ironically, even though it was the first time I'd met the majority of these people in person, I felt like I'd already known them for years and, of course, in a sense I had. Even now, as I sit here back in D.C., I know I'll continue to be connected with them for years to come, for we all share the common bond that is a love of Celtic Football Club. God bless each and every one of them."

"The Mighty Quinn"

Celtic's Scottish Cup win in 2011 caused my mind to wander as I strode back through the rain soaked streets of Glasgow's Southside in search of my lift home. Undoubtedly, that triumph will go down in history as the day on which Celtic won their first silverware under Neil Lennon, at the end of a season where football was rarely the main focus of everyone's attention, as explosive devices were intercepted within the mail system and an utter idiot, whose name I shall not dignify with a direct mention in this book, was pulled away from the Celtic manager on the touchline at Tynecastle. Regardless, the victory at Hampden inspired me to look back at one of Celtic's greatest Scottish Cup wins - the 1904 defeat of Rangers - and consequently, at the man who won the trophy almost singlehandedly. James Quinn, generally referred to as Jimmy, was born in the village of Croy, North Lanarkshire – a place few people would have heard of – that is if it wasn't for Jimmy. The village itself was built by the **"William Baird Company"** to house the Irish Catholic immigrants working in the nearby mining trade, in a separate settlement from the nearby, largely Protestant, town of Kilsyth. Jimmy was born on the eighth of July 1878, and grew up to work in the local mines, like the majority of men his age. In this sense, he was as ordinary as the next man, but it just so happened that when a football was placed at his feet, Jimmy Quinn became rather extraordinary. While he played for local junior side Smithside Albion, he rebuffed a contract offer from English league side Sunderland, as he felt it was too far away from his home and his family for him to consider a possibility. It was only at the age of twenty-two, relatively late for a footballer to start his professional career now, that Willie Maley went out to meet Quinn and attempt to sign him. Initially, Jimmy was unsure, but eventually he would come around to the idea.

He had a quiet and rather shy nature as an individual, and two factors above all others concerned him with regards to a potential move to Celtic. Firstly, he wasn't hugely keen on Glasgow as it was a fair distance from his home in Croy – however, in comparison to Sunderland, or any other footballing city, it was about as close an offer as he was likely to receive. Secondly, and somewhat incredibly with the benefit of hindsight, the great Jimmy Quinn genuinely doubted whether or not he was good enough to compete as a professional footballer at all, let alone at a Club like Celtic. Thankfully though, after a fair amount of discussion, Maley was able to persuade the young man that this was the right move for him, and that he should finally accept their offer and sign for the Parkhead side.

In saying that, he only managed this by assuring Jimmy that he could commute to Glasgow using the train line that ran through his hometown, and by highlighting that the Club and his new teammates would help him to develop as a footballer. After all, **"would Celtic really have been interested in signing him if they did not believe he possessed a significant level of talent? Of course not"**, said Maley. And so, on the thirty-first of December 1900, Jimmy signed provisionally with Celtic Football Club, before signing fully on the twelfth of January 1901. Only a week later, he made his debut and scored his first professional goal as Celtic defeated St Mirren by four goals to three in Paisley. The Celts started emphatically that day, leading by four goals to one at the break, with Quinn as the first goalscorer. However, in the second half, St Mirren attacked their opponents more strongly – in all senses of the word – as the match became rather physical. However, Celtic hung on for the victory, and Jimmy Quinn was off and running as a Celtic player.

At this early stage in his Parkhead career, Willie Maley played his new signing as a left winger, a position in which he was competent enough, but not entirely comfortable. Despite this, his natural ability shone through fairly regularly and yet, oddly, both the player and his manager couldn't quite decide what Quinn's best position was for sure, even after some experimentation in this regard.

However, in 1904, at the end of the first season in which Celtic wore their now iconic green and white Hoops, Celtic were scheduled to play Rangers in the Scottish Cup Final at Hampden Park. Having already lost both the 1901 and 1902 Scottish Cup Finals in the last few years to Hearts and Hibs respectively, Willie Maley made a tactical adjustment that would go down in Celtic folklore. He took the radical decision to take centre-forward Alec Bennett out of the starting line-up, to be replaced with Jimmy Quinn (moving Quinn from outside-left, where he had featured in both of the aforementioned Scottish Cup Final defeats, meant Bobby Muir started in that position instead).

In Willie Maley's book, **"The Story of the Celtic"**, he describes Celtic as besieging Rangers' goal for the first quarter of an hour, before Rangers woke up and Speedie scored two goals in two minutes at the new Hampden. However, the stage was now set for one of the greatest comebacks (and individual performances) in the Club's history. With his side trailing by two goals to nil, Jimmy Quinn received the ball around the halfway line and knocked it forward into the wind which was blowing towards him. He then used his speed and strength to push past two Rangers defenders and catch up with the ball, before sending a thunderous shot into the net from the edge of the opponent's box – Celtic one, Rangers two. Only minutes later, some great work by the replacement left winger, Bobby Muir, led to him sending the ball across the Rangers goalmouth for Jimmy Quinn to slot home once again – Celtic two, Rangers two.

At half time, as the estimated sixty-five thousand spectators in attendance mused over the first half's proceedings, many of them could have sensed that they were witnessing something special – at a new Hampden, a new star was rising – the Bhoy from Croy was about to write himself into the history books. With only minutes remaining and the scores still tied, Jimmy Quinn received possession of the ball around thirty yards out. He then feinted a pass towards a wide position, before turning and heading for goal himself. As he made use of now his infamous pace and power (the attributes that won him nicknames such as **"The Croy Express"**) he made his way through the Rangers defence before cleverly directing the ball past the helpless John Watson in the Rangers goal. While the Celtic fans (and several players) were sent into absolute hysteria by this late strike, Jimmy Quinn simply turned and walked back to the centre circle once he saw the ball pass through the posts in front of him. He had just scored the first Scottish Cup Final hat-trick of all time, and yet he was so determined not to let this chance of victory slip through his fingers, that he could not begin to even consider celebrating just yet. Rangers were unable to equalise, and after a truly sublime display by one man above all others, Celtic had won their first major silverware of the twentieth century, and the first 'glory years' at the Football Club had begun. Happily, there would be many more trophies to follow for Maley, Quinn, and everyone else associated with Celtic, as this victory gave the team the confidence to move forward and win an unprecedented six consecutive league titles (between 1904–05 and 1909–10) and three more Scottish Cups in the same time period. Whilst doing so, Celtic also became the first side to do something many people said **"could not be done"**, as they became the first Club to win a league and cup double in Scotland in 1906–07. They then proceeded to top even that mean feat by winning every one of the four competitions they entered in 1907–1908, something no Celtic squad would repeat until the Lisbon Lions. However, not everything was perfect for Jimmy. Over the course his career, he had several run-ins with the Scottish Football Association, generally after matches against Rangers (something many 'Celtic-minded' individuals know far too well nowadays).

Less than a month after his heroic performance in the 1904 Scottish Cup Final, Celtic faced the Ibrox side in the Glasgow Charity Cup Final at Hampden once more, and again, it was a hard fought match, with the tie ending five-two in favour of Rangers. However, before half time, Jimmy Quinn was forced to retire from the match having been injured by what he saw as a very rash 'tackle' from one of the opposition players, and before the match itself was even over, Jimmy found himself in hospital. The damage done to his leg was of such a severe nature that it kept him out of the Hoops' upcoming tour of Europe and it took him several months to recover fully. The nature of the challenge stuck with the quiet and unassuming Jimmy, and let's put it this way, he was not overly fond of Rangers or much to do with the club from then onwards.

However, prior to his next run in with the aforementioned blue-noses, Jimmy Quinn was awarded his first full international cap, as he was selected to play for Scotland as they took on Ireland at Celtic Park, on the eighteenth of March 1905. He scored the third goal that day, as the home side ran out four-nil victors in front of approximately forty thousand people in the East End of Glasgow. During the following season, Jimmy featured twice for Scotland, but he did not manage to score, and this fact, combined with some less than ideal overall team performances conspired to see him lose his place in the side for the next couple of years.

Returning to 1905, the first major incident of controversy involving Jimmy Quinn occurred at Celtic Park on the twenty-fifth of March, during the Scottish Cup semi-final between the teams already emerging as **"Glasgow's big two"**. By all accounts, it was a truly awful day with regards the Glaswegian weather, with relentless bands of rain making the pitch incredibly slippery. Rangers led Celtic by two goals to nil, and as Celtic delivered a cross into the Rangers box, a defender by the name of Alec Craig leapt for the ball, losing his footing on the slick surface when he landed. As he fell, he held on to Jimmy Quinn's leg to try and steady himself, causing Jimmy to fall with him and collide with Craig's head. Despite both Quinn, and to be fair to him, even Alec Craig, attempting to persuade the referee to change his decision, Jimmy was immediately sent off, and subsequently suspended from football for a month as **"punishment"**. I feel it is worthy of mention that the home support that day then took matters into their own hands. They were so outraged by what they saw as an absolutely unbelievable decision that they invaded the pitch and, initially, caused the match to be interrupted, as groups of fans: **"...mobbed the players and the referee, Mr Robertson, was assaulted and he had to be escorted from the field by several policemen. Some of the Celtic players were carried off of the field by their sympathisers."**

The match was then delayed for approximately a quarter of an hour, before another pitch invasion within minutes of the restart eventually caused the game to be abandoned entirely (forcing Celtic to concede the tie). Quinn's suspension also meant he missed an upcoming international fixture with England, and this only fuelled the belief within the Celtic support that their players were being discriminated against, not only in domestic matches, but also when it came to being awarded with international caps.

A little over a month after that disturbance, Celtic were set to face their increasingly intense rivals in a play-off match for the 1904–05 Scottish League Championship, as the two sides had finished on the same number of points at the end of the regular season – as is discussed in an earlier chapter. Jimmy played that day as the Celts won by two goals to one but, rarely for him, he did not actually score. Having said that, it should not be forgotten that Jimmy played a big part in the build-up to both of the Celtic goals that day. Also, there should be no doubts in the minds of anyone that it was the often critical goals from Jimmy Quinn which fundamentally allowed Celtic reach the points total to feature in the play-off match in the first place, as he alone was responsible for several of the points picked up over the course of the league campaign proper.

For example, Celtic defeated Port Glasgow Athletic in their second match of the season by four goals to one, with three of the four coming from Jimmy: **"Towards the end of the game, Quinn, who all through was playing in deadly style, received some injury to one of his legs, but this did not prevent him adding another goal for the Celts."** Quotes such as that one were not uncommon sights in Scotland's newspapers in those days, as Jimmy Quinn not only scored barrel loads of goals, but also regularly had injuries intentionally and unintentionally inflected upon him by his opponents. However, he rarely let it faze him, as he continually gave all he had for his team and their supporters.

In December, Jimmy scored the only goal of a one-nil victory at Morton; in February, he scored the first two of the four goals which would see the Celts take a critically important two points from their four-one victory at Ibrox in the league; and in March, as Celtic travelled to Fir Park for their final league match of the season, Celtic held a four point advantage over Rangers, who had two games in hand. The Ibrox side were not set to play that day, and so a win for Celtic would give the Hoops a six point lead at the top, with three games more played to be played by their closest competitors. This would leave Rangers requiring three victories to force a play-off and so the importance of this match cannot be understated, even more than a century on from it. The Hoops would go on to win by six goals to two against Motherwell that afternoon, with Quinn scoring yet another hat-trick.

However, we know now that Rangers did win their remaining three games, and therefore forced the play-off which Celtic won, but that day in Motherwell was simply another example of the goalscoring force of Jimmy Quinn that season, which drove Celtic Football Club forwards towards their first league title in seven years. Had Celtic dropped any points against the Fir Park side, and Rangers then went on to win their three matches in hand as they did, it would have been the Ibrox side who were crowned Champions, and therefore, the next few years may not have turned out to be as successful as they truly were for Celtic. Quinn's second run-in with the Scottish Football Association and the officials they employed came in the New Year's Day game against Rangers in 1907. Having beaten their rivals in the first league encounter that season, Celtic travelled to Ibrox in good spirits, for they led the league table by a relatively significant margin and Rangers were not playing as if they were serious contenders for the title. However, on another soaking wet Glaswegian day, Joe Hendry, of Rangers, had just fouled inside forward Jimmy McMenemy. Quinn was so disgusted with this foul (and possibly with the fact his side were trailing by two goals to one despite having had several good chances they were unable to convert) that he began to sprint over to the referee in order to put to him his view of the incident. However, he slipped on the treacherous surface as he approached the official, instead ploughing into Joe Hendry – temporarily injuring him – an action which the referee deemed to be intentional. The sending off he received resulted in an astonishing suspension no less than two months in length being handed down to him (clearly the S.F.A. liked doubling bans and suspensions for 'Celtic-minded' folk back then too), and Quinn was enraged. This time, the Celtic supporters were so mystified by the decision-making that they actually raised money to pay Quinn's wages over the course of his suspension and, indeed, even bought his wife a piece of jewellery as a token of their support.

Ironically, having served his punishment, Jimmy's first match back in the Celtic squad was to be a Scottish Cup quarter final match against Rangers at Ibrox. Whilst it would have been somewhat forgivable if Jimmy (or for argument's sake one of his teammates) had lost his temper that day, especially when one considers the prior circumstances which he had to endure, he did no such thing. In fact, the entire Celtic side, with Jimmy spearheading the forward line as ever, played coolly with an admirable level of maturity, calmly asserting their dominance when it came to sheer ability on the turf at Ibrox Park by defeating the home side three-nil. Whilst Jimmy did not score, he was once again in the thick of the action, bullying defenders and spreading the ball across the field of play for his teammates. This was an important step on the way to the first domestic double in the history of Scottish Football, and performances such as this should be both remembered and appreciated long into the future.

As the 1907–08 season got underway, Celtic started their campaign with five victories from five matches – scoring three times on every occasion – defeating Hamilton Academical, Motherwell, Morton, Dundee and Falkirk in the process, leaving them top of the table by a single point ahead of Rangers in early September. Of these fifteen goals, Jimmy Quinn provided four, but it is noteworthy that he was often heavily involved in the build up which led to some of his teammate's scoring strikes.

In October that year, Celtic faced Rangers in the final of the Glasgow Charity Cup at Hampden Park. Quinn scored the Celts' second goal in the match, which finished in a two-all draw. This led to a replay a week later, which ended in another draw and, subsequently, this resulted in the sides having to play each other for a third consecutive weekend in a row (with Jimmy featuring on each occasion). In the end, first half goals from Peter Somers and David McLean were enough for Celtic to finally defeat their rivals, on the third time of asking, by two goals to one. With each match bringing in four figure sums from entry fees and ticket sales (considered to be enormous totals in those days), it is understandable that some supporters felt that the Clubs were intentionally drawing big matches, knowing that they could both benefit financially from the income another tie would bring. This ill-feeling would boil over less than two years later at Hampden, after the 1909 Scottish Cup Final replay between the two clubs was drawn, as I shall describe in a moment. I have merely highlighted these three matches to prove that precedents had been set in the past, before referring to Jimmy's role in the events of that day.

In March 1908, Jimmy would pull on a Scotland jersey once again, as he featured in ties against both Ireland and England. The name **"Quinn"** appeared no less than four times on the score-sheet against the Irish, a feat which only a select few have ever matched in the colours of their native Scotland. However, despite featuring in a one-all draw with England, as well as leading the forward line in the premier domestic side in the country, Jimmy wouldn't appear for the national team for another two years thereafter.

As Celtic pushed for their fifth league title in a row and 1908–09 drew to a close, they were forced to play eight games in twelve days at the end of the season in order to fulfil their fixture list – a schedule which would be considered as unthinkable by top flight sides nowadays. Jimmy scored seven times in those eight games, all of which he played in, as he helped Celtic to attain an unprecedented run of five consecutive Scottish League Championships.

However, prior to those matches, there was of course the little matter of a Scottish Cup Final with rivals Rangers to attend to. As I have mentioned at other points in this piece, Celtic had done the double for the first time in 1907, a feat which many previously branded as an impossibility. To add insults to those critic's injuries, the Hoops had done it again in 1908 (winning every competition they took part in that season) and, as they entered May of 1909, a third consecutive domestic double appeared to be a serious possibility for the Parkhead Club. With minutes remaining at Hampden in the first Cup Final though, this potential triumph looked somewhat unlikely, as the Ibrox side led two by goals to one – that is until Jimmy Quinn forced the ball into the back of the Rangers net, as **"The Glasgow Herald"** describes below:

"In the last 10 minutes Celtic recovered somewhat, and Munro flashing a shot in to Rennie, the goalkeeper in evading Quinn [who attempted a shoulder charge] swung the ball over the line, and Celtic drew a sensational game."

For those of you who may not fully understand the significance of that quote, allow me to expand upon it somewhat. At that time, players were allowed and, in some cases actively encouraged, to **"charge"** opposition goalkeepers if they had the ball in their hands for more than a second or two. This was somewhat similar to a modern day shoulder tackle on steroids, and whilst it may seem rough looking back on it, in those days it was viewed as a normal part of the game. As such, players who were regarded as strong chargers were adored by their respective supporters, and with his broad shoulders and renowned physicality on the field of play, it will come as no surprise to you that Jimmy Quinn (also known colloquially as **"The Bison"**) made use of the tactic whenever he could. And so, in summary, Jimmy managed to force the ball over the goal line that day without touching the player or even the ball itself, as his reputation resulted in the Rangers goalkeeper's mind focusing on the approaching Bhoy from Croy rather than where the ball was in relation to his goal line.

A week later, Jimmy was involved in the critical events of the day once more, as he headed home a late goal to cancel out Rangers' one-nil lead, causing the replay of the Scottish Cup Final to end in the aforementioned draw. It is then said that whilst many of the Ibrox side headed to the changing rooms upon the sounding of the full time whistle, some of the Celts did not, caught up in the confusion of it all and expecting a period of extra time to be played. Upon seeing some supporters climbing the fences and invading the field, Jimmy did what he could to urge them to return to the terracing, before realising that his efforts were in vain and sprinting off towards the main stand at Hampden Park along with his colleagues. In the ensuing chaos, supporters of both sides (who had been so enraged by the prospect of having to pay to watch a third match; suspecting collusion between the two clubs) joined forces, breaking both sets of goalposts, tearing up large sections of the field, destroying lavatories and even setting fire to a couple of pay boxes. Extensive battles with the police followed, and several knives (as well as other weapons) were later found upon inspection of the field. However, the iconic image of that day remains a photograph taken from outside the ground, which shows large plumes of smoke rising over the national stadium.

The following is a letter entitled "**SCOTTISH CUP FINAL – CELTIC V RANGERS REPLAY**" from Queen's Park Football Club to the Scottish Football Association, highlighting not only their anger that such events were allowed to take place within their home ground, but also outlining their desire to seek significant compensation for all of the damage which was done:

"Dear Sir,

I regret exceedingly to inform you that at the conclusion of the replay at Hampden Park on Saturday last, the 17th, there was considerable damage done to the property and effects of this Club by the mobbing and rioting of a section of spectators, and the pay boxes on the northern side of the ground, containing 22 turnstiles, have been completed destroyed by fire or violence.

In addition to this, 5 gates and 4 latrines, at least, have also been completely destroyed, and damage to a considerable extent has been done to the playing pitch and terracing on the north side of the field. It is of course impossible at the moment to estimate the amount of damage done, but from what you saw on Saturday night, you should be able to give your committee some idea of it.

My object in formally writing to you now is to advise you of the fact, and, in view of eventualities, to give your committee an opportunity of having the debris inspected, and an estimate made of the damage done, should they desire to do so.

As it is extremely desirous, in the interests of public safety, that the ruined structures should at once be removed, I shall be

obliged by your making arrangements for the inspection at your earliest convenience. I may mention that I have given instructions to our groundsmen to leave the debris untouched, until all interested parties have had an opportunity of inspecting it.

Kindly acknowledge receipt,
Yours Faithfully,
C.B. Miller, Secretary, Queen's Park Football Club"

Putting the debatable rights and wrongs of the riot which followed to one side for a moment, the events of that day would mean the Scottish Football Association would withhold the trophy that year, and therefore Celtic were unable to determine whether or not they would win a third domestic double in a row. In fact, with the benefit of hindsight, we can now ponder whether Celtic could (and perhaps would) have made it an incredible four domestic doubles and five Scottish Cups in a row, as they won both major domestic trophies once again in 1909–10, as well as the Scottish Cup in 1911.

For the record, the S.F.A. eventually came to the conclusion that approximately one thousand pounds worth of damage had been done to Hampden Park that day – a remarkable amount for that period in history. However, Queen's Park were left infuriated as both Celtic and Rangers were only ordered to pay one hundred and fifty pounds each in compensation, with the Association covering the rest of the cost. Now, when one considers that both Celtic and Rangers made around one and a half thousand pounds each in ticket sales for the two matches, the anger of Queen's Park becomes all the more understandable. Subsequently, Hampden Park did not host another Scottish Cup Final until 1922.

However, returning to 1909, even after that infamous day and the fixture congestion it partly contributed to, Celtic still found themselves with a significant league deficit of nine points to leaders Dundee, who had played several more matches. Regardless, six victories and two draws from their remaining eight ties meant the Hoops would win the league by a solitary point from the Dens Park outfit.

Despite scoring four times in an international match in Dublin in 1908 (as previously discussed), Jimmy Quinn's international prowess would not truly be appreciated until 1910, when he was selected for all three of his country's British Home Championship matches that year. When Scotland faced England at Hampden in their final match of the short campaign, Jimmy proved himself to be almost unplayable on the highest level of them all as, after his Celtic teammate Jimmy McMenemy had opening the scoring, Quinn fired home the second from the edge of the penalty box, helping Scotland to a two-nil victory. Although they didn't know (and perhaps didn't expect) it at the time, these goals would be enough to win the Championship that year, as Wales defeated Ireland in their final match, leaving Scotland as the unlikely winners.

The following quote from one newspaper highlights that Quinn did far more that day that score a goal. In fact he and McMenemy ran the forward line, as if the pair were firemen fuelling an almighty Scottish football train with coal, making sure all was well and completing their jobs with expertise but, critically, without complacency. This was perhaps appropriate for Quinn in particular – after all, he was nicknamed **"The Croy Express"**.

"Quinn never showed such self-sacrifice. His game was to see that the English defence did not trouble his partners, and he carried that out admirably, staving off opponents and playing the real centre game by feeding his wings and sinking his individuality."

A year later, it was **"six in a row"** for Celtic, and the greatest side the Parkhead Club were fortunate enough to see in its early days began to disassemble. Jimmy started to miss the occasional match due to recurring injury and the increased recovery time that comes with age for any athlete, but he was far from **"past it"** just yet. In 1911, after one hundred and seventy minutes of goalless football in the replay of the Scottish Cup Final, he would open the scoring at Ibrox as Celtic defeated Hamilton by two goals to nil, as was discussed in **"The Scotsman"** newspaper:

"But though the Celtic pressed, and pressed persistently, they found the Hamilton goal difficult to locate. McMenemy worked

hard, and Quinn continued to be the outstanding shot of his side. Thus it was only fitting that when a goal did come, the famous Celtic centre had the honour of scoring it."

However, whilst **"The Glasgow Herald"** could not praise his efforts and talents highly enough, as you can see, they do allude to the fact the years may be just beginning to take their toll on **"The Mighty Quinn"**:

"...and the monotony of another prolonged Celtic attack began. Quinn, eager for goals, showed much earnestness when he rushed after the ball and tried to keep it in play with a capital header."

"After twice endeavouring to break away the Academicals lost their first goal, Quinn with a hard, oblique shot giving Watson practically no chance to save his charge."

"...while Quinn, still far from his physical self, was harshly dealt with – from our view – by the referees in the early stages, and was seemingly out of humour afterwards. He was always a keen trier, and his goal was a good one, but the old acute perception was lacking."

Jimmy would also feature in the Scottish Cup Final victory of the following season against Clyde, once again at Ibrox, but he would not score on that occasion. Sadly though, as the years passed, the name of **"Quinn"**, which had once been synonymous with virtually every Celtic line-up, whether it was in the league or cup, became a rarer and rarer sight on the Parkhead Club's team sheets.

Prior to the 1912 Cup Final, Jimmy would be rewarded twice more with the final international call-ups of his career, for matches against Wales and England. Whilst Scotland struggled against a **"robust"** (read as borderline dirty) Welsh team at Tynecastle, they would snatch victory thanks to a late Jimmy Quinn goal, which would turn out to be his last for his country. Whilst he may not have been at his peak anymore, it was clear the Welsh continued to believe he would present the main threat to their goalmouth, as they kicked the thirty-three year old up and down the park all afternoon:

"Quinn was not played fairly, as his countenance and body showed afterwards, but he had the satisfaction of knowing that

the very dread of him contributed to the miss which allowed Scotland to win. That the win was delayed until within two minutes of the finish was due to the concentration of the Welsh defence on Quinn and the senseless policy of the Scottish inside forwards plying the centre with the ball, knowing all the time that with him so well guarded they were asking him to attempt the impossible...from that period the game was flabby until Quinn terrorised Wales and won the game."

"He had got many bad passes, and this one from Walker was about as hopeless as others, but he raced away on the chance of something turning up. His luck was in this time, for Llewellyn Davies, with lots of time to clear anyhow and anywhere, took his eye off the ball and saw the man. That was sufficient, and Quinn, profiting by mistake, screwed the ball past the outcoming Evans. In ordinary circumstances, sympathy would have been extended to Wales in losing after 88 minutes against a better team, but when the manner of their comparative success is remembered regret that the defeat was not heavier replaces sympathy."

Having dragged Scotland to a hard fought victory against Wales, the newspapers were rather disappointed that Quinn was not given the opportunity to attack the English defence a few weeks later as he might have liked, having been played away from his preferred position in favour of a final stint on the wing. More than anything, I believe this shows that, even in his later years, when fitness and perhaps to some degree mobility were gradually deserting **"The Mighty Quinn"**, his natural talent never diminished. In all, Jimmy played eleven times for Scotland, scoring seven goals for his country.

"It is probable that Scotland would have won handsomely had Quinn been at centre forward, but placed as the forwards were Scotland must have done better had Hay not so palpably ignored Quinn. The famous Celt, if not boycotted, was starved, and Hay must bear to blame." In all honesty, towards the end of his career, all of the kicks he had taken began to catch up with Jimmy. He featured less and less regularly, until he played his final match for the team he loved in a one-all draw with Hearts at Celtic Park in January 1915. He had previously scored his final goal for the Football Club on Boxing Day 1914 against Hamilton Academical. It is a pity that only six thousand spectators were fortunate enough to witness the great man hit the back of the net for the final time, but such were the effects of the ongoing Great War.

In a reflection of his humble and shy character, Jimmy soon he took his chance to escape the limelight he had found himself immersed in for the last fifteen years and replace it with candlelight, returning to work in the mines in his hometown of Croy. His employment continued through the difficult times of the general strike of the mid-1920's and the depression that engulfed the United Kingdom in the early 1930's.

Tragically, Jimmy Quinn lived to hear of his son John's death on active military service in Holland in 1944, before he himself died at the age of sixty-seven on the twenty-first of November 1945. A vast number of people turned out at Jimmy's funeral to play their final respects, including Billy Meredith, a famous Welsh player whom he had made such an impact on when they met previously in international matches. Jimmy is buried in Kilsyth Cemetery and has been honoured in the recent past by those involved with the **"Celtic Graves Society"**.

Jimmy's grandson and namesake was a member of the renowned **"Quality Street Gang"** of the late 1960's and early 1970's at Celtic Park, alongside the likes of Kenny Dalglish and Danny McGrain, although he was ultimately unable to make such a significant impact at the Club as the two men mentioned previously, playing forty-one times and scoring a single goal. However, it would have been almost impossible for the young Jimmy to match his grandfather's record, something only a handful of Celts can claim to have done. In total, the legendary Jimmy Quinn scored two hundred and sixteen times for Celtic in three hundred and thirty-one appearances, making him the Club's fifth highest goalscorer of all time, with a goal per game ratio that has only been bettered by Jimmy McGrory and Henrik Larsson. Perhaps it would be fitting to leave the final words about **"The Mighty Quinn"** to the man who persuaded him that football was indeed the game, and that Celtic were indeed the Club, for him – his manager, Willie Maley:

"He was the keystone in the greatest team the Celts ever had."

"Glasgow Herald Death Notice"

"QUINN – At 45 Cuilmuir Terrace, Croy, on 21st November, 1945. James Quinn (ex-Celtic F.C.); R.I.P. – Requiem Mass in Holy Cross Church, Croy, tomorrow (Friday) at 10am; funeral thereafter to Kilsyth Cemetery at approximately 11.30am."

"Death of Jimmy Quinn"

"Jimmy Quinn, Celtic and Scottish international centre forward, who had been ill for some time, has died at his home in Croy, Dunbartonshire."

"Quinn, who joined Celtic from a club called Smithston Albion, had been described by Mr William Maley, then manager of Celtic, as definitely the club's greatest centre forward and possibly the greatest centre Scotland ever had."

"Once he had won his place in Celtic's team he never lost it. He was a strong, robust, but always clean player, and honours soon came his way. He gained a League cap in 1904 and played in his first full International match next year against Ireland. His last cap was against England in 1912 when Scotland was in difficulty for an outside left to match against England's renowned right back, Crompton. Quinn was selected for the job."

"Altogether he was awarded 19 caps."

"Quinn was a miner, and at the end of his playing days he went back to the pits."

"He was 67 years of age."

"Moscow Or Nothing?"

As the group stages of the UEFA Champions League began in 2012–13, Celtic endured a rather disappointing goalless draw at home with Benfica, whilst two late goals from Lionel Messi stopped Spartak Moscow from achieving a historic victory in Catalonia. And so, as the second match day of the group approached, a gentleman from Newton Mearns readied himself for a trip to Russia. Stephen Tait, a thirty-six year old originally from Rutherglen, had previously considered a trip to Helsingborg in Sweden in the qualifying rounds, but was put off of the idea by the fact he couldn't secure a ticket prior to travelling.

When the groups were drawn, Stephen was "**desperate to play a few teams we hadn't met recently**", and unsurprisingly he was then left somewhat "**disappointed**" when we were placed in Group G alongside Barcelona and Benfica. Of course, these were big sides and it is always great to play clubs of such a stature, but by Stephen's own admission, he was hoping to be able to travel somewhere he hadn't visited before. Having followed Celtic to both Barcelona and Lisbon in the past, this left him with a simple choice – Moscow or nothing?

Now, considering that you are currently reading about Stephen, I'm sure you have worked out that he did indeed choose to go to Moscow rather than simply sit at home in front of his television: **"I'd never been to Russia before, let alone Moscow, so I felt it was a unique opportunity for me to see one of the world's most famous cities. Being honest, it's not the sort of place I would have ever visited on holiday with my wife, so I knew if I didn't go to see Celtic play there I'd likely never do so."**

Rather than paying for one of the official travel trips sanctioned by the Football Club, Stephen found it was far cheaper to make his own way there, flying from Edinburgh to Amsterdam, and then on to Moscow sometime later, with a group of around twenty-five other supporters (with whom he would eventually travel to the match with whilst in the city).

Having arrived in the middle of the night, Stephen said he was surprised by the lack of traffic on the roads: **"Before we travelled, I'd read all of these articles on websites warning about how bad the congestion in Moscow could be, with traffic jams lasting half the day and people having to sleep in their cars and stuff. Now, it was the middle of the night when we arrived but still, I found myself wondering whether there were even any other vehicles in the city – the roads were deserted, as was the airport itself."**

In time though, Stephen would find the Moscow traffic he had been searching for. He awoke the next morning, and set out to explore the most populous city in Europe. Upon entering Red Square, Stephen felt slightly overawed by his surroundings and even his situation at first: **"In years gone by, I would have just gone straight to the pub around lunchtime, but I had decided to stop drinking earlier in 2012, so it meant that this was to be my first trip abroad with Celtic without touching a drop of the stuff. In all honesty, I was a little nervous about it for a time, because obviously the vast majority of the support would be having a lot to drink, but I was put at ease when I came across an old pal in Red Square who doesn't drink either. Ironically, I hadn't seen him in years – since another trip abroad with the Hoops in fact – but there he was."**

"It was funny actually because it turned into one of those trips where you seemed to meet a lot of people in a fairly short space of time. For example, I had bumped into Tony Hamilton earlier in the day in Subway of all places, whilst we were getting something eat, and then in Red Square I met not only the other non-drinker I mentioned, but also two lads who had come all the way from Philadelphia."

"The square was actually pretty quiet early on in the day because our travelling support wasn't huge. Anyway, as we wandered about admiring our surroundings and passing the time of day, these two American accents sounded out from behind us, as two guys, who had clearly spotted our Hoops from a distance, wandered over and introduced themselves. They were fantastic. We all thought that coming from Scotland to Moscow was a fair trip, but as I said, they'd flown all the way from Philadelphia.

I dread to think how much it cost them, but they were great – some of the nicest lads you could hope to meet."

And so, having enjoyed a bit of a sing-song in one of the most famous squares on Earth and having had photographs taken with Celtic flags in front of the likes of the Kremlin and St Basil's Cathedral, the travelling supporters began to make their way out of the city centre towards the Luzhniki Stadium using a variety of different transportation. Whilst some travelled using the underground metro system, Stephen and the rest of his group leapt into two prearranged minibuses a few hours before kick-off, and in doing so, they finally were introduced to Muscovite traffic at rush hour.

"It was just mental," said Stephen. **"We literally moved almost nowhere in an hour. There were six or eight lanes of traffic that were virtually static, and it became increasingly clear that we were not going to go anywhere fast if we stayed in the minibuses. Drivers were playing games on their phones or tablets in their cars, and other people actually had books out, flicking through the pages whilst sat at the wheel. I couldn't believe it considering how quiet it had been during the night and earlier in the day. Anyway, after a bit of discussion, we all decided to bail out and find another way to the stadium. It seemed our best bet, as part of me wonders whether we'd still all be in the minibuses today had we not chosen to jump ship!"**

Of course, this was an admirable pursuit, but by all accounts the vast Russian capital is not an easy city to navigate, especially if none of you read or speak any Russian. Unsurprisingly, this quickly became an issue when they eventually found a metro station and attempted to decipher the large maps and diagrams adorning the walls. Having seen the group in their distinctive green and white Hoops, a local policeman (who spoke no English) essentially pointed to a station on the map repeatedly with his finger, indicating where to get off of the train, before guiding them to the appropriate platform for departure.

"We thought this was great," Stephen recalled. **"We were finally moving and thought we would be at the stadium in no time. We had memorised how many stops it was until the station which we were meant to get off at, so it was just a case of counting them**

down – or so we thought. There were several Spartak supporters on the train, but there was no evidence of any animosity. People were swapping scarves and shaking hands with us, and whilst our differing languages were an issue, there were certain words which both sets of supporters could understand – like "McGeady" and even "Larsson"."

"Eventually, our train emerged from the subway tunnel into a station which was absolutely heaving with Spartak fans. The majority of the red and white clad supporters in our carriage departed here, and so we decided to follow them. A few of us wondered whether it was one stop too soon, but we weren't fussed since we knew the home support wouldn't get off here without reason. However, when a couple of police there saw the group of us exiting the station itself they went nuts, and soon they'd told us they would be escorting us to the stadium."

In truth, this didn't bother Stephen or the other supporters around him initially. They presumed that whilst the police were perhaps being a little overprotective, they would certainly guide them to their destination, meaning there was no chance they could get lost. However, this feeling would alter somewhat as they began their journey towards the ground.

"We turned a corner, and as we started to walk through a few residential streets, we encountered some of the locals. I wasn't bothered until we came across a group of men who were standing in the street drinking beer, none of whom appeared to have anything to do with Spartak Moscow though, I hasten to add. However, I noticed one of them was holding his bottle oddly, as if he was about to throw it, rather than drink from it. Nothing happened, other than the odd shout here or there, but something about it unnerved me slightly. It was one of those times where you begin to get a bad feeling in the pit your stomach – it wasn't pleasant."

"A few minutes later, we passed under a small bridge and finally we could see the stadium in the distance, some way across a large park. The only problem was that there was about ten thousand Spartak Moscow supporters between us and the ground itself, with no other green to be seen anywhere in amongst the vast expanses of red and white. In fact, it reminded me of walking into one of those pubs where everyone stops what they're doing and stares right at you as soon as you go through the front door. With the police marching us across this park, we stood out like sore thumbs, and as we began to pass through the crowd, we got a bit of a mixed reception to say the least."

"Some of the people were lovely, shouting "Celtic!" or wanting to swap scarves like the folk on the train, but a lot of the more hardcore supporters were really quite scary. It was only later that we found out we had walked straight through a large section of the Spartak ultras, and whilst we weren't too bothered by the insults being thrown our way, it was a different story when physical objects like rocks and bottles began to fly."

"At this stage, I should highlight that there were only about twenty-five of us in our group, and it was a mixed bunch. There were a few older couples, one or two fathers with their young sons, and then a mixture of men and women, some of which had travelled alone. It's not like we were all young guys who could handle ourselves. Some of them were tired enough by the lengthy walk, let alone any prospect of it all kicking off!"

"There were a lot of young Russian men who were visibly angry to see us, and also a few skinheads, but nowhere near as many as some stereotypes may suggest. Most of the guys just looked rough and ready if nothing else. In fact, the language barrier between us and them probably didn't help matters, but I have to say I was pretty intimidated for a bit. When the happy shouts of "Celtic" morphed into chants of "Fuck you Celtic" and bottles started landing every now and again, there were a certainly a few nervous expressions being exchanged amongst us, with a lot of the kids and women naturally moving into the middle of our group."

"At this point, there were only two cops escorting us – one in front and one behind. They were decked out in the camouflage gear you would normally associate with the army, and whilst they looked like they were as hard as nails, I couldn't help but think that they wouldn't have been able to do much about it if all hell had broken loose. When we finally reached the stadium it felt like we'd been walking for an eternity and the sense of relief was palpable amongst us all. We had all been loud and jovial on the

subway, but for the latter stages of our walk we were almost silent, trying to keep our heads down as much as possible. It was the most intimidating atmosphere I've ever experienced as a Celtic supporter, and I'm no stranger to those."

For the record, Stephen has also attended the Sarajevo derby, a match which pits two of the biggest clubs in Bosnia and Herzegovina, F.K. Željezničar Sarajevo and F.K. Sarajevo, against each other. It may not be as glamorous as many of the world's derbies but, according to Stephen, the atmosphere which is produced (often by a relatively small number of supporters) is immense. If you have a chance, look it up on **"YouTube"** and enjoy, but be sure to mind the flying fireworks – it certainly wouldn't be a match for people who don't like pyrotechnics anyway. Returning to the topic at hand though, I would therefore suggest that Stephen would not claim that points of his trip to Moscow were particularly intimidating lightly.

Once inside the Luzhniki Stadium, which Stephen described as being **"far from full, but a very impressive football ground,"** the small band of a few hundred faithful Celtic supporters stood at one end, facing three sides housing Spartak supporters. **"The noise they produced was remarkable. The singing and chanting was so low and guttural that, again, it was, quite intimidating for a time. There was a lot of security present too. Thankfully though, the team would shut them all up with their performance on the field."**

Celtic ran out the victors in Russia that night in dramatic fashion, as two late goals from a deflected James Forrest shot and a Georgios Samaras header sealed a three-two win. Regardless of the relatively small size of the away support, the Greek's goal sent those who had made the trip across Europe absolutely crazy, with people falling over rows and one lad even jumping about waving a seat in the air.

For Stephen, the nerves and unease he felt prior to the game had been replaced with utter elation, and I have no doubts in my mind that his experience of his journey to Russia will live long in his memory, as he recalls a few thoughts to conclude:

"Gary Hooper scoring early on was about as good a start as we could have hoped for, but when we let the lead slip and then

eventually went behind, I couldn't help but think "oh no, here we go again – we could end up losing by two or three here." However, the team fought back tremendously well and they showed great character in doing so. When Juan Insaurralde was sent off, I turned to my brother-in-law and said: "If we can score soon, we'll win this." A few minutes later, Forrest's strike was turned into the Spartak net by one of their own men, and then it was just a case of whether or not Celtic could find that one piece of magic to win the game. As usual, they left it late, but when Samaras headed the third goal beyond the goalkeeper, the away supporters went wild."

"We were all so proud of them. It was one thing to win our first away match in the Champions League proper, but to do so in such a foreign country amidst an intimidating and at times scary atmosphere was magnificent. In truth, I think the cultural differences, and particularly the language barrier as I mentioned earlier added to the intensity of the fixture. The locals often didn't come across as being the friendliest bunch, but I wonder how much of that was simply down to our collective lack of ability to communicate with them. It wasn't like a trip to Spain or Germany where a lot of the locals speak some English. I mean, if I'm honest, the only places we ate were Subway or our hotel because we had no grasp of their language, so it can't have been easy for the Russians either. After all, we were foreigners in their city, but I must admit, whilst I would maybe return to Russia, I don't think I would be crazy about making another trip to Moscow."

"It was the best Celtic game I've ever attended in the flesh mind you, and I was so proud because of what we had achieved. We'd all followed Celtic across Europe and watched them lose time and time again, through a combination of poor performances and bad luck, but finally, we'd done it. I saw men and women who had travelled to countless games in the past hugging each other, shaking hands, and even wiping away the odd tear. It meant so much to them – and to me. What a performance, what a result and what a trip."

"It Was Like The Hoops Had Taken Over"

Australia is an enormous country. Now, that may sound somewhat obvious, but I've met countless people in my time who don't seem to truly grasp this point. After all, the vast majority of people in Scotland, including myself, have only ever seen this country on a map or on the television. Due to the fact it is surrounded by water on all sides it is, of course, an island and this may be part of the reason so many people don't seem to appreciate the magnitude of the place itself. For example, if you were to overlay a scale map of Australia over a similar map of the United States of America, you would find that they are almost identical in size (excluding Alaska and Hawaii, of course). And yet, unlike America, Australia has a very small population for its relative size.

For instance, if I was to tell you that less people lived in Australia than within the United Kingdom, you'd probably think I was mistaken, but I am not. In fact, countries such as Thailand, Italy, Ukraine, Iraq, Uzbekistan and even Nepal have higher numbers of people living within their borders than the largest country wholly in the Southern Hemisphere. To contextualise this point somewhat, let me put it this way. Australia is a little over ninety-eight times the size of Scotland in terms of area, and yet they only have a little over four times the population living there.

Now, put that to the back of your mind for a little while but remember it, and please allow me to introduce Sean McGinlay, a twenty-five year old born and bred Australian, with a passion for a Football Club based over ten thousand miles away from his home in Adelaide, South Australia. This love was fostered and encouraged by Sean's father and grandfather, a man who was a regular at Celtic Park in the 1940's and 1950's.

In 1969, his grandparents (Colin and Teresa), swapped the country of Dumbarton Rock for that which boasts Ayers Rock (more commonly known by its Aboriginal name **"Uluru"**) in search of work. And so, the pair arrived in the industrial community of Whyalla, which was then growing rapidly into the city it is today. Colin had been guaranteed a job at the new steelworks there, and so the family, made up of the two parents and their four year old son (Sean's dad) began their new life **"Down Under"**.

A little under twenty years later in 1988, Sean was born and as he grew up, he developed a love of sport and music, thanks mostly to Australian Rules football and his guitar. Now, whilst the guitar still forms a large part of his life, the Aussie Rules has, as you may have guessed, been largely overtaken by soccer. Coincidentally, the first **"Adelaide Celtic Supporters Club"** was also born in 1988, but sadly it dissolved midway through the following decade. The men and women initially involved with the organisation could not get live coverage of Celtic matches at that point in time, and Sean recalled how they would all wait until V.H.S. (video) recordings were mailed over from Scotland so they could gather together and watch them days, if not weeks, later as if they were live matches.

In more modern times, the capital of South Australia has seen the resurrection of its Supporters Club, thanks largely to the internet and the commitment of several Celtic fans, including Sean. **"It's not a fully organised Club yet"**, Sean said, **"It began with the occasional pub meet-up, but now we're actively looking to find premises where we can all meet regularly and watch matches, rather than just in the twenty-four hour sports bar where we do so now".**

"A couple of years ago we all travelled up to Gosford to see Celtic play the Central Coast Mariners, and while we were there we met a lot of the lads from the other Supporters Clubs dotted around Australia. Every city seemed to have one or more, whether it was Sydney, Brisbane or Perth – even the Papua New Guinea C.S.C. were there, despite the fact they were only made up of a few guys who watch games on a laptop. I suppose that sort of inspired us to make the Adelaide Club a reality, and we're all really proud of it".

At this time, I'd suggest considering the implications of following Celtic from Australia. I must confess that, albeit very rarely, I have heard a small number of Celtic supporters question the commitment of their counterparts overseas from time to time. Of course, this is a farcical view to hold, as I believe that the men, women and children who support Celtic Football Club around the world show the same levels of dedication as those of us much closer to the Club's home – they just do so in differing manners. For example, early rises for coach trips to away grounds can be replaced with getting up in the middle of the night to watch matches in a city centre bar. Regardless of where one individual may support Celtic from, we all embrace the same attitudes that come along with it; we simply exhibit them in our own unique ways.

Obviously, being on the other side of the globe, there is, most noticeably, a significant time difference between Scotland and Australia, and therefore the Celtic supporting men and women **"Down Under"** can find themselves watching games at particularly odd times of the day. For example, matches kicking off in the evening in Scotland last through till dawn in Australia, and therefore seeing the clock tick past 5am when you're watching Celtic in the Champions League is something you must be prepared for. Equally well, you often need to be ready for work only a few hours later, and this requires a significant level of not only emotional, but also physical commitment. As Sean joked, **"Maybe we Aussies are the only supporters on Earth who like to see Celtic kicking off at lunchtime!"**

Equally, as an Australian Celtic supporter, you would have to face a question which can be annoyingly common throughout the modern footballing world: **"Who are your English team?"**

This is perhaps no surprise considering the amount of coverage the English Premiership receives in the country, but nonetheless: **"Some folk do seem to find it odd when you tell them you support Celtic above any English side"**, according to Sean. In saying that, he continued, **"I do have a soft spot for West Ham United and, of course, I follow Adelaide United in the A-League, but nothing really comes close to Celtic for me."**

Now, towards the beginning of this chapter, I discussed the true size of Australia as a country and asked you to put it to the backs of your mind. Well, now I'd like you to recall it, as I tell the short story of Sean's first Celtic game and, more importantly, what it meant to him. In 2009, only a year or so after the loss of his grandmother, Sean was looking forward to Celtic travelling to the Southern Hemisphere to take on Brisbane Roar for the **"Translink Cup"** (also known as the **"Roar Against Racism Cup"**) for what was Tony Mowbray's first match in charge of the Club. Unsurprisingly, Celtic supporters from all across the country travelled to the capital of Queensland to see the match, which was held at the SunCorp Stadium (host of a 2013 British and Irish Lions test), with the McGinlay family being notable members of the aforementioned travelling support.

Whilst reflecting on the trip, Sean said: **"One of the best things about it was the number of Celtic tops – from the plane to the airport to the city centre, they were everywhere. It was like the Hoops had taken over Brisbane, and it was fantastic."**

The match itself was organised by none other than Lisbon Lion Willie Wallace, a man who moved to Australia decades earlier after retiring from professional football. Prior to the game, Willie spoke eloquently at a Celtic Supporters breakfast which the McGinlay family attended. Sean's grandfather, Colin, had not seen Celtic play in over four decades at that point in time (Wallace was still a Celtic player when Colin left Scotland), and therefore he felt compelled to make the one thousand mile trip (the approximate equivalent of Glasgow to Barcelona or Warsaw) to see the Bhoys – one last time. Understandably, this journey meant an incredible amount to both Sean, his father, and his grandfather, as they grasped the opportunity to enjoy watching Celtic play live together (with a few beers thrown in for good measure). Sadly, only a couple of years later, Colin would pass away.

Incredibly, Sean still has relatives in Clydebank whom he keeps in touch with and, as I write this, he is only days away from beginning an epic trip to take in the sights of Europe, Scotland, and Parkhead. Having saved up some money and left his job as a computer programmer (operating laser cutting machines), he is destined to spend a month following Celtic around Britain, including trips to Brentford and across Scotland, whilst visiting his family's home in Clydebank.

Having asked Sean what he is anticipating most about his trip (with seeing his family being excepted) he told me that **"I'm just looking forward to being able to see the stadium with my own eyes. I've watched countless matches held there on television, and I've celebrated and commiserated just like any other supporter depending on the result, so to finally be able to experience it for myself will be something very special. I've already booked my tickets for the first home game of my time there against Inverness Caledonian Thistle, and apparently my cousins are going to take me out on the Gallowgate after it, so it should be great!"**

Whilst the Celtic Park that Sean will visit will look remarkably different from that last graced by his grandfather, and whilst many of the faces will have changed, the soul of the place remains very much the same. The raw energy the supporters can generate within the cauldron that is now a sixty-thousand seater stadium is just as it was all those years ago, before one family took an incredibly brave, life-changing decision to leave their home in search of a better life for themselves and the generations to follow. Undoubtedly, this homecoming of sorts for Sean McGinlay will be an emotional one at times, but it will be a journey he never forgets. The weather may not be too memorable, but I'm sure the hospitality will be second to none and I, for one, thoroughly look forward to welcoming him to his green and white home from home, before placing a nice cold pint in his hand.

"The Human Torpedo"

There are very few people who possess a love of Scottish Football who will not know the name of Jimmy McGrory (or James Edward McGrory, to give him his full title). Born into the then desperately poor Irish immigrant stronghold of the Garngad, Glasgow, on the twenty-sixth of April 1904, Jimmy drew his first breaths only ten days after Jimmy Quinn had scored a historic hat-trick against Rangers to win the Scottish Cup for Celtic. At that stage, no-one could have known that this baby boy would go on to not only to achieve similar stardom to that held by the man from Croy, but in certain senses, to eclipse it. From an early age, Jimmy endured not only the hardships of day to day life in the Garngad, but also the type of unique tragedy that is bound to change a person forever, when he lost his mother, Kate, at the age of only twelve years old. Of course, this affected Jimmy very badly, but the manner in which he conducted himself and worked hard throughout the rest of his life was tremendously admirable, as such an event always has the potential to adversely affect a young man or woman.

In his formative footballing years, Jimmy played for junior side St Roch's, helping them to win their first and only Scottish Junior Cup in the spring of 1922. Having provisionally signed for Celtic sometime earlier, he continued to play with his local team for a short while, before signing fully and joining up with his new Club at the end of the 1921–22 season. Initially played at inside right, Jimmy would soon find himself playing as a centre forward. Despite standing only five feet and six inches tall, he possessed an incredible talent to score goals, particularly with his head. Now, this is something that I, as a young man, can only liken to the great Henrik Larsson, whose ability to spring into the air (seemingly hanging there as long as required) and redirect the ball towards goal is something I hope to tell my grandchildren about one day.

In Willie Maley's book, referenced previously, he describes how there had been interest from both himself and the Club in Jimmy, throughout almost the entirety of his footballing career prior to their approach for the forward, as well as discussing some of the attributes which made him such a prized target for the Football Club. He wrote: **"We were first told about him when he played in a Boys' Guild team. We kept a watchful eye on him. He stepped into junior football. His Club was St Roch's. Our watchfulness increased. I was struck not by his ball play but his adaptability, his versatility, and by his tremendous enthusiasm and virility."**

Maley then proceeds to describe the ambition McGrory possessed with regards to signing for his beloved Celtic: **"When our time to take Jimmy came, we had no difficulty in making him a Celt. His heart was ours long before he was ever offered a peg in our dressing-room. He brought with him a fervour and a freshness which revealed the real Celtic spirit."**

Jimmy made his Celtic debut in a disappointing one-nil away defeat to Third Lanark, on the twentieth of January 1923. Replacing the great Patsy Gallacher for the match, Jimmy, at the age of just nineteen, was one of the youngsters the Celtic support would look to in the future to provide them with some much needed goals, as Celtic languished in the middle of the league table, barely managing to score more goals than they were conceding at the time. According to one newspaper report, **"for a first appearance he made a credible show."**

He proceeded to score his first goal for the Club only a fortnight later, as Celtic lost by four goals to three against Kilmarnock at Rugby Park. In the summer, after featuring only four times for the senior Celtic side, Jimmy was sent out to the now defunct Clydebank on a season long loan, where he appeared thirty-three times and scored sixteen goals. Despite the fact he scored a third of Clydebank's league goals that season, he could not help them avoid relegation in the end. Regardless, Jimmy learnt a lot from the vital experience he gained there, as the relatively few chances that were created for him during matches helped to emphasise the importance of converting them as often as possible.

In 1924, during the new football campaign, Jimmy's dad Henry, an Irish Catholic immigrant from County Donegal, tragically lost his life in an accident in his mid-sixties, leaving his children without a surviving parent. Obviously, Jimmy was distraught, and Maley attempted to become a new father figure to the boy, as he had tried to do with so many others during his time at the Club for one reason or another, with both relative success and failure. It is reported that the pair attended Henry's funeral on the final morning of August that year, and then travelled to a Celtic match away against Falkirk in the afternoon, in which the young Jimmy scored for the Hoops. After this event, Maley enquired as to whether Jimmy would need some financial assistance in order to keep his family, as he was now the main breadwinner, but McGrory turned him down, highlighting that he still had far more in his pocket than many of the people around him in the city every day. Even before Jimmy began to earn significant sums as a footballer, he would still regularly save some change to hand to many of the hungry children of the Garngad, and in his old age, he never forgot where he had come from, and how comparatively lucky he had been in his life in many regards, for he was a humble man.

In the weeks following the death of his father, Jimmy McGrory found his best goalscoring form as a Celtic player thus far, scoring nine goals in the five games after the aforementioned match against Falkirk. One newspaper report, published after Celtic's convincing four-two victory over Third Lanark in the Glasgow Cup said: **"McGrory, who scored three goals, proved himself to be a daring and resourceful leader."**

Later that same season, Jimmy would score the first of his truly famous goals. In the last minutes of the Scottish Cup Final against Dundee, with the match tied one-each (the equaliser having come from the legendary Patsy Gallacher somersault goal), Jimmy threw himself at a low cross and scored a powerful diving header (described as a **"beautiful goal"** by **"The Glasgow Herald"**) which gave Celtic only their second Scottish Cup triumph in eleven years. Having been clattered by an opponent in the process of scoring the winner, it is reported that McGrory later spoke of how he only regained an awareness of his senses whilst lying flat out on the grass, as an immense celebratory roar emanated from the Celtic supporters in attendance.

Having held on to win the trophy, the Celtic team celebrated with each other and thanked the crowd for their support, before disappearing inside the main stand. In those days, the Scottish Cup was not presented to the Club captain for all of the fans to see, but rather given to the Club chairman and other relevant officials in private. When Mr Maley later returned to the dressing room with the trophy, Jimmy was still visibly shaking with the excitement and nerves of the day. Seeing a chance to build the confidence in the young lad, who was only a few weeks away from his twenty-first birthday, Maley invited Jimmy to stand with the trophy at the front of the team bus as they drove back to Celtic Park through packed city streets. This would not be the last time that the Garngad Bhoy would have his hands on a piece of silverware, but it is clear it was a tremendously important moment in Jimmy's life nonetheless.

As is so often the case, winning a competition one season gives a team the momentum, the desire and most critically the belief, to go on and replicate such successes in the coming season. This was just what happened with this Celtic side, driven forward by the young and exciting McGrory – the new star in the Celtic sky now that the great Patsy Gallacher had departed – as they went on to win the League Championship by a significant margin in the 1925–26 season. During this time, Celtic scored ninety-seven goals in the league, over a third of which of which came from Jimmy McGrory alone.

Throughout the 1926–27 campaign, Celtic were not so dominant in the league, despite scoring more goals than they had managed during the previous season. They eventually finished in third position, having scored one hundred and one goals in thirty-eight games (more than any other side in the league), but defensive lapses let them down too often for them to be serious challengers for the title. How many of these Celtic goals came from the great Jimmy you ask? Well, Mr McGrory scored no fewer than forty-eight league goals that season and a staggering fifty-nine in all competitions, despite the fact he only made forty-one appearances that year. Celtic did have one notable success though, as they won the Scottish Cup once again, defeating East Fife by three goals to one in the final (although Jimmy missed the match through injury). Despite this, James Edward McGrory was, remarkably, the highest goalscorer in Europe over the course of that season.

Interestingly though, in terms of goalscoring at least, 1927–28 was actually Jimmy's greatest season, despite the fact he wasn't the highest scorer in Europe that year. Celtic finished second to Rangers in the league, having scored ninety-three goals, forty-seven of which came from McGrory this time. In all competitions, Jimmy scored on sixty-two occasions in forty-six appearances, the sort of record that only global superstars like Lionel Messi or Cristiano Ronaldo could hope to achieve nowadays. However, during this period, Jimmy did something which either of those two present day masters of the game would struggle to equal. On the fourteenth of April 1928, the name **"McGrory"** would appear no less than eight times on a single competitive score-sheet, as Celtic annihilated Dunfermline Athletic by nine goals to nil. For the lovers of trivia amongst you, it is perhaps noteworthy that Celtic's other goal that day was scored by Alex Thomson (no, not the journalist), an inside forward McGrory once said **"used to lay on beautiful passes for me"**.

Throughout his playing career, Jimmy was known to be one of football's gentlemen as well as a great goalscorer. Despite the fact he went from a relative unknown to the new superstar of the Celtic support after the dramatic Scottish Cup Final victory over Dundee, and people began to mob him any time they spotted him walking down the street, Jimmy always did his best to be friendly and accommodating to the Club's supporters. That is not to say that he was fully suited to the aforementioned stardom, as being the centre of attention was not something which came to him naturally, but he did well regardless. This good nature made him many friends in the game, and not only those of a Celtic persuasion. For example, Bob McPhail, the Rangers inside forward (a great player himself), was a firm friend of Jimmy's, so much so that he would visit the ill McGrory in hospital only a week before he died in the early 1980's.

One story which I feel exemplifies McGrory's character actually spawned from the act of kindness of an opposing goalkeeper. During a match at Celtic Park, Jimmy threw himself towards the ball in an attempt to power a diving header into the net as he had done so many times before. As usual, he connected brilliantly, but unusually, he missed his target as the ball flew high over the bar. Anyway, as the crowd naturally followed the flight of the ball high into the Glaswegian air, McGrory's momentum took him towards the post, and just as he was set to sustain a nasty injury, the opposition goalkeeper, Jack Harkness, dived and pushed him away so his head avoided the obstacle it would have struck dangerously hard otherwise.

The actions of the Scotland international goalkeeper (who played with both Queen's Park and Heart of Midlothian during a twelve year long professional career), went unnoticed by many inside the ground, but not by Jimmy. Perhaps unsurprisingly, as the two men exchanged words immediately after the incident, the **"boo's"** rang out as the supporters in attendance presumed Harkness was guilty of some crime against the great Jimmy and that was why the two men were conversing. For the remainder of the tie, Jack was berated by the home fans whenever he touched the ball. This deeply troubled McGrory, who knew that the quick thinking of his opponent had saved him from enduring a nasty collision, so he decided to do something about it.

In the style typical of Jimmy McGrory, he later insisted that the Football Club printed his recollection of the event in the subsequent match day programme at Celtic Park, in which he cleared Jack Harkness of any wrongdoing and proverbially pulled his name from the gutter in the process. Having realised the error of their ways, the Celtic support responded magnificently whenever Harkness took the field against the Hoops in the future, not only applauding him, but actively cheering many times whenever he had the ball. Harkness' act of kindness has not been forgotten by the Celtic support, and I hope it never will be.

Moving on, in terms of international football, the man who scored over forty goals a season for no less than six consecutive domestic campaigns received a paltry seven international caps for his country. Yes, a man who will forever be known as one of the greatest goalscorers of all time, not just in Scotland but around the world, was rewarded for his effort with just seven caps. During these outings Jimmy scored six times – hardly the sort of strike rate that would make a football fan think, **"he's not doing the business, I hope we drop him"**, but nonetheless, he was rarely given any serious international recognition.

Indeed, without James McGrory, the now famous **"Hampden Roar"** may never have become the household phrase and marketing slogan that it is today. On one of his few appearances for his country, on the first of April 1933, Scotland faced England at Hampden Park, in front of a then world record crowd of a little over one hundred and thirty-six thousand (of course, the true figure was most likely higher due to people finding 'unofficial' ways inside). Regardless of the exact attendance though, this was a truly gargantuan match and most certainly a footballing sight to behold.

The tie was part of the 1932–33 Home Championship series, which had already been won by Wales. However, this is not to say it was a meaningless tie, as this match would decided who finished second, with Scotland needing a win to achieve the feat. As tens of thousands packed the terraces on all sides of the ground, Jimmy McGrory, playing at centre forward, opened the scoring within five minutes of the first whistle. England eventually equalised through international debutant George Hunt, to leave the scores at tied at one apiece at half time.

In the second half, with both teams searching for a winning goal, Jimmy McGrory scored with less than ten minutes remaining to give the Scots one of their most famous victories over their rivals from south of the border. The noise created by the Scotland support as a result of McGrory's winner was likened to nothing that had ever erupted from a football ground before and, when the noise was reported to have travelled far across the city, it led to the conception of a phrase to describe the phenomenon, the so-called **"Hampden Roar"**. The following excerpt from **"The Glasgow Herald"** not only describes the excitement prior to the winning goal and the pandemonium which followed it, but may also prove to be one of the initial sources of the now famous phrase mentioned above.

"Then came the Scottish rally, and the most exciting part of the game. The huge crowd on the terracing swayed this way and that way, and cheers of encouragement and groans of disappointment followed each other in rapid succession."

"The English defence was now thoroughly rattled, but when Duncan, McPhail, Crawford and Marshall all missed chances to put Scotland in the lead it looked as if the winning goal would never come. Then, with about ten minutes remaining for play, McPhail sent a clever pass to McGrory, who withstood Cooper's challenge and then carried on towards goal."

"What excitement prevailed. On went McGrory, with Hibbs and Blenkinsop rushing to tackle him. Down came the Celtic player's foot on the ball, and it sailed past Hibbs into the net. Then a hush of expectation was shattered by one of the mightiest roars ever heard at Hampden; the game was won, and once more Scotland had triumphed over the "Auld Enemy" from south of the border. It was a good game, played in a sporting manner and watched by an orderly crowd."

However, whilst many Celtic fans still despair to this day regarding the number of caps awarded to some of the Club's early greats, it is intriguing to think that Jimmy, like many of his colleagues throughout the years, were not too bothered by the whole fiasco. In their minds, their job was to give their all for the team they had supported as boys and had subsequently become lucky enough to star for. Any international football was simply a bonus, albeit a prestigious one, and should have been treated as such.

Returning to the tale of his domestic career, this devotion was proven beyond all doubt by Jimmy when he rejected the opportunity to become the highest paid footballer in British Football when Arsenal offered to buy him in 1928. It is widely reported that the Celtic board hoped the transfer would go through at the time, in order to provide the Club with some much needed funds for the redevelopment of the main stand, but Jimmy simply could not force himself to leave the Club he loved. **"I felt McGrory of Arsenal did not sound right. It wasn't like McGrory of Celtic"**, he said famously.

In 1931, Jimmy scored late in the second half of the Scottish Cup Final to give the Hoops a fighting chance of finding an equalising goal (with less than ten minutes left on the clock and the score then poised at two goals to one in favour of Motherwell). In the final seconds of the match, McGrory's marker was panicked to such a degree by his presence behind him that he diverted a crossed ball into his own net, earning the Parkhead side an unlikely replay, and meaning that **"pandemonium prevailed on the terracing."**

When the sides met again, Jimmy scored twice as Celtic ran out relatively comfortable four-two winners. In truth, despite the crucial importance of those two goals in the replay, McGrory would later admit they were two of the simplest finishes he ever had the pleasure of making over the course of his career (both were tap-ins, one with his foot and the latter with his head). However, whilst McGrory's goals were important, his overall performance, which encapsulated the natural sporting determination of the man himself, helped to make life especially difficult for Motherwell's defence, as well as their goalkeeper, Allan McClory.

The following quote alludes to this show of spirit somewhat: **"McGrory was very eager in his charges, and on one occasion he went right over the heads of the crouching press photographers..."**

Regardless, Jimmy's goals, combined with his overall display of skill and endeavour, helped Celtic to Scottish Cup glory once more. A brief glance at **"The Glasgow Herald"** from the following morning gives us an insight not only into the match itself, but into the supporters who attended it, as well as the logistics of dealing with such a large crowd of people in those days (officially totalled at over ninety-eight thousand that Wednesday):

"The crowd came well up to expectations, especially in view of the fact the game began at five o'clock, while the rain during

the day was not calculated to induce a large attendance. As was the case on Saturday, when the teams met in a drawn game, the spectators faithfully observed the police arrangements for packing the terracing in an orderly way, and there were very few casualties."

"The only serious one cannot be put down to the press of people, since the person involved had gone to the match while suffering from a trouble for which he was already on the waiting list of the Victoria Infirmary. He and three other spectators, who were later able to go home, were the only persons admitted to the Victoria Infirmary during the game."

"It was largely a hungry multitude who filled the ground. While some were able to leave work early for the occasion, the vast majority found that a five o'clock start necessitated going straight to the ground. It was not the well-groomed crowd, dressed in holiday clothes, which attended Saturday's match. Instead, one saw hundreds whose dungarees proclaimed that they had come direct from bench and forge, and mingling with the crowd were others whose grimy hands and faces spoke eloquently of penetrating coal dust."

"The police and ambulance arrangements at the park worked admirably. The systematic and organised packing of spectators on the terracing was carried out just as it was on Saturday. An officer stationed in the police box and commanding a view of the entire field was in constant telephone communication with another officer on the turret above the main entrance, the latter having control of the squad of runners who conveyed instructions to the constables on duty at each of the 37 sections of terracing."

"The result was that the crowds as they arrived were evenly distributed, and there was no evidence of unoccupied space, while at the same time everyone seemed to have adequate room. An ambulance squad of 50 men and 12 nurses was on duty, supplemented by three wagons, one of which was stationed inside the ground. In all they dealt with about 20 cases, most of which were minor in nature."

Following their Scottish Cup triumph, Celtic travelled to North America for their first tour of the continent. Previously,

Third Lanark, Rangers and even Kilmarnock had travelled there, all to be met with mixed receptions and variable, often somewhat disappointing crowds. However, with their notable Irish connections, as well the large Diaspora spread across the United States and Canada, Celtic were welcomed unlike any other side before them. Some of the challenge matches were some of the highest attended soccer matches of all time on the entire continent at that stage, as over thirty thousand people packed out several stadia on a few occasions in order to see the famous Glasgow Celtic play.

McGrory was one of the most talked about talents within the American press prior to the team's arrival, and in the first match (a six-one victory over Western Pennsylvania) he did not disappoint, scoring three goals and leading the forward line with **"marked cleverness"**. Upon the sound of the final whistle, an adoring crowd invaded the field of play and McGrory, as well as several other Celts, were carried off on the shoulders of their fans amongst much singing and dancing. The following day, McGrory scored twice more, including a last gasp winner, as Celtic edged past the New York Giants (no relation to the American Football team) by three goals to two in front of more than thirty thousand spectators.

A week later, despite another goal from Jimmy, Celtic suffered their first loss of the tour against the New York Yankees (no, not the baseball team) at Fenway Park, in Boston. Whilst in the city, McGrory told one journalist that it was his **"favourite place he had visited so far"**, as its quiet easy going nature reminded him somewhat of Glasgow. However, Jimmy's enjoyment of the trip would be significantly lessened when, after two more defeats, he would suffer a broken jaw during a five-nil victory over the Brooklyn Wanderers (he had scored twice prior to his retirement from the tie). Whilst the injury was wholly accidental, it is notable that many of the matches on the tour had become rather heated, with fights breaking out on several occasions between opposing players. Maley was scathing regarding the quality of the officiating upon his return to Scotland, highlighting the risk to his players, but to be fair, the Celts often gave as good as they got, as tackles reigned in and punches flew.

Incredibly, Jimmy was back in a Celtic jersey around two and a half weeks after the infliction of his injury, as Celtic played Michigan All-Stars, winning by five goals to nil, one of which came courtesy of the returning McGrory. Interestingly, this was the first match Celtic Football Club ever played under floodlights, although the players seemingly had no difficulty in adapting to their new artificially lit footballing environment. Jimmy would chip in with another couple of goals towards the end of the tour, before the Celtic team left the eastern coast of the United States and sailed back to Glasgow. However, as the team disembarked in Scotland and supporters on the riverside flew green and white banners to welcome them home, Jimmy McGrory was the only member of the side not to disembark from the vessel.

This was due to the fact he had departed the ship via tender near Moville in Donegal the previous night in order to marry his fiancée, Veronica Green, the following day. Whilst Celtic's American tour was definitely not your typical stag trip, the players and the staff involved are said to have enjoyed the experience, but this likely paled in comparison to the emotions experienced by the many Irish-Americans who, for the only time in many cases, had revelled in the opportunity to see the team their relatives before them had adored and spoken of so often.

As Jimmy grew older, and the regular injuries began to take their toll, the number of goals he scored waned. In saying that, throughout the course of thirteen consecutive seasons (of his seventeen in total with the club), the lowest number of goals he scored was still an impressive nineteen. In his early thirties, after a couple seasons of scoring around the range of twenty goals per season, some may have thought Jimmy's best days were behind him.

However, in his later years, Jimmy went on to prove his critics wrong and show them that he still had a few pieces of magic, and two final pieces of silverware, up his green and white Hooped sleeve. During the 1935–36 season, he once again went past the iconic fifty goals mark, scoring fifty-one in a mere thirty-seven appearances for the Celts. A staggering fifty of these came in the league, which Celtic won for the first time in a decade, with the entire team scoring one hundred and fifteen goals in all (this was only the second of two League Championship medals McGrory would win during his lengthy career). On one memorable day in March 1936, Jimmy scored three times in as many minutes against Motherwell at Celtic Park. Unsurprisingly, this remains one of the fastest hat-tricks of all time, and once again, if Lionel Messi or Cristiano Ronaldo were to do something similar nowadays, the football world would ignite almost immediately with praise for the player in question.

A writer for **"The Glasgow Herald"** described the feat as follows: **"McGrory was the man mainly responsible for the rout. He scored three goals in three minutes, all in his best style, and thus provided a memorable feature of a rather disappointing match...McGrory's three goals came midway through the second half. He shot the first after Delaney crossed the ball. A minute later Buchan let Murphy away, and when the wing man crossed McGrory met the ball with his head, and it went at lightning speed into the net. In another minute a similar cross from Murphy was treated in the same way by the Celtic centre."**

In 1937, Celtic reached the Scottish Cup Final where they would take on an Aberdeen side who were debutants to such an occasion. Of course, Jimmy was used to playing in front of big audiences, but this was to be the largest of them all. To this day, that match, held on the twenty-fourth of April 1937, remains the highest attended national Cup Final in history. Debatably, it may actually have been one of the highest attended games of all time.

Officially, there were one hundred and forty-seven thousand, three hundred and sixty-five spectators in the ground that day but, having consulted with experts at the Scottish Football Museum who referenced the original architect's plans for the time and this man's own personal estimates, they believe that in all likelihood, the real attendance may have been **"somewhere around the one hundred and eighty thousand mark"**, with the aforementioned plans of Hampden predicting it's true maximum capacity to have been about one hundred and eighty-two thousand at that stage (at a time when the stadium was as large as it would ever be).

The match itself was an engrossing affair. Celtic started well and took the lead after only eleven minutes through Johnny

Crum. Only sixty seconds later though, Aberdeen equalised via Matt Armstrong, and so began a tactical battle for the Scottish Cup. In the second half, Celtic largely dominated, controlling the midfield against a determined and organised Aberdeen side which defended valiantly. In the end, with around twenty minutes to go, it fell to the great Jimmy McGrory to create the chance for Willie Buchan to score and win Celtic their fifteenth Scottish Cup.

Buchan himself said this of the match: **"Even now I still remember the incredible volume of sound that greeted us as we ran onto the field. I have never heard anything like it and initially I found myself slightly overawed. The memory of my winning goal is still vivid in my mind too. The ball was played through from our own half, and Jimmy McGrory flicked it on, allowing me to move in on the keeper from the right hand side of our area. The two full-backs closed in and I remember as the keeper came out, the goal seemed to become smaller. I just managed to squeeze the ball past him, and it went in off the post."**

This was to be the final trophy McGrory won in his extraordinary career, and he eventually retired during the 1937–38 season, having only scored a mere six times in eleven appearances in that period. Jimmy made his final appearance for Celtic on the sixteenth of October 1937 against Queen's Park and, typically, he opened the scoring that day, as the Hoops ran out four-three winners at Celtic Park. Nobody knew this would be the last time he would play for the Hoops, but one newspaper report did say the following of Jimmy's goal and his performance: **"McGrory appeared to concentrate too much on making openings for McDonald and Buchan, and although his scheming was always full of subtlety his methods were inclined to hold up the attack...White fumbled a ball from Crum to allow McGrory to head through Celtic's first score."** And so, the footballing career of one of the greatest strikers of all time was over – on the field at least.

During his time with Celtic, the supporters coined several nicknames for McGrory. A prominent example of this was **"The Human Torpedo"**, because Jimmy was seemingly unbreakable, always heading for his target until the ball exploded into the net from his boot or head. He suffered an almost endless list of injuries, as opposition defenders knew no other ways of stopping him other than attempting to hurt him. For example, he suffered a broken nose on more than one occasion, and of course, he had his jaw broken at one stage after being kicked in the face. However, none of this could stop **"The Mermaid"**, the man who had such a talent for heading the ball, whether he was jumping or diving to do so, that he earned this slightly unorthodox tag for a footballer.

All in all, Jimmy McGrory from the Garngad scored five hundred and fifty goals in five hundred and forty-seven appearances for Celtic. He firmly holds his place within the top ten greatest goalscorers in the history of the beautiful game, and finished his career with the mind boggling statistic of boasting 'goal to game ratio' higher than one. He has been immortalised in song, and will always be remembered as one of the **"football greats"** who **"have passed through Parkhead's gates, all to play football, the Glasgow Celtic way!"**

At the end of 1937, only weeks after another injury in his final match for Celtic had ruled him out of action for the foreseeable future, Jimmy became the manager of Kilmarnock Football Club, a position which he would hold until the end of World War Two. The highlight of his tenure there was a run to the Scottish Cup Final in 1938, where they lost by four-two to second division East Fife in extra-time. This was only the club's fifth appearance in a major domestic final, and a notable piece of success for a team who were largely a mid-table side at the time.

When Willie Maley published his aforementioned book in 1939, he said the following of one of his greatest players, continuing on from the excerpts cited earlier: **"Jimmy McGrory leaves memories of the finest and of deeds in our colours that will never fade. As a goal-getter, McGrory stands supreme."**

Some years after his final appearance as a player, tragedy would again strike the life of Jimmy McGrory, as his wife Veronica (often referred to as Nona) died during a medical procedure which aimed to determine why the couple had been unable to have a child thus far. The loss of his wife struck Jimmy terribly hard, and it was only his strong connections with his family, as well as his friends at Celtic Football Club, that kept him on the proverbial 'straight and narrow' through another tremendously traumatic period of his life.

In 1945, Jimmy McGrory returned to Celtic Park to become the Club's third manager, replacing Jimmy McStay, the man who had taken over from Willie Maley only five years previously. Personally, his life would once again take a turn for the better in 1946, as he married his second wife, Barbara Schoning, with whom he would go on to have two daughters (Barbara and Elizabeth) and one son (John). During his time in charge of the Football Club, Celtic experienced some fantastic highs as well as some sobering lows. After all, at the end of the 1947–48 season, Celtic finished only four points clear of the relegation places.

In truth, part of the problem during this period was Jimmy McGrory's good manners and overall amicability. The board of directors and Robert Kelly, who became the Club's chairman only a couple of years after Jimmy took on his managerial role, incessantly interfered with footballing matters, such as team selection and which players were bought and sold. The players knew this all too well, and many of them voiced their anger about the way in which the Club was being run, even if many of them only did so once they were no longer affiliated officially with the Football Club (see Bobby Evans as an example).

Most managers, especially those in the modern era, would have walked straight out of the front door to the media in the face of such treatment. However, McGrory saw it as an honour to manage Celtic, and felt he could not walk away from the Club he loved. He did not rock the boat, and at times had almost as little managerial influence as you or I – well, perhaps that is an exaggeration, but you will understand my point. However, he always did his best and gave his all, and this must not be forgotten.

In saying all of this though, I must highlight the triumphs (albeit they were not as numerous as we may all have hoped for) that the Club achieved under Jimmy McGrory. With their greatest goalscorer at the helm, Celtic did win the Scottish Cup in

1951; the Coronation Cup in 1953; a league and cup double in 1953–54; the Club's first League Cup in 1956; and of course, the famous seven-one League Cup Final victory in 1957. In his later years as manager, Jimmy would also lead Celtic to the semi-finals, and very nearly to the final, of the European Cup Winners Cup in 1963–64. While the Coronation Cup win and the day of **"Hampden in the Sun"** will forever be remembered with fondness by the Celtic support, Jimmy McGrory's tenure as manager will never really be looked upon as some of the glory days of the Club. Granted, much of that was not Jimmy's fault, with various factors affecting his ability to do his job.

In reality, to progress in footballing terms, Celtic needed a significantly more strong-willed, somewhat stubborn individual to lead them. In 1965, just that man, in the form of Jock Stein, became the fourth manager of the Football Club. It wasn't exactly a proud moment for Jimmy, who was demoted by the board of directors to another position within the Football Club without much of a say in the matter, but he was still happy to be playing his part at Celtic Park.

In his later life, Jimmy continued to follow the Club he supported as a lad, reflecting on Celtic's most famous victory of them all in Lisbon in a book entitled **"A Lifetime in Paradise"**, which was published in 1975:

"I actually broke down in tears that night, the first time in all my years in the game that I had cried. What a thrill it was to see young boys like Murdoch, McNeill, Johnstone, Gemmell, Clark and Lennox coming of age. What a thrill it was to the see club I had served all my life reach its pinnacle."

Jimmy McGrory died on the twentieth of October 1982, at the age of seventy-eight years old, leaving behind him a legacy of goalscoring that will never be forgotten and, poignantly, one that will likely never to be beaten by another Celtic player. While the number of medals he accumulated throughout his career may not have quite lived up to his individual talent, and while his tenure as manager may not have been quite as successful as we all would have hoped, one thing is certain; James 'Jimmy' McGrory loved Celtic Football Club with all of his heart and soul, and he gave a tremendous amount of time and effort throughout a long, and at times difficult life, to that end.

Following his death, "**The Evening Times**" featured a few words from the previously mentioned Bob McPhail, the Rangers inside-forward whom Jimmy had befriended decades previously. He said: "**I like to think I was a good friend and I am privileged to say so. I had a tremendous regard for him and found him a great man to have on my side. On the other hand, I played against him a few times for Rangers and that wasn't so much fun. He always scored against us. But that won't stop me remembering his name with affection.**"

From a personal point of view, I remain somewhat disappointed that Mr McGrory was not voted into the "**Greatest Celtic Team Ever**" by the Club's supporters, as I feel his record calls for it more than any other individual featured in my fictional eleven. However, as I have always maintained, the differing opinions football supporters possess are a critically important part of the game itself, and regardless, there is no doubt in my mind that the name of James Edward McGrory will live as long as Celtic Football Club itself. In this regard, he will live forever.

Upon his death, Ian Paul of "**The Glasgow Herald**" began his memorial article as follows: "**Great footballers will always be remembered. Great footballers who were gentlemen are entitled to be revered. Jimmy McGrory managed to fit the bill on both counts with ease. From the day he joined Celtic until the day he died, Jimmy McGrory could not find an enemy. Speaking to people who watched, played alongside, or just knew him, the prevalent theme was simple, McGrory was a nice man. It is an epitaph all of us must envy.**"

Jimmy is buried alongside his wife Barbara (who died in 1997) in Dalbeth Cemetery on London Road, Glasgow, within sight of his beloved Celtic Park. For anyone interested, he can be found by passing through the cemetery gates, turning left past the small red brick house, and continuing fifty yards along a path, where he lies on the end of a row on the left hand side.

In 2013, Jimmy's old junior side, St Roch's, imparted a tremendous honour upon the man they still regard as their greatest son. They renamed their stadium (which was previously known as **"Provanmill Park"**) by popular demand, and it is now known as **"James McGrory Park"**. Had Jimmy been alive to see this, I'm sure he would have been incredibly proud to find his name adorning the stadium.

Finally, I would like to round off this chapter with a mention for my grandfather, who turned ninety only weeks prior to the publication of this book. Having lived in England for many years, he has never been a big supporter of any Scottish Club, although he does remember visiting Rugby Park in the early 1930's occasionally before moving south. Anyway, when I first described the nature of the book I was writing to him, I made a reference to Jimmy McGrory, and almost immediately, my grandfather's eyes lit up as a memory entered his head – perhaps slightly dusty – but phenomenal nonetheless.

"It's always the same old story, another goal for Jimmy McGrory..." he sounded out, before pausing for a moment and saying, **"I'm sorry, there's more to it, but I can't seem to remember the rest!"**

Now, in the days before mobile phones and prior to any sort of serious television coverage, many of the old songs from the Celtic terraces have been lost or forgotten, but by nothing other than chance, I have since come across a slightly different version of the song my grandfather remembers. In all likelihood, there were probably a few different versions of this song, or perhaps even differing verses. Regardless, I'll simply let the words speak for themselves, and Granda, thank you for bringing a smile to my face yet again, as you have done so many times over the years.

"Tell me the sweet old story, a hat-trick for McGrory,
Another victory for the Celtic, he will carry us through,
He'll carry us through the hue, to beat the Rangers in blue,
Look forever to McGrory, he will carry us through!"

"You Guys Are Absolutely Awesome!"

As I write this, it is a little under twenty-four hours since I returned home from a memorable trip to Barcelona and, as with all stories, I suppose I should start from the beginning. I had, prior to this journey, only travelled abroad to see Celtic play on one occasion. This pilgrimage to Seville in 2003 is discussed at some length in another section of the book. Of course, I was only twelve at that time, and so any future trip as an adult would almost inevitably take on a very different, somewhat alcohol fuelled, dynamic.

And so, when Celtic booked their place in the Champion League group stages in early 2012–2013, the thoughts of both me and my father began to turn to a potential European jaunt to follow the Bhoys. In truth, if we could have chosen anywhere before the draw, we would both have picked a trip to the Bernabeu. The reasoning behind this was simple of course – José Mourinho.

I do not believe myself to be a bitter individual, or the type of person to hold a grudge. However, when it comes to José, I must admit there is an exception to this rule. Firstly, I'd like to state that José Mourinho is a truly fantastic manager. Somehow he manages to bind teams full of expensive players with enormous individual egos together into units which would do almost anything for each other. His record, like it or loathe it, speaks for itself. With regards to a potential trip to Madrid though, I have always wanted a chance to tell **"the special one"** what I think of him. He is an enigma, as despite the fact I rather dislike him, part of me cannot help but admire him.

Anyway, without digressing too much, we wanted Real Madrid for this reason above all others. However, we were delighted when Celtic were drawn in Group G alongside one of the greatest teams in the world – Barcelona – a team whom, in my mind at least, will go down as one of the best sides the game has ever known. Once my mum had persuaded my dad that a trip to Moscow wasn't the best idea (with regards to both the view of a trek to Russia itself and the potential impact on the family's bank balance), we quickly agreed that we fancied a visit to Catalonia.

And so, within a couple of hours of the draw, my parents and I huddled around the family computer (no pun intended) and set about trying to find flights and accommodation. Tickets would become an issue at a later stage of course, but having quickly decided we weren't interested in paying the often extortionate prices charged by the official travel company, we knew we would have to cross that bridge when we came to it. With prices leaping upwards around us, and as flights and hotels filled up in the time it took us to enter our details on several websites, we were eventually fortunate enough to purchase two seats on planes flying Sunday-Thursday (with the match on Tuesday night), as well as a twin hotel room somewhere between the city centre and the stadium itself.

In the days following our booking, I created **"Maley's Bhoys Barca"** (@MBBarca on Twitter) in order to provide supporters with somewhere to share information and ask questions about their upcoming journeys. As I did so, I began to tread through unchartered waters (at least personally) as I attempted to learn all I could about a city which, in truth, I knew very little about. Several websites, as well as a few Celtic fans with local knowledge (these people will know who they are), were tremendously useful as I began to develop a basic guide for supporters travelling to the city. This included a subway map; a guide to prominent pubs (Irish bars mostly, of course); advice with regards to Barcelona's infamous pickpockets; bus and taxi prices; where to eat; the weather we were all likely to face; where we were all likely to congregate on the day of the game and details of how people may be able to get their hands on tickets for the upcoming match.

I was pleasantly surprised by the response I received from my fellow Celtic supporters, as is so often the case, and I would like to state in writing once again that it really was a pleasure to be of some service to them. Having now visited the city, I feel I could almost write a small book in itself with regards to my experiences there, as well as hints and tips on what to do and what to see, but for the purposes of your sanity I will try to keep it brief.

Around a month before the match, I phoned Celtic's ticket office in Glasgow for the umpteenth time, enquiring as to when any remaining tickets for Celtic's official allocation would be made available to other travelling supporters. I was told that **"any leftover tickets will be sold to season ticket holders who are successful in the upcoming ballot". "Fair enough"**, I thought. However, I was subsequently told that (and I was certainly not the only one judging on what other people have told me) we had **"no chance of getting tickets in the ballot if we hadn't recently attended an away match in Europe"**.

Now, in principle, I'm not overly opposed to that idea. There are individuals, some of whom will be reading this, who follow Celtic far and wide across the globe with some regularity. I cannot praise these people enough, as the travelling Celtic support is one of the traits synonymous with the reputation of the Football Club. Anyway, I begrudgingly accepted this situation and, once again, I checked Barcelona's official ticket website that night.

Previously, I had been warned by a local that any away supporters buying tickets for a match at the Camp Nou would not be able to pick them up with a foreign passport if it matched the nationality of Barcelona's opponents for the match. However, since being told this, I had been reassured by several supporters who had contacted the Catalan club directly that this would not be an issue with regards to the upcoming game against Celtic.

I published this information and many people, like me and my father, went on to buy tickets within the home sections of the ground with some trepidation and excitement. Fortunately, we managed to hold fire long enough for two seats together (in the second of the Camp Nou's three vast tiers) to become available, before we snapped them up.

In the coming week, Celtic would announce, contrary to all previous correspondence, that they would begin the general sale of away tickets to any season ticket holders who turned up at the ticket office with their travel documents. Despite accepting an allocation of several thousand briefs from Barcelona, they had struggled (perhaps unsurprisingly) to sell particularly many through the rather expensive official deals, and were therefore forced to sell them directly to supporters who had made their own travel arrangements instead.

For those without tickets, this provided a fantastic opportunity and fans began eagerly purchasing them. The result of this was, rather oddly, that several supporters ended up with more tickets for the match than they actually required, as many had already bought tickets for the Barcelona end when away tickets became readily available. This led to an almost continuous stream of people looking for help with regards to selling their tickets for the home end. This proved to be rather tricky in certain senses, as people were trying to sell tickets they would not have in their possession until they travelled to Barcelona and picked them up. Nonetheless, we were happily successful in coupling many ticketless individuals together with tickets for the match, and this is something I am proud to have been a small part of.

Sadly, in one last display of a lack of common sense, those at Parkhead's ticket office proceeded to publicise the deadline for season ticket holders to purchase away tickets, before leaving many non-season ticket holders disappointed when they subsequently sent the remainder for the allocation back to Catalonia without a general sale. Of course, the glut of home end tickets in the hands of Celtic supporters essentially remedied this issue, and I think almost everyone who travelled to Barcelona was eventually able to attend the match, although the tales of how certain people got there and the hassle which sometimes went along with it will live long in the memories of many.

And so, on the Sunday prior to the match, myself and my father set out for Barcelona. Flying straight from Glasgow to the closest of the three airports which service the Catalonian city, El Prat, this was to be a fairly relaxed and enjoyable trip. A short delay allowed us an extra hour in Glasgow Airport's main bar (somewhere I'm sure many of you will know all too well) and, with a Catalan flag in hand, we waited for our flight to be called.

Prior to boarding, I decided a trip to the gents was required thanks to several pints of Guinness, whereupon I was confronted with a rather unexpected sight. As I pushed open the first of the two doors to the toilets, a man with a face like thunder came storming past me. As he did so, I noticed he was wearing a peculiar top, which on closer inspection I found to be a bright orange polo shirt with a rather fetching mural featuring **"King Billy - 1690"** on the breast (ironically apt for the tit wearing it, I must say).

Now, I can't say for sure, but perhaps the fact the airport was crowded with several groups of happy looking Celtic supporters (myself sporting a bright green Jimmy Johnstone shirt) had put him in a bit of a bad mood. I proceeded into the gents where I was met with a few other lads bound for Barcelona, who were already midway through the following discussion.

"Did you see that guy with the King Billy t-shirt on?"

"Aye mate, his coupon was an absolute picture! He looked absolutely raging!"

"Ach well, no wonder I suppose! Imagine thinking you're going your holidays to get away from all the abuse about Sevco only to find the airport's full of us when you're flying out!"

"Aye, right enough, wonder where he's off to anyway? It'd be funny if it was Barca!"

It was at this point, after a couple of pints of the aforementioned black stuff, I simply could not resist making a joke about the previous gentleman's situation, and I chipped in with the following line: **"You never know lads, maybe they're doing chartered flights to Annan nowadays!"**

Anyway, having had a bit of a laugh, we went our separate ways and boarded our flights. Other than the eternally interesting airline food, my flight was, for the most part, rather uneventful. Seated near the front of the plane, occasional bursts of the Victor Wanyama song could be heard from some distance behind us. As time passed, and more alcohol was consumed, these bursts became louder and more prolonged, although all of the singing was good natured and polite.

As we approached El Prat, you could have been forgiven for thinking the remainder of the journey was a given, but then we were informed over the tannoy that we would have the fun of landing in the middle of a lightning storm. **"Great,"** I hear you think! Well, being someone who isn't hellish keen on flying at the best of times, my thoughts were vaguely similar in nature, but they were perhaps a little vulgar to publish here.

With around twenty minutes to landing, the ride began, as the cabin crew dimmed the lights and ensured all of the window visors were fully open for the approach to El Prat. In the distance, flashes of light could be seen in the clouds whilst, at the rear of the aeroplane, the singing continued undaunted.

"Don't sell McCourt, Paddy McCourt, I just don't think you understand!" was the cry.

At this point, we entered the main body of the thunderstorm, and began to fly through the sheet lightning itself. As the aircraft moved up and down with the inevitable turbulence which followed, flashes surrounded the plane and illuminated the cabin in an eerie glow which lasted for several seconds at a time. By now, the chanting had progressed a little, before it stopped dead immediately after the first large flash.

"Cause if you sell McCourt, Paddy McCourt, you're..."

Clearly, even those who had drunk a fair bit both on and off the plane had become aware of the situation they found themselves in. Now, don't get me wrong, this wasn't a particularly bad landing. Nobody's lives were ever in danger and I'm sure that, on the grand scheme of things, it was all fairly routine. However, I'm sure many of the three hundred or so Glaswegians on the aircraft would have been more than a tad relieved to arrive safely in Barcelona and finally feel the ground under their feet once again – I know I was.

The next morning, as we had previously agreed, my dad and I hastily munched our way through a rather unremarkable hotel breakfast before heading straight for the Camp Nou. A short trip on the Metro system (the first of many that week) took us to the Maria Christina stop, around ten minutes walk from the stadium. On exiting the station, it is not entirely apparent where the stadium is, as there is no obvious signage and tall buildings block the ground from view until you are fairly close to it.

In my family, there is a long running joke that you either possess an innate sense of direction or you do not. To put this in context, my father would openly admit that when it comes to this sort of thing, he is largely clueless, and will generally rely on either myself or my mother whenever he is abroad. Having glanced at **"Google Maps"** before leaving Glasgow, I remembered that the stadium was somewhere south west of this subway station. Much to my dad's amusement, I quickly worked out which way that was thanks to the position of the sun and pointed in what I believed to be the correct direction. Despite the inevitable mockery which ensued as we blindly went where neither of us had gone before, I was soon proven right as we found ourselves facing the stadium whilst strolling along **"Pope Pius XII Avenue"**.

"Now, there's a street name you wouldn't see in Glasgow," quipped my father.

Even from afar, the Camp Nou is an impressive sight. For those of you who may not know, the stadium is built into the ground, meaning that the pitch is some way below ground level. As we strolled around the behemoth itself, we came to the glass front of the structure to find the Barcelona megastore (and it is truly a megastore; imagine Celtic's shop and add two floors to it) and the arena which houses the Barcelona basketball team.

Anyway, once we had been bounced from pillar to post, from desk to desk and from building to building asking where we could pick up our match tickets, we were eventually directed down the access road away from the stadium to a rather rickety old building with a red tin roof which stood next to the bus park. Ironically, whilst the front of the ground and the nearby amenities are all remarkably modern, this building was, in fact, the main ticket office.

Upon our arrival here, we immediately knew we were in the right place as we noticed many other Scottish and Irish accents, whilst a couple of groups clambered together near the ticket queues discussing whether or not they would be able to pick up, or even purchase, briefs for tomorrow's game. The ticket office is so small that only the staff members are allowed inside, with customers being addressed through small iron barred windows, in keeping with the old feel of the small building. Before we had even introduced ourselves to the other Celtic fans there, touts were openly approaching us all asking us what tickets we needed and how many, assuring us that they could **"get whatever we wanted"**. Having quickly decided that turning to a ticket tout was only to be a final resort; we joined the queue behind a Glaswegian couple and awaited our fate.

As the queue moved steadily forward, we began chatting once again with those around us, and we soon discovered that the couple in front were trying to buy tickets, not simply pick them up. A nervous husband bit away at his fingernails as his wife showed off the one line of Spanish she knew, which from memory was something similar to **"quisera dos boletos por favor"**. This apparently meant, **"I'd like two tickets please."** At this stage, I didn't have the heart to tell her that most people in Barcelona speak Catalan. Of course, they all spoke Spanish too, so I knew this wouldn't be too big an issue. And, to be fair to the lady in question, she strode up to the little window when her time came and, in a typically Glaswegian attempt at a Spanish accent, said her piece, before proudly walking away with tickets for herself and her slightly stunned husband.

However, neither I nor my father knew any Spanish or Catalan, with the exception of obvious words such as those for **"hello"** and **"thank you"**. For this reason, when we approached the window, we simply stuck to **"ola"** and **"gracias"** and tried to say as little as possible. Thankfully, we were successful, and soon found ourselves in possession of two tickets for the opposite side of the ground from the away support.

A few seconds later, as we hastily put the tickets away to keep them safe for the trip back to our hotel, the lad who had been behind us in the queue and his father passed by muttering under their breaths. Having given them a shout, they came over and explained they had been turned away when they attempted to buy tickets for the match. Now, I have no idea as to why the little woman in the office refused to sell them tickets, but perhaps the fact the guys were both decked from head to toe in Celtic gear may not have helped them in their quest.

However, not ones to see fellow supporters go without, we suggested that they should chase after the couple who had previously managed to buy tickets. They soon did so, and persuaded the lady with the one line of broken Glaswegian Spanish to join the queue for another window, in an attempt to buy them two tickets. Low and behold, ten minutes later, the two gents left delighted as the woman triumphantly returned with tickets for the Barcelona end once more. So, the moral of this story is – if you're ever travelling to a foreign country without a ticket, learn a few basic phrases of the native tongue, don't dress like **"Hoopy the Huddle Hound"** and hope for the best!

Anyway, having picked up our tickets we bought a couple of Barcelona scarves for the next day and headed back into the city centre. There, I was fortunate enough to meet a couple of folk I'd spoken to previously on Twitter, who were incredibly kind when it came to offering to buy me a pint. Had I accepted all of the offers, I think I would have ended up more than a bit worse for wear, and perhaps that's putting it lightly.

Having sampled the delights of **"The Temple Bar"** and **"Molly's Irish bar"** just off Las Ramblas, we went in search of somewhere to eat. As we did so, the relative quiet of the day was broken by a tremendous bang somewhere in the distance. In time, we would witness a large protest march make its way past us – banners, firecrackers and all – before the people surrounded what we presumed was a government building of sorts.

Leaving them to it, we plumped for that definition of culinary excellence, **"Kentucky Fried Chicken"**. We'd find ourselves somewhere a little more exciting to eat another night, but on the Monday, we'd had a couple of drinks and, having watched the aforementioned protest for some time, we were rather hungry. Having eaten something quickly, we returned to **"The Temple Bar"** and were met with around one hundred fans singing and dancing in the street outside the pub.

This show of support will not surprise any of you reading this. I'm sure most of us have, at some point at least, spilled out of a pub for a sing song, whether it was in Glasgow or further afield. It was at this point that a woman with a foreign accent, which I first thought was American in origin, tapped me on the arm and the following conversation ensued (most of which was shouted over the din of our supporters going crazy):

"Excuse me sir, can you tell me what's going on here?"

"Ah, hello! We're Celtic fans here for a match against Barcelona!"

"Oh! Soccer? Okay! What was the score?"

"Yes, soccer! The game is tomorrow night!"

(At this point, the obligatory Huddle typically broke out in the street next to us).

"Tomorrow night? Wow! What's caused the celebrations then?"

"Nothing! This is just what we do! We all travel, sing, drink, and try our best to enjoy ourselves!"

"Ah ok, are you all from Ireland?"

"No! Celtic play in Glasgow! Scotland!"

"Glasgow? Ah! That explains why I've met so many people from Glasgow during the last few days! Is this all of your fans?"

(I couldn't help but laugh when she asked that question).

"All of us?! No! There will be at least five thousand of us in the city tomorrow!"

"Five thousand? But you've come so far! You must be crazy!"

"Well, there might be something in that! Where are you from?"

"Canada!"

"Ah, very good. Are you enjoying your trip?"

"Yes! Very much!"

"Should I stay indoors tomorrow in case things turn violent?"

"Violent? No, there's no chance of that! Don't worry, we'll just drink and sing! Other than that we pose no threat to anyone!"

"Ok! Thank you very much! I hope you do well tomorrow night! You guys are absolutely awesome!"

Now, over the years, I'm sure many people will have had conversations like that. However, what was really interesting was just how amazed this little woman was by the entire spectacle of the events unfolding around us. She had never seen football supporters, or anyone in fact, behave in the same manner as the Celtic fans did that night. In fact, all of the jumping about, singing, dancing, and huddling caused not only some travelling supporters, but also many locals and tourists to take both photographs and videos. Most of all, the Canadian lady was amazed with regards to how friendly we all were, especially considering many of those in front of her had clearly drank rather a lot.

Fundamentally, that little woman will have gone home to Canada and told those around her of what she saw and heard. It is stories like this that help to add to the incredibly positive reputation Celtic Football Club has around the world. She came to Europe and had, by her own admission, never even heard of Celtic, and yet now, I feel she won't forget us in a hurry. Of course, that's what it's all about. People can fall in love with Celtic over the course of several decades, or in the space of a few minutes.

Later that night, we returned to the bar in our hotel, only to find that, unlike the night before, we were not the only Celtic fans to have had the same idea. As we clambered up onto bar stools and ordered a couple of rather large, cold Estrella's, we were greeted like brothers by people who neither of us had met before. Fathers sat with their sons, husbands with their wives, and both those young and old spoke with fervour and expectation about the upcoming match against the mighty Barcelona.

Soon though, things would take a rather unexpected turn as one of the lads, wee Johnny from Leeds, pulled out a deck of cards and started to perform a few magic tricks. I must confess I was initially sceptical when I was first asked to **"pick a card"**, but within moments both myself and the rest of the group were taken in by wee Johnny's ability to manipulate the deck and, seemingly, do things which were **"magic"**. It was a thoroughly enjoyable way to spend a few minutes actually, before Johnny's dad (also called John) introduced himself to my father and I.

A member of the **"Wim the Tim Celtic Supporters Club"**, John was born in Leeds and has no obvious connection to Celtic Football Club. When I say that, I mean that he does not have, for example, a parent who lived in Glasgow before moving to Leeds and settling down. By his own admission, he is simply someone who developed a love for a particular Football Club, and that

Club just happened to be Celtic. Nowadays, both John and wee Johnny are season ticket holders, rarely missing a match and regularly making the four hundred mile round trip to Celtic Park (and beyond).

The next morning, me and my dad, as well as several others no doubt, were nursing hangovers of varying severities. We spent the morning sightseeing in the area around the Plaça d'Espanya, where a couple of Australian tourists shouted: **"Hey Celtic fans! We hope you don't lose too badly! Hail Hail!"**

After a few hours more to recover in the hotel room around lunchtime, we headed out on the subway to the main square (the Plaça de Catalonia), in the hopes of finding the party. Even as we stepped off of our train, we knew we were in the right place as, even over the noise of the trains, distant Glaswegian voices carried the chants of **"Victor Wanyama! Victor Wanyama! Wanyama! Wanyama! Wanyama! Oh-oh!"**

Upon exiting the station, we were greeted with a sight that I, certainly, will never forget – green and white Hoops, tricolours and Catalan flags everywhere – Celtic fans as far as the eye could see. It was a scene reminiscent of Seville although, of course, there were many less of us in Barcelona that day.

Directly next to the subway station on the corner of the main square is a typical, traditional Mediterranean bar. Known as **"Cafe Zurich"**, it was the closest source of alcohol to the gathered masses and therefore, it was doing a roaring trade, with four Euro pints of lager flying out the door with a staggering regularity. All of the tables, both inside and out, were packed and there wasn't a seat to be had anywhere. Once we had grabbed a couple of pints each at the bar, we wandered through the array tables and supporters sat on the outside of the establishment. At this point, I watched an elderly waiter with a moustache, waistcoat and bow tie, skilfully navigating the crowds in front of him, before delivering a tray full of drinks to a thirsty, expectant table.

As we left the bar and headed for the centre of the square, we reached the main road separating the two and found that the back and forth chanting was already in full swing, as the folk on either side of the street attempted to better their opponents:

"Celtic! CELTIC! Celtic! CELTIC! C'mon you Bhoys in green (etc)!"

Whilst this was remarkably competitive, it was incredibly friendly, and provided a great spectacle for the many passing locals. When we eventually managed to cross the road, we entered the square itself, where I quickly noticed a football was being punted about from one side of the crowd to the other. Now, a football isn't normally anything to be concerned about, but when you are carrying eight Euros worth of Estrella each, it becomes a notable hazard, especially when you are wandering straight across the proverbial shooting gallery.

Inevitably, as we neared the safety of the trees, the ball landed right in front of me – I was fortunate enough to dodge it, but my dad was not. Much to the amusement of the hundreds who witnessed it, two pints became one and a quarter in an instant, and suddenly he was feeling a bit cooler than he had been a few moments before. With a shrug of his shoulders and a mildly embarrassed smile on his lager soaked face, we continued on before finding somewhere to sit and enjoy the remaining beer which survived the journey.

Having relaxed for a few hours, there was a collective mood shift within the support, as afternoon turned into early evening and thirst became hunger. Many, including ourselves, then decided a quick trip to the local McDonald's was in order, before travelling out to the stadium itself. Whilst in the rather long queue inside, a mixture of bewildered tourists, awestruck locals, and bemused staff were treated to several renditions of the **"Don't Sell McCourt"** song. This caused the counter staff to smile and start shouting **"No! No! Quiet!"** before a couple of police officers appeared a few minutes later. Unsurprisingly, this still didn't stop the singing, and soon the atmosphere was, for a McDonald's restaurant at least, really rather impressive.

Anyway, we had our fill, before making our way into the square's subway station alongside hundreds of other Celtic supporters. Whilst we weren't expecting any trouble, the arrival of a few dozen riot police in the square just as we had finished eating signalled to us that it was probably a good time to head.

In truth, the police were just aiming to begin to shepherd the supporters out of the square and on to trains, nothing more.

Between the subway and the stadium itself, having met a couple of my pals, we enjoyed a quick pint and posed for more photographs with Barcelona supporters. Having seen both sets of fans enjoy each other's company in Glasgow a few years earlier, it was great to see that the same welcome which Barcelona fans received in Scotland being reproduced by the locals of the Catalan capital.

Having grabbed a couple of baguette style sandwiches wrapped in tin foil (the popular choice amongst Barcelona fans for half time food), we began to search for **"Access Nine"**. Unlike Celtic Park, the Camp Nou has a large fence set around a hundred yards out from the stadium itself and to approach particular turnstiles, you must pass through an allocated access gate in this fence. It was only as we followed this structure around the perimeter that we realised just how large the area owned by Barcelona was. The stadium seemed fairly small in comparison to the grounds, which held shops, stalls, and the basketball arena to boot. As well as this, Barcelona's 'B' team has a sixteen thousand seater stadium across the road. In a way, it reminded me of Lesser Hampden but on a ridiculous scale.

Finally, we reached our gate and, once we had covered up our Celtic colours, zipped up our jackets (no mean feat in weather which would be hailed as **"glorious"** in Scotland) and donned our Barcelona scarves, we proceeded through the outer fence and through the interior turnstiles. In this time, we were only stopped to produce our tickets and to have the lids taken from our bottles of water. Yes, there are people employed to do this on match days as, unlike in Scotland, Barcelona will happily allow you to take a bottle of juice into the ground. However, the agreement is that you must surrender the cap from your bottle so that you cannot seal it and throw it as a missile. Of course, without the cap, any liquid would spill out midflight and reduce the potential injury incurred by anyone struck with said bottle. Common sense seems to be a big part of the match day experience at the Camp Nou, and I feel this is something we could all learn from in Scotland.

However, one thing that I must admit I did find rather odd was being met with someone trying to sell me a cushion for my seat within seconds of entering the stadium itself. It was only as me and my father discussed this oddity that we noticed several locals wandering past with cushions they had clearly brought with them from home. I have to say I can't see that catching on in Glasgow, but I suppose you never know.

Anyway, moments later this bewilderment was forgotten as I walked out onto the second tier of the Camp Nou. It was still around an hour before kick-off and fairly quiet, but under the powerful floodlights, I was greeted with an awe-inspiring sight. I had never in my life been more impressed by a football stadium than Celtic Park up until that point (despite trips to the likes of Old Trafford and the Estadio Olímpico in Seville), but I can now categorically state that the Camp Nou is the most impressive stadium I have ever had the pleasure of setting foot in.

As I looked around the truly vast arena and gazed at the Champions League banner already laid out in the centre circle, voices from the Gods of the stadium caught my ear and I looked up to see our away allocation, already more than half full, in the highest tier on the opposite side of the field from myself. It was only as we reached our seats that we noticed a group of Celtic fans around twenty-five feet away, all decked out in Hoops with flags. On the tier below us behind the goal, we spotted were several other groups openly displaying their colours without any problems, and so, with a sigh of relief, we happily took the chance to take off our jackets and cool down.

Around half an hour before the start of proceedings, as the stadium became to fill up, I ventured back up the stairs in search of the toilets. At the top stood someone I immediately recognised as a fellow Glaswegian. Despite the fact he was wearing a Barcelona shirt, a Barcelona scarf and even a Barcelona hat, I was confident enough in my estimations to wander up to the lad and say: **"Alright mate, how you doing?"**

Mildly stunned, he looked back and said, **"Alright man. I'm good cheers, but how did you know I wasn't a Barca fan?!"**

With a wry smile on my face, I replied, **"Ah it was just a funny feeling pal...that and the fact I can see your Hoops sticking out from underneath your Barca top!"**

"Aw shite! So much for my master plan eh?" replied my new friend in typical Scottish style as he glanced down at his waist, **"I see you're not hiding your colours though, so I'm guessing I should be alright?"**

Once I had pointed out a few other groups openly displaying their support for the visiting team, I left the lad, who was rather happy at this point, and proceeded to my original destination. Upon my return, he hadn't moved anywhere, but now had his Celtic shirt on top of its Barcelona counterpart. Once we worked out where his seat was, he happily came down the tier to take a few photos of me and my dad and, of course, we returned the favour. The next and final time I would see the man, who was perhaps slightly older than myself, was when Georgios Samaras opened the scoring less than twenty minutes into the match, but I'll come back to that.

Moments later, the first bars of the iconic Barcelona theme song began to reverberate around the Camp Nou, signalling the entrance of my two favourite football teams. I have always enjoyed watching Barcelona from afar, but there was only one side I truly wanted to see triumph that night, and they were wearing the distinctive green and white Hoops which are now synonymous with a brand of football, a Club, and its supporters. As the Champions League theme tune played through the tannoy, a tremendous roar erupted from the upper tier across the stadium, as the away fans visibly and audibly showed their support for the Bhoys. However, the locals remained relatively subdued, quietly clapping throughout the song.

I suppose it is worth remembering that, when you take their recent Champions League record into account, the fans of Barcelona expect their side to progress from the group stages without too much hassle, and this was reflected in the fact there were around twenty thousand empty seats in the nigh on one hundred thousand seater Camp Nou.

Unsurprisingly, Barcelona began to dominate the game in terms of possession straight from the kick-off. Whilst the Celtic supporters produced the majority of the noise coming from all four sides of the ground, the home players on the park began to pass the ball beautifully and probe the Celtic defence, constantly looking for an opening. Other than one or two early scares, Celtic resolutely held out, attempting to break up the field whenever the opportunity presented itself.

A little over fifteen minutes in, one such break resulted in the Hoops being awarded with a free kick just outside the box. As Charlie Mulgrew addressed the ball, we held our breath, as did thousands of other Celtic fans inside the Camp Nou. As the ball flew through the night air, Georgios Samaras rose to meet the cross and it soon found its way into the back of the helpless Victor Valdés' net. Immediately, all noise from the Barcelona fans stopped dead, replaced only with the cacophony coming from travelling fans.

Having instinctively leapt to our feet and began jumping about hugging each other in celebration, it was only after around forty-five seconds that my dad sat down and I turned to do the same. At this moment, I glanced back up the tier to be met with an image that will never leave me. I saw hundreds, if not thousands, of stunned faces staring at me – Barcelona fans – some open-mouthed, others shaking their heads, and even a few gesticulating wildly about the poor defending from their side only moments before. However, what really makes this memory special is the lad I mentioned earlier, whom I had encountered at the top of the stairs.

Around twenty rows above us, a little off to the side, stood this guy, in amongst all of the aforementioned home supporters. Alone, with no Celtic fans for some distance around him, he was, suitably, still going mental; waving his scarf in the air, jumping up and down, and screaming at the top of his lungs. To the credit of the locals, nobody bothered him nor any of us, they simply allowed us all to celebrate our goal, before upping the volume levels inside the stadium significantly as the match kicked off once more.

The Camp Nou is certainly one of, if not the, most difficult place in the world to achieve a positive result. With this in mind, it goes without saying that Barcelona do not drop points at home very often and, with over seventy minutes to go, every Celtic supporter around the world knew it would take a truly gargantuan effort, mixed with a rather large sample of good fortune for the Bhoys to maintain a clean sheet for the rest of the night, especially as Barcelona began to move their play up a gear.

In the minutes which followed, Lionel Messi would send two free-kicks from distance just over Fraser Forster's bar. On each occasion, this was met with an **"ooh"** from the home supporters around us, before a **"wayyy"** filtered down from the away allocation across the park. The home supporters didn't seem too worried about this, as it was masked somewhat by other noise. However, when the Celtic supporters started to audibly shout **"olé"** after every successful pass in a sustained period of Hoops possession, the Barcelona fans began to become somewhat riled.

With the benefit of hindsight, I suppose it should come as no surprise that a group of supporters who are not used to losing were a tad upset at having the Mickey taken out of them by a team from a league of a lower calibre. It is also worth remembering that Spartak Moscow had pushed them close in the first Champions League match in the Camp Nou that season, and they definitely did not want a repeat of that. In truth, whilst they viewed us all as a great novelty in terms of the manner in which we support our team, the fans of Barcelona wanted three points from their opponents just as they always did.

As half time approached, Celtic finally succumbed to the pressure, as three of the best footballers in the world, Iniesta, Xavi and Messi, combined sublimely to level the scores. Had someone offered me a one-all scoreline at the half way point before kick-off, I think I (and all of my fellow supporters) would have gladly accepted it. During a discussion with my dad, we concluded that the match would most likely end in a three or four-one victory for Barcelona, as we felt Celtic would begin to sit deeper and deeper (having lost Samaras, and therefore our **"out ball"**, to injury), and as Barcelona began to turn the screw and their incredible quality began to show.

However, during the second half, as the seconds ticked slowly away, hope began to spring eternal amongst the Celtic supporters inside the Camp Nou (not to mention those around the world). The Hoops, under incredible pressure from their hosts, stood firm in the face of adversity, even when Barcelona decided to introduce David Villa to the fray. To put this substitution in context, David Villa (who was sat on the Barcelona bench for the first hour of proceedings), cost more than twice the amount of the fourteen players who featured for Celtic that night combined!

Regardless, Celtic continued to break with the ball whenever the opportunity presented itself, but these chances were few and far between. The Hoops continued to threaten from set pieces, and one particular counter attack looked particularly dangerous, but Kris Commons was unable to complete a very tricky cross field pass at its climax.

Throughout the entire second half, my father had been saying to me: **"they'll score...don't get your hopes up, because they'll score"**. However, I must confess that as the match entered stoppage time, and Barcelona struck the post with a little over a minute remaining, I did begin to get my hopes up – we were going to hold out for a draw; an hour and a half had become seconds – we were only seconds away from glory – and then the unthinkable, and yet almost inevitable, happened. Adriano crossed the ball, which bounced between Fraser Forster and James Forrest. On another day, the ball would have gone harmlessly past the post, or Forster would have been able to gather it without fear or favour. However, fate was to deal a cruel blow to the players, the staff, and the supporters of Celtic Football Club that night as the ball glided just inside the far post and into the net.

Around me, the home supporters erupted in celebration, and I sunk my head into my hands. It would have been much less painful to concede with fifteen minutes remaining, rather than fifteen seconds. Whilst the Barcelona supporters shook our hands as the final whistle went, it was clear to see the smiles on their faces were not those of pleasure, but those of relief. As the stadium emptied, the Celtic players marched over to the corner of the stadium where their supporters were housed and applauded them accordingly. You could tell the team felt like broken men. They had just given everything they had to give, and more, in the pursuit of an almost impossible dream. They had been so close.

As we left the Camp Nou, thousands of home supporters streamed past us. Many of them gave us a look which transcended the barriers of language. It was a look of **"we were lucky there"**, but it did little for how I, personally, was feeling at that moment in time. If I'm honest, the word **"gutted"** really doesn't do it justice. One Barcelona fan who spoke fluent English actually stopped me and said **"You were very unlucky tonight – that was the best performance we have seen from an away team all season. It was nice to see a side compete fairly, rather than simply kicking us at every opportunity. We all hope Celtic go far this year."** As we continued around the perimeter of the stadium, glimpses of green and white shone through a sea of red and blue, the colours of our hosts, as small parties of Celtic supporters trudged away from the ground, despondent but proud.

It was only upon our return to the hotel, when I had a cold pint of Estrella in my hand, that things began to sink in. The bar sat eerily quiet, as more and more supporters arrived back from the Camp Nou. People spoke in hushed tones, almost as if there had been a death in the family. Even the staff looked like they felt sorry for us.

Eventually, conversation began to return to the fans present. Perhaps it was the alcohol, or perhaps we'd simply had time to recover a bit (both mentally and physically), but this was when the enormity of the task previously in front of us began to truly hit home. As a Football Club, we had taken on one of the greatest football teams in the world on their turf, and it had taken a fluky last minute goal to defeat us.

Our supporters had conducted themselves impeccably as always, even in the face of such a painful defeat. There was no fighting between the two sets of supporters, only looks of respect and admiration, as well as the swapping of scarves, shirts, and flags. The single tricolour, which flew amongst the Barcelona ultras that night, didn't go unnoticed by many amongst the travelling support either.

Having had a night's sleep, the remaining Celtic supporters in Barcelona began to emerge from hotels and hostels across the city the following morning. The newspapers were covered not with pictures of Lionel Messi or Tito Vilanova, but Fraser Forster, Neil Lennon and, of course, Jordi Alba. Photographs of Celtic fans filling the city's main square were everywhere, and the local media praised our supporters to an enormous extent. One newspaper even said we didn't have the **"Rangers mentality"** and we were the direct opposites of our old rivals.

In summary, it had been a truly phenomenal trip to a truly phenomenal city. The fans of Barcelona had, once again, conducted themselves magnificently. I know there are some people within our support who believe that we shouldn't have such a close relationship with the Catalan giants (unsurprisingly, most of these people support Real Madrid, which is entirely reasonable) but personally, I must disagree.

It's very hard to pin down why, exactly, our two Clubs and the two sets of supporters get along so well, but nevertheless, we do. If anyone tries to tell you that there is no special relationship between Celtic and Barcelona then they are sadly mistaken. I know there is because I have seen it with my own eyes, heard it with my own ears, and been part of it on more than one occasion now, in both Scotland and Catalonia.

I can only thank the people of Barcelona for their incredibly welcoming and friendly attitude, and my fellow Celtic supporters for helping to make those few days a time which I shall never forget.

Of course, the players, staff, and supporters would not know that they would go on to defeat the Catalan giants a fortnight later – a night which will go down as one of the greatest in Celtic's long and illustrious history. As Tony Watt ran through on goal and calmly slotted the ball home, Celtic Park erupted, and what followed were a couple of minutes of absolute carnage. Someone from the row behind landed on me, and I very nearly took a tumble as well.

However, when my attention once again turned to the football itself, nerves began to grip me, and I doubt I was the only one. As

Lionel Messi scored for the visitors, I found myself being transported back to the Camp Nou.

"Not again. Not again. Not again!" I screamed inside my head, as Barcelona began to probe for a late equaliser. Had I been offered a draw prior to kick-off, I would have happily accepted it. However, having led Barcelona two-nil only minutes before, I don't know if I could have coped with us conceding another goal.

Thankfully, as the final whistle went (at last), elation gripped us all. Cries of: **"Wembley! Wembley! We're the famous Glasgow Celtic and we're off to Wembley"** rang round Celtic Park, albeit with an obvious degree of satire attached. Regardless, Celtic had done it. Bhoys who had joined the Club from Airdrie United, Cardiff, Germinal Beerschot, Newcastle, Nottingham Forest and Scunthorpe United (to name but a few) had beaten Barcelona, and become men.

"Music At His Fingertips And Celtic In His Heart"

As those of you who have driven along and through them will no doubt know, the East Kilbride Expressway and the Raith Interchange can be mildly chaotic places, even at the best of times. As I travelled to Coatbridge, that bastion of the Celtic support in the west of Scotland, in early 2013, I found myself to be rather enjoying the hustle bustle of navigating the afternoon traffic, whilst listening to my suitably loud car stereo. I was thoroughly looking forward to the few hours ahead of me, as I have always enjoyed listening to the tales of years gone by from those Celtic supporters more senior in their years than I.

Soon, I pulled into the car park next to a couple of high rise flats and sat there, trying to decipher the seemingly simple puzzle of which one was which, with only the address of my interviewee scribbled on a crumpled piece of paper to help me. I soon realised that I wasn't making any progress sitting doing nothing, and so I ventured out of the warmth of my Volkswagen into the chilly Lanarkshire air, heading towards the buildings themselves. As I did so, I happened to glance up, and soon saw the name of the tower block which I was looking for emblazoned in giant letters more than ten floors above where I stood.

"I've found it! At least that's the difficult bit over", I thought. Sadly, this wasn't to be the case. Firstly I tried to enter what turned out to be the back door (and emergency exit) of the tower block to no avail, before I strolled around the other side of the building and found the main entrance. I was then faced with the keypad to call the flat I was heading to. I typed in the numbers, and waited... nothing. So I pushed in the keys once more...nothing. Finally, after a couple of minutes of standing around, I tried once again, and with some degree of relief, the door buzzed loudly and I was able to get out of the cold. Had this not happened, I was simply going to wait for the people to get out of an approaching taxi and hope to slip into the tower block behind them before the door closed, but thankfully I managed to avoid the potential awkwardness that scenario may have brought along with it.

A few moments later, as I stood in the lift, I found myself wondering whether I'd caused any offence by dialling the number of the flat on several occasions outside. For some reason, I've always seemed to have hassle with these innately simple devices. In the past, I've dialled the wrong number; I've dialled the right number, but at the wrong set of flats; and I've tried to push doors which were **"pull only"** (and vice versa). This fear was soon to be quelled though, as I chapped on the door of my destination and was warmly greeted by a man named Billy Davidson. As he shook my hand and welcomed me into his home, I was immediately struck by the fact there was a mobility scooter and crutches in the hall, with Mr Davidson using a Zimmer frame to support his short walk into his living room. For a moment, I felt awkward as I was concerned that I may have hassled Billy by forcing him to get up, but he quickly reassured me that it was fine and that he'd just been busy with something else when the buzzer first went. After all, I was actually a little early, and that's a fairly rare occurrence on my part.

And so, as I took a seat in his living room, I couldn't help but notice some of the items which adorned the walls. On one hung a picture of Pope Benedict XVI, with a couple of other religious images. On another hung a signed Celtic shirt from a season gone by, along with various other pictures, including one of the team who defeated Rangers by seven goals to one in the famous League Cup Final of 1957. Now, in one sense, Mr Davidson's flat is quite unique, because I don't think there is another wall on this Earth where images of Henrik Larsson, Muhammad Ali, and Carol Vorderman hang side by side, but I suppose I could be mistaken.

Against another wall was a bookcase, crammed to, and perhaps beyond capacity, with Celtic books amongst other bits and bobs, as Billy settled himself down on a seat with his back to the window, high over an icy cold Coatbridge. With a guitar case leaning against the couch I was sitting on and a jumper with an intricate musical logo currently upon his chest, it was clear from the outset that Mr Davidson's love of music was just as strong as he had described during a phone call around a week or so earlier.

Undoubtedly most, if not all of you, will currently be wondering who Billy Davidson is, as he is certainly not a celebrity or an ex-player. In my mind, I consider him to be the literal **"face in the foreground"**, as he will forever be associated with one of the most famous moments in the history of Celtic Football Club in his own small way, despite the fact that very few people know his name. When Celtic returned from their greatest triumph in 1967, the team paraded the European Cup through the streets of Glasgow, before arriving at a packed Celtic Park to show off their prize to the supporters gathered on the terracing of the famous old ground.

As the team did so, they clambered onto the back of an old builders' lorry, and drove slowly around the track which surrounded the pitch, receiving the adulation of a crowd who could never have dreamed of such success only years, and perhaps even months, previously. In front of the vehicle, an Irish band, made up of around fifty young men (as well as two majorettes) marched around trackside, playing music for the supporters in attendance, and heralding the victory of Celtic Football Club over Europe's elite. For the record, Internazionale had won the tournament in both 1964 and 1965, and been eliminated by eventual winners Real Madrid at the semi-final stage in 1966, so they were certainly no pushovers. Anyway, Billy Davidson, now in his mid-sixties, played the accordion that day – and what a day it was.

Born on the third of January 1947, Billy Davidson has been a Coatbridge Bhoy all his life. He emphasised this point by telling me that he was born around a hundred yards from the base of the block of flats we were currently sat in, at his granny's old house. Like many families in Scotland (including my own), Billy's is made up of one side of Scottish ancestry, and the other of Irish descent. His mother's family originally hailed from the Antrim Glens of the North of Ireland, before moving to Scotland in the 1880's, whilst his father's family, who hold the name Davidson, hail from central Scotland.

Billy's father, Frank, was originally a miner by trade. However, at the outbreak of World War Two, he put his name forward as a volunteer for active duty, and soon found himself as a serving member of the Royal Navy in the fight against Hitler and the fascist Third Reich, as well as the Japanese in Asia. During his time on the world's oceans, Frank saw deployment in the Far East and the fearsome Northern Atlantic around Iceland. Billy's mother was originally named Kathy McMullan prior to her marriage to Frank.

In his early years, Billy attended St Bartholomew's Primary School in Townhead, before progressing to St Augustine's Secondary School when he was a little older. One of six boys, Billy had two older brothers and three younger than himself. Sadly, only four of the six are still alive, with one currently living in the somewhat warmer, sunnier climate of Spain. As for Billy himself, he suffered from tuberculosis as a child and spent the majority of his time from the age of three, until the age of six, inside Stonehouse Hospital. He would have more health problems in his later life – hence the motorised scooter – but I shall discuss these in more detail as his story progresses.

By his own admission, Billy was never a particularly gifted footballer, unlike a couple of his brothers. Nevertheless, he always enjoyed playing the game when he could, albeit at no serious level. He told me that he had always preferred watching the games, enjoying the emotional rollercoaster that followed and dissecting the tactical nuances of the display before him, but there was a time when he certainly wasn't opposed to a kick-about himself.

Now, Mr Davidson absolutely adores statistics, and his ability to quote not only the scores from matches long gone by, but the teams and relevant match details is simply stunning. Considering these are, as you may have guessed, something I too share an interest in, I knew I was in the company of a man I could learn a lot from.

And so, at the age of ten, Billy's older brother, Frank, took him to see Celtic for the first time. On the twentieth of April 1957, Celtic defeated Airdrieonians by three goals to nil at Celtic Park, in front of a crowd of only six thousand or so. The Scottish Cup

Final, contested by Falkirk and Kilmarnock was scheduled for the same day and, for this reason, the attendance at Parkhead was unusually low. It was also on this date that Celtic signed one Johnny Divers, the son of 1930's Celtic star Johnny Divers and the grand-nephew of Patsy Gallacher from Glentyan Thistle. That same week, the legendary Jimmy Delaney **"called it a day at last"** according to **"The Evening Times"**, having **"told Elgin City that he had finally decided to stop playing."**

Whilst most of the Celtic supporters were happy enough with the result of their trip to Celtic Park that day, Billy was not. He can still remember growing bored, crying and wanting to go home midway through the match, and this eventually led to his brother taking him back to the supporters bus early, much to his displeasure. On the way back to Coatbridge, Frank said that he would never take his little brother to Celtic Park again because of what had just happened and, remarkably, he never did. Ironically, having read the match report in the aforementioned newspaper, Billy may well have had a case to be suffering from boredom. Its verdict of the match was as follows: **"This game, despite the goals, was almost too tiresome to be taken seriously."**

When Billy next attended a match around a year later, he was now eleven and felt much more comfortable in his surroundings, even without his brother by his side. His interest in all things Celtic, both on and off of the pitch, began to flourish and within a few years, his milk round was funding regular trips to matches, both home and away. Of course, his mother would only let him travel so far at that age, and felt that journeys to Dundee and Aberdeen were too big a step for a young Bhoy. However, he often travelled to Edinburgh and Kilmarnock (amongst other places), and soon formed strong friendships with other members of his hometown's supporters buses. **"The older lads always kept an eye on us, to make sure we were alright"**, he reflected with a hint of a smile.

As Billy attended his first Scottish Cup Final as a Celtic supporter in 1961, he was hopeful that he would soon see his heroes lift a major trophy for the first time in the flesh. However, it wasn't to be, as Dunfermline Athletic (managed by Jock Stein), won a replay by two goals to nil, after the first encounter had finished goalless. At this point, Billy could never have foreseen that he would find himself watching Celtic feature in a European Cup Final, live, less than a decade later.

A couple of years after the defeat to the Pars, Billy saw Celtic win their first silverware (albeit somewhat minor) of his time as a spectator, as the Hoops defeated Third Lanark in the replayed final of the Glasgow Cup by three goals to two (with the first tie ending in a one-all draw).

The next season, 1963–64, was to be one of mixed emotions. On the twenty-second of November, President John Fitzgerald Kennedy was assassinated in Dallas, Texas. Celtic played the next day, beating Kilmarnock five nil at Celtic Park. Bill recalled that, prior to kick-off, a minute's silence was impeccably observed, with more than a few tears being shed for the slain President.

"You could have heard a pin drop. It had a huge impact on almost everybody," he said, before continuing, **"There was only one football ground across Britain where there was any problems upholding such a silence, and that was in Dunfermline where Rangers were playing."**

Returning to happier affairs, with Celtic having made their first appearance in European competition in the Inter-cities Fairs Cup a year earlier, the Hoops recorded their first victories, both home and away, against F.C. Basel in the first round of the European Cup Winners' Cup. Billy saw Celtic win for the first time at home as they beat the Swiss side five-nil at Celtic Park in the second leg of the first round. In his own words: **"Celtic were fantastic in Europe that season on that run, beating Basel, that Yugoslavian team** [**"Dynamo Zagreb?"** I interjected – **"Aye, them!"** came the reply]**, and Slovan Bratislava, but we still couldn't manage to beat Rangers domestically."**

Looking back on it, this view is most certainly valid. Celtic lost five times in five attempts to Rangers in 1963–64, finishing in third place behind then Champions (and treble winners) Rangers, and runners-up Kilmarnock. Despite this, the Hoops went to M.T.K. Budapest with a three goal lead from Celtic Park for the second leg of the European Cup Winners' Cup semi-final, and looked set to progress to the final tie. However, the frailties and inexperience of a young squad, still at a stage of early growth, were all too clear to see in Hungary, as the Celts suffered a sickening four-nil defeat and crashed out of Europe. For the record, M.T.K. Budapest eventually lost a replayed final to Sporting Lisbon of Portugal.

Nowadays, it is clear that Celtic are the Scottish team who have achieved the most on the European stage. However, in the 1960's, prior to Celtic reaching the semi-finals of the European Cup Winners' Cup, Dundee and Rangers were the only sides to have reached such a level, albeit in the bigger competition, that of the European Cup. Whilst I have referred to the European Cup Final of 1960 in another part of this book, it is of note that Rangers were defeated six one and six three by Eintracht Frankfurt in the semi-finals of the competition that same season. With a wry smile on his face, Billy recalled a joke from the time, where someone would ask: **"What's the telephone number for Rangers Football Club?"** with the response being **"Ibrox, six one, six three"**. Interestingly, Wolverhampton Wanderers also made the quarter finals of the tournament that season, before being annihilated by Barcelona, who would lose to the eventual winners of the competition, the great Real Madrid, in the other semi-final.

Returning to the tale of Mr Davidson, he saw his beloved Celtic win the Scottish Cup for the first time in 1965, as the Hoops banished the demons of four years hence by defeating Dunfermline Athletic by three goals to two at Hampden Park, with Mr Stein now the manager of the Glasgow side. At that time, Billy said he felt that it was **"the start of a revolution"** and that **"there were good things to come"** and, with the benefit of hindsight, we all know how correct those predictions would turn out to be.

A little over two years later, almost to the day, Celtic played out a goalless draw with Dukla Prague to seal their place in a European Final for the first time. With the result came scenes of joy across the Celtic supporting world and, as we would now expect, the scramble to find a way to the final began. Billy, who did not have the money to go, had never really considered the prospect due to his financial situation. However, only days before the match in Lisbon, his mother told him that his granny had asked to see him. Having rushed around to his grandmother's house, mildly concerned that something may be wrong, the old lady instead presented him with the results of a six pence endowment policy she had been adding to since his birth, twenty years previous. It totalled approximately twenty-eight pounds, and she asked what he planned to do with it.

"I'm going to try to go to Lisbon" was the reply from Billy, and his grandmother was very pleased with this, saying **"I can't think of a better way to spend it, myself."** In truth, it was no coincidence that after all those years his granny decided to withdraw her policy in the run-up to the game; she clearly wanted him to have the opportunity to see Celtic on the grandest stage of them all, and to this day, it is clear that the magnitude and kind heartedness of this gesture is not lost on the Coatbridge man.

However, when Billy left his grandmother's house and headed to Phil Cole's, a local pub that had plane tickets to Portugal, he discovered that the last available seat had been sold only hours earlier. In truth, while he was somewhat disappointed, Billy recalled that he wasn't totally distraught by that news as he had expected he may struggle to find a seat with only days to go before the match. In his mind, he suddenly had more money in his pocket that he had ever had previously and his favourite football team would soon compete in the European Cup Final for the first time, so his spirits remained high.

And so, the big day for Celtic arrived. On the twenty-fifth of May 1967, Billy arrived home from a nightshift at his work in the local MacKinnon's Knitwear Factory, read the morning newspapers, ate some dinner and went to bed whilst the majority of Coatbridge was waking up full of anticipation. A colleague had left Billy's work early that morning with a parting remark, asking if he could bring in his accordion to play for everyone if Celtic managed to win in Lisbon. Billy, who was a member of the **"Coatbridge Shamrock Accordion Band"**, agreed, but Mr Davidson recalls now that he did not think Celtic would win against Inter Milan.

"We were the underdogs, and Inter were a fantastic side" he said. "I watched the match in the house because despite the fact I was twenty, I looked so young that I knew I wouldn't get into any of the pubs and I didn't really drink much at that stage. Anyway, they were all absolutely packed and I had my work to get to later that night, regardless of the result."

"When they scored their penalty, I thought we were probably done and we'd struggle to come back...ah well, we've become the first British side to reach the final, and that's some achievement," he thought during the early stages of the match.

"Inter just didn't lose games when they went ahead back in those days. It was virtually unheard of son, but when Tommy Gemmell equalised I began to get a good feeling that it might just be our day, and so it was! We absolutely pounded them; it was attack after attack once they'd taken the lead! I couldn't believe it, and I literally couldn't wipe the smile off of my face for days. Later that night, I took the accordion into work, and what a time we had. Almost all of the workers were big Celtic supporters, and we were allowed to turn off all the machines for over an hour just so I could play my music and we could celebrate. It was great!" reflected Billy, clearly enjoying the memories which still provide him with a good feeling several decades later.

At the end of his shift, Mr Davidson said he headed straight for the local newsagents and bought every single newspaper he could lay his hands upon because they were all covering Celtic's triumph in extensive detail. Having looked them over in the house, he retired to bed, only to be awakened in the afternoon by his mother, who told him that Mick Boyle (one of his fellow band members who had a telephone in his house) had been at the door and said he'd to be at the band's hall in an hour and a half "because they were set to play the team around the pitch at Celtic Park later."

Obviously, Billy was absolutely thrilled at this piece of unexpected news: "Celtic had just won the European Cup and I thought life couldn't get any better than that, but then you're told you'll get to play in the band that accompanies the team upon their arrival at Celtic Park – it was just incredible."

However, his mother, whilst delighted for her son, had her world thrown into frenzy with Mr Boyle's visit, as she had to feed Billy, as well as clean and iron his band uniform in less than an hour's time. As so many fantastic mothers do on countless occasions worldwide every day, Billy's mum pulled off such a superhuman feat, and he was there for the bus pick up at five o'clock sharp. The band, which was affiliated with the **"Ancient Order of Hibernians"**, had played to several large crowds before, both in Scotland and across the sea in Ireland, but this was, by Billy's own admission, to be their biggest audience of all.

As the bus carrying the chosen ones weaved its way through the streets of Glasgow, more and more people began to line the pavements as they approached Celtic Park, until they found themselves travelling up London Road with supporters not only packing the pavements, but hanging out of windows and perched on top of any potential vantage point, all waiting to catch a glimpse of the men who conquered Europe. At that time, the enormity of what Celtic had achieved began to really sink in for Billy, and as the band clambered off of their bus outside Celtic Park, a representative from the Club asked if they could play a few songs to entertain the crowds outside for a time. They then duly obliged, much to the applause and adulation of the people who were unable to gain access to the stadium itself, which was already full to capacity with other supporters. However, as Billy recalled, a section of terracing wasn't opened for fans because of ongoing maintenance work, which reduced the number of people able to squeeze into the ground.

Having played outside, the band made their way inside a delirious Celtic Park, and as they strolled out onto the track next to the pitch, they passed the vehicle which would soon shepherd the Champions the Europe around their home ground – the much fabled builders' lorry. When Mr Davidson recalled this machine, he produced a hearty laugh, followed by a little bit of a sigh. Nowadays, when teams return to their stadium with the European Cup, coordinated fireworks shoot around the ground upon their entrance, and brightly coloured confetti fills the local air. There are light shows, big screen montages, and announcers working the crowd to a frenzy to be found all across Europe nowadays for the new Champions. However, all those years ago in the East End of Glasgow, the only thing being produced from the builders' lorry was some rather nasty fumes, and as for pyrotechnics, the closest they got was probably a few people lighting up a match or two on the terracing to smoke their pipes.

Continuing on with Billy's involvement, his band began to play for the gathered Celtic support. Whilst they had indulged in some Irish music outside the main stand, the band stuck to tunes such as **"The Celtic Song"**, **"Celtic, Celtic, That's The Team For Me"** and **"We Shall Not Be Moved"** inside Celtic Park.

Leaving 1967 for a time, it was only a year later that Bill made his first trip to a European away match. Having initially drawn Hungarian side Ferencváros in the first round of the European Cup (1968–69), Celtic lodged a protest with UEFA due to the recent invasion of Czechoslovakia by the Warsaw Pact countries (which the Hungarian military played a part in). With this in mind, UEFA rescinded the original draw, and Celtic were told they would instead face French opponents St Etienne. Alongside this, all of the teams from the Warsaw Pact countries were drawn against each other in a separate section for the first round, with most of them then deciding to withdraw from the tournament entirely in a protest of their own.

Having discussed the prospect of an away trip with his mother, Billy had already saved up the required money before the draw was made. With Celtic initially set to face the Hungarian Champions, Billy headed to a travel agent's in Partick which was becoming increasingly well known for their football trips. However, having presumed that Partick was near where Partick Thistle ply their trade, Billy first headed to Maryhill. After wandering around for some time searching for the travel agents, he asked someone in the street for help, before realising he had made a rather naive mistake. Having finally travelled to Partick and found the shop, Billy booked his place for a trip to Hungary, before handing over twenty-eight pounds for the privilege. This was subsequently reduced to twenty-two or twenty-three pounds as the destination was altered to France.

Billy estimated that somewhere between one hundred and fifty and two hundred Celtic supporters travelled to the away leg: **"The plane was full, but a few folk had made their own way there, I'm sure. It was the first time I'd ever flown, and I absolutely loved it. I still do, in fact"** said Mr Davidson. Personally, I rather admire that, as you already know flying is not an endeavour which I particularly enjoy. Returning from that slight tangent, Celtic lost by two goals to nil against St Etienne in the first leg. While Billy remembered the disappointment of the result, he did say: **"It could have been a lot worse. Ronnie Simpson made a fantastic save with a couple of minutes left. Thankfully, we hammered them in the return leg so we got through anyway."**

Billy's next trip onboard a plane would see him travel with Celtic to Milan, for the European Cup Final of 1970. However, prior to that, there was the small matter of Leeds United to attend to. Billy travelled down to Yorkshire for the first leg without a ticket. He recalls standing around outside Elland Road trying to get a brief with kick-off quickly approaching: **"I couldn't afford what the touts were charging. I thought I was stuffed, but when I found out one of them was trying to shift a youngster's ticket not long before the match started, I bought it since it was cheaper and decided to chance my arm."**

And so, at the age of twenty-three, clearly with his youthful good looks intact, Billy Davidson managed to get into Elland Road with a child's ticket, only moments before George Connelly's early strike put Celtic in front.

As you all know, Celtic took a one-nil lead into the return tie at Hampden. This match still holds the record for the highest official attendance of any match in UEFA competition, with over one hundred and thirty-six thousand officially inside the national stadium. Once again, Billy was there supporting the Hoops. However, actually watching the game wasn't as easy a feat as you may imagine. Thousands of people were stuck outside the stadium in the build up to kick-off, with thousands more inside the turnstiles but unable to reach the top bank of the terraces so they could view the playing surface. For those of you who may not know, the old terraces rose away from the field at Hampden until they reached their peaks at the top of each hill, before sloping down towards the turnstiles and access points on the other side. This meant that even if you managed to make it through the turnstiles at these mammoth matches, you still had to force your way over the brow of the hill on to the terracing so that you could see the pitch.

Once Billy had finally managed to work his way inside the North Enclosure at the national stadium, he said could **"just about reach the back of the terracing"** but even then, he was unable to see the field past the sheer mass of humanity in front of him. After all, I'm sure Billy would admit that he's not exactly the tallest man in the world. Anyway, this is where a little bit of luck and some creative thinking on Bill's part was to come in handy. As the match kicked off, he noticed that one of the small pie stalls at the back of the enclosure was closed, and so he managed to clamber up onto the stall, with his feet on the counter and his arms hanging on to the metal of the roof above, giving him a perfect, if somewhat unconventional view of the historic Celtic victory. Afterwards, many of the people from Billy's supporters bus, who had ventured into other areas of Hampden Park, told him they had seen little if anything of the match because it was simply too busy.

Anyway, Celtic had defeated Leeds United and were set to compete in their second European Cup Final in only four years. Having been eliminated by A.C. Milan (the eventual winners) last season, the San Siro wasn't an unfamiliar environment for this Celtic team. They'd played out a goalless draw with Milan on their last visit there, whereas Feyenoord, who had played A.C. Milan on their run to the final, had lost by a single goal at the stadium only a few months earlier.

However, that record would matter for nothing when it came to the European Cup Final itself. Billy recalled that he got a ticket for the match, which was officially attended by approximately fifty-three thousand people, without too much hassle. Inside the ground, he was sat next to an Italian father and son pairing boasting the colours of Internazionale, both of whom were, according to Billy, fully behind Celtic: **"They clearly admired the**

way we had played in 1967, because they were shouting for the Celts just as loudly as we all were."

"It was impossible for Celtic to lose," recanted Mr Davidson, **"Everybody wanted us to face the Dutch side in the final if we got past Leeds because they were seen as the easier opposition. Nobody, and I mean nobody, wanted the Poles. Feyenoord were a ridiculous price to beat us at the bookies – I remember that. We'd just beaten Leeds United twice, who were seen by many as the best side left in the competition, so we thought it would be a doddle...how wrong we were."**

"I've only cried twice in my life about football, and that was the second time. I just couldn't bear to go out after it, so I went back to my hotel and tried to get some sleep through the tears. As I lay there, I could hear the Celtic support singing in the street. There was no trouble or animosity, just the good old Celtic fans doing their best to enjoy themselves, even in spite of the result. I imagine that is what Seville was like. I must admit though, it took us all a while to recover from that defeat. It was a sore one – a really sore one."

Less than one year later, Billy attended the now infamous New Year derby clash at Ibrox, during which sixty-six Rangers supporters tragically lost their lives in a crush. In the modern age of mobile phones, Twitter, and twenty-four hour news cycles, it is perhaps difficult to truly appreciate the panic that ensued following the horrific events of that day, as news filtered through the city, fear took hold, and rumours spread with a terrifying pace. Upon leaving the ground just after Celtic had opened the scoring in an attempt to avoid any hassle outside, Billy heard sirens off in the distance but thought little of it. As he travelled home, via the "**Hutton Street Celtic Supporters Bus**", Billy first heard on the radio that **"five people had died."** As the miles passed en route to Coatbridge, he said, **"five became ten, then fifteen and then thirty"** as he finally reached his street. When he opened the front door, his mother gave him the **"biggest, tightest hug he had ever received"** when she found out he was alive and well. Understandably, his family had been utterly terrified as confusion shot across the country, and only in the coming hours and days would the true scale of the horrific events that day be clarified.

In the years which followed, Billy's friends and family began to notice he had developed a bit of a limp. Presuming it was nothing serious at first, he continued with life as normal. However, in the mid-1980's, Billy would seek medical advice regarding his worsening stride, only to discover that he had a condition whereby his spinal cord was slowing but steadily crushing the nerves in his back, to such a point that nowadays he is all but unable to walk unaided. This had nothing to do with the aforementioned tragedy at Ibrox, but rather his childhood battle with tuberculosis. However, with the use of his motorised scooter, Billy still enjoys the ability to venture outdoors when he chooses, and continues to lead an active social life which includes the occasional drink at his local pub with a few of his mates.

I then asked Mr Davidson, like I do with all supporters of a certain age, if he was at the Scottish Cup Final in 1980, which saw the infamous large scale riot break out on the field following Celtic's extra-time victory. Billy assured me that he wasn't there, but did proceed to discuss his attendance at the Scottish Cup Final eight years later. Billy had a terracing ticket for that match, but happened to come across someone outside Hampden looking to swap their brief, which was for the main stand, for an equivalent **"Celtic end"** terracing ticket. With Mr Davidson not quite as young as he used to be, and with the prospect of a seat and a good view of the match itself to boot, this seemed like a fairly good deal, and so before long, he took advantage of it and made his way inside the main stand.

Moments later, as Billy found his seat and kick-off approached, he realised that he was within yards of the Prime Minister, Margaret Thatcher. According to Mr Davidson, while **"he certainly didn't like the woman"**, he did admire her ability to **"remain as cool as a cucumber, even while people threw insults her way."**

"She seemed to be just unshakable," he said. **"She just sat there, and from time to time she would turn to say "Could you kindly stop that?" after another verbal barrage reached her ears, before her gaze returned to the pitch. It was quite a sight."**

Returning to what is really important though, the match, Billy thoroughly enjoyed it, as did the rest of the Celtic supporting crowd in attendance. In typically late and dramatic style, the Hoops won the trophy and secured the domestic double in the glorious sunshine of the city's Southside.

In more recent years, as Billy's health has deteriorated, he has given up his long held season ticket at Celtic Park and now watches every Celtic match from the comfort of his home or from the local pub. One of the last matches Mr Davidson attended was to be one of the final home matches against Rangers, as Joe Ledley's header separated the sides on a windswept night at Paradise. Sat in the South Stand for the Rangers game, Billy found himself only rows behind Paul Riley (who played Winston in **"Still Game"**), and only rows in front of Frank Mulholland, the Lord Advocate (another Coatbridge Bhoy). Alongside Mr Davidson was a Church of Scotland Minister, who apparently **"went absolutely nuts celebrating"** when Celtic scored.

And now, if I may, I'd like you to cast your minds back to my initial description of Mr Davidson's living room, upon the walls of which hang pictures of Muhammad Ali, Henrik Larsson, and Carol Vorderman. Like many people, including myself, Billy is an avid fan of boxing, and he was lucky enough to meet **"The Greatest"** himself in Waterstones (which is a book shop for any foreign readers) in 1994. To this day, his photo with Ali continues to take pride of place in Billy's home. Unsurprisingly, Henrik Larsson's image also adorns the wall in a similar manner to several other Celtic pieces, but then there's Carol Vorderman.

In 1999, Billy featured as a contestant in three episodes of the famous afternoon game show, **"Countdown"**. For those of you unfamiliar with the rules, it is essentially a letters and numbers game, whereby contestants predominantly attempt to form as large a word as possible from a particular selection of letters. The show operates a **"winner stays on"** format, and therefore by the time he was defeated, Billy had won two matches on the trot.

Whilst he was there, six episodes of the programme were filmed in a single day, although only five were actually broadcast each week. For this reason, all of the contestants had to have several changes of clothes with them in order for it to appear as if the shows are filmed on different days when they are, in fact, often only minutes apart. Being a massive fan of one particular Football Club, Billy took several Celtic Supporters Clubs t-shirts along with him, as well as a set of Hoops. However, due to sponsorship issues, he wasn't allowed to wear the Celtic jersey itself. Anyway, a picture of Billy on the set, with each of the presenters (including Carol Vorderman) and the famous **"Countdown Clock"** still hangs on his living room wall, as a memento of Mr Davidson's moment in the literary spotlight.

Returning to football, Billy is relatively confident about the future of Celtic Football Club under the current regime, although the same cannot be said of his views regarding Scottish Football as a whole. By his own admission, Billy has no time for Rangers, but feels that without a form of them in existence, the rest of the game in this country will suffer financially. **"Celtic don't need them, but the rest do"**, said Mr Davidson. As we went on to discuss the national team, and the quality of players making their way through to the upper echelons of the game, Billy was also rather pessimistic.

"Too many good youngsters get drawn down to England and fade into obscurity nowadays" he said, before highlighting that, **"with the exception of Darren Fletcher, who is by far and away the best player we have produced in a long time, Wales have brought through more talent than us. Look no further than Gareth Bale and Joe Ledley for prominent examples, and yet they have a much smaller population than we do! Something is clearly not right."**

And finally, back on that evening in 1967, as the arrival of the European Champions drew nearer, the buzz in the crowd became more and more noticeable, until the emergence of the European Cup, Jock Stein, Billy McNeill, and all the rest, sent the Celtic supporters in attendance absolutely wild. As the band marched twice around the ground, it was understandable that most of the eyes inside Celtic Park were firmly focused on the lorry behind them. However, the fact that Billy did play a role that day has put him in the history books, and nobody can ever take that away from him. While you may not see his name mentioned in the newspapers from the time, you will see his face, as it featured on at least one front page the morning after the event.

Billy Davidson, a man with music at his fingertips and Celtic in his heart, will forever be associated, in his own small way, with the achievements of the Lisbon Lions and Jock Stein. The proverbial **"face in the foreground"** that I mentioned earlier will live forever in this regard, captured at what he himself described as **"his proudest moment as a Celtic supporter"**, and it has been an absolute pleasure for me to feature his story in this book.

"Napoleon"

James 'Jimmy' McMenemy was born in Rutherglen on the twenty-third of August 1880. At such a time, the Football Club he would go on to star with for almost two decades in his later life did not even exist, but soon, the name of **"Napoleon"** would become synonymous not only with a French military leader of old, but with Scotland's greatest football team. As he learned the basics of the game through his participation in junior football, Jimmy was scouted by Celtic, and eventually signed from Rutherglen Glencairn in June 1902. Willie Maley states in his book that Jimmy had received many offers to become a professional during his time in the amateur game, but that he had refused all of them in the hope that, one day, his ambition to become a Celtic player would a reality.

Several characteristics had attracted the Football Club to Jimmy, not just the fact that everyone knew he wanted to play for them, although this show of loyalty prior to having any official connection with the Club probably did work in his favour to some degree. No, more than anything, it was Jimmy's ability, physical attributes and temperament which won him his dream move – after all he was a young, exciting winger with two gifted feet, memorable agility, a few tricks up his sleeve and critically, he was tough enough to take a knock or two and get back up again without any fuss. Whilst he wasn't a big man by any means, he was robust and determined, and that meant even more in the olden days of the sport than it does now, when it is still a trait which is both admired and much sought-after.

A few months later, in November of the same year, he proceeded to make his debut for the Club at the age of twenty-two, as Celtic travelled to Port Glasgow Athletic and came away with a three-nil victory, with one of the goals being scored by the debutant himself. However, it was clear that the young man did suffer from some nerves on that day, as an account in one newspaper said that **"McMenemy missed the easiest of chances to**

score" prior to the half time whistle being sounded. Criticism such as that though was to become a rarity, as Jimmy began to settle into his role at Celtic Park, adapting not only to his on field partnerships with his teammates, but also having to accept the fact that he was now a celebrity of sorts away from the football pitch.

This was the start of a beautiful relationship between Jimmy and the Celtic support, who would in time nickname him **"Napoleon"**, as they felt he possessed the power to control and conquer Scottish Football with his skills. He had that **"je ne sais quoi"** so to speak, to make use of our French theme once again. Fundamentally, you could write a book about the skills of Jimmy McMenemy alone, and some have. However, for the sake of relative brevity, I shall simply say that he could read the game around him unlike almost any other, conjuring goalscoring opportunities out of nowhere, either for himself or his teammates, through nothing other than sheer imagination.

Sometime later, in January of 1904, Jimmy scored the first hat-trick of his Celtic career, as the Celts eased past Motherwell on a frosty day in Glasgow by the total of six goals to nil. Whilst newspaper reports regarding the game are somewhat short in their nature, one did say that the sixth and final strike came from **"McMenemy with a brilliant individual run"**.

Jimmy was to become an integral part of the side which won six League Championships in a row between 1904–05 and 1909–10. Although he had been eased in to a degree during his first season at the Club, by the time that first league winning campaign was underway, **"McMenemy"** was a common sight on the Celtic team-sheet, alongside the likes of Jimmy Quinn. As the Celts looked to win their first title since 1898, they travelled to Ibrox to face their closest rivals for the league title on the eighteenth of February 1905, in the middle of a severe rain storm.

Going into the match, Celtic held a slender advantage at the top of the table, but critically, Rangers had matches in hand. A defeat for the Hoops would have allowed their opponents to open up an almost unassailable lead (presuming they won their matches still to come), and a draw would have been a better result for the home side than the visitors, but few could have predicted an emphatic Celtic victory – by four goals to one no less. McMenemy, along with the rest of his teammates, shone like a footballing sun through the darkened clouds and the howling wind of Glasgow that afternoon and, for the first time in recent years, the Hoops found themselves with a serious chance of being crowned the Champions of Scotland.

However, before the domestic campaign was to come to an end, Jimmy made his international debut in the same match as his fellow forward Jimmy Quinn, as Scotland eased past Ireland by four goals to nil at Celtic Park exactly one month on from the Celtic victory at Ibrox. However, unlike Quinn who would be recalled after only a year, McMenemy would have to wait another four years before he was selected for international duty once more, despite producing almost wholly consistent sterling performances for Celtic. Perhaps the fact that the newspaper reports following his international debut do not give McMenemy's performance any significant mention alludes to the fact that he had a relatively quiet game for Scotland that day.

Returning to the domestic front, once the normal season came to a close, Celtic and Rangers would finish level on points, and would therefore face each other in a Championship play-off match, as is discussed in detail in another chapter. Regardless, the match was played and, early in the second half, with the tie goalless, Jimmy McMenemy shot and scored to send the Celtic supporters in attendance wild. A minute later, a high cross from David Hamilton following a corner kick evaded the Rangers goalkeeper, who could not prevent the concession of second quick-fire goal. Despite the Ibrox side's best attempts, they could only manage a consolation goal, as Celtic were ultimately crowned the Champions of Scotland.

Of course, this was to be the first of many Championship medals for Jimmy. As Celtic continued to improve, beginning to truly dominate the Scottish game, so did **"Napoleon"**. He became the well known second name listed off by those referring to Celtic's famous forward line of **"Bennett, McMenemy, Quinn, Somers and Hamilton."** Jimmy, as an inside forward, composed many of the Celtic attacks which led to goals over many years.

With a habit of dropping deep, he would often find the ball at his feet, and with both incredible vision and jaw dropping accuracy, he would regularly deliver passes which one of his colleagues, predominantly Jimmy Quinn, would run on to before guiding the ball into the back of the net as if it was easy.

In both 1907 and 1908, with Jimmy as a key component of the green and white Hooped machine, Celtic won both the Scottish League and Scottish Cup consecutively, attaining fifty-five league points on both occasions, and comfortably winning Cup Finals against Hearts and St Mirren respectively. Of these two matches, McMenemy featured in both, and was praised highly for each of his performances as, now in his late twenties, he added his second and third Scottish Cup medals to his résumé.

Regarding both of the aforementioned triumphs, I feel it that is safe to speculate that without Jimmy McMenemy, neither of them may have came to be, for his knack of popping up with important goals or critical passes helped Celtic not only through those respective Cup Finals, but also through a few of the earlier rounds of the competition as well. For example, on their way to success in the 1907, the Hoops faced a tie with Morton in the second round of the tournament after they edged past Clyde previously. For the record, Morton had it somewhat easier in the first stage of the competition, as they took on lower league side Maxwellton Volunteers (who would later reform before going on to merge with another club to form the modern day Queen of the South), eventually winning by three goals to one.

Anyway, whilst Morton would proceed to finish thirteenth from eighteen teams in the top flight that season, losing to Celtic both home and away, they proved themselves to be remarkably stubborn opposition when it came to the country's greatest knockout tournament, as they forced Celtic into not only one, but two, replays of their second tie. The first match, played at Cappielow, finished goalless. The second, played at Celtic Park, concluded with both sides having scored once, with the Hoops' goal coming from none other than Jimmy McMenemy himself. Of course, this meant that a second replay would be necessary (the only one of the entire second round of the competition), and this was to take place at Celtic Park once more. Finally, at the third time of asking, Celtic would defeat their opponents narrowly by two goals to one, with McMenemy scoring and playing a great game to boot.

Prior to reaching the Scottish Cup Final itself, Celtic would then ease past Rangers before requiring another three matches to dispose of Hibernian at the semi-final stage, in which Jimmy added his name to the list of goalscorers once again. In the final, **"The Glasgow Herald"** reported simply that **"Somers and McMenemy were the pick of a good all-round forward line"**.

The following year, Celtic and Jimmy were at it again, as is highlighted above, reaching the Scottish Cup Final before hammering their opponents St Mirren when the day finally came. However, once again, McMenemy's goals (and one of them above all others), were crucial with regards reaching Scottish Football's biggest occasion in the first place. In the tournament's quarter final stage, Celtic eased past their opponents Raith Rovers by three goals to nil away from home, with two of the three goals coming courtesy of Jimmy. When one takes a moment to consider how a band of truly awful weather across the country affected the playing conditions that day (leading to a couple of upsets), the comfortable nature of Celtic's victory becomes even more impressive, as the following quote dictates:

"Ground and weather had no bearing on Celtic, who suited themselves to both in a manner which marked them as a heady eleven, and after establishing a three-goal lead with the wind, they were not unduly stretched to maintain their advantage when they faced the gale".

And so, on the twenty-first of March 1908, the attention of all those with a love for Aberdeen or Celtic turned to Pittodrie, as the two teams took to the field to fight it out for a place at Hampden Park in a little under one month's time. Celtic started brightly, but were unable to open the scoring and, inevitably, the home side fought back as the match wore on. Midway through the second half, with the enormity of what was at stake becoming increasingly prominent in the minds of the players and spectators alike, nerves began to become evident with regards some of the play from both teams. Despite this, as **"The Glasgow Herald"** of the time said: **"Even play followed, and there was every indication that the game would end in a goalless draw when three minutes from time McMenemy headed through a corner kick, and Celtic won by 1 goal to 0".**

However, all was not well in the Granite City after the match, as the same newspaper article continues: **"Our Aberdeen correspondent says a good deal of hostile feeling was shown by the crowd towards the referee, Mr J. S. Ferguson (Falkirk), whose decisions had not given entire satisfaction to the supporters of the Aberdeen team. While Mr Ferguson was leaving the grounds in a cab a stone was thrown, which smashed one of the windows of the vehicle, but fortunately the occupant received no bodily injury. It is also stated that some stones were thrown by boys at the members of the Celtic team while they were being driven away from the grounds, but there was no hostile demonstration at the railway station when the visiting team left the city in the evening."**

Regardless, Celtic would go on to triumph in the Scottish Cup Final as previously discussed, teaching St Mirren a thorough footballing lesson in a five-one victory. Such results, combined with their accompanying performances from one Jimmy McMenemy, eventually earned the Rutherglen man another call-up to the international squad where he would feature in a Scotland jersey once again. It was to be a joyous outing too as Scotland trounced Ireland by five goals to nil, two of which came courtesy of Jimmy McMenemy on this occasion. Coupled with ex-teammate Alec Bennett, now a Rangers player, he tore the opposition apart, as the following quote highlights: **"Bennett's running and crossing and McMenemy's judicious inside work were factors in the game by which the opposing defence were greatly harassed."**

A few years later, at the end of a relatively poor 1910–11 season which ultimately resulted in a fifth place league finish, the Scottish Cup came home to Celtic Park once more after a replay win over Hamilton Academical (one of only two Scottish Cup Final appearances the Lanarkshire club have made in their history). At this point, the **"six in a row"** side began to disband, and Jimmy reached the age of thirty years old at a time when significantly fewer footballers continued to such ripe 'old' ages as they do nowadays.

However, at that start of the next season, it was clear that Jimmy McMenemy still had a lot left to offer in a Celtic shirt, as he strung together goals in six consecutive league games between the nineteenth of August and the twenty-fifth of September, epitomising not only Jimmy's ability, but his consistency and calm with regards to taking chances when they fell his way – something experience had taught him over the years (contrast and compare this with his debut upon which he is said to have missed what would now be colloquially referred to as **"a sitter"**).

Anyway, the first of the six came against Falkirk, as: **"Good play from McMenemy made an opening for Hamilton, which the latter was not able to take advantage of, and then the latter crossed beautifully for McMenemy, who put his team three up".**

The second arrived during a one-all draw versus Morton (despite the poor English that forms the quote itself), when **"Celtic displayed more vigour than in the opening period. McMenemy after 17 minutes had gone equalised".**

Third-up was a goal amidst a three-two win over Clyde at Celtic Park: **"McMenemy cleverly netted the second from a cross of Hamilton..."**, and the fourth came as Celtic slumped to a disappointing away defeat to Dundee: **"After ten minutes play McMenemy opened the scoring from a corner kick taken by McAtee."**

Fifth and, finally sixth, occurred via wins to nil against Kilmarnock and Partick Thistle respectively as: **"Towards the close, McMenemy scored a fine goal..."** and **"five minutes later, Brown narrowly missed heading a second goal, but McMenemy made amends by putting the ball into the net for a second time".**

Upon the emergence of a young Irish forward named Patsy Gallacher, few would have criticised Jimmy too heavily if he had decided that he may have been getting **"past it"**, before moving on and allowing his career to quietly draw to a close as so many others had done before him. Keep in mind that, even prior to World War One, Jimmy was already considered a Celtic great by the Club's avid followers. However, to give up was never a personality trait of our "**Napoleon**" and, accordingly, instead of trying to battle with the young Irishman for his position, Jimmy chose to work with him and their manager, Willie Maley, whom he respected greatly, in an attempt to find a solution which suited all three men. Having seen the talent possessed by Patsy, Jimmy went to Maley and suggested that he move sides, from inside-left to inside right respectively, in order to allow Gallacher to take over his old position. This gesture, as well as the overall attitude displayed by Jimmy, which said that whatever was best for Celtic was best for him as an individual, did not go unnoticed by Maley, and undoubtedly, it was greatly appreciated by Patsy Gallacher too, especially in the years to come.

And so, with a mixture of exuberant youth and reliable experience, not simply in the forward line but throughout his whole squad, Willie Maley began to build another team which would become Scotland's footballing powerhouse. The following year, a resurgent Celtic faced Clyde in the Scottish Cup Final and would go to prevail by two goals to nil. However, in order to better understand the victory, it is perhaps worthwhile to refer to a couple of excerpts from the newspaper accounts of that April day, as both McMenemy and Gallacher scored, displaying the mixture of youth and experience employed by the Hoops was a potent one indeed.

"The Celtic attack at length told, for McMenemy when close in on goal scored after a mistake by Gilligan."

"Half-time: Celtic 1 Clyde 0. With the wind in their favour Clyde were expected to have a good chance of winning but the ripe judgement of the older players and the cleverness of the younger members in the Celtic eleven made the Shawfielders' task a difficult one."

"The Celts continued to display rare caution, and seldom allowed a chance to slip of invading Clyde territory. A smart movement on the left took them to Grant's end, and another goal fell to the ultimate winners, Gallacher beating Grant, who had previously failed to properly get rid of the ball."

A couple of years later, before the Great War ignited in late July, Celtic (who found themselves in serious contention for the

Scottish League Championship for the first time since 1910), faced rivals Rangers at Celtic Park in the New Year's Day match of 1914. The match set the record attendance for the fixture at the time, with over seventy-five thousand spectators paying a fee to take in the spectacle for themselves. The Hoops had previously beaten their opponents at Ibrox in October that same season, in front of a then record crowd of sixty-four thousand, but Jimmy did not feature on that occasion. Regardless, he would have his say on derby day this time around, as he scored one of his most famous goals - jinking past several defenders, displaying all of the poise and technique which continued to make the thirty-three year old one of Scotland's great talents, before finishing coolly with a well placed shot as Celtic ran out four-nil winners. For the record, the other goals that day came from 'Sunny Jim' Young and John Browning, the latter of whom scored twice.

"McMenemy scored a second goal after a magnificent run, in the course of which he outwitted five opponents..."

Thanks to both individual and team performances like that described above, Celtic would win the 1913–14 Scottish League Championship, the seventh of Jimmy's time at the Club, as well as the 1914 Scottish Cup, thanks to a replay victory over Hibernian, the sixth with McMenemy as a Celtic player.

Having rounded off the previous season so well after such impressive performances throughout, it would have been yet another chance for Jimmy to relax somewhat from a sporting perspective as war engulfed Europe, playing from time to time before retiring somewhere near his peak, but as I mentioned earlier, he was not the sort of individual to give up on things. Instead, he continued to play in the green and white of his beloved Celtic with a sparkling attitude, and helped the Club to another three consecutive titles after their 1913–14 success.

Having worked in a munitions factory during the war, thanks partly to both his relative age and his profession, Jimmy was never called up for active service during World War One. However, it is now thought that, towards the conflict's end, he very nearly was, as both human and physical resources became increasingly scarce on both sides of the divide, but thanks to Germany's eventual surrender, he was saved from that hardship.

In 1918, the option of retirement once again loomed after he had suffered an injury which would keep him out for a significant amount of the season. There remains some speculation as to whether Jimmy actually retired for a season around the turn of the decade, or whether he simply kept away from proceedings as he recovered from his injury. Regardless, upon his playing return to Celtic Park, Jimmy McMenemy was greeted as a hero.

Sometime later, Jimmy would run out onto the field at Somerset Park, Ayr, for the final match of the 1918–19 season. With Celtic and Rangers separated by only a point, the Hoops knew that a win over an impressive Ayr United side (who would finish a notable sixth) would be required to guarantee the Club a fifteenth League Championship. Rangers, on the other hand, were set to face second from bottom Clyde. At one point that same season, the Ibrox side had been five points clear of Celtic, looking well on their way to being crowned Champions. However, thanks to a horrendous run of results in January (kick started by the Hoops managing to come away with a draw in the New Year derby match at Ibrox), Celtic had been able to claw back their lead and, towards the end of the campaign, nip ahead of their closest competitors.

"...the first place on the league table was held almost from start to finish by Rangers, and at one point no fewer than five points separated the two city clubs. Nine consecutive victories credited to the Ibrox club, and with the ninth success achieved at the Celts' expense, it should have been something more than an auspicious beginning. It ought to have been an earnest of ultimate triumph, and against any other than Celtic, the initial advantage thus gained would have sufficed for the championship. But while Celtic had to forego the services of McMaster, McStay, Dodds, McAtee, Cringan, Cassidy, and McMenemy at different periods, and McColl, Gallacher, and Browning were occasionally laid low by injuries, the management were successful in assembling an eleven sufficiently strong to avert defeat in a series of games extending over five and a half months."

Celtic went on to defeat Ayr United by two goals to nil that day, in front of approximately ten thousand spectators. The

Hoops had done it once again, but sadly, it would be the last honour of Napoleon's Celtic career, other than a final international cap, which would come against Ireland in March 1920. In all, Jimmy McMenemy played on twelve occasions for Scotland, scoring five times. This is, of course, an impressive record for any player. However, it becomes all the more incredible when one considers that Scotland never lost whilst Jimmy McMenemy was selected for the national side (a run which included three matches against England). His first and last Scotland outings were separated by fifteen years, once again highlighting his longevity and talent. Critically, had war not broken out in Europe, suspending international football in the process, it is likely that Jimmy would have racked up several more appearances (and likely a few more goals) for his country.

Having spent some time researching this point, I believe that his final competitive appearance for Celtic was during a two-all draw with St Mirren, on the twenty-second of April 1920 – seventeen years and five months on from his debut for the Football Club.

"The Glasgow Herald" from the following day refers to Celtic's first goal and attributes an assist to Jimmy, without knowing at the time that this would be his last match for Celtic, at the age of almost forty:

"After 30 minutes play a concerted movement taken part in by Cassidy, McMenemy and McInally ended in the last mentioned equalising."

Upon his departure on a free transfer in the summer of 1920, Jimmy McMenemy left Celtic Park having won eleven of the Club's fifteen Scottish League Championships, and six of their nine Scottish Cups with them during his tenure at the Club. Notably, for a player with such a reputation with regards his love for cup competitions, I feel I must mention that, incredibly, over the course of his entire stay at Celtic Park, Jimmy McMenemy only missed four Scottish Cup matches from a potential fifty-seven (discounting those played in his first season when he was still fighting to be given a chance in the first team) – a truly incredible statistic.

He had been an integral part of some of Celtic's greatest sides, but even at the age of forty, his playing career wasn't done quite yet, as he moved to Partick Thistle. In the eyes of many, this was expected to be simply a farewell style walk into the sunset, but to Jimmy, it was simply another chance to prove his abilities to the Scottish public, and help the team he was now a member of, whilst enjoying the increasingly short time he had left in him as a professional football player.

And yet, with this in mind, Jimmy would still manage to finish off his career in the limelight, a victor once again. However, before the end, he would find time for a couple more visits to Celtic Park as a player, but in the colours of the Firhill side on these occasions. On his first return, Partick Thistle suffered a one-nil defeat in December 1920. Jimmy was described as **"Thistle's best forward until he retired from injury ten minutes from the finish"** and, unsurprisingly, he received a rapturous welcome back home from the Celtic supporters in attendance.

As Jimmy's last taste of glory approached, he could, in fact, have faced his old Club in knockout competition, had they not been knocked out of the Scottish Cup by Hearts at home in early March. Having edged past the Edinburgh side via a replayed semi-final, Partick Thistle soon found themselves in the Scottish Cup Final for the first time, where they were set to take on huge favourites Rangers at, incredibly, Celtic Park. In the days before the match, few would have bet on the team from the north of the city pulling off an upset of such mammoth proportions.

However, after resisting sustained pressure from the Ibrox side, who had not won the famous competition in almost two decades, a passing move, which saw McMenemy heavily involved, resulted in the only goal of the match midway through the first half. In the second period, as Rangers pressed for an equaliser, newspaper reports described how McMenemy, along with other Thistle forwards, began to **"play as a defender"**, giving every ounce of energy he possessed and **"throwing himself into challenges"** as Rangers' attacks became more and more frantic in their nature. As the final whistle went, it was all worth it, as Jimmy McMenemy lifted the Scottish Cup for the seventh and final time, and Partick Thistle took the trophy back to Firhill. This remains the only occasion upon which **"The Jags"** have won the tournament.

One famous McMenemy story regards a conversation he had with his wife after he helped Thistle win the Scottish Cup that day in 1921. The story goes that Jimmy's wife asked him where he would like her to put his medal and it is rumoured that then he turned to her, smiled cheekily and simply stated: **"Just chuck it into the drawer with all of the others dear!"**

Like many stories, whether this is actually true is virtually impossible to say for certain, but it is a good tale nonetheless – what is certain though is that Jimmy McMenemy was one of the greatest players ever to pull on the famous green and white jersey of Celtic Football Club. He was tremendously skilful both on and off the ball, he was able to control virtually any ball that came towards him, and he could then distribute it to one of his fellow teammates without so much as a glance, such was the ability he had in his feet and inside his footballing brain. He was one of those players with an incredible talent for reading the game and knowing where, in all likelihood, the ball would end up before it was even struck. This gave him the edge on defenders when he was making runs and it also helped him when it came to delivering the ball to other runners, such as the aforementioned Jimmy Quinn.

"The football pitch to him was a chess-board; he was continuously scheming and plotting" said Willie Maley, before going on to describe him as **"one of the finest inside forwards of all time."**

In truth, there was only ever one side which **"Napoleon"** wanted to play for, and he was both fortunate and talented enough to have that opportunity, for eighteen years no less, from June 1902 until June 1920. Jimmy finally retired from football in 1923. A couple of years later, his son John signed for Celtic from St Roch's (the same Club which helped to develop Jimmy McGrory), and over the course of the mid to late 1920's, he made sixteen senior appearances for the Hoops, scoring two goals, and featuring in the Scottish Cup winning side of 1927 (an achievement which I'm sure his father, with all of his success in the same competition would have been tremendously proud of). With regards to his performance that day, one newspaper journalist said the following:

"Faced with the loss of their record goalscoring centre forward, it was characteristically courageous of Celtic to install an untried youth in McMenemy in their attack, but their acumen and judgement were justified, McMenemy fitting into the scheme of the attack with facility and distinction."

In October 1928, John joined Motherwell where he would enjoy more consistent football and notable success winning the Scottish League Championship in 1932 and reaching the Scottish Cup Final in 1931 and 1933, although his old side ran out the victors on both occasions. However, John's brother, Harry, was not to be outdone on the footballing stage, as he became a regular feature in the Newcastle United line-up's of the 1930's. Whilst footballing ability clearly ran in the family, it cannot have been easy for either of these young men to attempt to break out of their father's long shadow, for the pressure put upon them by supporters and teammates alike must have been huge, but to their credit, both John and Harry followed their individual paths, adding to the McMenemy family story in their own unique ways.

In the mid-1930's, Jimmy returned to Parkhead for a fairly brief tenure (at least by his own standards) of a little over five years as a trainer and assistant manager to Willie Maley, who was gradually approaching the end of his time in charge of the Club. This contribution to the Football Club should not be overlooked however, as Jimmy was significantly more **"hands on"** with the players he was coaching than Maley ever was, taking training sessions and providing the players with a friendly face they could talk to and feel they could trust. During his time as assistant manager, the Celts won the Scottish League Championship and Scottish Cup again (albeit in different seasons) as well as the Empire Exhibition Trophy in 1938. Notably, he is pictured on the field after the epic 1937 Scottish Cup Final along with the team themselves in a photograph which features several Celtic legends, including Willie Maley, Jimmy Quinn, Jimmy McGrory, and of course, **"Napoleon"** himself.

In fact, there is an argument which says that it should have been Jimmy McMenemy and not Jimmy McStay, who eventually took over from Willie Maley when he retired. Undoubtedly, McMenemy would have been some of the players' first choice, but that is no slight on McStay. It also remains unclear as to whether Jimmy would have actually wanted the job anyway, but I can't help but wonder whether he would have been able to turn down the offer had it come his way, regardless of what his personal feelings may have been.

Even after he officially cut ties with the Club just after the start of World War Two, Jimmy McMenemy continued to follow Celtic for the rest of his days, through the poor spells in the 1940's and 1950's, and as the Club began to truly recapture its old vigour in the early 1960's. He was always adored by his fellow supporters, both those old enough to have seen him play and those young ones who were unlucky not to have marvelled at his talents firsthand. He once told a Celtic Supporters Association rally **"we will soon be back on winning terms"**, and he would be proven to be correct.

Jimmy died in the summer of 1965, only weeks after he had seen the beginnings of Celtic's greatest age, as many of the team that would go on to become the Lisbon Lions – managed by the young, energetic and innovative Jock Stein – won the Scottish Cup in front of almost one hundred and ten thousand people at Hampden Park in May.

In his time as a Celtic player, James 'Jimmy' McMenemy racked up a staggering five hundred and fifteen appearances for the Club which he had supported all his life, scoring one hundred and sixty-eight goals in his time there. To this day, he remains the Football Club's ninth highest goalscorer, one strike ahead of Kenny Dalglish, and tenth in terms of his total number of appearances as a Celtic player, highlighting again (as if there was any need) just how important a figure he was, and continues to remain, within the Club's long history.

His talent was a joy to behold and his ability to read a football match as it developed around him was virtually second to none. It seems that he was just as proud to be a Celtic player when he last wore the shirt as he was when he first pulled on the jersey, persisting through war and injury, almost until his fortieth birthday. For a player who made his debut in 1902 to achieve such a feat was virtually unheard of, and even now, with sports scientists and nutritional advisers aplenty, few men manage to play competitively at such an age. All in all, Jimmy was a phenomenal footballing talent and, undoubtedly, stories of his abilities will be told for generations to come. With all of this in mind, there is no doubt that he would be worthy of a place in any Celtic eleven.

"Nap Dies At 85"

"Jimmy McMenemy, one of the all time great men of Scottish Football, died in Robroyston Hospital yesterday at the age of 85."

"McMenemy was such a great player with Celtic at the beginning of this century that he was promptly nicknamed "Napoleon" – top general in the game."

"He signed for Celtic in 1902, and after being farmed out to Stenhousemuir he was quickly brought back to Parkhead, where he won every honour in the game, including 12 full international and 13 Scottish League "caps"."

"In the twilight of a great career he moved to Firhill, but was still so good that he helped Partick Thistle beat Rangers in the Scottish Cup Final of 1920–21."

"Mr McMenemy won in all seven Scottish Cup medals."

"Guess Where I Am?"

Young men have always possessed the ability to act like idiots. I know this to be true because I am a young man and, from time to time, my natural idiocy shines through. This innate talent can be strengthened by the presence of several factors, such as alcohol, football, money or women (or any combination of these and more depending on the individual in question). Perhaps it is no surprise then that an away day in Europe can produce a comedic story of such idiocy, especially when a group of seventeen young men head to Portugal following Celtic. One member of this party was Gerry Currie, who was kind enough to pass this tale on for you all to enjoy. One of Gerry's mates, James, was also there, but there'll be more on him later.

As we all know, travelling Celts have a bit of a reputation when it comes to taking somewhat interesting routes to their eventual destination. Often, these choices are motivated by the high demand for places on simpler routes and, at other times, considerations such as cost can come into the equation. And so, the group left their respective homes in Kilsyth for Edinburgh Airport, the day before Celtic's Champions League group stage match against Benfica in Lisbon, and took their first flight, to Heathrow, at 2pm. Having landed in London, they awaited the next stage of journey, which would take them on to Madrid sometime later. From the Spanish capital, they flew, finally, to their destination in Portugal, landing at around 11pm.

Once they had all arrived in the city and dropped off their stuff at the hotel, the first destination for the Bhoys was, unsurprisingly, the closest pub. Having sampled some of the local culture (and undoubtedly some of the local beer), the lads then returned to their hotel for a well earned sleep, before heading towards the city's main square a little before lunchtime on match day. Unsurprisingly, it was already full of singing Celtic supporters, with flags and banners flying left, right and centre. As the afternoon wore on and the songs grew louder in the square, the alcohol aisle of the local supermarket became increasingly bare, which inevitably led to certain members of the travelling support buying some of the remaining scraps, regardless of what they happened to be. As a result, there were, by all accounts, some rather odd mixtures of drinks being consumed in Lisbon that day; causing a few folk to really enjoy themselves, and, as you may have guessed, this is where James comes in.

When it came time for the Bhoys to head to the stadium, they chose to make use of the city's numerous taxis rather than taking the subway. Having split into groups and leapt into several different vehicles, they headed to the ground and, once inside, continued to indulge in the party atmosphere which had carried over from the square. Around an hour later, just before kick-off, James appeared and proceeded to be rather vague as to where he had been when Gerry asked him about it. However, this was quickly forgotten as the teams appeared from the tunnel and the match began, with Celtic attempting to qualify for the knockout stages of the Champions League.

According to Gerry, **"The atmosphere inside the ground was incredible from start to finish, and I have to say that it was a great stadium to visit. Even after Benfica had taken the lead, we did what the Celtic support always does and simply began to sing even louder than we had been doing previously. When Samaras levelled the scores I must have literally hugged everyone within about ten yards of me in all directions – it was total carnage."**

Despite the fact the Hoops eventually lost on that wet night in Portugal, it didn't dampen the spirits of the travelling support, who continued to party on through the night: **"When the match finished, there was, of course, a tinge of disappointment in the air, but I don't really think that's quite the right word to use to describe it in all honesty. Perhaps it would be more accurate to say that we simply wondered what could have been. In truth, we all felt that we had played pretty well and we certainly believed we were still in with a fantastic chance of qualifying for the last sixteen. Yes, it was a setback, but it was far from being a disaster, and so we continued to look forward. We went out for a while after the match and enjoyed ourselves, although there**

were a few hangovers present the following morning as you would expect."

The next day, Gerry and the rest of the group flew to Madrid once more, where they passed a lengthy wait drinking beer from McDonalds and enjoying a few songs before they eventually returned home several hours later. However, before he continued on with the remainder of the tale regarding James and his bizarre period of unexplained absence, Gerry reflected on the city of Lisbon itself (somewhere the Celtic supporters who travelled there in 1967 loved passionately): **"It was a beautiful city, with endless wee streets which all seemed to lead to something interesting. Whenever the locals spotted our Celtic shirts, they would smile at us, give us a thumbs-up or shout "Celtic! Celtic!" regardless of whether they were fans of Benfica or Sporting. Despite the fact it's almost fifty years since our European Cup win in the city, it was clear that the people of Lisbon still have a place for Celtic in their hearts and the feeling is mutual – that's something I think we should all be very proud of."**

Gerry then chuckled as he told me that he is **"still finding out things which happened during the trip to this day."** With this in mind, Gerry recalled how funny it was when he finally found out exactly what had happened to his friend James, sometime after the trip was over when he found himself sitting in the pub with another mate of his, Chick. According to Gerry, James was **"the worst member of the group"** with regards drunkenness that day in Lisbon. **"He was hammered as early as lunchtime,"** Gerry said, before adding that he **"could barely stand in the square later in the day"**. Anyway, unbeknown to Gerry, as the lads clambered into various taxis around two hours before kick-off, James climbed into a taxi too – but he did so alone.

Around forty-five minutes later, a mobile phone back in Scotland began to ring. Chick, another lad who had been unable to travel to Lisbon, picked up to find a somewhat inebriated James proudly declaring: **"Guess where I am mate? I'm sitting in the centre circle!"**

Obviously, this was met with something along the lines of **"what you talking about?"** from Chick. James then proceeded to go into some more detail, boasting about where he was and the game later that night before mentioning that **"it was still a bit quiet"** at the ground. After a brief pause, Chick asked what colour the seats inside the ground were, and James said **"they're white mate!"** With that, it all made sense to the previously confused Chick, as he yelled: **"You're at the wrong fucking stadium you idiot!"**

Yes, whilst Gerry and the rest of the Bhoys were standing in the away section of the Estádio da Luz, James was sat there alone, blind drunk, in the centre circle of the Estadio Nacional, where Celtic won the European Cup in 1967, approximately ten kilometres away.

Having sobered up enough to realise he had made a mistake and that kick-off was fast approaching, James presumably found another taxi and made his way to the correct stadium just in time to catch the game. If nothing else, his antics made for a good story from a trip which was thoroughly enjoyed by all those involved. I suppose it just goes to show that, as long as you're not the most drunken member of the group on any European jaunt, then the chances are you'll be one of the people doing the laughing at the end of the day, rather than the unlucky individual being laughed at.

"From Govan to Greece"

Crete, Greece. Rolling hills, bathed in grape vines and fruit trees, form the countryside, filling the gaps between little old villages and the occasional rustic farmhouse. For large parts of the year, the vibrant Mediterranean sun bakes down on the deep red soil of Greece's largest island, whilst the locals enjoy the weather almost as much as each other's company. So, forgive me for assuming that this is not the sort of place you would necessarily expect to hear a broad Glaswegian accent emanating from a local establishment as you strolled past one afternoon. Incredibly, in one village, this isn't as rare a scenario as you would think, as Govan Bhoy Jim Brown regularly perches himself at the end of his favourite bar with the Hoops on his back and a cold beer in his hand, supporting his team from halfway across Europe.

So, **"how do you go from Govan to Greece?"** This was a question that Jim, who is a man with an infectious love of a good laugh and a wind up was quick to explain. Having attended his first Celtic match in 1974 (a one-nil victory over Arbroath), he'd found himself at the majority of home and away games for the next thirty seasons or so. Even when a mixture of work and family commitments meant he moved to Yorkshire, he still continued to travel up the motorways of Britain every week for eight years, come rain, shine, or hail (hail)!

However, as his work with petroleum companies continued to take him to sites across Europe, the thoughts of a potential move to warmer climes began to creep into Jim's head, as well as that of his girlfriend. Having befriended one of the his company's executives with his slight knowledge of the Greek language, through nothing other than sheer chance and a little bit of pluck, Jim was soon offered the opportunity to move to Crete, and he jumped at it. In doing so, he acknowledged that there was one thing more than any other that he would miss about **"home"**, and it wasn't the weather.

"I'll always have an emotional attachment to Scotland, and particularly to Celtic Park, but I don't have any regrets. We have a better life over here – a healthier life. It's all fresh fruit and vegetables, sitting outside and enjoying a bit of fresh air. Greece is corrupt – I haven't been paid in months because the country is absolutely skint, but don't get me wrong, we wouldn't live here if we didn't love it – and when it's hot, it's scorching."

Returning to earlier in his life for a moment, Jim grew up in what he described as a **"largely Protestant street"** in Drumoyne. His next door neighbour for a time was a member of the **"Orange Order"**, and whilst the jokes and quips would fly back and forth between the residents of two houses for most of the year, when a particular date in July approached, his neighbours would, annually, simply stop speaking to him and his family. To this day, the divide within certain sections of his native country continues to both baffle and trouble Jim, and whilst he admits he misses winding people up, he certainly doesn't miss the nastier, more visceral side of things.

Back in 1974, Jim had his first encounter with the Greek people, as Olympiakos travelled to Celtic Park to take on the Hoops in the European Cup. This was Jim's first experience of European Football, and although he cannot remember it in great detail, he still recalls the generally chaotic scenes to this day, as an incredible atmosphere was generated by the thousands in attendance.

As he grew somewhat older, Jim went on to attend St Gerard's High School in Govan. It was at this time in his life that he began to get his earliest tastes of one of the game's often forgotten relics, the **"football special"**. For those of you who may not know, these were special trains laid on by **"British Rail"** in order to transport away football supporters from one city to another. However, to say they were anything **"special"** in terms of their niceties would be a lie. In fact, the trains were often packed to within an inch of bursting, as if they were transporting livestock.

Generally, whenever you see one of these trains nowadays, they tend to be featured in a relatively low budget movie about football hooliganism, with supporters of a fictional team or a side with an infamous, if somewhat stereotypical history, such as West Ham or Millwall, playing major roles. As many of you will know though, the world of the casuals was not confined to England, with long running feuds and rivalries between different supports in Scotland often dominating the headlines in newspapers post match day.

And so, as a fourteen or fifteen year old, Jim boarded a special to Aberdeen with a few of his mates. Upon arriving in the Granite City after a lengthy journey, it was not igneous rocks the Celtic support were met with, but glass – and lot's of it – as bottles, as well as other missiles, began to rain down on the station platform from the bridge above.

Having avoided any injury, unlike a couple of less fortunate individuals, Jim and his pals headed for what was then the away end at Pittodrie, down by the beach. As supporters were corralled into their relevant pens, it was clear that the atmosphere was still rather nasty. Upon the completion of ninety minutes, the away fans were herded out of the stadium to the road outside, the other side of which had a sandy hill separating the city from the beach itself.

Due to the large crowd gathering on the road as the fans awaited the police's orders to move back towards the train station, many supporters took up positions on the hill, including Jim and his mates, with some sitting and others standing. Whilst there was still some tension in the air at this point, it had been notably diluted somewhat as the adrenaline of the game itself began to wear off and the day's previous incidents faded further into the memory.

However, soon a scene of relative calm was to transform into one of utter chaos. As a small boy further along the hill ran down its steep incline, he gathered up so much momentum that he could not stop immediately when he reached the bottom of the hill. As he moved downwards, a police vehicle was driving along between the stadium and the hill, and fate conspired to see the boy be struck by the car in question.

As many supporters rushed to help the injured boy, another section of the fans who had seen the incident were incensed, as they felt the police vehicle could have easily stopped earlier and avoided the collision. Within moments, the car was surrounded with the police officers still inside. As the vehicle was rocked from side to side, Jim watched on as several other motorised units, and well as police on horseback began to rush to the scene, having clearly been radioed by the cops in the car.

As the police struggled to gain control of the crowd, they forcibly marched the away supporters **"the long way around"** to the station, leaving the injured lad to receive medical treatment. Once the fans had eventually boarded the train, officers began to file on to the platform. At this point Jim, who knew himself that he had been present when the incident which had led to this latest band of trouble had occurred, was sitting silently, thinking **"uh-oh"**.

A moment or two later, officers began to board each carriage, picking out people from the crowd and dragging them out onto the platform. To Jim's disbelief, the other supporters, whom he could tell were fuming with anger, did not try to prevent this happening to their fellow fans. Once the selection process was over, and Jim had **"passed"** the test of a cop standing in front of him staring to see if he could garner any sort of a reaction, the police drew their batons on the platform, and began to **"lay into"** those fans unlucky enough to have been picked out.

At this point, according to Jim, **"the train erupted"**. Glass began to fly as windows were smashed and, as the train began to pull away, missiles were thrown and insults hurled at the cops still on the station platform. Such was the bad feeling that day that the officers who were to remain onboard the train barricaded themselves inside the top carriage before the beatings at the station had begun, as they clearly knew what their colleagues' intentions were.

A little over twenty miles outside of Aberdeen, the train came to a halt, and a black bus drew up alongside it. Once again, officers made their way on board in numbers and pulled another twenty supporters or so from the various carriages. A similar scene awaited the remaining fans at Glasgow's Queen Street Station, as countless police stood awaiting the arrival of this 'troublesome' football special. Having clearly been contacted by their partners up north, the police in Glasgow had descriptions of people they were looking for. At this point, Jim was, once again, worried that he was going to get caught up in something far beyond his control. Yes, he had seen what had happened but that wasn't his fault, was it? As he approached the police cordon, he intentionally attempted to look and frightened as young as possible, and was fortunate enough to be able to squeeze through without any problems, as were his friends.

Regardless of whether it was the story I have retold above, or another one involving **"metal spikes being thrown like javelins"** by Burnley supporters, it was clear that Jim, and no doubt many other football fans from the 1970's and 1980's were no strangers to the sight of violence, even though they took no part in it themselves. Unsurprisingly, Jim is pleased to see that, largely, things have changed and times have moved on, but he still resents how certain sections of the media portrayed Celtic supporters decades ago, as well as now.

In 1980, Jim travelled to Madrid for the return leg of our European Cup quarter final tie with Real Madrid. Whilst Celtic lost the match three-nil, meaning they went out by three goals to two on aggregate after a sterling home display, Jim will forever remember the events before the match, as well as the game itself. Having spent the day enjoying the sunshine and a couple of drinks, he was introduced to a local spirit in one of the bars, the name of which evades his recollection. Typically, being young, he made the mistake of drinking several shots of this stuff in an attempt to impress his mates. **"I'm from Govan"**, I thought. **"How strong can this stuff be?"**

Now, since there's clearly a story to follow this, I'm sure you've worked out that the spirit turned out to be rather strong stuff. Sometime later, Jim climbed up onto a table outside a bar, which was packed with Celtic fans, and started to sing. However, his fun was to be rather short lived as a searing pain from his leg suddenly encapsulated his mind. As he fell from the table, he felt himself being dragged along the ground, before hearing a clang. Once he regained a grasp of his situation, he found that he was in the back of a police van, with two rather irate Spanish officers shouting and bawling at him, asking to see his passport and a ticket for the match.

Having showed them his ticket and told them his passport was in the safe at his hotel, the van moved off and Jim began to worry. **"I tried to tell myself we must be going back to the hotel, but I had a bad feeling about these guys"**, he recalled. Once a significant amount of time had passed, Jim found himself becoming increasingly concerned. Eventually, the van began to drive over a bit of rough ground, before it came to a halt. As the doors opened, Jim was all too aware that he no longer found himself in the bustling city centre of Spain's capital city, but rather on some waste ground near to a motorway exit.

"These guys are going to kill me", he thought. **"The papers back home will be full of "Celt Found In Shallow Grave" – that is if anyone ever finds me!"** Once more, the police drew their batons and began to batter Jim, whilst shouting angrily in Spanish. **"I just curled up in a ball, covered my head and face as best I could and prayed they stopped"** he said.

Soon though, Jim would open his eyes. The potent mixture of alcohol, dehydration and intense pain had caused him to pass out mid-beating, and he now found himself propped up against a tree, some distance away from the motorway access ramps.

"My leg was killing me", he said, **"I could barely walk. Obviously, I couldn't just sit about though, so I began to limp towards the motorway. I had no idea how long I'd been there, or whether I'd be ok or not. I soon realised my ticket for the match was gone too, since those bastards must have wanted to prove a point. I was crying like a baby at this stage – my leg was agony; I had no idea where I was; no money; no ticket; and I didn't speak any Spanish – but other than that things were brilliant."**

Upon reaching one of the motorway ramps, Jim hobbled up it and began to attempt to flag down some of the passing traffic for help. Having been initially unsuccessful in his efforts, he persisted having no other option and soon heard the sound of screeching tires, as a bus skidded to a stop not far past him. As it slowed, Jim noticed a wooden plaque in the front window, which read simply **"Madrid"**.

As the door opened, Jim looked up and was greeted with the sight of a middle aged man, with a Celtic scarf around his neck. **"Jesus Christ son. What the fuck are you doing out here? Are you alright?"** Whilst this was perhaps not the greeting Jim expected from a random vehicle on a Spanish motorway, it was more welcome than he could truly describe.

"For the first time in what seemed like ages, I felt safe" said Jim. **"These lads were legends. Not only did they look after me and take me back into the city, but they also sorted me out with another ticket for the game. They couldn't believe what had happened to me, but they did everything they could to help me out, and while I have no idea who they are now, I just want to thank them again for what they did for me."**

Upon arriving back in the city, Jim left the supporters bus behind him, and went in search of his pals. Eventually, after a bit of a search, he found them casually sitting outside another local bar as if nothing had ever happened earlier on.

"Alright Jim! You look like shite mate! Where have you been? It's your round!" came the shout. Friends eh?

"The Mighty Atom"

It is hardly a surprise to think that some talented very Irishmen have pulled on the famous green and white Hoops of Celtic Football Club over the years when one considers the Club's notable Irish connections. Perhaps the greatest of them all signed a little over a century ago, in October 1911. Patrick 'Patsy' Gallacher was born in a poor house in the town of Milford, Donegal, on the sixteenth of March 1891. To this day, his name continues to be spelt in two differing manners by many people. The continuing literary debate is made somewhat more ironic when you consider the fact that both of Patsy's parents were wholly illiterate. However, whilst it is believed that **"Gallagher"** was the original spelling in their homeland, the family appear to have adopted the Scottish spelling **"Gallacher"** upon their immigration. Regardless of the previously discussed arguments, **"Gallacher"** is the name which appears on Patsy's gravestone, and thus I shall refer to him as **"Gallacher"** in this piece.

Early in his life, he moved with his family to Scotland in an attempt to escape the poverty and hardship they faced in their native land at the time. Many historical accounts, as well as the few surviving fans that saw him play for the Club still say that Patsy, popularly nicknamed **"The Mighty Atom"**, was the greatest Celtic player of all time. When you consider his goalscoring record and the list of honours he won with the Club, it is not hard to see why this opinion was, and still is, held by a significant number of people. Patsy scored one hundred and ninety-two goals in four hundred and sixty-four competitive appearances during fourteen years with Celtic, making him the Club's sixth highest goalscorer. In truth, this figure could have been much higher considering the fact he continued to play at a high level for several years after his eventual departure from the Celtic Park. It is also worthy of note that Patsy was, predominantly, a winger and not a centre forward, so I feel such a goalscoring record should still be considered a marvel to this day.

Patsy was a fine example of someone that could be, and probably often was at stages of his life, viewed as an unlikely superstar. Nowadays, when kids are far too often driven away from football in Scotland because they are too small, it is refreshing to consider the staggering success story of a man who was met with the same misguided stigma over a century ago. At only five feet and seven inches tall, with a very slight build (and a weight reported by Willie Maley as only **"just over seven stones"** at one stage), many would have presumed Patsy wouldn't have been a fair match for the hugely physical defenders of the era, many of whom enjoyed nothing more than booting a small skilful player into the air whenever the opportunity presented itself. This aspect of Gallacher's footballing persona undoubtedly added to his popularity within the Celtic support, who are well known for their feverous support of an underdog. The retention of this attitude may be attributed somewhat to the perceived position of the Club's supporters within society over many generations.

Upon his attendance at the Holy Redeemer Primary School in Clydebank, Patsy, still a young child, found that he would have to work rather hard in order to indulge his growing passion for football. The school itself was fully staffed by women, and since none of them held any interest in the game (unlike many women nowadays I hasten to add), Patsy had not only to play football, but to take on the administrative side of things as well, organising matches and picking which players would play in any given game because none of his teachers saw any benefit in doing so themselves. His endeavours would pay off in both the short and the long term though, as he helped Holy Redeemer to victory in a schools tournament, before a spell with another team, Benvue, set him up for a move to junior side Renfrew St James.

Having joined Renfrew St James around the time of his sixteenth birthday, he plied his trade there for a few years, constantly developing his ability and knowledge of the game, before securing a move to Clydebank Juniors in 1910. However, despite the fact he continued to impress the majority of those who saw him with his abundance of ability and regular displays of trickery, there were still those who felt, as is discussed previously, that Patsy would be overpowered or hurt at any serious level of the game.

Thankfully though, Celtic manager Willie Maley always believed that sheer physicality alone could only bring you so much on a football field, and that a raw and natural talent of this significance simply had to be given a chance to evolve and mature. For these reasons, Maley offered Patsy a trial with the Club before signing him in late 1911. During this trial period, Gallacher scored five goals, with two coming against Dumfries and three against a British Army 'Select XI'.

Decades later, shortly after Patsy's death, Willie Maley would write a column for **"The Evening Times"** eulogising not only his great player, but his firm friend. In it, he gives us an insight into the decision, which appears to have involved a vote, which was made in order to sign the rather diminutive Patsy:

"The Celtic management decided to watch him specially in a friendly game at Dumfries in 1910, when on a heavy, wet ground, the future hero played a masterly game on a ground all unsuited to his height and weight. He looked a very little chap then, but his cleverness, enthusiasm and genuine pluck won the day, and despite two strong votes he became a Celtic player, and one whose name will live in the annals."

Patsy made his debut in a three-one home victory over St Mirren in front of approximately six thousand people, at a windy Celtic Park, on the second of December 1911. Playing up front alongside the likes of the great Jimmy Quinn who, coincidentally, is one of the five players to have scored more goals for Celtic than Patsy, it would have been a special moment for the young Irishman. It is said that Quinn, who was just returning from injury himself, came out with the following remark that day as the teams prepared for the match: **"You can't put that boy on the park boss! If you do it'll be manslaughter!"**

However, to be fair to him, I doubt Patsy's new teammate could have envisaged the success that was to come in time for the slight of build winger. In fact, it would have be interesting to know what Patsy Gallacher and Jimmy Quinn would have thought of the fact that their surnames would be intrinsically linked in one of the most famous Celtic songs in existence over a century later.

"Gallacher and Quinn have left their mark! And they gave us..."

Returning to the match against St Mirren, much of the hype surrounded the return of the aforementioned Quinn, who suffered from a few long term injuries over the course of his career, as has been described previously. This aside, the debut of Patsy was mentioned by **"The Glasgow Herald"**, which stated **"The winners introduced a forward – Gallacher – in McMenemy's place, who should go far..."** – and how correct that correspondent would turn out to be.

A week later, as Celtic ran out to face Queen's Park at Hampden Park, Gallacher was once again a feature in the starting line-up, leading to this follow up comment from the previously referenced newspaper: **"What we said about Gallacher last week has to be repeated now – the youngster has come to stay".** Having scored the last goal in a four-one victory, the article continued: **"Gallacher, who gave a clever display throughout, scored a fourth goal."**

Patsy's first major honour with the Club came less than six months into his Celtic career, as he scored the second goal in a two-nil win in the 1912 Scottish Cup Final against Clyde at Ibrox. Having played in the side which defeated Hearts on the same ground only a week earlier in the semi-final, Patsy's contributions to the Club's success, even in his first season, remain worthy of recollection and respect.

"...and another goal fell to the ultimate winners, Gallacher beating Grant, who had previously failed to get rid of the ball."

Patsy would go on to win his first Scottish League Championship in 1913–1914, as Celtic won the league by six points from Rangers, losing only three times and conceding only fourteen goals in the process. On the first day of that season, as Celtic began their campaign against Ayr United, Patsy scored as the Hoops eased past their visitors by the margin of five goals to one. As the season progressed, Gallacher would also take part in emphatic victories at both Ibrox and Celtic Park against Rangers which helped the Hoops on their way to the title. In the same year, Celtic won the last Scottish Cup Final before the outbreak of World War One, as they defeated Hibernian by four goals to one in a replay held at Ibrox Park. A couple of weeks later, as Celtic ended their league campaign as Champions, Gallacher would do what he did on the first day of the season and score again. However, on this occasion against Raith Rovers, he did so twice, as Celtic defeated their opponents two-one.

"Young missed an open goal, but Gallacher made amends by placing, rather than shooting, the ball past Wallace..."

The following season, Patsy would score the deciding goal in a two-one win over Rangers at Celtic Park in late October, which made it five consecutive league victories for the Hoops over their increasingly fierce adversaries. However, please do not allow me to purvey an image whereby Patsy Gallacher only performed well against Rangers, as he regularly excelled against any and all opposition he came up against. For example, in January 1915, Celtic faced Partick Thistle and Patsy scored a hat-trick as Celtic won by six goals to one. Victories such as this one would prove to be vital as the campaign continued and drew to a close, as the Hoops managed to overturn Hearts' advantage at the top of the league and win their second consecutive Scottish League Championship.

There would be more celebrations too, as in the spring of 1915, Patsy Gallacher married his girlfriend Mary Josephine Donegan (a housekeeper in the city), at the end of April.

Returning to the world of football, Celtic's third consecutive League Championship was won the next season in a manner unlike any other in the Club's past. I could have conceivably decided to cover this tale in one of the other chapters dedicated to another great Celtic player, but there has been method in my madness holding off until now, in my mind at least. So, what made the fifteenth of April 1916 so special? Well, remarkably, Celtic were forced to play two league matches on the same day, with an almost identical squad for each match, and in doing so they secured themselves as the Champions of Scotland for the thirteenth time.

As interesting a story as this is, it is noteworthy that Celtic were already on the verge of winning the league title going into that day, only requiring a point from their remaining five matches (or alternatively for Rangers to drop a point in any of their last four matches) to secure the retention of the title of Scottish Champions. However, to play two top flight matches in a single day is an achievement nonetheless. And so, as the teams, and Patsy, ran out for their first match of the day, they found themselves at Celtic Park, along with approximately ten thousand spectators and their opponents, Raith Rovers. With a clear desire and determination not only to win the league as soon as possible, but to do so upon their own ground and on their own terms, Celtic went on to hammer the Fife side by six goals to nil. By all accounts, Patsy Gallacher, now twenty-five, was the star of the show, scoring an impressive hat-trick which all of the Celtic fans undoubtedly enjoyed.

Later in the day, instead of being able to enjoy the fact they had just won the league, the Celtic team, Patsy, and many of the Celt's supporters had to make the journey to Fir Park to face Motherwell. Incredibly, they too had played earlier in the day, losing three-nil to Ayr United at home. The Hoops would go on to win three-one that evening in Lanarkshire, thanks to goals from Jimmy McMenemy, Joe Dodds and John Browning. And so, by the end of that memorable day, Celtic had won twice, both home and away; Rangers had been heavily beaten, conceding five to Partick Thistle, and Celtic were the Champions of Scotland once again. Patsy too, the player whom some felt wasn't big enough to compete at the highest level, had scored a hat-trick earlier in the day, and completed one hundred and eighty minutes of top class football at two different Scottish stadia. Whilst this is incredible to look back upon, the newspapers of the time were very complimentary about Celtic's achievements, as well as their character.

"The Parkhead officials hoped at one time to be able to play the same eleven in both matches, but McColl and Johnstone were unable to assist their club in the final stages of a memorable contest. Their enforced absence merely emphasised that feature which has been the distinguishing trait of past and present Celtic championship teams, the adaptability of the players and their facility for taking up a new position in an emergency."

Finally, for a Club which always has, and likely always will, pride itself on the attacking manner with which it attempts to play its football, I feel it is worth highlighting that on that day, Celtic set a new league record for the number of goals scored after thirty-four matches (thirty-four being the number of games that were played for many years in a single league campaign, although it was thirty-six that season). By the end of the 1907–08 season, so often remembered for the famous victories of Celtic, many people have forgotten that Falkirk, who came second, would manage not only their highest league finish ever (they would be runners-up to Celtic once more two years later), but they also set the record for the highest number of goals scored by a single team in the league – an incredible one hundred and three, or an average of just over three goals per match. At the time, **"the Bairns"** were, rightly, very proud of this total.

However, having played only thirty-one games thus far, Celtic, who were set to face Raith Rovers on that day in 1916, had already scored on ninety-eight occasions. Thanks partly to Gallacher's hat-trick and a late goal from Joe Dodds the Hoops made it six on the day, and one hundred and four for the season. Three more goals at Motherwell, combined with a goalless draw with Hearts the following week left Celtic at one hundred and seven goals for their thirty-four matches. When the season came to an end, the Celts' record read: **"thirty-eight matches played, with thirty-two wins, three draws, and three losses."** In this period, one hundred and sixteen goals were scored, with thirty-two conceded, leaving them with a goal difference of plus eighty-four and, interestingly, a points total of sixty-seven. Of course, that number had no significance at the time, but hindsight is a wonderful thing at times, isn't it?

As Patsy's career continued, success after success followed, and Celtic went on to win five out of six possible League Championships, until he was eventually rewarded with an international debut in 1919, in front of a reported fifty thousand fans at Windsor Park, Belfast, as Ireland took on England (the game ended in an one-all draw). In all, Patsy would play thirteen times for his country (eleven for the Football Association based in Belfast, and two for the Dublin based equivalent – a notable difference at that point in time). It is worth remembering that at that time, although there were two football associations fielding two different sides, they were both considered to be **"Ireland"** and several players played for both teams over the years.

Patsy won his sixth and final Scottish League Championship with Celtic at the end of the 1921–22 season, having helped the Hoops to win edge the title race by a single point from their city rivals Rangers. Subsequently, he would go on to win his third and fourth Scottish Cup medals with the Club in 1923 and 1925. As some of you will undoubtedly know, Patsy would be the recipient of a great deal of the plaudits on both occasions, from fans and media alike.

Dealing with the 1923 Scottish Cup Final firstly, Celtic faced Hibernian, who had not won the trophy since 1902 (and still haven't, as of the start of the 2013–14 campaign, that is), and neither side had featured in the few Cup Finals which had been held since the end of World War One. Patsy was the only non-Scotsman on the park that day, as over eighty thousand people packed Hampden to see the battle of the 'green and whites'. Interestingly, the match also saw a dual between Maley's, as Willie, manager of Celtic, took on his younger brother Alex, manager of Hibernian. By all accounts, the Edinburgh side started the brighter: **"to such an extent that their supporters at the interval were justifiably confident that their team held a winning chance"**, according to one newspaper reporter of the time.

"Celtic's forwards were badly out of the game for a bit, but a great run from Gallacher, in which he beat three opponents and shot straight for goal, was the turning point in the game for Celtic. Gallacher continued to urge on his colleagues, and Hibernian's defence broke under the strain of the constant attacks. For quite ten minutes Celtic practically besieged their opponents' goal, and at the end of that period it fell in rather peculiar fashion. McFarlane bobbed the ball into goal, where it descended between the two backs. Harper hesitatingly left his goal to clear the danger, and here he neither reached the ball nor could recover his position as Cassidy dashed in and headed the bouncing ball into the vacant goal."

Two years later, as Celtic strived to reach another Scottish Cup Final, they found themselves set to face Rangers at Hampden Park. Despite the massive scoreline which followed, this match has largely been forgotten amongst a plethora of great Celtic results. Regardless, Patsy Gallacher, as well as many of his teammates, delivered magnificent performances that day, as Celtic annihilated Rangers by five goals to nil. In the following days, Patsy was described by **"The Glasgow Herald"** as **"the inspiration of an attack in which wing players Connelly and McLean played probably their finest game for Celtic."** Such references clearly highlight the fact that, despite Patsy's increasing age and slight loss of mobility, he was still one of the best players around when it came to controlling not only a ball, but a match itself. One additional point of interest is that this was, at the time, the highest attended Club match Scotland had ever seen, with almost one hundred and two thousand people officially inside Hampden Park that day.

Less than a month later, Celtic found themselves a goal down with less than twenty minutes to go in the Scottish Cup Final against Dundee, before Patsy scored a truly unique equaliser which left all of those at Hampden Park in awe. With both the Celtic players on the park and the fans on the terraces looking increasingly despondent, Gallacher is reported to have received the ball at his feet, before he began to dribble towards the Dundee defenders in front of him. Once he had ridden and avoided several attempted challenges, he was heavily tackled in the box. While most players would have immediately gone to ground, turned to the referee and shouted for a penalty, Patsy somehow managed to keep the ball between his feet and somersault over the oncoming goalkeeper into the net to make the score one-all. This was not only a show of skill from Patsy, but a sure sign that he possessed a vision and daring few footballers could hope to match and, unsurprisingly, the newspapers were gushing in their praise for the Irishman, now in his mid-thirties, but still the envy of many admirers of the beautiful game.

"...Celtic got the goal that always seemed imminent, Gallacher crowning a daring and devious bit of play by throwing himself

bodily into the net and carrying the ball with him. It was a positive relief to a great section of the crowd, who were wrought up to an almost painful degree of excitement over the long-continued battle between the Celtic attackers and Dundee's unflinching defenders."

"Celtic's second-half display will long be remembered for the part taken in it by W. McStay and Gallacher. These two experienced players were at once the inspiration and the example to their team, and the value of their coaching, particularly the skill and determination of Gallacher, at a time when signs were not wanting that Celtic were faltering before the daring and capable opposition, could not be overestimated. The feature of the exciting contest was Gallacher's equalising goal, and in a career of much distinction it is questionable if the clever Celt ever accomplished anything so sensational and clever."

According to one newspaper, the match was, at that point in time, **"the second most highly attended Scottish Cup Final ever"**, with a little over seventy-five thousand individuals paying to watch the spring encounter. Despite the large crowd, **"the game was carried out without a hitch and practically without accident."** However, tellingly, it continues **"Some half-dozen cases were treated by the efficient ambulance section, the excitement when Celtic scored the equalising goal being responsible for the majority of the casualties..."**

As the match continued, Jimmy McGrory netted an eighty-seventh minute winner to assure the Scottish Cup would be returning with Celtic to the East End. In press reports after the match, several Dundee players begrudgingly praised Patsy's skill and endeavour, saying the equalising goal was **"out of this world"**, with one even stating that it was **"the greatest feat of skill and determination they had ever seen on a football field"**.

Regrettably, the wonder goal of the aforementioned Cup Final would be Patsy's last as a Celtic player. He would only make one more appearance in a Celtic jersey, as the Hoops lost by five goals to one away at Airdrieonians on the third of October 1925. Ironically, a Gallacher stole the show that day, but it was not Patsy. Instead, it was the rising talent of Hughie Gallacher, who would move south only a couple of months later and go on to keep Jimmy McGrory (who netted Celtic's single goal that day) out of the Scotland squad on many occasions for years to come.

In sad and in fact rather acrimonious circumstances, Patsy Gallacher would soon leave Celtic, the team he had been served for no less than fifteen years, although there remains some debate as to when this actually occurred. The most common story appears to be that the Club (possibly via Willie Maley) announced the player would be retiring in the summer of 1926, only for Patsy to categorically deny these claims and prove his former employers wrong by going on to play for Falkirk for another six years. Speculation is still rife to this day that Patsy was forced from the Club because the board no longer wanted to pay his wages, which were reported to be a step above those the rest of the players received, rather than because the manager felt he was no longer of benefit to the playing squad.

Patsy's absence from a Celtic jersey for the final six years of his footballing life has also led many a supporter to look back and think **"what if he had stayed?"** How many more titles and trophies would Patsy have helped Celtic to win, and just how many more goals would he have scored for the Club? This feeling was only strengthened by Patsy himself, who displayed some of his old skill and trickery upon Falkirk's first meeting with Celtic in the following season. Celtic won by three goals to one, thanks largely to their superior finishing, but Gallacher was praised as **"the greatest source of trouble to his old colleagues"**, and described as providing **"fine football"** for the spectators in attendance.

On a more serious note, away from the world of football, Patsy and his family were to suffer the tragic loss of their wife and mother Mary, in 1929, as she gave birth to the couple's sixth child. She was only thirty-five years of age, and suddenly Patsy was left to care for his children alone. To his credit, he faced this wall of adversity like he had done so many times on the football field, with a gritty fortitude which must be admired. With the help of a housekeeper, he not only raised his children, but helped two of them, William and Thomas, to follow in his sporting footsteps. Willie, as many of you will know, made over fifty appearances for

Celtic whilst Thomas played for Dundee. I feel it is also noteworthy that Patsy's grandson, Kevin, played for both Dundee United as well as a selection of English sides in a career which included a memorable opening goal in the Scottish Cup Final of 1988.

Patsy finally retired from the professional game in 1932 (at the age of forty-one) and went on to own a pub in Clydebank, in which the walls were covered with football memorabilia, much of it related to the owner or the other great men he was fortunate enough to have played alongside at one point or another. Earlier that same year, in January, Scottish Football came together at Celtic Park to honour the services of Patsy Gallacher to the game of football. A Celtic and Falkirk select side, including Patsy and some of his former teammates, took on a Scottish League select and defeated them by ten goals to seven. As was perhaps rather apt, Patsy scored once more at Celtic Park.

Even after his retirement, every weekend, with a humbling consistency, Patsy would return to Parkhead, paying to watch the first team or, alternatively, the Celtic juniors if the senior side were away from home. Always able to pass on a few words of wisdom, or to offer constructive criticism on the odd occasion it was required, Patsy continued to endear himself to the Celtic support long after his playing days were over. His hair may have been a little grey, and he may not have moved with the speed and agility that he once did, but his footballing brain and his sterling reputation were still firm features of his character.

Patsy Gallacher died of cancer, aged sixty-two years old, on the seventeenth of June 1953, less than a month after the Club he loved so much famously won the Coronation Cup. A plaque, presented by Celtic Football Club and Patsy's son Bernard to the people of his **"hometown"** of Ramelton, in Donegal, adorns the first house which he lived in. I have highlighted the use of the word **"hometown"** previously because Patsy was actually born in Milford, and not Ramelton, which is where he later lived and went to school, but I digress.

Whilst we may be accused by some of looking through rose (or, in fact, green) tinted spectacles at some of the true greats of old who have played for Celtic, we must not underestimate the vast amount of technical ability that Patsy, and many of the other players from that era, possessed. Nowadays, people can compare modern players by looking up countless films of them showing off their talent at its best. However, with players who starred in sides the length and breadth of the country before the serious introduction of television coverage at football matches, we sadly cannot do this. After all, what Celtic supporters wouldn't want to see for themselves just how good the likes of Gallacher and Quinn were if they had the capability to do so?

For many older Celtic supporters to genuinely and wholeheartedly believe Patsy was the greatest Celt ever, he must have been a very special player indeed, and to earn the following plaudits from Celtic's highest ever goalscorer, Jimmy McGrory, he must have been a truly incredible talent to behold:

"Many people have asked me how Patsy would have stood up to the rigours of the modern game. He would have strolled through it. There is no present day player in this country that I would put anywhere near his class. Even Jimmy Johnstone, with all his talents, never reached the Gallacher heights. Gallacher was always advancing; there was no doubling back and playing across the field. Everything he did was positive."

Indeed, from the descriptions of Patsy's play which I have read, I know that McGrory was not the first person to make the comparison between these two wizards of wing play. Gallacher was, in many aspects, the Jimmy Johnstone of the 1910's and 1920's or, depending on your viewpoint, perhaps Johnstone was actually the Gallacher of the 1960's. Regardless, such comparisons do hold some merit, as despite a seemingly endless line of opposition players trying to kick the smaller and more skilful men out of the game, they both continued to get up, time after time, and simply infuriate defenders by running rings around them.

"During the fifty years of the Club's existence many brilliant players have played their part in making history and not the least of these was Patsy Gallacher, who many declare was the "finest o' them a'". Well, I am not going to express any opinion on that or make comparisons, but I will say, and without any fear of contradiction, that there never was one who gave better service

to the Club and with so little to commend him in the way of physique." – Willie Maley

Now, I do not know which of these two players (Gallacher and Johnstone) was superior to the other, as I have not been fortunate enough to watch either of them play live, but I will say I have no doubts that the two men would have been great admirers of each other's abilities had they ever been able to play together. Regardless, one thing is certain; the name of Patsy Gallacher will forever be synonymous with exceptional skill, footballing underdogs, and his many glorious successes with Celtic Football Club.

"There never was a player like him, and I often wonder if we shall see his like again. I wish we could, just to show the present day players that we of Patsy Gallacher's time had something to boast about." – Alan Morton, Rangers

"I am privileged to write a little appreciation of one of the old Celtic players whom I brought out and whom achieved fame in the colours still so dear to me. Patsy Gallacher, to my mind, was one of the greatest players who ever played for the old club."

"Frankly, I had thought Patsy (who was a special friend of mine) would have been attending my funeral instead of the other way about, as when I saw him last I thought his fate was fixed, although with his usual pluck death seemed far away."

"As a player I have never seen one cleverer with the ball or so passionate in his love of the game and of the very ball itself. In training, Patsy delighted in juggling with the ball, and his form of training often consisted of his trying all sorts of ideas he had in his mind."

"I shivered at times to see him going into the tackle with men stones heavier. Nevertheless, he combined his bravery with a knowledge of the real game which surprised all who saw him."

"For swerving in the tackles, I never saw his equal, and his powers of lasting were marvellous, as he would play on when others, bigger and stronger, were falling."

"The Celtic, to my mind, have ever been lucky to have such men, and I remember Quinn, McMenemy and Patsy Gallacher as

outstanding. Their spirit has been the Celtic's salvation on many a hard fought field."

"It was with great sorrow I attended the funeral. While it reminded me of great days of footballing success, I regret the passing of one of my greatest heroes. May the turf which Patsy loved so well in life rest softly on him in his last rest, and may he rest in peace." – Willie Maley, "Evening Times" Obituary

"The Superstars Of Their Day"

And so, there you have it – **"John Thomson, Dan Doyle, Alec McNair, Willie Loney, Willie Lyon, Bobby Evans, Charlie Tully, Jimmy Quinn, Jimmy McGrory, Jimmy McMenemy, and Patsy Gallacher."** In my opinion, this fictional side would have been capable of defeating virtually anyone on their day, and I mean that in every sense. Each of these men was regarded as an incredible talent by the Celtic supporters who have gone before us. Whilst in more recent years fans have flocked to see the likes of Henrik Larsson, Lubomir Moravcik and, yes, even the **"Greek Gazelle"** Georgios Samaras, it is clear that individuals with an abundance of skill and a unique character have always drawn crowds to follow Celtic.

From Doyle in the 1890's, to Tully and Evans in the 1950's (1960 included in Bobby's case), these men were the superstars of their day. Had replica kits existed in the manner they do now, names such as Gallacher and Quinn would have been commonplace upon them. Instead, the Celtic fans of old idolised their heroes with whatever was available to them, in the form of rosettes, badges, Brake Club banners and that most important, most treasured medium – song. Fans did not sing **"You'll Never Walk Alone"** or **"Oh Ah Samaras"** in the late 1800's and early 1900's, but they did sing, both loudly and proudly. Their voices filled the air of decades and centuries gone by, and it is a tragedy that many of their songs and chants have been lost to the mists of time.

In a similar vein, it is a shame that so little of the early days of the Football Club was caught on camera. Whilst I may be able to sit as a pensioner and reminisce about how I saw Henrik Larsson play live to any of my future grandchildren, they will be able to watch recordings of almost all of his career goals with ease. They will be able to see the saves of Fraser Forster in Barcelona, or watch John Hartson thunder a shot into the top corner at Anfield with nothing more than a few pushes of a button.

However, prior to the glory days of the Lisbon Lions, very little was recorded at football matches. Not only was there no **"YouTube"** or camera phones, there was often nothing more than a fifty word match report or a grainy black and white photo to consume at that time – if you were lucky! To watch Celtic, you literally had to travel to wherever they were playing, pay your entrance fee and stand there, taking in the sights and sounds with nothing more than your eyes and ears. And yet, critically, the three most important factors have always been there, regardless of the period of our history in question – the players, the fans, and the stories.

Whether such tales refer to modern day players and, for example, a prospective move elsewhere, or players of old and a gripping finish to match long since gone by, they still capture the imagination and the attention of the majority of Celtic fans, and that is what I have attempted to capture for you within my greatest team. Those of you who are historical experts may not have learned much if anything, but I wholeheartedly hope that most Celtic supporters who have picked up this book and read the historical section have not only enjoyed it, but learned something from it too.

The history of our Football Club is, in my mind at least, tremendously interesting. We have the ability to enjoy the high points and taste the elation of victory to this day; we can experience the pain of defeat; we can almost tangibly touch the sadness of the illnesses and deaths; and we can look to the future with unmatched pride, proud of our history, playing a part of our present and looking to our future with optimism. That passion and pride is something which I have attempted to convey within these pages, as I tried to tell the stories not only of these player's achievements, but of the men themselves.

Continuing with this theme for a moment, allow me to indulge you once again with regards to my greatest team – and what a side they would have been. Put simply, I believe they would have been all but unstoppable in the old days.

In goal, of course, we had the incredible John Thomson – a young man who had not only his career, but his life cut short far too soon – a young man who amazed those who saw him with his agility, bravery, and skill.

At full-back, I chose Dan Doyle and Alec McNair, my 'odd couple', if you will. The former was a character to say the least. Fun loving and at times, unreliable, he provided a source of frustration for many on occasion. However, gifted with both sparkling skill and an infectious personality which often made up for the aforementioned frustrations, this Celtic captain would bring a lot to any side, providing he wanted to play and arrived on time. Alec McNair was on the other hand, the perfect servant. Consistent, reliable and coolheaded with a dedication to his fitness, he would have been the proverbial yin to Doyle's yang, allowing them to form a fearsome partnership on the field of play.

In the middle of the park, we would find our half-backs, the engine room of this greatest eleven. With this in mind, I could not find three better candidates than Willie Loney, Willie Lyon and Bobby Evans. Each was as strong and powerful as the biggest footballers of their respective days, able to dominate the game even against the toughest of opponents, but critically, each of them were tremendously gifted with the ball at their feet. Both Lyon and Evans were Club captains in their time, and Loney in particular was capable not only of defending one goal, but a causing serious threat to that located the other end of the field, with a notable talent from set pieces.

Moving to the forward line, we shall consider the outside forwards on the wings first, Charlie Tully and Patsy Gallacher. Both of these men, with their own distinctive styles, wowed terraces full of excited spectators more than any other wingers at the peak of their powers. Each would go on to be described as **"the greatest footballer of all time"** by some of those fortunate enough to watch them, and the flamboyance of their play would be greatly appreciated even today. With regards to our fictional team though, both would earn a place not only because of their abilities to beat several defenders at once, but other assets too. Gallacher was a great goalscorer, played at inside forward predominantly but pushed out to outside forward for the sake of this fictional side. Tully, whilst not as prolific in front of goals as

Patsy, had an almost unmatched talent for creating goalscoring chances for his teammates, and this would prove vital if this team were ever to stand up in comparison to any other.

Finally, the front three forwards, 'The Three Jimmy's' - Quinn, McGrory, and McMenemy. Beginning with the latter, Jimmy McMenemy not only scored goals but created countless chances, capable of playing on either side of the centre forward but playing at inside right in this side. His unselfish attitude to the game led to him being the envy of many players and clubs alike and, whilst his name may not be quite as well known as that of the other forwards I have selected, I have no doubt that he would have shone in this prospective line-up. As for Jimmy Quinn and Jimmy McGrory, their goalscoring records, as well as their quiet, unassuming characters speak for them better than I can. Whilst they were incredibly determined on the field, playing with both tenacity and vigour which helped them to become the greatest strikers of their respective eras, they were gentlemen off of it, and this must not be overlooked. Of course, Jimmy McGrory simply had to take the role of my centre forward, and therefore Quinn would feature at inside left in my team, where I have no doubt he would have excelled alongside such incredible teammates.

Having considered all of this though, I must confess that I could have decided on a slightly different eleven. In fact, I could rather easily assemble another team, using totally different players, who would have been utterly magnificent also. Men such as Charlie Shaw, Joe Dodds, James Kelly, Peter Wilson, Sandy McMahon, James Young and Peter Somers could have easily featured, to name only a few. In all honesty, the difficulty with which I made my choices only highlights how many fantastic talents graced Celtic Park over the years, many of whom are now names some would not recognise. With this in mind, I attempted to mix some of the more famous names, such as McGrory and Tully, with some of those which are perhaps less prominent in the minds of many, such as McNair and Loney, and I hope I have been somewhat successful in this regard.

Finally, to conclude the point I am attempting to make, I shall compare the records of my side, with both the greatest Celtic team ever as voted for by the fans, and also with the Lisbon Lions, whom most people would regard as the greatest Celtic side that actually played together. If we consider the number of years of service given to the Football Club (excluding those spent in managerial roles for men like McGrory and McNeill), we can see that whilst the Lisbon Lions gave over one hundred and twenty-five years between them, and the fans greatest eleven a little over one hundred and forty years, my pre-Lions greatest eleven gave over one hundred and fifty years cumulatively to Celtic Football Club.

Continuing this theme, we discover that of the three teams in question, my greatest eleven made fewer appearances than both of their counterparts, making little over four thousand, one hundred competitive outings for the Club. The Lions made a little over four thousand, three hundred whilst the supporters' greatest eleven made just over five thousand between them. However, when you note that both European Football and the Scottish League Cup were non-existent for much of the period discussed in the previous chapters (as well as remembering that John Thomson died at the age of just twenty-two years old and that Willie Lyon had his career cut short by war) then it becomes clear there are contributory factors to the 'more years service, less matches played' discrepancy.

All in all, I believe there is no doubt as to who the greatest 'real' Celtic team ever was. Despite all of the information discussed above, I firmly hold the Lisbon Lions as the best of the best, and their achievements speak volumes in this regard. However, I wholeheartedly believe that, although we may not have seen them play, we cannot afford to forget the greats of years gone by. Without these men and their efforts, Celtic Football Club would not be what it is today. Even without one player or one match, the list of honours may read differently, or the memories and stories cherished by so many may not be the same. Of course, every man who pulls on the Hoops play their part in one way or another, but a select few achieve far more than that. They ignite the hopes and dreams of the Celtic support, and their legacies will outlive us all.

The Oxford English Dictionary describes a **"legend"** as being **"an extremely famous or notorious person, especially in a particular field"**. In a sporting sense, I feel that the eleven men I have discussed previously define the meaning of the word far better than any such dictionary can, so if you're looking for legendary figures, look no further.

"Your Friends Have Gone – They Have Left With Everything"

The fifth of December 2012. Glasgow. Celtic are awarded a late penalty by German referee Felix Brych. As Kris Commons stands over the ball, the Hoops are drawing one each with Spartak Moscow, requiring a victory to seal their place in the knockout phase of the Champions League. Neil Lennon cannot watch. He turns around and buries his head in the shoulder of one of the seats in the home dugout. Almost sixty thousand people hold their breath – a number which is almost ten thousand higher than the equivalent attendance within the Camp Nou, where Barcelona's tie against Benfica remains goalless. If Celtic do not better Benfica's result in Catalonia, then they will drop into the Europa League.

Soon, Kris Commons starts his run up, believing that Barcelona are currently leading Benfica due to a previous noise from the home crowd, and rattles the cross bar. Time seems to stop as the ball thunders downwards into the ground, before bouncing upwards and ultimately nestling in the roof of the net, causing somewhat restrained celebrations inside Celtic Park. Neil Lennon jumps from the dugout when he hears the roar circulate around the stadium, but soon tells his players they must continue to focus on the task at hand. Everyone keeps one eye on the score at the Camp Nou, continually checking their phones or asking someone near to them with a radio, until the final whistle in both games confirms Celtic's success, sparking more characteristic, more exuberant celebrations from the Parkhead faithful.

A couple of weeks later, the 'real' draw for the last sixteen replicates that drawn in UEFA's rehearsals exactly, with Celtic set to face Juventus, the team who won Serie A without losing a single league match the previous season. Having suffered a tremendously disappointing three-nil defeat at Celtic Park, one would be forgiven for thinking that the Celtic supporters facing a trip to the north of Italy for the return leg would be feeling somewhat deflated, but that was far from the case. Of course, very few of them seriously believed we would overturn such a deficit and progress to the quarter finals, but that wasn't going to stop them enjoying themselves.

One man destined to make the journey to Turin was Grant Kelly, a twenty-five year old from Glasgow's Southside. As a lifelong Celtic supporter, he had previously travelled to Blackburn and Milan following Celtic abroad, and he would return to the latter on this trip. Upon the scramble to arrange travel to Italy when the aforementioned knockout draw took place, many supporters realised that very few flights flew directly into Turin itself, and many of those which did were remarkably expensive. For this reason, countless Celtic fans instead chose to fly to Milan, a city located less than a couple of hours drive away from Turin. And so, when the time came, a ticketless Grant set off amidst a group totalling between twenty and twenty-five people in size, although only five or six of them were his well-known friends.

Having stayed in Milan overnight prior to the match, the lads had a few beers and then boarded a minibus which would take them along the motorway to Turin. Upon their arrival, they headed for what had become the main meeting point for Celtic fans in the city – **"The Shamrock Inn"** – where one of Grant's mates met a lad he had previously seen in Barcelona a few months earlier. As Grant set off in search of another bar in which he was meant to pick up a ticket he had arranged to buy, all of his mates headed for the Juventus Stadium. After all, kick-off was fast approaching and reports of slow turnstiles and long queues were already filtering through. Clutching a piece of paper with the address of the aforementioned meeting point on it, Grant wandered around the streets of Turin in search of a taxi. However, after an extensive yet fruitless search, it became clear to Grant that his ticket was not going to materialise as time ticked away. And so, Grant simply did what he could and returned to **"The Shamrock Inn"**, where he watched Celtic lose two-nil on a rain soaked night in Italy. Of course, Grant was not alone, as hundreds of other ticketless Celts crammed **"the pub so full you could barely move."**

Now, it goes without saying that once the match was over, Grant still had to meet up with his pals in order to return to Milan on their minibus. However, when factors such as the consumption of significant quantities of alcohol and a general lack of knowledge of the city's geographical layout were added into the equation, this seemingly simple task became somewhat tricky. With this in mind, as he attempted to locate his mates, Grant took a picture of a street sign where he was standing with his phone and sent it to his pals so that they could come to find him, rather than the other way about.

However, having done this, his phone battery died, and with his charger back in Milan, Grant was unable to make contact with his mates again. Despite Grant proceeding to wander around in search of the aforementioned minibus and his friends for over an hour, his endeavours were in vain, as his mates were nowhere to be seen. After some time, the fact that they had left without him became increasingly clear to the twenty-five year old, and this forced him to change tact.

With this in mind, Grant decided to return to the pub, as he recalled the fact that the aforementioned friend of his friend was still there and, by his own admission, he **"had no other ideas"**. Having explained his situation to this lad, the group he was with were kind enough to allow Grant to sleep in their room in Turin, but not before they all enjoyed several more drinks celebrating Celtic's magnificent Champions League run. Now, most of us who have enjoyed a drink from time to time will be familiar with two feelings – the first being the end of the night before, when you feel as if you don't have a care in the world – and the second being the feeling of dread the next morning when you wonder whether or not you did something stupid whilst in your drunken state of mind.

And so, as the next morning dawned, Grant awoke on a couch. He was actually somewhat comfortable at first, as he tried not to think about how rough he felt and slowly opened his eyes. As is so often the case when a person is hungover, it can take a few seconds longer than normal sometimes for things to register inside their heads. With this in mind, it is no surprise that "**it took thirty or forty seconds before I started to look about and thought "I don't recognise this place. Hang on, this isn't my hotel room. Where the hell am I?**" according to Grant, before he leapt to his feet in dread.

Moments later, Grant spotted one of the lads from the night before and asked "**Where am I?**" before he was subsequently told "**you're still in Turin mate!**" At this point, Grant looked at a clock on the wall and, after seeing that it was already after 9am, the severity of his situation began to truly sink in.

"I knew the check-in for our flight home was sometime in the early afternoon, but I didn't know exactly when. I tried to look at my phone to contact my pals but then I remembered it had no battery. All of my stuff was in Milan – my clothes, my bag, my passport, my mates, and my flight! All I had with me were the clothes I was wearing, a dead phone and ninety Euros in cash. I didn't even have a watch so I had no grasp of what time it was unless I was near a clock. To say I was panicking would be an understatement."

Once the other lads in the flat had stopped laughing at Grant's predicament for a minute, they hastily guided him to the main train station in Turin where he boarded the first train to Milan. This journey cost him thirty Euros, as well as around an hour and a half in terms of time. As Grant ran out of the station on to the streets of Milan, he spotted a clock and predicted he had somewhere between two and three hours until the check-in for his flight would close.

"I sprinted out to the taxi rank and started trying to find a driver who knew where my hotel was. I couldn't remember the address, but I could remember its name – "Hotel America". However, even with the name, all of the taxi drivers just gave me a blank stare" said Grant.

"I couldn't believe it," he continued. **"I was running out of time, so I had a quick think and decided all I could do was to start looking for an internet cafe in the hope I could find the address of the hotel there, because I had absolutely no idea where it was**

and neither did anyone else I asked. The only problem was that I had no clue where an internet cafe was either, so I started asking people in the street, but nobody seemed to know what I was going on about. I mean, you would think the word "internet" would be recognised by most people regardless of which language of they spoke, but apparently this wasn't the case in Milan. I suppose my accent probably didn't help."

"Anyway, I just started to aimlessly run about the streets looking for anything which remotely resembled an internet cafe. I was sticking my head in almost every open doorway I could see, meaning I stumbled into the likes of clothes shops and even a hairdresser's before quickly looking around like an idiot and then leaving again. Eventually, through nothing other than determination combined with a bit of luck, I finally found what I was looking for, and as I wandered in I said "Internet cafe?" to the person behind the desk, and they just nodded and looked at me like I was stupid."

Hastily, Grant scribbled down the street address of his hotel, and having paid five Euros for his use of the computer, he leapt up and ran back towards the taxi rank. This time, thankfully, one of the drivers looked at the address and said "ok!" before driving him to his hotel, whilst Grant sat in the back seat praying his mates hadn't left for the airport yet. Once he had paid the taxi driver another twenty Euros, he raced into the hotel reception where the little Italian woman behind the desk looked at him quizzically. Before he could even ask about the location of his mates, she told him through broken English: "Your friends have gone - they have left with everything."

"At that stage I was just standing there thinking: "You cannot be serious. Don't tell me they've gone." I stood there stunned for a minute and then asked if I could use the computer behind the reception desk to contact my friends on Facebook. Initially the wee woman wasn't having it, but once I explained what was happening she gave in. Once I worked out how to navigate the Italian version of the website, I finally managed to get a hold one of my mates, who told me "We're at the airport and we've got

everything. You've got less than an hour to check-in or we're away!""

"Now, I'll openly admit that this was one of the scariest moments of my life. I had about ten Euros left on me (since I'd spent a good bit on some food and a few bottles of water during my trip to Turin on the train), no passport, no clothes, and a useless mobile phone. If I didn't manage to get to the airport in time, I would have been stuck and I would have had absolutely no idea what to do. In fact, I'd probably still be stuck in Italy!"

Having explained all of this again to the hotel staff, they led him out to a nearby bus stop and put him on the first coach destined for the airport. As Grant sat there, unable to alter the speed with which the bus winded its way through the city and out on to the motorway towards the airport, he grew increasingly anxious: **"I had no watch, so I had no idea how long it was since I'd spoken to my mate. How much time was left? How much longer would the bus take? Would I make it? I was absolutely terrified."**

"Eventually, the bus pulled into the airport and I leapt off of it almost as soon as it had stopped moving and opened the doors. I sprinted into the airport terminal, and before I could even get my bearings, all I heard was the sound of Glaswegian accents shouting at me. I looked up and there were my mates, as well as the rest of the larger group, all giving me pelters – "There he is! Grant mate! You fucking fanny!""

"To be honest, I must have looked quite the sight. I had the same clothes on as the previous day, which had beer stains all over them, and obviously I looked pretty awful myself, but I'd made it – with less than fifteen minutes to spare. Despite all of the abuse I received, nothing could shake the feeling of relief I experienced. I was just delighted to be going home."

And so, Grant Kelly became one of, if not the last, person to check-in for that particular flight to Scotland. Having awakened in the wrong city in a foreign country, without a working mobile phone or any idea where he was going, he had pulled off a remarkable feat of recovery and made his return flight. Of his original ninety Euros, only four Euros remained, and Grant told me: "I don't even want to think about what would have happened if I hadn't got there in time."

Nowadays, Grant says that "it's funny looking back on it all now, but it wasn't remotely amusing at the time. I suppose the moral of this story is stick with your pals and don't get so drunk, but that's hindsight for you! Next time I'll be sure to make sure my bloody phone is fully charged too, but I'd still do it all again to follow Celtic."

"A Section, A Row And A Seat"

At the end of the 2003–04 season, Celtic Park bid farewell to Henrik Larsson, our Swedish star; our unique talent; our proverbial King of Kings. When Henrik left the field for the final time as a Celtic player (recent charitable appearances excluded), he cried - and I doubt he was the only one, as the emotion around the stadium that day was raw to say the very least. Football has always had a funny knack of starting the waterworks in some people, regardless of whether they're ecstatic or heartbroken. Every season, you're bound to see at least one boy or girl adorning the colours of their favourite team, bawling their eyes out on the last day of the season as their Club narrowly fail to avoid relegation, and they realise they'll be playing in a lower division in a few months time. In fact, television stations seem to feed off scenes such as these as the domestic season draws to a close, almost as if they feel they have to repeatedly prove to their viewers that football supporters do indeed care deeply about their club of choice. In a similar manner, it's not too long since we all witnessed Rod Stewart enjoy a good blubber as Celtic defeated Barcelona at Celtic Park (yes, we beat Barcelona, just in case you'd forgotten about it!).

And so, as Henrik left Parkhead in May, with the eyes of everyone upon him, I arrived in August, without so much as a second glance from anybody. As I mentioned earlier, my dad has been a season ticket holder at Celtic Park for over thirty years now. I, on the other hand, only got to attend a game every now and again prior to 2004. My birthday falls in the summer, and that year, as my fourteenth such celebration approached, I was told my parents had **"something special"** lined up for me. Obviously, the thought of this surprise set my mind racing. Naively, I was thinking along the lines of a games console or a guitar. Obviously, I was too young for cars or alcohol or all of that other fun stuff at that stage in my life, and I already owned a fair selection of merchandise from the Celtic store, so it had to be one of those two things, surely? Or so I thought at least.

When my birthday eventually came around, they simply presented me with an empty season book from the football campaign which had just ended. I must confess that it took a few seconds for the proverbial penny to drop inside my head. For the past two seasons, I'd actually been the owner of a Queen's Park season ticket, such had been my desire to take in some regular, live football. For the record, I rather enjoyed my time at Hampden Park (which is a stadium I've never been a big fan of). However, it was easy to get to, I could choose wherever I wanted to sit because of the small crowds and I now feel that enjoying a different style of football there helped me to appreciate the success of my own team to a larger degree. To this day, I continue to check to see how **"The Spiders"** have fared when I return home from matches at Celtic Park or elsewhere; although I must confess I don't miss being able to hear the ball flying off of someone's boot every time it was struck or the individual players shouting at the referee.

Anyway, returning to my fourteenth birthday, it was only upon looking inside and seeing my older cousin's name did the nature of my present begin to dawn on me. My parents then proceeded to tell me that since my cousin John had recently become a father, he was going to give up his season ticket for **"a couple of years"** and that they'd bought it from him for me on a supposedly temporary basis.

Obviously, this absolutely thrilled me. I couldn't believe it; Celtic Park and every home game! Nowadays, I must say I'm fairly used to the idea, but I do find myself just looking around the place in wonder from time to time, both before and after matches, remembering all of the things I've witnessed and pondering what may yet lie ahead. Most folk stand and curse the weather or bemoan the quality of the half time pie, and of course I do indulge in such pastimes too, but I must admit that occasionally my mind wanders on to bigger things at the football.

For those of you who have never visited the stadium, allow me to say that Celtic Park is a truly wonderful place, especially at night. On a cold, dark evening in Glasgow, you generally see a few things; the orange glow of street lights; people hurrying about with their heads bowed low against their chests, and puddles galore thanks to the famously tropical weather. However, you simply cannot help but look up if you find yourself outside Celtic Park at night. The bright white of the floodlights can be seen for miles around (and I mean miles as the city sits in the middle of a huge valley), as it shoots over the South Stand and out into the Glaswegian night. Colour erupts from the interior of the stadium, and lures the Hooped worshippers in from the dreary grey and orange of the city streets.

Returning to 2004, my first match as a season ticket holder was to be Celtic versus Motherwell, on the eighth of August. Of course, my father sits in the South Stand, and therefore, on the majority of my previous visits to Celtic Park, I'd taken in the match from that side of the ground. In fact, I'd only sat in the upper tier anywhere in the stadium on one occasion, and that was towards the lower reaches of the Jock Stein upper on a Champions League night. You may find it somewhat amazing that the height of my new seat genuinely didn't enter my mind until I passed through what is now my favourite turnstile (yes, I have a favourite turnstile, but I'm not telling you which one) for the first time, and began to climb the stairs.

Looking back on it, the first ten flights were no bother at all. The following five were a little bit tiring. The next five were rather demanding, and the final five, well, they were downright knackering. Of course, I made the rookie mistake of running up each of the twenty-five flights of stairs as if someone had set my tail on fire. I was a young, fit lad (and I still am thankfully), but the seemingly endless stairs did give me cause to wonder what height I was in the process of climbing to. Nowadays, I'm rather used to it, but back then, it was all new to me.

And so, after reaching the main concourse, I ventured out onto the upper tier of Celtic Park's North Stand for the first time. Back then, I had no idea that it was, and continues to be the second largest club stand in British Football (behind the truly enormous Sir Alex Ferguson Stand at Old Trafford), housing a little under thirty thousand supporters when full. Once again, I began to climb stair after stair until I finally reached my row, not too far from the top. I moved inwards from the stairway, past a few folk who took no notice of a fourteen year old, and soon set my eyes upon my seat for the first time. Even saying it now makes me smile, **"my seat"**. From that day, I could rhyme off the seat number, row, and section without a moment's hesitation. I could repeat it now, but I'd rather not have everyone knowing exactly where I sit, so I'll refrain from doing so (after all, I could very well be that guy seated a row or two behind you who has been annoying you for years on end!).

Once I had spent a good twenty seconds or so checking my ticket, and then the seat, and then my ticket again, and then the seat once more, I finally accepted that I was in the right place and turned around. In hindsight, it would have been wise to have made sure I was holding onto something, or perhaps even sitting down as I did so, because my eyes almost popped out of my head subsequently. The height of the stand, especially from the point of view of a young lad who'd never been that far up in any football ground, was absolutely spectacular. However, it wasn't the height that frightened me; it was the steepness of the tier itself. In later years, I'd find out what it was like to fall over into the row in front (which is a significant drop) during goal celebrations against Shaktar Donetsk, A.C. Milan and Rangers.

Anyway, at that moment, it seemed like I had been left standing on a window sill at Glasgow's famous Red Road Flats. However, having taken a few minutes to adapt to my new environment somewhat, I was distracted as the teams emerged from the tunnel opposite to a rapturous applause. A minute's silence for the late Bertie Peacock was observed magnificently, and the flag of the Scottish Premier League Champions was unfurled to an adoring audience. As I have previously mentioned, when the teams were read out by the stadium's announcer, an iconic name was missing, and this was not lost on anybody in attendance that day.

As the Club and its supporters began to adjust to life without Henrik Larsson, and I continued to adjust to the gradient of the upper tier, Celtic started brightly and one Jackie McNamara scored a beautiful goal from the corner of the box, less than ten minutes into my debut as a season ticket holder. Early in the second half, Chris Sutton would score the second goal of the campaign for the Hoops. The match would then go on to end two-nil to the home side, and we were off the mark with regards our league campaign.

Celtic Park was almost full that day, and as I sat there captivated by the spectacle before my eyes, I must admit that I took fairly little notice of those around me as no one asked where the previous inhabitant of the seat was. Perhaps they presumed he was simply away on holiday, therefore missing the first game of the season? After all, it was August, or perhaps the thought simply never even entered their heads?

At the request of my mother, I'd sat in the South Stand for the second home match of the season, purely because it was against Rangers, so I could get a feel of the derby's atmosphere without being left on my own at first. Personally, I had thought I would have been alright in my own seat, but to keep my mother happy, my father and I swapped tickets that afternoon. With the benefit of hindsight, I think it may well have been a wise move, as it was not the intensity but the vitriolic nature of the stadium's atmosphere that day which took me a little while to become accustomed to.

A few weeks later, I appeared in the Gods once more, as Celtic put three past Dundee. Once again, nobody seemed to take any notice, and no one spoke a word to me. To be fair, I'm rather quiet by nature, and I was still pretty young at this age – therefore maybe not the best half time chat on offer for a fully grown adult.

And so, the matches and the months went by, without any words being passed between myself and those around me. Yes, we'd score in the Champions League or derby matches and leap about like lunatics together, but we never really spoke, not properly. Immediately to my right sat a quiet man in his late twenties or early thirties. Every week, he'd wear a khaki green jacket with a large furry hood. In truth, I knew very little about him, other than the fact he would consistently blow his nose throughout every match with what was, if I am wholly honest, a mildly irritating regularity. He seemed like a nice enough bloke to be fair to him though, it simply seemed as if he always had the cold. In reality, it didn't really matter to me – I was watching Celtic play live every week or two, from the unique vantage point provided by my own seat, so I didn't care. On my left sat two men who looked notably alike, and therefore I presumed they were likely brothers, perhaps in their late twenties or early thirties at that point in time. The pair largely kept to themselves, and other than exchanging the odd phrase such as **"how did he miss that?"** I never really spoke to them.

On one particular occasion in my first season, with Celtic playing our rivals of old, Stefan Klos (the Rangers goalkeeper) made, to his credit, a rather impressive save. This was met with the usual shouts of frustration and despair from the home supporters – well, except from the lad next to me, that is, who decided to vent his fury by screaming a rather long drawn out insult which continued for several seconds before finally ending with the immortal words: **"you fucking diddy!"**

Now, all I had heard throughout the afternoon thus far was **"bastard"** this and **"prick"** that, but this gentleman stayed true to his Scottish heritage and chose **"diddy"**, which I rather appreciated. In my eight years at Celtic Park, I've never again heard that word shouted with such venom. It was fantastically amusing (the shout that is, not Klos' save, good goalkeeper though he may have been) and to this day, the thought of it still brings a wee smirk to my face – but maybe you had to be there.

The Hoops would ultimately go on to lose the league on the last day of the season at Fir Park (the less said about that the better) and, as is the way of things, we all returned for the 2005–06 campaign full of renewed hope for the coming battles which lay ahead. Whilst events would be different on the field during the next season as I saw Celtic become the Scottish Premier League Champions for the first time, it was more of the same in my row – silence. Once again, this wasn't anyone's fault. It was simply a mixture of my innate shyness and the fact I was still only fifteen. As you may or may not have gathered, I've never really been the type to spark up a conversation with somebody

I don't know, and obviously this didn't help me much in this regard.

The following August, Celtic were set to face Kilmarnock in the first competitive match of the new domestic season. Oddly, I was rather early for the game, and so I sat there (now fully accustomed to the height of the seat and the steep tier it was situated on) waiting for the usual faces to appear. As the teams ran out and the match kicked off, the seat to my right lay empty but on my left sat the two brothers who were always there. In later years they would take turns using their two seats, each alternately appearing with their respective son, unless of course it was a derby when the two adults would be reunited for ninety minutes of madness once more.

Around fifteen minutes into the match, the man sat two seats to the right of me, whom I'd never spoken to much, leant over and asked, **"any idea where he is?"**, pointing at the empty seat between us. I shrugged my shoulders, gave him a blank look that said **"no"** and returned my focus to the game which was unfolding in front of me. As the season continued, the seat remained empty, even during the first Glasgow derby of the year. In time, the man I'd previously spoken to began to chat to me more and more, passing comments on the games themselves and occasionally treating me to one of his now infamous jokes.

He soon introduced himself as Gerry, a man from Govan who had owned his seat since the North Stand opened in the mid-1990's. Despite the fact he had a couple of decades on me in terms of age, we got on rather well. In November 2006, we were both there, as per usual, as Celtic took on Hearts. In what was a tight affair, the match remained goalless until around twenty minutes from the end, when a mistake from our beloved captain (who has since turned manager), Neil Lennon, allowed Hearts to break forward and open the scoring through Andrius Velička.

As the clock ticked ever closer to full time, it began to look as if the Edinburgh side were set to return to the nation's capital with all three points. However, when Jiri Jarosik headed home a Shunsuke Nakamura corner in the eighty-sixth minute, everyone inside Celtic Park knew they were set to witness a frenetic finish, whatever the final outcome may be.

In stoppage time, Celtic won another corner kick, and up stepped the Japanese master of the dead ball. Perhaps some people expected Nakamura to pull a piece of magic from his bag of tricks, putting it on the head of one of his teammates to convert and give Celtic the victory; perhaps some others expected it to be headed away by our opposition who were, to be fair to them, probably worthy of a point from the match on balance. However, I am almost certain that no one could have predicted what would happen next.

As the ball came in, it was met by a defender who only managed to head the ball as far as Gary Caldwell on the edge of the penalty area. As **"Heid"** (as he continues to be lovingly known by many members of the Celtic support) and his marker fell to the floor, he scrambled the ball forward to his central defensive partner Stephen McManus, who directed a shot goalwards. However, Craig Gordon, the Hearts goalkeeper, got his hands on the ball for an instant, before he lost it and it spun up in the air over his head. Clearly panicking and concerned that the ball was heading for the net, Gordon lunged back towards his own goal in a desperate attempt to catch it. Uncharacteristically though, he got it all wrong and as he went to grasp the ball, he missed by some way, essentially throwing it into his own net in the fourth minute of stoppage time. Inevitably, this sent all but a small maroon corner of Celtic Park barmy.

As the ball crossed the line, I leapt to my feet, thrusting both arms out in the air to my sides in delight. In the ensuing melee, it was not until around a minute later that I noticed Gerry was holding the side of his head, with a slight grimace just permeating his celebratory smile. In truth, I was far too ecstatic to dwell on this at the time and I quickly forgot all about it. Soon though, the final whistle blew, and everyone made their own way home. It was only a week later when I arrived at the next home match that Gerry decided to inform me that I'd accidentally punched him when I leapt up, leaving him with earache for around half of the week just gone. However, to this day, Gerry still says the three points were worth all of the pain. Anyway, I'm sure he'd agree that his jokes can be equally painful on the ears sometimes, so maybe that was just fate's way of returning the favour!

Of course, I am just having a laugh there. In the long run, this incident only led to me and Gerry talking more and more at the football, and becoming firm friends. Ironically, had Gordon chosen not to dive back after the ball, his defender would have almost certainly cleared it off the line, and he could have saved both himself and Gerry a lot of hassle, but that's life (remember, it's chaotic!).

Years later, I consider having a laugh with Gerry to be an integral part of my match day experience at Celtic Park. If, for some reason, he's not there, and the usual pre-match handshakes and greetings aren't exchanged, it feels like something is missing. Through him, I've now spoken with many of the other people who sit around me, some of whom I honestly hadn't uttered a single word to in years. Everyone knows Gerry where I sit – to say he's a character would be an understatement. In truth, he's a fantastically friendly individual, and someone whom I would miss dearly if he were ever to decide he'd had enough of me or the stairs and move seats. In the same vein, whenever my father has floated the idea of me moving to the South Stand in the past, my friendships with Gerry and the other folk around me have been one of the main reasons why I have stayed where I am.

However, I must mention that some of the people who have sat near to me over the years have been well, loveably mental to say the least. I recall one season, for example, when a young priest sat a couple of rows behind me. I had seen him several times previously, as his distinctive collar made him stand out from the crowd to some degree. As the matches passed, and the weeks and months ticked by, I never heard him raise his voice or shout at the referee. In fact, on occasions I'd forgotten he was there at all. In truth, he always came across as a rather quiet individual – well, that is until the first derby match of the season at Celtic Park came around.

Within the first ten minutes of the game, as were so often the way of things, two opposing players flew into a challenge for a fifty-fifty ball, with the man in Hoops subsequently coming off much worse. Large sections of the home support leapt to their feet screaming for a card to be produced by the official on the field (myself included), although typically no such punishment appeared to be forthcoming. However, through the cries, one particular shout seemed to emanate above all others from behind me. It was so noticeable in fact that many people stopped midway through their own sentences, and turned around. Upon looking over my shoulder, I was greeted with the sight of the aforementioned priest, with a vein throbbing on his neck, bawling his head off at the referee. In all seriousness, he was going absolutely nuts, and it was quite a sight.

Eventually, he finished his insult with something along the lines of "**...you dirty cheating bastards!**" Having uttered his final words, he clearly began to realise that several people were staring straight at him. There then followed an awkward silence for a second or two, during which you could see the man becoming rather embarrassed, and he swiftly began to apologise to those around him. However, before he could finish his first sentence of reconciliation, a cry from a few rows in front of me bawled: "**Aye! Spot on! You fucking tell them Father!**" and many of us erupted into fits of laughter (and even a few ripples of applause in some cases). I never heard the priest shout another word at that game, or at any other in fact, before he was replaced by someone else come the start of the following campaign. Regardless, it is funny how these things stick with you. Clearly even a man of God can be left utterly infuriated by some of the refereeing decisions we all have the pleasure of witnessing every year in Scotland!

On another occasion, a few years later, the good folks in my section were treated to some rather unique half time entertainment. For those of you who may be unaware, Celtic have held a raffle known as the "**Paradise Windfall**" for many years now at Celtic Park. Thousands upon thousands of people buy tickets every time they enter the stadium and, as only a couple of folk ever actually win anything, the tickets soon become nothing other than worthless bits of paper to the majority of their owners midway through the half time interval. In the upper tier, especially towards the top where I sit, many supporters carefully craft their losing tickets into paper aeroplanes, competing to see whose creations can make it the furthest down the tier. In eight years, I've seen only two which have managed to clear the upper tier itself, much to the admiration of their owners and peers. I, myself, have never been particularly successful in my attempts with regards these flying machines, and sadly, I've never won the windfall either.

Anyway, during one such half time period, perhaps five years ago now, the winning ticket was drawn and within minutes the aeroplanes started to take flight around the stadium. As usual, many of these hit people further down the respective tiers in the back of the head or body. However, one stereotypical Glaswegian 'ned' in front of me didn't react particularly kindly to this when it happened to him, and he turned around and began to scream at those in the rows behind him, accusing them of **"throwing a pie at him"**. Quite how he came to this assertion – considering there was no obvious evidence of any meat-filled pastry-covered missile – is beyond me, but nevertheless, he persisted with his claims.

Soon, he pointed at the gentleman in front of me. Now, this individual whom I believe to have been in his thirties was, shall we say, not someone you would mess with lightly. With broad shoulders, a skinhead, a beard and facial piercings, he was certainly an imposing figure from a visual point of view. To be fair, those who knew him were aware that he was actually a very nice guy to converse with and enjoy a joke or two, but on that day, the aforementioned 'ned' chose the wrong person to have a go at.

As the minutes ticked by, he continually berated the man in front of me, screaming and balling about how **"he'd hit him with a pie"** and saying that he was going to **"do him"**. Eventually, the big lad returned a verbal volley of his own, but the abuse from below continued and soon I saw the lad walking out of his row and down the stairs towards the offending 'ned'. As they squared up to each other, I heard someone say **"this isn't going to end well!"**

Within seconds, the gentleman had head-butted the 'ned', who fell to the ground like a proverbial tonne of bricks. Having proceeded to receive a few swift kicks to the body, the 'ned' scrambled to his feet and ran off, never to be seen again. As the man who sat in front of me walked back up the stairs, he was greeted with a round of applause and a few pats on the back. When he finally reached his seat, he said simply: **"Fucking dick. I don't even like the pies in here. They're shite."**

A couple of seasons ago, for the first time in several years, the seat between me and my good friend Gerry was filled. For the record, I've never repeated my Ali-esque display (which, to be fair, was probably more Ali G than Muhammad Ali), having learned from my previously discussed mistake. In all honesty, both me and Gerry had grown rather used to having an empty seat between us by this point, and always joked throughout the winter months of asking Peter Lawwell to install a power socket so we could bring an electric heater along with us and plug it in. However, suddenly, we found an older gentleman sat between us, by the name of John from the Calton. It took him a few months to really open up to us, and even longer for him to get used to Gerry's jokes, but he's now as firm a fixture as the rest of us in our small section of Celtic Park's North Stand. A few of his family members are also situated in the row behind us, which only adds to the sociable atmosphere around my seat.

I'll never forget the day when John, who I would guess to be in his late sixties if not his early seventies (please forgive me if I'm wholly incorrect John and I'm doing you a disservice), turned to me and said, **"I've been getting into this Twitter thing lately."**

I must confess that I thought I'd heard him wrongly. My mother has always told me not to make presumptions about people and not to believe stereotypes for all they're made out to be, but I'm sure this is a fairly common message from parents to pass to their children. Despite this, I suppose we are all guilty of it to an extent from time to time, and I was most certainly caught out there – I'm man enough to admit that. I was gobsmacked, but delightfully so.

"Twitter?" I asked, with a slightly quizzical expression on my face.

"Yes, Twitter. You're a young lad, you must have Twitter?" he replied.

Having never spoken to John in any detail about my online presence before, I began to explain what I did, which website I ran and that, obviously, I had Twitter. Jokingly, John refused to accept this until I proved it by producing my mobile phone, upon which he said: **"I can't believe it! I follow you!"** before turning around and introducing me to his family in the row behind us.

I suppose the lesson which I was taught on that occasion was to never judge a book by its cover (no pun intended). For the record, I think it's absolutely fantastic that John enjoys using Twitter, and I'd love to see more and more of the older generations becoming involved with the online world in the future. On a personal level, I absolutely adore sitting next to John at the football. In a similar sentiment to that expressed in the chapters devoted purely to older supporters within this book, I feel I should highlight that I consider sitting next to someone on a regular basis who possesses such an experience of supporting Celtic to be an absolute privilege.

In recent times, only a few months before this book was released, I was browsing the internet one night and opened the inbox of my email account. Within it, I found an email from Celtic Football Club, telling me that there was **"still time for me to purchase my ticket for the first home match of the season."** Having had my ticket on an automatic renewal policy since my first season several years beforehand, I considered this to be an oddity of a significant enough level for me to check the online ticketing service, which proceeded to tell me that my old seat was **"available for purchase"** within the online general sale.

Obviously, this revelation startled me and within moments of the premises opening the following morning, I found myself on the phone to the Club's ticket office seeking some clarification, having the spent the previous night worrying someone would snatch my seat from me through no obvious fault of my own. However, once I contacted the ticket office, they told me that my seat was still available and I was therefore able to renew it once more, although they were not able to tell me what had gone wrong previously with the automatic renewal. Regardless, I kept a hold of my seat, but it did make me think and, in part, it inspired sections of this chapter somewhat. After all, it wasn't the physical seat I was so concerned about the prospect of losing, but my individual vantage point with its unique soundtrack of jokes, quips and stories.

Football is often referred to as **"the beautiful game"**. In many circles, this description has become somewhat overused, if not wholly clichéd. Undoubtedly, the sport itself can be a tremendous spectacle to behold, but it would be naive to presume that there were no downsides associated with it. I mean, if we're being honest, everything from players attempting to cheat in order to win a penalty to fans rioting on the terracing can be associated with the **"ugly face of the beautiful game"**.

And yet, football remains an immensely beautiful sport, as it allows us to appreciate the talents of a few and provides us with an opportunity with which to form relationships with many. Without Celtic and without my season ticket (which still has my cousin's name on it to this day), I would not be able to call Gerry, John, or any of the others not directly mentioned by name in this chapter my friends. In fact, it is likely that I would never have met them at all. However, because Celtic is a big part of all of our lives and we happen to enjoy the experiences that come along with it together, we are friends, and firm friends at that.

I am confident that this story and many tales like it can be found not only at Celtic Park, but at football stadia across the globe. As Jock Stein famously said, **"Football without the fans is nothing"**, and if I was left to attend Celtic Park alone for the rest of my days, as the only supporter there, I wonder if I would soon give up and simply watch the games on the television, because it's not just the players or the manager that make you brave the cold, dreary Glaswegian nights, it's your friends; your family; your Football Club as a whole.

And all because of a section, a row, and a seat number which happen to put you in the same place as some likeminded individuals with a love of life, laughter, and Larsson.

Anyone fancy a pie?

“Unbowed, Unbroken and Unforgettable”

This is, by my own standards at least, a rather short chapter, detailing a fairly brief moment which I happened to bear witness to. However, whilst it may seem to take a somewhat bizarre path at first, stay with me, for a relevant point does lie at the end of this winding literary road.

Early one afternoon in the spring of 2013, I found myself sitting inside the main reception at Celtic Park. The reason I was there is neither here nor there really (nothing too interesting I assure you), but as I sat in one of the leather armchairs positioned around the large flat screen television mounted on the wall, the double doors adjacent to the reception desk opened, and in strolled a Lion. Of course, I do not refer to one of the four legged variety with their distinctive manes, but a gentlemen with notably less hair which was somewhat silvery in colour. He was wearing a Celtic t-shirt, tracksuit bottoms and trainers, whilst clutching a dinner plate wrapped in tinfoil in his right hand.

And so, suddenly I found one of the eight remaining Lisbon Lions, John Clark, standing in front of me. Now, despite the fact I wasn’t born for more than two decades after the European Cup win in Lisbon, I should state at this stage that I regard it as an honour to even breathe the same air as one of these great men, and I’m sure I’m not alone in this view. To say they are held in high esteem by the Celtic support would be an understatement of utterly colossal proportions.

Anyway, John wandered across the room with the aforementioned dinner plate, before greeting the receptionist by her first name and handing over her lunch. Having had a brief chat, passing the time of day if you will, he turned and headed for the doors from which he had entered the room a few moments earlier. Once he had taken a few steps, he turned on his heels in a similar, if somewhat slower fashion than he used to do on the football pitch, and returned to the desk as if something had sprung into his mind.

"Sorry hen, is there any chance I could use the phone? I need to give wee Bertie a ring while I remember!" said John.

As you would expect, the receptionist happily handed the receiver to John, and he leant over the desk to dial the number. Within a few seconds, his voice filled the otherwise quiet air once again as Bertie Auld picked up the phone at the other end: **"Bertie! Bertie! It's John here. How you doing? ... I'm ok Bertie, I'm ok. I'm just wondering if you're coming to the game tonight or not?"**

Now, as you will understand, I could only hear one side of the conversation, hence the lack of any corresponding dialogue, but I still found it fascinating nonetheless.

A few moments later, he continued, **"Aye I'm at the ground ... Aye, yes ... Are you going to Hampden at the weekend as well? Uh-uh? Good! Are you coming down to the ground before it to head over to Hampden with us? Great! No bother. Great!** [At this point there was some reference made to **"Big Jock"**, regarding how **"he always said that"** but sadly I have no idea what Bertie said to prompt such a reply] **We'll make sure we get a cup of tea before it then, eh? Danny's going to be there too ... Aye, Danny McGrain ... No problem. That's great Bertie, I'll see you tonight anyway! Ok. Great. Bye-bye."**

With this, John put the phone down, thanked the receptionist for her help, smiled at me and the other gentleman sitting by the television, turned and walked towards the doors, before disappearing out of sight. Now, you may be wondering what I am going on about here, as all I have done so far is describe a fairly mundane telephone conversation (I know, phone calls are much less mundane when there's a Lisbon Lion on either end of the phone, but still). Anyway, you'll be pleasantly surprised to know that we've now reached the crux of the matter, or at least my perception of it.

As I write this, John Clark is in his early seventies, with Bertie Auld a few years his senior. On the grand scheme of things, it isn't too long until the fiftieth anniversary of the Football Club's greatest day under the scorching Portuguese sun, and yet here these men are, still the best of friends, and still heavily involved at Celtic Park.

John is currently the Club's kit man, and he is a regular on the Celtic bench, often sitting directly behind Neil Lennon, quietly considering the intricate details of the game being played out in front of him. Ironically, a man who once stood atop the European footballing mountain now fades into the background in many camera shots, as people see our enthusiastic manager discussing tactics with Garry Parker or Johan Mjallby shouting instructions into the ear of an eager substitute. Regardless, John is clearly a man who is very content within his role at Parkhead and someone who is still very proud to be a part of the Football Club he loves so dearly. Similar plaudits apply to Bertie Auld and the rest of the Lisbon Lions (even those who are sadly no longer with us), who are (or were) all renowned for their willingness to use their time to benefit Celtic Football Club and its supporters, as well as numerous worthy causes away from football.

In the modern era, we all see certain players acting irresponsibly, selfishly, or just plain petulantly on a relatively regular basis, whether they do so on or off the field of play. Of course, many footballers now are ideal role models for men and women of all ages, living clean, healthy lifestyles and working hard to maximise their potential, but some of them are quite the opposite. In saying that, to act in such an extravagant manner can add to the reputation of a footballer, and undoubtedly this notoriety is something which a section of these young men seek. However, in my opinion at least, with the support of a fan base and a Football Club comes great responsibility for your own actions. This does not mean that every footballer needs to act like a modern day saint, but a bit of respect and common sense wouldn't go amiss at times with regards to some of their actions. For example, when you pull on a Celtic jersey, whether you are a player or a supporter and whether you are aware of it or not, you are seen as a representative of Celtic Football Club. Granted, this responsibility is significantly higher with regards our players, as they have significantly higher public profiles than your average supporter, but the point stands regardless.

Focusing on the players for the sake of this chapter, whether they take ridiculous dives, demand exorbitant wages, treat money as if it is an endless resource, spit at other players or even supporters (three guesses who I'm referring to there), or a countless list of other such offences, their actions do nothing to promote the image of **"the beautiful game"**.

However, in stark contrast, as I sat in the reception of Celtic Park, I saw a man who continues to be a beacon of sanity in a time when the game today seems like a soap opera in many regards. There are numerous large egos in the world of football, some of which are somewhat justifiably inflated, and others which are simply pumped full of hot air and nothing more.

To win the European Cup is to become a legend, regardless of who you play for. This is an undeniable fact. It is the absolute pinnacle which any player can achieve at their respective Clubs in Europe, and in truth, it would be very easy for John Clark or any of the Lisbon Lions to consider themselves as legendary figures, and expect to be treated as such. However, whilst the Celtic support do hold them in a truly iconic light, the men themselves have always been, and continue to be, admirably humble with regards to their achievement, whist remaining fiercely proud of it.

The spirit which Jock Stein, Sean Fallon and the countless members of the Celtic support instilled in those men is still clearly evident inside each and every one of them who remains with us. For example, could you see a modern football player, who essentially believes that they are **"a gift to the sport"** winning the European Cup and then, years later, happily handing workers their lunches wrapped in tinfoil, before laying out the kits for men less than half his age (and, with all due respect to them, with less ability than himself or his teammates of old) without complaint or query? I know that I can't.

This is, of course, only a criticism of certain modern day footballers. There are countless honest, hardworking players who can be found from the lower levels of the game all the way up to the very top who disprove the stereotype of money grabbing, fame seeking morons who are more interested in what headlines they can get on to the front page of a newspaper rather than the sports pages at the back.

However, even with this in mind, it goes without saying that the Lisbon Lions are unique. From their first days at Celtic Park, through their glory years and even now as pensioners, they have been, and continue to be, a credit to themselves and Celtic Football Club. The humility and contentment of John Clark only goes to prove this fact. They see themselves as small parts of something much bigger than themselves as individuals, whilst some other footballers seem to believe quite the opposite. Therein lays the beauty of the beast I suppose, highlighting that while the Persian cats of the modern game may feel they look fantastic and are tremendously important without justification, our proud Lions will continue to rule the proverbial footballing jungle for evermore – unbowed, unbroken, and unforgettable.

"The Footsteps of My Forefathers"

Ladies and gentlemen, as finally I draw this book to a close, I must thank you once again for taking the time to read it. One of the main themes which I have tried to explore and highlight is my belief that, above all else, anyone can support Celtic. From the earliest years of the Club, everybody has been welcome, and this inclusiveness continues to this very day. This is something which we should all be tremendously proud of, and we must all continue to strive to spread the good name of the Football Club and its supporters around the world. Whether we haven't missed a Celtic match in decades or we have just witnessed our first game, whether we only ever watch the ties from the stands or on **"Celtic TV"** in a basement on the other side of the world, we all stand together as equals – rich, poor, Catholic, Protestant, Muslim, Hindu, Buddhist, Sikh, Atheist, straight, gay, bisexual, white, black, and any colour in between – we stand together as one living, breathing entity.

With every match, every goal, every card, every signing, every departure and every season, Celtic Football Club continues to grow that little bit bigger; with every clicking turnstile, every new supporter, every veteran, every chant, every shout and every song, the Celtic support continues to stand that little bit taller; and critically, with every passing hour of every passing day, the history of Celtic Football Club becomes that little bit longer.

I have been lucky enough to speak to some fantastic people while writing this book, be it in the flesh or through the wonders of modern technology, and it has been an absolute joy to put this piece together. Once again, I cannot thank all of the individuals featured in this book for not only taking the time to speak to me, but for helping a dream of mine to come to fruition. I sincerely hope that you all have enjoyed reading this, and I hope it will not be the last piece of my work you decide to read. Of course, my day to day ramblings can be found on the **"Maley's Bhoys"** website, an outlet I am immensely proud of, but whether you choose to visit it is not massively important on the grand scheme of things. However, what is important, above all else, is not you or me, but our Football Club, its support and its influence on the world as a whole. As the future becomes the present, we must carry on our charitable, open ethos, regardless of results on the field of play or the situations we find ourselves in. This must be our primary objective, for these were the mantra upon which Celtic Football Club were founded and through which so much good has been achieved.

This matters to me tremendously, because when I walk to Celtic Park, whether it's along the Gallowgate, down from Parkhead Cross, up Springfield Road or along London Road, I walk in the footsteps of my forefathers. Not only do I walk the same steps as generations of my family before me, I walk in the footsteps of the men and women who built our Football Club from nothing; the individuals who set out to feed an impoverished, forgotten community in the East End of Glasgow; those who broke down religious and social barriers, providing a beacon of hope for anyone of any background; those men who conquered Europe, and those men and women who continue to wear the famous green and white Hoops to this day. In a similar vein, our footsteps will outlive us all, as generations of Celts to come will continue to represent not only a Football Club, but a people and a cause – and I wouldn't change it for the world – for upon the shoulders of giants on which we stand, the view is not only utterly spectacular, it is uniquely ours, it is uniquely Celtic.